European Banking and Financial Law

In recent decades, the volume of EU legislation on financial law has increased exponentially. Banks, insurers, pension funds, investment firms and other financial institutions all are increasingly subject to European regulatory rules, as are day-to-day financial transactions.

Serving as a comprehensive and authoritative introduction to European banking and financial law, the book is organised around the three economic themes that are central to the financial industry: (i) financial markets; (ii) financial institutions; and (iii) financial transactions. It covers not only regulatory law, but also commercial law that is relevant for the most important financial transactions. It also explains the most important international standard contracts such as LMA loan contracts and the GMRA repurchase agreements.

Covering a broad range of aspects of financial law from a European perspective, it is essential reading for students of financial law and European regulation.

Matthias Haentjens is Professor of Financial Law and director of the Hazelhoff Centre for Financial Law at Leiden University.

Pierre de Gioia-Carabellese is Associate Professor of Business Law at Heriot-Watt University, Edinburgh.

European Banking and Financial Law

Matthias Haentjens and
Pierre de Gioia-Carabellese

Routledge
Taylor & Francis Group
LONDON AND NEW YORK

First published 2015
by Routledge
2 Park Square, Milton Park, Abingdon, Oxon, OX14 4RN

and by Routledge
711 Third Avenue, New York, NY 10017

Routledge is an imprint of the Taylor & Francis Group, an informa business

British Library Cataloguing in Publication Data
A catalogue record for this book is available from the British Library

Library of Congress Cataloging-in-Publication Data
Haentjens, Matthias, author.
European banking and financial law/Matthias Haentjens and Pierre de Gioia-Carabellese.
pages cm
Includes bibliographical references and index.
ISBN 978-1-138-89796-0 (hbk) – ISBN 978-1-138-89797-7 (pbk) – ISBN 978-1-315-70851-5 (ebk) 1. Financial institutions – Law and legislation – Europe. I. de Gioia-Carabellese, Pierre, editor. II. Title.
KJC2188.H34 2015
346.4′082 – dc23
2015001809

ISBN: 978-1-138-89796-0 (hbk)
ISBN: 978-1-138-89797-7 (pbk)
ISBN: 978-1-315-70851-5 (ebk)

Typeset in Times New Roman by
Florence Production Ltd, Stoodleigh, Devon, UK

MIX
Paper from responsible sources
FSC® C013056

Printed and bound in Great Britain by
TJ International Ltd, Padstow, Cornwall

Outline contents

Contents

Preface

In recent decades, the sheer volume of European legislation in the domain of financial law has swollen exponentially. Banks, insurers, pension funds, investments firms and other financial institutions are all finding themselves increasingly subject to a European regulatory framework. Furthermore, financial transactions too are, to an ever-greater extent, governed by precepts that originate in Brussels. Within such a context, this book is intended to serve as an initial introduction to the field of European banking and financial law. It covers not only regulatory (European) law, but also includes elements of commercial and financial law that have a bearing on the most notable financial transactions.

Thus, this textbook analyses European financial law legislation as a starting point, but it also clarifies the most salient international standard contracts (usually governed by English law), of which LMA and GMRA contracts feature prominently. It is organised around the three (economic) themes that are central to the financial industry: (i) financial markets; (ii) financial institutions; and (iii) financial transactions. Within these three themes, the primary focus is on banking (as our title indicates), for it is our contention that the bank continues to prevail as the most important financial institution in the European financial sector.

As the book revolves around European financial law legislation, the task of writing it while keeping pace with the tempo set by the Brussels legislator was a challenge. Nonetheless, we have sought to account for all important recent developments. Of the legislation that has been enacted in 2014 alone, we cover, for instance and inter alia: the Single Supervisory Mechanism, the Bank Recovery and Resolution Directive, the Single Resolution Mechanism, the Markets in Financial Instruments Directive II, the Market Abuse Regulation and the Residential Credit Directive. We have chosen to review only statutes that have been enacted by the European legislator irrespective of whether or not they have been implemented at national level by the relevant Member States. MiFID I, for instance, was still in force at the national level upon the completion of this textbook, but in due course, it will be replaced by national implementations of Directive 2014/65 (i.e. MiFID II), which has already been enacted. At the relevant places, we have highlighted the similarities and differences between MiFID I and II. In so doing, we hope to prepare the reader for the imminent (financial) future.

This is a book aimed at the needs of lecturers and students alike, while also providing a valuable resource for practitioners (lawyers, chartered accountants, financiers and bankers) working in a global environment. We wished to provide a textbook that gives an initial introduction to European banking and financial law and jointly covers both regulatory and commercial law, as it became clear to us that these typologies of topics are now being taught with the same breadth in several universities across Europe and indeed globally. For the same reason (the educational purpose of the textbook), we deemed it useful to include both questions and references for further reading so that it can be readily used for teaching purposes.

As is befitting for a textbook, our words of thanks are due, first and foremost, to our students, most in particular our PhD student Robert Colhoun, our student assistants Boudewijn Smit, Dorine Verhey and Daan Helleganger, and the students of International Banking and Financial Law at Heriot-Watt and of Financial Law at Leiden University. Also, we are grateful to our anonymous reviewers for their most valuable comments and suggestions.

Finally, as this is a textbook to be used principally in *academia*, by definition it is neither finished nor complete. Conversely, this work is intended to serve as a basis for daily interaction between students and lecturers and, therefore, it is expected to be adapted in the future to the ever-changing needs of both. In light of this, we would be delighted to hear any comments you might have with a view to ensuring the further improvement of our work going forward.

Matthias Haentjens
Pierre de Gioia-Carabellese

List of (abbreviated) statutes

(1) European directives

(2) Non-European Union legislation

Part A

Introduction

Chapter 1

Sources of European financial law

Chapter contents

1.1 Introduction

In financial law, ends commonly mark a beginning, as will be seen when charting the evolution of any legislation relating to banking and finance in general, not only that confined to the specific focus of this textbook, i.e. the EU legislative framework which regulates banking activity, credit institutions and financial markets. For instance, a pertinent illustration of the above dictum can be found in the wake of the Great Depression when the US responded by devising and implementing robust legislation on the financial markets as a riposte to the collapse of the stock markets in 1929. Furthermore, with the recent financial crisis still fresh in our memories having left an indelible mark on the latter half of the past decade and having wreaked havoc on a global scale, the European Union has felt compelled to wage a drive, not only relatively speedily, but also boldly and powerfully, towards the increased integration or 'harmonisation' and even (in part) unification of financial law. At the national level in countries such as Britain, the same crisis which resulted in the collapse of major financial institutions has brought to light the inability of the supervisor to prevent this systemic failure, thereby establishing the need for a creation in law of a brand new system of supervision. In Britain, the Financial Services Act 2012[1] has made the Bank of England and its new operational arms[2] together with its subsidiaries in charge of prudential supervision.[3] In between pushes for more stringent legislation and harmonisation as just discussed, periods of liberalisation stimulating the financial industry can be discerned. Nonetheless, a constant factor has been the ever closer integration of EU banking and financial law, which will be the subject of this chapter.

1.2 European Union statutes and their hierarchy

The focus of this book is on European banking and financial law, yet the key issues it addresses should not be considered in isolation but rather by drawing a wider perspective and glancing at the entire canvas on which this complex and wide-ranging composition has been orchestrated. In other words, an understanding of each specific theme (e.g. market abuse, prospectus, listing and consumer protection) cannot be considered in a vacuum, independent from the overarching legal structure of that complex and increasingly integrated phenomenon called the European Union. Any analysis of international banking and financial law, particularly with respect to that

1 In force as from 1 April 2013.

2 More specifically, for instance, the Financial Policy Committee. For recent commentaries to the new supervisory system in Britain, see G Walker and R Purves (eds), *Financial Services Law* (3rd edn Oxford University Press, Oxford 2014) 29, 51.

3 The Financial Conduct Authority and Prudential Regulation Authority. Similarly, almost 120 years before in late nineteenth century Rome, the bankruptcy and ensuing political scandal which engulfed Banca Romana – the Italian credit institution (at the time, just one of six in that country authorised to issue currency) which by way of an adherence to loose practices had far exceeded the permitted threshold of banknotes to be printed and dispatched into circulation – lit the blue touch paper for the subsequent creation, in that country, of radical reform hinged upon the formation of a unified central bank, the Banca d'Italia.

applicable in Europe and within the European Union, must therefore be preceded by a brief discussion of the legislative 'sources' existing in this area of law.[4]

1.2.1 The Treaties

Beyond the domain specific to banking and financial law, the formative pillar of European solidarity, i.e. the European Economic Community, in an early tentative step towards the current 'federation' known as the European Union, was born and shaped from the ruins of the Old Continent where values and institutions had been torn asunder and lay strewn across the deadly battlefields of WW2. It is from those battlefields that the conviction arose that a future war could and should be avoided by a commercial and financial community. This community is first and foremost a product of the European Treaties.

Of the various EU legislative sources, those which carry the most weight are the Treaties. Remarkably, what are now referred to in the plural (Treaties) began life as a singular Treaty – more specifically, the Treaty of the European Economic Community or the Treaty of Rome, signed in the Eternal City on 25 March 1957.[5] The original Treaty was concluded by the six founding states (i.e. France, Germany, Italy and the 'BeNeLux') although the ensuing years have witnessed a progressive rise in the number of signatories to arrive at the current formation of 28 Member States.[6]

The Treaty of Rome has evolved, following a succession of subsequent Treaties and an ever-increasing number of signatory countries.[7] Most significantly, the Maastricht Treaty, dated 7 February 1992, established the European Union, a denomination replacing the European Economic Community, while the Treaty of Lisbon, dated 13 December 2007, resulted in a three-fold constitutional chart replacing the Treaty of Rome, specifically hinged upon: (a) the Treaty on European Union ('TEU'); (b) the Treaty on the Functioning of the European Union ('TFEU'), consisting of the basic principles of the Treaty of Rome and, thus, the de facto successor to it; and (c) the Charter of the Fundamental Rights of the European Union.[8]

As far as the TFEU is concerned, within it are still enshrined the four fundamental freedoms of the Union, to all intents and purposes mirroring (albeit not replicating

4 In law, a source is the way a precept has come into existence and, more significantly, an answer given to the following question: why is a precept binding and what is the addressee of that precept expected to comply with? (H Thirlway, *The Sources of International Law* (Oxford University Press, Oxford 2014) 4. Sources are usually divided in material or formal. The former denote the place where 'the terms of the rule can be found conveniently' (ibid.) whereas the latter (formal sources) refer to the 'legal element that gives to the rule its quality as law' (ibid. 5).

5 Remarkably, the signing of the Treaty of the European Economic Community was preceded by the agreement, among the same six founding countries, the Treaty of the European Coal and Steel Treaty, achieved in Paris on 18 April 1951, entered into force on 23 July 1952 and expired on 23 July 2002 (A Kaczorowska, *European Union Law* (2nd edn Routledge, Abingdon 2011). This Treaty, relating to the specific market of coal and steel rather than the more generic economic market, is generally perceived as the build-up to the signature of the Treaty of Rome. A different Treaty, also signed in Rome by the six founding countries, on the same day as the Treaty creating the European Economic Community, is the Treaty establishing the European Atomic Energy Community. This Treaty, relating to the niche market of atomic power, is still in force, as a parallel Treaty to the current three EU Treaties.

6 The United Kingdom, for instance, together with Ireland and Denmark, joined in 1973.

7 In 2007, Romania and Bulgaria became, respectively, the 26th and 27th EU members. In 2014, Croatia became the 28th EU Member State.

8 The 'Charter' was initially adopted by the Nice Council, although without any legal effect. It was the Treaty of Lisbon that made that Charter a binding document (L Woods and P Watson, *Steiner and Woods EU Law* (11th edn Oxford University Press, Oxford 2012) 140, 141).

word for word) those initially established under the Treaty of Rome: free movement of goods; free movement of persons; free movement of services; and free movement of capital.[9] In regard to the banking and financial sector, the last two principles are of particular significance, while aiding a better (methodological) understanding of the following chapters of this textbook. If a bank established in one of the (current) 28 Member States wished to offer its banking services in one, some or all of the other Member States, it is permitted to do so, in light of the free movement of services principle and the body of laws which, as a result of it, have been effectuated to render this concept practically applicable. Likewise, the free movement of capital permits individuals and legal entities of a Member State to freely export their assets to another EU country, unhampered by any legal barriers. Therefore, a consumer availing of a particular banking product, for instance a bank account, may well conclude that the range of banking services presented in his 'home country' falls short of those on offer in another Member State. To take advantage of the preferable option, the consumer would only have to open the more advantageous bank account in the alternative Member State and transfer his money to it. To reiterate the point specified above, as a matter of principle, this transaction should not be hampered between the relevant EU states, as this might infringe the core principles laid out by the TFEU.

While refraining from lingering on the characteristic concepts of EU law, it is nevertheless worth noting that a Treaty provision is 'directly applicable', in that each individual in a Member State is entitled to raise a claim before a national court requesting its application, specifically in cases where the relevant national piece of legislation contains a provision to the contrary. Simply put, Treaty provisions take precedence over national norms and, once presented before the local adjudicator, the latter shall yield to the supremacy of the supranational one.[10]

1.2.2 Regulations and Directives

As can be inferred from the analysis conducted in the previous section, the Treaties are the primary sources of European Union law. Other statutes and official decisions adopted by the European Union and its multifarious bodies are considered as of 'secondary nature'. Such secondary legislation can be binding (a category incorporating the Regulations, the Directives and the Decisions) or non-binding (Recommendations and Opinions).

First and foremost, binding legislation is adopted by the European Union in order 'to fulfill a specific function in the development of the Union law',[11] which means, in a nutshell, that the legislation must demonstrate a legal basis and fall within the scope of the EU Treaties.[12] A Regulation, according to art. 288 of the TFEU, is 'binding in its entirety and directly applicable in all Member States.' Furthermore, a Regulation

9 C Barnard, *The Substantive Law of the EU: The Four Freedoms* (4th edn Oxford University Press, Oxford 2013).

10 S Weatherill, *Cases and Materials on EU Law* (8th edn Oxford University Press, Oxford 2007) 85–94 and, more recently, S Weatherill, *Cases and Materials on EU Law* (9th edn Oxford University Press, Oxford 2010).

11 A Reid, *European Union* (4th edn W Green, London 2010) 14.

12 For instance, because defence is not included in the Treaties, it would be illegal to enact a Directive on it and have the purpose to legislate or to force a certain conduct of Member States in this matter, notwithstanding that such Directive could have been legally approved by the Council. Consistently with this, art. 296 of the TFEU requires that legal acts must clarify the reasons they are hinged upon.

is self-executing by virtue of the fact that, although domestic administrative measures of implementation are sometimes required, Member States are not permitted to enact any implementing norm in order to apply it. Accordingly, the norms of each Regulation are identical across the spectrum of Member States, given the lack of discretion afforded to them.

Conversely, a Directive is 'binding, as to the result to be achieved, upon each Member State to which it is addressed, but shall leave to the national authorities the choice of the form and methods.' Its implementation is mandatory within each Member State and is bound by a strict time frame; although the manner in which the specific norms are worded within the relevant domestic legislation is left to the discretion of each EU country. As a general rule, Directives are not directly enforceable; although, according to a well-entrenched line of case law of the European Union Court of Justice, such an eventuality could transpire should the relevant Directive provisions turn out to be sufficiently detailed.[13]

1.3 Financial law legislation from Brussels

1.3.1 Introduction

To chronicle the history of European banking and financial law would be to draw on an evolution of what, in essence, is the business of lending money and raising funds from the public. In a way, this business is not dissimilar to the functioning of any other entrepreneurial activity, such as a bakery or a butcher. Nonetheless, there is a clear demarcation line between the two forms of business to the extent that they sit at polar ends of public perception, where an awareness exists among the community at large that the manner in which a bank is managed (or mismanaged) carries far greater implications for the entire economy of a country, its financial system and sometimes also the economy outside of its own national borders. Accordingly, the bank and, more generally, other financial businesses such as investment firms and insurance companies enjoy a special status: the ability to commence that activity (i.e. to open a bank, with branches offering services to the public), even in the most 'liberal countries', is not nonchalantly left to the arbitrary decision of any individual or entity. Rather, any resolution to open a bank is, as a matter of protocol, preceded by a request to the relevant incumbent authority in each respective country (traditionally, but not necessarily, the Central Bank), whereupon it will be subject to the fulfilment of a series of more or less rigorous prerequisites.

Pursuant to the more accentuated implementation, within the European Union, of a Single Market in the 1970s and 1980s coupled with a steady increase in the number of participating Member States, a profound change of tack became evident in the modus operandi favoured by Brussels in regard to legislating on the banking sector. Manifested by a clear departure from the previously fragmented national rules, and in preference

---

13 See, e.g. (Case 9/70) *Grad v Finanzamt Traunstein* [1970] ECR 825. Among scholars, see also A Dashwood, M Dougan, B Rodger, E Spaventa and D Wyatt, *Wyatt and Dashwood's European Union Law* (6th edn Hart Publishing, Oxford and Portland 2011) 235, 285.

to the ensuing adherence to a set of pan-European norms applicable in a homogeneous way across the European Union, this revised course of direction can be regarded as a revolution, even when viewed from the perspective of the traditionally conservative jurist. This advancement in legislation, which gained a dramatic degree of impetus in the wake of the 2007/08 financial crisis, cannot be regarded as having charted a steady and progressive course, but rather as a slow and tortuous journey in arriving at its current configuration. It will be discussed below.

1.3.2 First Banking Directive

More specifically, in relation to the banking sector, an early example of the formation of common rules applicable exclusively to credit institutions is the so-called 'First Banking Directive', which originated in the 1970s.[14] This Directive, no longer operational, specified that any banking activity ought to be preceded by communication of the relevant authorisation from the competent authority, subsequent to the fulfilment of certain prerequisites. However, this statute was rather poorly forged as, on the one hand, it failed to clarify the precise nature of these prerequisites while, on the other, it maintained the obligation that authorisation be granted not only by the home state, but also by each and every host EEC Member State where the authorised bank wished to conduct its business.

1.3.3 Second Banking Directive and European passport

The obvious flaws of Directive 77/780/EEC were addressed and subsequently rectified by the ensuing Directive 89/646/EEC (the 'Second Banking Directive').[15] This time around, the 'reserved activities' detailed in the preceding Directive were better aligned with the principle that authorisation granted to a banking business in one Member State will suffice and does not therefore require that the process be repeated in another. This principle – nowadays almost sacrosanct as a European principle of banking and financial law – is commonly referred to as 'passporting', which will now be discussed more extensively.

The notion of a 'European passport' is inexorably linked to the parallel concept of 'passported activities'. Such activities are detailed in a list and termed the 'activities subject to the mutual recognition'. The list, in the most recent version, can be found in Annex I of Regulation (EU) No 575/2013 (which Regulation can be seen as a successor to the Second Banking Directive and forms part of the new capital requirements legislation package, see below, section 1.3.4).[16] Although the relevant details will be comprehensively explored over the ensuing chapters of this textbook,[17]

---

14 In full: First Council Directive 77/780/EEC of 12 December 1977 on the coordination of the laws, regulations and administrative provisions relating to the taking up and pursuit of the business of credit institutions.

15 In full: Second Council Directive 89/646/EEC of 15 December 1989 on the coordination of laws, regulations and administrative provisions relating to the taking up and pursuit of the business of credit institutions and amending Directive 77/780/EEC.

16 Previously, the list of the activities to mutual recognition was within Directive 2006/48, and even before, in Directive 89/646/EEC (Second Banking Directive).

17 See Chapter 6.

it would not go amiss to already say that the main reserved activities are, on the one hand, the '*acceptance of deposits or other repayable funds*' and, on the other, the '[l]ending including, inter alia: consumer credit, mortgage credit, factoring, with or without recourse, financing of commercial transactions (including forfeiting).'[18]

Further to the above explanation of passported activities, it might also be useful to clarify the three pillars on which the concept of the EU passport rests. First and foremost, upon authorisation by the relevant authority in its EU home Member State, this green light must also be deemed to sanction all the passported activities that the financial institution wishes to perform in other host EU Member States without this requiring the further (additional) consent of a different supervisory authority in the 'host countries'. Whereas no additional consent may be required, the relevant host authorities must be notified. Also, it is important to note that this universal green light applies to the activities a financial institution wishes to perform in another Member State either by means of cross-border, distant services, or by means of a branch office in that other Member State. As a matter of principle, the green light does not apply to the activities of a subsidiary company established in another Member State, which subsidiary company – as a separate legal entity – must apply for its own authorisation(s).

The second pillar underpinning the EU passport concerns the increasing harmonisation of legislation regulating the banking industry in terms of standards and requisites applicable to the entire spectrum of EEA countries, thereby giving rise to a reduction or minimisation in disparities among the relevant legislations. We refer to 'EEA countries' here, because much EU financial legislation not only applies to the EU, but also to the broader European Economic Area, which comprises the 28 EU Member States plus Iceland, Norway and Lichtenstein (but not Switzerland). The process of harmonisation just mentioned has not yet accomplished an unqualified neutralisation of the prevailing 'legal barriers' among the EEA for two reasons, both following from the European law principles of proportionality and subsidiarity. First, in many instances, harmonisation occurs only at a minimum level leaving Member States the freedom to implement EU Directives more broadly, rather than at a rigid, mandatory level (maximum harmonisation). Second, EU legislation tends to be specialist and geared towards specific products or institutions, while refraining from harmonising general areas of law. Consequently and most notably, general private or commercial law is not harmonised.

---

18 Other activities subject to 'mutual recognition', also referred to as 'passported activities', are:

- financial lending;
- money transmission services;
- issuing and administering means of paying (e.g. credit cards, traveller's cheques and bankers' drafts);
- guarantee and commitments;
- trading for own account or account of customers in money markets instruments (cheques, bills, certificates of deposit, etc.), foreign exchange, financial futures and options, exchange and interest-rate instruments, or transferrable securities;
- participation in securities issues and the provision of services related to such issues;
- advice to undertakings on capital structure, industrial strategy and related questions and advice as well as services relating to mergers and the purchase of undertakings;
- money broking;
- portfolio management and advice;
- safe-keeping and administration of securities;
- credit reference services;
- safe custody services.

The 'home country control' principle constitutes the final pillar of the EU passport. Upon the authorisation by the relevant authority in an EEA country, that consent automatically identifies the authority in charge of supervising the stability of the financial institution, irrespective of where in the EEA that enterprise wishes to perform its business activities. In this scenario, the host authority will play a supervisory role where it concerns the business conducted in that host country, but, as a matter of principle, it will have no competence in the matter of the stability of the bank.

1.3.4 Lamfalussy Report

A discussion of the main legislative architecture of the EU concluded, attention can now be trained on the specificities of the current EU legislative process in the financial sector, where it must be stressed that an initial foray into this area, as an autonomous EU tenet, came to light by way of the Maastricht Treaty in 1992. There, for the first time, principles aimed at shaping the organisation of an Economic and Monetary Union were set out,[19] in accordance with the overarching purpose of the European Union to 'establish the foundations of an ever closer union among the people of Europe'.[20]

Remarkably, a significant step in the change of pace of the EU legislative process specific to the banking sector emanated from the so-called Lamfalussy Report. This report,[21] drafted by Baron Alexandre Lamfalussy and a group of like-minded 'wise men' he chaired in the late 1990s, was, upon appointment of the EU Council, entrusted with assessing the efficiency of the legislative progress in the financial sector. Ultimately, it consists of a document detailing a set of recommended guidelines conducive to a more efficient law-making process in the Union, in regard to the financial sector. The EU legislature has embraced the recommended process, which is now commonly referred to as the Lamfalussy process.

In brief, the Lamfalussy process discerns the following four levels of regulation:

- the adoption of Directives or Regulations by the EU, in accordance with the co-decision procedure (Level 1);
- the implementation of additional legislation at EU level, the purpose of which is to fill in the details (Level 2);
- a focus on cooperation among national supervisors, so that 'consistent implementation and enforcement' can be ensured (Level 3);
- a more effective enforcement of the EU legislation (Level 4).

The interaction between Level 1 and Level 2 of the Lamfalussy Report is fundamental and fully deserves some further explanation. A piece of legislation appearing at the first level, usually a Directive but on occasion a Regulation, allows the EU law-maker to expedite the enactment of basic principles, on the grounds of the fact that the co-decision process requires a simple majority, as opposed to complete agreement.

---

19 Although this move has been hampered by the decision of two countries, the UK and Denmark, to opt out of it.

20 A Kaczorowska, *European Union Law* (2nd edn Routledge, Abingdon 2011) 22, 23.

21 Final Report of the Committee of the Wise Men in the Regulation of European Securities Markets, Brussels, 15 February 2001, http://ec.europa.eu/internal_market/securities/docs/lamfalussy/wisemen/final-report-wise-men_en.pdf, accessed 4 August 2014.

This greases the wheels of EU law making as otherwise reaching a consensus on a detailed statute would be inherently more problematic and time consuming.

Coupled with the first level, is the correspondent piece of legislation represented at the second level (also, in this case, either a Directive or a Regulation with implementing provisions) where the detailed norms are provided. In other words, the impasse that traditionally transpired as a fly in the ointment of the EU legislative process is cleverly sidestepped by the Lamfalussy process, based on an interaction between the first level Directive (or Regulation) and the second level Directive or Regulation. Moreover, as a result of the implementation of the De Larosière Report, to be discussed below, section 1.3.5, three European Supervisory Authorities have been created, which authorities consist of the cooperating national supervisors and are empowered to issue Regulatory Technical Standards and Implementing Technical Standards which serve as detailed implementation norms of the second level. On the third level, the same European Supervisory Authorities may issue recommendations and guidelines.

Since the introduction of the Lamfalussy procedure, the Second Banking Directive has been superseded by an even more organic statute (i.e. Directive 2006/48/EC),[22] the latter being recently amalgamated within Regulation (EU) No 575/2013,[23] and ancillary Directive 2013/36,[24] together referred to as 'CRD IV'. This progression of the aforementioned chain of Directives paints a picture of EU banking legislation which can be identified with a number of salient features. First and foremost, the banking business is a reserved one on the grounds that the typical banking activities (not only to lend money and to raise funds, but also those which are ancillary)[25] are not available to anyone, but rather exclusively to those who/which, in satisfying the minimum legislative requirements such as having the necessary capital and adequate managerial skills, are permitted to commence such a business by means of a licence or authorisation. Additionally, the business is supervised to such an extent that the sword of Damocles hangs over the head of each financial institution, thereby subjecting them to the mercy of an authority (the supervisor) who can decide, in accordance with the objective parameters, whether that business can continue to operate or, alternatively, if it should be excluded from the market by revoking its licence.[26] Finally (and this is a particularly important factor at EU level and in a market which is expected to be highly integrated), banking activities are passported. In other words, once authorisation has been granted to a bank in a given country, no further authorisation is required in other Member States where it wishes to operate, subject to the conditions discussed above, section 1.3.3.

---

22 In full: Directive 2006/48/EC of the European Parliament and of the Council of 14 June 2006 relating to the taking up and pursuit of the business of credit institutions, also referred to as the Capital Requirements Directive.

23 In full: Regulation (EU) No 575/2013 of the European Parliament and of the Council of 26 June 2013 on prudential requirements for credit institutions and investment firms and amending Regulation (EU) No 648/2012 Text with EEA relevance.

24 In full: Directive 2013/36/EU of the European Parliament and of the Council of 26 June 2013 on access to the activity of credit institutions and the prudential supervision of credit institutions and investment firms, amending Directive 2002/87/EC and repealing Directives 2006/48/EC and 2006/49/EC.

25 See in this respect Chapter 2.

26 See also Chapter 7, dealing with the insolvency of credit institutions.

1.3.5 De Larosière Report

The broad picture of the legislative sources pertaining to banking and financial law is completed by the De Larosière Report. In October 2008, Jacques de Larosière de Champfeu was entrusted with a mandate, administered by the President of the European Commission (José Barroso), the purpose of which was to chair a group of experts uniquely qualified to devise practical proposals in the area of financial regulation and supervision. The report was commissioned against a challenging backdrop of economic crisis and recession. In the months pursuant to the eruption of both the Eurozone crisis and the public debt crisis in 2009, the latter affecting most notably the peripheral countries of the Eurozone, the European Union faced a critical juncture: on the one hand it could opt for a 'chacun pour soi' solution (each country independently makes its own decisions on how to proceed) or, on the other, it could choose to strengthen cooperation within the EU countries to provide a united front against the testing economic landscape of financial recession. The latter solution found the favour of the De Larosière Report,[27] which essentially emphasised three steps to guard against any likelihood of a future collapse: (a) a new regulatory agenda; (b) stronger coordinated supervision; (c) effective crisis management procedures.

Significantly, the De Larosière Report does not seek to alter the legislative architecture of the EU, as forged from the foundations by the Treaties and, as far as the financial legislation is concerned, specified by the finishing touches of the Lamfalussy Report. In other words, the Report of 2009 does not (methodologically) amend the manner in which legislation is crafted in Brussels. However, it certainly provides the legislator with important pointers on what kind of norms and principles shall be promoted in the financial sector to address the issues and problems which crawled (or rather, leapt) out of the woodwork as the first decade of the twenty-first century neared its conclusion.

As emphasised by the De Larosière Report, the regulatory framework in place prior to the recent crisis lacked 'cohesiveness', and therefore homogeneity. As the EU Member States were afforded a significant degree of leeway over the extent to which they could implement and enforce the Directives, such 'options [led] to a wide diversity of national transpositions related to local traditions, legislations and practices'.[28] The reason for this lack of harmonisation was the overly accentuated vagueness which characterised the first level of legislation (the Directive), where the national legislator had at his disposal a multitude of options with the outcome that, at the lower level (the Level 3 committees of the Lamfalussy report), it was very difficult, if nigh on impossible, to 'impose a single solution'.[29]

The De Larosière Report, and its remarks on the manner in which legislation in the financial sector should be adopted in the EU, has not gone unheard or indeed unheeded. First and most significantly, the De Larosière Report has resulted in the creation of a European System of Financial Supervision ('ESFS'), the purpose of which is to ensure the supervision of the Union's financial system. The ESFS consists of

27 J de Larosière, *The High-Level Group on Financial Supervision in the EU*, Brussels, 25 February 2009, http://ec.europa.eu/internal_market/finances/docs/de_larosiere_report_en.pdf, accessed 5 August 2014.
28 See ibid. 27.
29 Ibid.

three European Supervisory Authorities: the European Banking Authority, having its seat in London ('EBA'); the European Securities Markets Authority, having its seat in Paris ('ESMA'); and the European Insurance and Occupational Pensions Authority, seated in Frankfurt ('EIOPA').[30] As stated previously, in these authorities the relevant national supervisors participate and, unlike their predecessors, are empowered to issue binding Regulatory Technical Standards and Implementing Technical Standards in addition to non-binding guidelines and recommendations. In addition, a European Systemic Risk Board ('ESRB') forms part of the ESFS, which is:

> responsible for the macro-prudential oversight of the financial system within the Union in order to contribute to the prevention or mitigation of systemic risks to financial stability in the Union that arise from developments within the financial system and taking into account macroeconomic developments, so as to avoid periods of widespread financial distress. It shall contribute to the smooth functioning of the internal market and thereby ensure a sustainable contribution of the financial sector to economic growth.[31]

Moreover, as analysed in this textbook, many areas of financial law underwent significant change so as to limit the level of discretion in the hands of each Member State. For instance, as mentioned in Chapter 7, the deposit guarantee scheme which was previously based on a minimum harmonisation Directive[32] and which thus left relative discretion to each country on the level of protection afforded to the depositor, has been replaced by a more robust maximum harmonisation Directive[33] where this discretion is significantly curtailed, if not entirely removed. In other cases, Directives have been or will be replaced by Regulations, so as to accomplish unification. Also, where no trace of harmonisation was to be found,[34] a legislative framework is in the pipeline and shall be presently administered accordingly.

1.3.6 Single Supervisory Mechanism

Despite the tumultuous evolution of the financial sector over the past 30 years, prior to the recent financial crisis a truly European integration of supervisors had remained conspicuous by its absence. Therefore, until relatively recently, a sort of paradox

30 See, respectively, Regulation (EU) No 1093/2010 of the European Parliament and of the Council of 24 November 2010 establishing a European Supervisory Authority (European Banking Authority), amending Decision No 716/2009/EC and repealing Commission Decision 2009/78/EC; Regulation (EU) No 1095/2010 of the European Parliament and of the Council of 24 November 2010 establishing a European Supervisory Authority (European Securities and Markets Authority), amending Decision No 716/2009/EC and repealing Commission Decision 2009/77/EC; and Regulation (EU) No 1094/2010 of the European Parliament and of the Council of 24 November 2010 establishing a European Supervisory Authority (European Insurance and Occupational Pensions Authority), amending Decision No 716/2009/EC and repealing Commission Decision 2009/79/EC.

31 Article 3 of Regulation (EU) No 1092/2010 of the European Parliament and of the Council of 24 November 2010 on European Union macro-prudential oversight of the financial system and establishing a European Systemic Risk Board.

32 Directive 94/19/EC of the European Parliament and of the Council of 30 May 1994 on deposit guarantee schemes, OJ L 135.

33 Directive 2009/14/EC of the European Parliament and of the Council of 11 March 2009 amending Directive 94/19/EC on deposit guarantee schemes as regards the overage level and the payout delay, OJ L 68.

34 For instance, a guarantee scheme in the insurance industry.

prevailed within the European Union where, on the one hand, a fully integrated market of credit institutions reaped the benefits of a single market which afforded them the tools to expand and operate at a greater pace across Europe while, on the other, the fragmented subsistence of a body of supervisors as numerous as the various countries constituting the EU was evident. This asymmetry, replete with myriad organisational distortions, in hindsight may have been a contributory factor in the collapse of several major financial institutions in the late 2000s, too vast and pan-European to be supervised by the assemblage of authorities existing in each respective country. This flaw in the architecture of the EU banking system has recently been revisited by the creation of the Single Supervisory Mechanism.[35] This legislative structure is hinged upon the European Central Bank,[36] which, in assuming this new additional role, is responsible, in conjunction with the national supervisors, for the prudential supervision of the credit institutions of all banks operating in the Eurozone. It is hoped that this mechanism will confine to the annals of history the predicaments of the past (in other words, a largely fragmented body of supervisors dwarfed by the giants among the credit institutions which in the interim had grown exponentially beyond the borders of a specific Member State) and thus curtail the likelihood that such disarray could once again be catapulted into the public spotlight.

1.4 Conclusion

The hierarchy of legislative sources existing in the banking and financial sector bears many similarities with that in operation, at EU level, in any other industry. Nonetheless, for the financial industry a dual layer blueprint of legislation (levels 1 and 2 of the Lamfalussy Process) has been developed for more than a decade and as early as the Lamfalussy Report, where, for each financial sub-area, each topic is legislated upon in general terms by a Directive, which is subsequently adopted by means of a co-decision process and detailed in the relevant ensuing Directive.

In the aftermath of the tripartite crises which wreaked havoc across Europe between 2007 and 2010 (the financial, Eurozone and public-debt crises), the possible demise of the European legislative architecture in the financial sector and the likelihood of the same fate befalling the very essence of the Union has been averted, in part, it seems, due to a new philosophy – echoed strongly in the vision of the De Larosière Report – which dictates that certain rules and regulations are homogenously applied among the various Member States.

35 By virtue of Council Regulation (EU) No 1024/2013 of 15 October 2013 conferring specific tasks on the European Central Bank concerning policies relating to the prudential supervision of credit institutions, OJ L 287.

36 The European Central Bank already existed in its capacity of bank in charge of the monetary policy.

1.5 Further reading

Barnard, C, *The Substantive Law of the EU: The Four Freedoms* (4th edn Oxford University Press, Oxford 2013)

Dashwood, A, Dougan, M, Rodger, B, Spaventa, E, and Wyatt, D, *Wyatt and Dashwood's European Union Law* (6th edn Hart Publishing, Oxford and Portland 2011)

Kaczorowska, A, *European Union Law* (2nd edn Routledge, Abingdon 2011)

Reid, A, *European Union* (4th edn W. Green, London 2010)

Weatherill, S, *Cases and Materials on EU Law* (9th edn Oxford University Press, Oxford 2010)

Woods, L, and Watson, P, *Steiner and Woods EU Law* (11th edn Oxford University Press, Oxford 2012)

1.6 Questions

1.1 What were the flaws affecting the 'First Banking Directive'?

1.2 Can you describe the principle of 'EU passport'?

1.3 What are the differences existing between an EU Treaty, a Regulation and a Directive?

1.4 Is the 'Lamfalussy Report' a piece of legislation?

1.5 What was the main reason the EU commissioned the drafting of the 'De Larosière Report'?

Part B

Financial markets

Chapter 2

The stock market

Chapter contents

2.1 Some history

Historically, an ancestor of the modern stock exchanges was created in the Italian Renaissance, more precisely in the 1300s, by Venetian bankers. The Republic of Venice or *La Serenissima* – at that time an independent sovereign state with overseas territories and colonies across the Mediterranean – boasted an extensive network of trades. It was, together with Florence, the most opulent city of Europe. The active and ambitious merchants of the Venice city-state, in order to support their increasingly booming commerce overseas and the enormous financial resources required to prop them up, needed fresh capital from outsiders. These outsiders ('investors' in contemporary finance terminology) demonstrated no knowledge of the business, but they had an interest in investing money to make a future profit. Therefore, bankers in Venice set up a system of exchange (a primordial form of the modern stock exchange), where traders were permitted to buy and sell corporate debt obligations and also government debt obligations issued by the Republic of Venice. These debt obligations represented an early form of 'bonds', i.e. promises to pay an amount of money, issued by a merchant (in respect of corporate obligations) or the Republic of Venice (in respect of government obligations) for a nominal value to finance a specific venture; the issuer received money as a result. The remuneration for the investor would transpire, upon maturity, in the capital originally lent to the issuer, plus the interest promised, should the relevant venture reach a successful conclusion.

This system was expanded upon the discoveries of Asia and the Americas and the resulting need for more extensive investments in the 'new world'. The new ventures were decidedly hazardous, given the new inter continental and trans oceanic arena in which they were played out. The mechanism envisaged was therefore to separate the risk of the investment from a single venture through the release of 'shares'. By investing in shares, the investor did not speculate in a single venture by buying the relevant bond (as was the case in the initial period), but rather he spread the risk over different ventures and/or businesses, organised by the issuer of the shares, de facto an entity bearing some similarities to a modern joint stock company. In this new scenario, it is remarkable to note that the Dutch East India Company – a legal entity with various business operations and ventures scattered across Asia – was the first company whose shares started being traded, continuously, in the Amsterdam Stock Exchange, as early as 1611. The London Stock Exchange began operating in a coffee shop in the eigtheenth century, as a place where shares of companies masterminding the organisation of several ventures across the ocean, were initially exchanged or, to use the contemporary term, traded.

Thus, the term 'stock market' traditionally conveys a venue – by definition, a trading venue – where transactions relating to financial instruments take place. From an economic point of view, the functions of a stock market are multifarious, but first and foremost it is to facilitate the exchange between demand and supply of transferrable securities or, more generally and applying the relevant technical terminology, financial instruments.[1] The conclusion of transactions within an organised stock market is

1 The concept of 'financial instruments' is described in more detail in Chapter 7. Here, it suffices to note that, according to Directive 2014/65 ('MiFID II'), particularly Annex I, Section C, financial instruments are 'transferrable securities', such as 'shares' and 'bonds', but also 'money-market instruments' (e.g. covered bonds), 'units in collective investment undertakings' and the important category of 'derivatives'.

rendered all the more secure as transactions therein are concluded by qualified professionals, specifically authorised as market participants to ensure such an outcome. Ultimately, these factors increase the liquidity of the market and, therefore, the prospects for firms to unearth capital in order to operate more dynamically. A salient feature of a stock market, from an organisational point of view, although this reverberates also on the way these special 'venues' are regulated,[2] is the fact that the financial instruments traded in that market are granted entry through a process of authorisation. Additionally, the dealers entitled to place orders in the regulated market are exclusively dealers authorised by their own organisation (usually from qualified investment firms and banks) and the market is an organisational structure, which is overseen by a management department charged with ensuring the best functioning of it.

2.2 The rules governing a stock exchange

Before addressing the details of the legal provisions governing the stock markets, it is essential to touch on the way in which the legislation existing in this area is articulated in relation to each EU Member State. The legislation in question is to large extent of EU origin, the reason being that the Brussels law-maker regards the relevant *sedes materiae* as adhering to the fundamental principles of the EU (particularly, the principles of free movement of capital). Accordingly, the interaction between European and national statutes in this area of law is mainly based on a dual layer, where an EU piece of legislation (usually in the form of a Directive) fixes norms, and at national level these norms are subsequently implemented by each Member State.[3] This implementation tends not to materialise in a homogenous fashion across the spectrum of countries presently in possession of EU membership. However, as long as the specific provisions do not infringe the relevant Directive, legislative divergences do not give rise to any concern in terms of legitimacy and legality.[4]

Each stock market is typically the product of a certain country, and its relevant legislation and regulations, where it is incorporated and operates. Nonetheless, globally, stock markets have undergone a dramatic transition over the past three decades, advancing from a scenario where they were formerly purely 'public' (i.e. managed by an authority which was de facto an emanation of the government) to a more competitive system, where each market is perceived to be 'private' and the entity in charge of its organisation – terminologically the 'market company' or the 'operator' – considered a 'private' company, incorporated and functioning in accordance with

---

2 See below, section 2.2.

3 See also Chapter 1.

4 In Chapter 1, more details were provided about the fact that the EU legislative process in the financial sector has been given a significant acceleration as a result of the so-called Lamfalussy Report. For the purposes of this chapter and, in general, for this textbook, the interaction between Level 1 and Level 2 of the Lamfalussy Report is quintessential, for the reason that with a piece of legislation of the first level, usually a Directive but also a Regulation, the EU law-maker sets forth basic principles, whereas in the correspondent piece of legislation of the second level (also in this case, usually a Directive with implementing provisions) the detailed norms are provided. The Lamfalussy Report can be accessed at http://ec.europa.eu/internal_market/securities/docs/lamfalussy/wisemen/final-report-wise-men_en.pdf.

the corporate law rules on private companies. Needless to say, this liberal approach does not prevent the market company from falling under the supervision of a local authority instituted at national level. The organisation and business of a stock exchange is predominantly a regulated activity, to be authorised by the national authority and thereafter subject to its supervision, which is carried out, constantly and systematically, during the pursuit of the relevant business.

At EU level, the matter of the stock market has been profoundly influenced by the harmonisation process; the initial Directive 2004/39/EC of 21 April 2004 on markets in financial instruments (henceforth 'MiFID I')[5] shall be soon phased out as a result of the passing, in 2014, of a new EU piece of legislation, Directive 2014/65/EU (henceforth 'MiFID II').[6]

More specifically, art. 44 of MiFID II, basically corresponding to art. 36 of MiFID I, details the principle that the regulated market is a reserved activity,[7] permitted exclusively to those systems complying with the provisions of Title III of the Directive. The authorisation hinges decisively on the 'home authority' being satisfied that both 'the market company' and the systems of the regulated market (i.e. the organisation and structure of it) are consistent with the requirements set forth at EU level, particularly the provisions disclosed by art. 44 (and following) of MiFID II.

MiFID I required a specific dual layer pattern as a prerequisite to a regulated market being granted authorisation: the organisation (the market itself) and the entity,

5 In full: European Parliament and Council Directive 2004/39/EC of 21 April 2004 on markets in financial instruments amending Council Directives 85/611/EEC and 93/6/EEC and Directive 2000/12/EC of the European Parliament and of the Council and repealing Council Directive 93/22/EEC. MiFID I needs to be read, until its full replacement by Directive 2014/65, in conjunction with two additional EU pieces of legislation:

- The MiFID Implementing Directive 2006/73 ('Commission Directive 2006/73/EC of 10 August 2006 implementing Directive 2004/39/EC of the European Parliament and of the Council as regards organisational requirements and operating conditions for investment firms and defined terms for the purposes of that Directive').
- The MiFID Implementing Regulation 2006/1287 ('Commission Regulation (EC) No 1287/2006 of 10 August 2006 implementing Directive 2004/39/EC of the European Parliament and of the Council as regards record-keeping obligations for investment firms, transaction reporting, market transparency, admission of financial instruments to trading, and defined terms for the purposes of that Directive').

Both these implementing statutes represent 'Level 2 measures' in the 'Lamfalussy process' described earlier in this chapter. On MiFID, see also Chapters 4 and 8.

6 In full: Directive 2014/65/EU of the European Parliament and of the Council of 15 May 2014 on markets in financial instruments and amending Directive 2002/92/EC and Directive 2011/61/EU. Directive 2014/65 has been published in the Official Gazette of the European Union on 12 June 2014 and has entered into force, according to its art. 96, on the twentieth day after its publications (i.e. on 2 July 2014). According to its art. 93, the transposition of its main rules, including those concerned with the regulated markets, dealt with in this chapter, shall take place by 3 July 2016. Directive 2014/65 shall be read in conjunction with EU Regulation No 600/2014. Together, MiFID II and the Regulation should 'form the legal framework governing the requirements applicable to investment firms, regulated markets, data reporting services providers and third country firms providing investment services or activities in the Union' (see Recital 7 of MiFID II).

7 Different from the regulated market is the 'multilateral trading facility' (MTF), therefore 'a multilateral system, operated by an investment firm or a market operator, which brings together multiple third-party buying and selling interests in financial instruments – in the system and in accordance with non-discretionary rules' (art. 4(1)(22) of MiFID II). Although the MTFs are not officially recognised regulated markets and, therefore, not subject to the relevant rules of authorisation, MiFID II, and previously MiFID I too, makes sure that in each Member State the investment firms and operator in charge of them establish and implement 'non-discretionary rules for the execution of orders in the system' (art. 19(1) of MiFID II). A new typology of system, introduced by MiFID II, and unknown in the architecture of the previous MiFID I, is the 'organised trading facility'; the latter is defined (art. 4(1)(23)) as 'a multilateral system which is not a regulated market or an MTF and in which multiple third-party buying and selling interests in bonds, structured finance products, emission allowances or derivatives are able to interact in the system'.

distinct from the market, operating the latter, and therefore called the operator.[8] Conversely, MiFID II seems to postulate two possible options, either a market managed and operated by an operator or a regulated market managed by itself.[9]

The operator,[10] given that it is ultimately responsible for the correct functioning of the regulated market, is tasked with requirements, not simply at the start of the business but also later, for the duration of its lifespan. For instance, all information relating to the programme of operations and the organisational structure of the regulated market shall be provided to the relevant competent authority by the regulated market.[11] On the other hand, the authority shall be empowered to ensure that the market itself complies with the provisions specified by MiFID II, in addition to implementing national provisions.[12] A stock market is by definition global, as it aids both domestic and international intermediaries in gaining access to dealings on financial instruments traded in that market, but it shall be subject to the regulations of the country in which it is authorised.[13] For instance, if for public policy reasons the authority of the country where the market is authorised suspends transactions, that order shall take effect on the relevant regulated market of that Member State.

At EU level, no time limit is specified in regard to the number of days by which the authorisation to carry out a regulated market must be granted; entailed to this is the principle – inferable indirectly – that any national legislation will have a certain discretion to this end. On the other hand, MiFID II accounts for the circumstances upon occurrence of which the competent authority may withdraw the authorisation or, in some cases, suspend it.[14] In this respect, first, attention must be drawn to a lapse of 12 months from the time the authorisation was granted during which time the operator failed to engage in any business, an express repudiation by the market company,[15] or a lack of activity in the preceding six-month period. Additionally, the authorisation shall be withdrawn in cases of fraudulent activity, where the authorisation has been obtained 'by making false statements or by any other irregular means'.[16] Furthermore, a variation of the original conditions under which the authorisation was granted as well as a serious and systematic infringement of the provisions adopted pursuant to MiFID II may prompt a revocation of the authorisation.[17] Finally, art. 44(5)(e) of MiFID II,[18] with its generic wording, would suggest that the applicable national law may contemplate additional provisions for the withdrawal of the authorisation.

8 Art. 36(1)(3) MiFID I.

9 This seems to be inferable from art. 44(1), para. 3, MiFID II: 'In the case of a regulated market that is a legal person and that is managed or operated by a market operator other than the regulated market itself'.

10 Or the regulated market, in cases where the latter managed itself.

11 Art. 44(1), para. 1, MiFID II. However, according to the following art. 44(1), para. 3, if the regulated market was managed or operated by a market operator other than the regulated market itself, 'Member States shall establish how the different obligations imposed on the market operator under this Directive are to be allocated between the regulated market and the market operator.'

12 Art. 44(2) MiFID II, corresponding to the previous art. 36(2) MiFID I.

13 Art. 44(4) MiFID II, previously *mutatis mutandis* art. 36(4) MiFID I.

14 Art. 44(5) MiFID II, previously art. 36(5) MiFID I.

15 The language used by MiFID II is slightly different: '[The regulated market] expressly renounces the authorisation'.

16 Art. 44(5)(b) MiFID II, previously art. 36(5)(b) MiFID I.

17 Art. 44(5)(c) and (d), equipollent to art. 36(5)(c) and (d) MiFID I, respectively.

18 *Mutatis mutandis*, art. 36(5)(e).

Akin to any other regulated entity such as a bank, those effectively directing the business and the operations of the regulated markets (more specifically, the 'management body'[19]) must be endowed with 'sufficiently good repute', 'sufficient knowledge', 'skills and experience to perform their duties'.[20] Coupled with this provision is the obligation on each operator of the regulated market to communicate to the competent authority the identity of those in charge of the regulated market, and any ensuing change of personnel at that executive level.[21] The standard imposed on management of the regulated market (or its own operator, if different) is extended by the Directive, albeit in terms of mere 'suitability', to the 'persons exercising significant influence over the management of the regulated market'.[22]

Although the regulated market is typically a private organisation and the new legislative framework would appear to encourage this form of business (with the consequence that the selection of the appropriate personnel to shepherd the business is a matter of limited public concern or open to limited public interference), the competent authority shall be fully entitled to veto the appointment of management personnel in exceptional circumstances where, on the one hand, it is not satisfied that the 'members of the management body of the market operator are of sufficiently good repute, possess sufficient knowledge, skills and experience and commit sufficient time to perform their functions', on the other hand, there are 'objective and demonstrable grounds for believing that [they] pose a threat to its effective, sound and prudent management and to the adequate consideration of the integrity of the market.'[23]

Attention has been drawn, at the outset, to the fact that the stock market is an arena in which exclusively 'admitted financial instruments' are listed. This concept of the regulated market as a 'restricted club' of financial instruments is echoed in MiFID.[24] The Member States must have 'clear and transparent rules regarding the admission of financial instruments to trading'. These rules are engineered to ensure that 'any financial instruments admitted on a regulated market are capable of being traded in a fair, orderly and efficient manner and, in the case of transferrable securities, are freely negotiable'.[25] For instance, a pertinent example of shares not being 'freely

19 The 'management body' is a very neutral definition of the Directive at stake, fitting both into national legal systems where exclusively a board of directors is contemplated (e.g. the UK one), and jurisdictions (e.g. Germany) which conversely lie on a two-tier body, the board of directors itself and a more enlarged supervisory board.

In the terminology of MiFID II, the 'management body' is defined as 'the body or bodies of . . . a market operator, which are appointed in accordance with national law, which are empowered to set the entity's strategy, objectives and overall direction, and which oversee and monitor management decision-making and include persons who effectively direct the business of the entity.'

20 Art. 45(1) MiFID II, correspondent to art. 37 MiFID I.

21 Art. 46 MiFID II.

22 More specifically, according to art. 46(1) MiFID II (in the past, basically but not identically, art. 38 MiFID I), Member States 'shall require the persons who are in a position to exercise, directly or indirectly, significant influence over the management of the regulated market to be suitable.' According to this line of reasoning, the operator of the regulated market shall be required, on the one hand, 'to provide the competent authority with, and to make public, information regarding the ownership of the regulated market and/or the market operator, and in particular, the identity and scale of interests of any parties in a position to exercise significant influence over the management' (art. 46(2)(a) MiFID II), on the other hand, 'to inform the competent authority of and to make public any transfer of ownership which gives rise to a change in the identity of the persons exercising significant influence over the operation of the regulated market' (art. 46(2)(b) MiFID II).

23 Art. 45(7) MiFID II; in the past, albeit in a more loose wording, a similar provision was contained in art. 37, second part, MiFID I.

24 Art. 51(1) MiFID II, previously art. 40(1) MiFID I.

25 Art. 51(1), para. 2, MiFID II, previously art. 40(1), para. 2, MiFID I.

transferable', would be shares of an issuer, in the bylaws of which clauses are embedded so that any transfer of shares is not possible without first seeking, and being granted, authorisation from the board of directors of the issuer. An issuer which requested the listing of its shares with bylaws drafted in such a fashion should not receive the consent of the stock market to the admission of the listing; likewise, if the clause was added at a later date (e.g. as a result of a resolution reached at the shareholders' meeting), in all likelihood the issuer would receive notice from the stock market to remove the relevant clause and be cautioned that an exclusion from trading could ensue, should this order not be heeded within a specific timeframe.

Because the listing renders the issued securities 'public', the admission to the market of financial instruments is generally accompanied by a prospectus, i.e. a document disseminating and disclosing to the public not only the characteristics of the securities but also of the entity issuing the securities (the issuer). The prospectus obligations, albeit also incorporated within MiFID II,[26] are the subject matter of a specific piece of legislation – the Prospectus Directive – an analysis of which will be undertaken in the following section.

2.3 The admission of securities to a stock market

The admission of securities to a regulated market is a decidedly complex process which must negotiate several steps. Aside from the legal aspects connected with the listing, which will be discussed forthwith, it is worth acknowledging that entailed to the listing is the decision of the issuer to go 'public', thereby accepting that its financial instruments will be traded publicly and, therefore, acquired by individuals and entities not necessarily known to, or welcomed by, the issuer.

It is rare that the issuer itself organises the listing, rather it relies on the cooperation of one or more financial entities (a bank, specifically an investment bank, an investment firm or a combination of them), to which a mandate is given to aid the specific securities of that issuer being admitted to the market. This financial advisor is also called the 'arranger'. Traditionally, the mandate of the arranger involves the organisation of two activities: (i) the listing of the securities on the regulated market; (ii) the drafting of the prospectus and its subsequent submission to the competent authority for approval, if indeed this is required.[27] From a financial point of view, the activities of the arranger may also include what is called 'underwriting'. The underwriting can be of three typologies: (a) firm commitment underwriting (the underwriters purchase securities from an issuer, or one of its main shareholders, at an agreed price); (b) best efforts underwriting (an underwriter makes its best efforts to sell the securities of the offeror/issuer); and (c) standby underwriting (the offeror/issuer offers securities, with the commitment of the underwriters to purchase the remaining securities that are not purchased).[28] The issuer is typically advised by its own legal team, as are the arrangers.

26 And previously MiFID I too.

27 As explained later in this chapter, there are cases where the issuer is exempt from the prospectus.

28 Cf. LD Soderquist and TA Gabaldon, *Securities Law* (Foundation Press and Thomson West, New York 2004) 30): 'Underwriting refers to the function of helping a company, or one or more of its major shareholders, see securities to the public through an offering'.

In some cases, the same team of legal advisors may be retained by both parties (issuer and arrangers), although, to avoid any conflict of interest, the more likely scenario is that two separate law firms are employed.

The understanding reached between the arranger(s) and the issuer is typically contained within a contract, with terms and conditions dictating the duties which the arranger is expected to fulfil (including any relevant indemnities and penalties), and the rights and obligations of the issuer giving the mandate. Among such terms is obviously the right to remuneration owed to the arranger for its advice on the listing process.

The offer of securities to the public has been, for some time, the subject of a harmonisation process at EU level. A piece of legislation dating back to 1980, Directive 80/390/EEC[29] represents the earliest attempt by the European Economic Community to create a legislative framework setting forth guidelines for the drawing up, scrutiny and distribution of the relevant documentation (the listing particulars) to be published for the admission of securities to the stock markets. Directive 80/390 was later subsumed within Directive 2001/34/EC ('Listing Directive'),[30] which codifies, among additional features, a number of previous Directives existing in this area, more specifically: (a) Directive 79/279/EEC of 4 March 1979, coordinating the conditions for the admission of securities to official stock exchange listing (the 'Admission Directive'); (b) the 'Listing Particulars Directive', already cited above[31] of 17 March 1980, coordinating the requirements for the drawing up, scrutiny and distribution of the listing particulars to be published for the admission of securities to official stock exchange listing; (c) Directive 82/121/EEC of 5 February 1982, on information to be published on a regular basis by companies the shares of which have been admitted to official stock exchange listing (the 'Interim Reports Directive'); (d) Directive 89/298/EEC, relating to the drawing up, scrutiny and distribution of the prospectus in its published format when transferable securities are offered to the public (the 'Public Offer Prospectus Directive').

A further pillar of legislation in the broad area of the public issue of securities is Directive 2003/71/EC,[32] which offers guidelines on the 'prospectus to be published when securities are offered to the public or admitted to trading'.

As a result of the above, the legislative framework currently prevailing in this area is two-fold: (a) first, guidelines relating to the 'prospectus' and enshrined within Directive 2003/71 ('Prospectus Directive'); (b) second, guidelines relating to the 'listing', where the relevant rules are those incorporated within Directive 2001/34 ('Listing Directive'). The intention of these two pieces of legislation, alongside the third one, the 'Transparency Obligations Directive',[33] ultimately, is to promote the

---

29 In full: Directive 80/390/EEC of 17 March 1980 coordinating the requirements for the drawing up, scrutiny and distribution of the listing particulars to be published for the admission of securities to official stock exchange listing, OJ L 100 ('Listing Particulars Directive').

30 In full: Directive 2001/34/EC of the European Parliament and of the Council of 28 May 2001 on the admission of securities to official stock exchange listing and on information to be published on those securities, OJ L 184.

31 Again, more specifically, Directive 80/390/EEC.

32 In full: Directive 2003/71/EC of the European Parliament and of the Council of 4 November 2003 on the prospectus to be published when securities are offered to the public or admitted to trading and amending Directive 2001/34/EC, OJ L 345.

33 In full: Directive 2004/109/EC of the European Parliament and of the Council of 15 December 2004 on the harmonisation of transparency requirements in relation to information about issuers whose securities are

concept of a single EU passport for issuers, so that the raising of capital can be facilitated across the EU, both as regards a listing to the regulated markets and as regards the issue of securities.

2.3.1 The listing process

2.3.1.1 Listing Directive

Within the EU, the admission of securities to a regulated market is governed, as already mentioned, by Directive 2001/34 (Listing Directive), which again relates to the admission of securities to the official stock exchange listing and to the information to be published on those securities.[34] From a more general perspective, its purpose is to establish a level playing field across the Union in terms of setting minimal requirements which securities must adhere to prior to listing.

The first general rule is that '*securities* [emphasis added] may not be admitted to official listing on any stock exchange situated or operating within their territory unless the conditions [of the Directive itself] are satisfied.'[35] To simplify, a national piece of legislation which had incorporated a decidedly loose interpretation of the guidelines, thereby not requiring any form of authorisation for securities to be listed, would undoubtedly fail to comply with the rules of the Directive and, potentially, would prompt the EU Commission to initiate an infringement procedure against that country in accordance with the principles of the Treaty. In other words, the harmonisation of securities markets, manifested in standardised guidelines on authorisation, aims to ensure that an investor may safely invest in a security market with the 'EU brand'. Although the EU legislation, as a matter of course, does not give any guarantee on making a return on the investment, it does provide a minimal 'floor' of rules which each country will be obligated to implement so that a minimal level of protection has been afforded to the investor.

A second rule, also inferable from the Listing Directive, is one which requires that all *the issuers* of securities to be admitted to official listing be subject 'to the obligations provided for by this Directive'.[36] The provisions are intended to guarantee that the issuers operating in the EU market uniformly comply with the Directive at stake. All issuers, i.e. 'companies and other legal persons and any undertaking whose securities are the subject of an application for admission to official listing on a stock exchange',[37] operating in the Community engaged in the issue of securities shall be obligated to comply with it.

The Listing Directive, when analysed further, sets forth two sets of guidelines: (a) for shares (or 'equity securities'), i.e. securities representing the share capital of a

---

continued

admitted to trading on a regulated market and amending Directive 2001/34/EC, OJ L 390. A brief commentary to the Transparency Obligations Directive can be read in HS Scott, *International Finance* (17th edn Foundation Press, New York 2010) 273, 274.

34 Among authors such as S Grundmann, *European Company Law Ius Communitatis, Vol. I* (2nd edn Intersentia, Cambridge, Antwerp and Portland 2012) 480, the Listing Directive is sometimes also referred to as the 'Stock Exchange Directive'.

35 Art. 5 Listing Directive.

36 Art. 5 Listing Directive.

37 Art. 1(a) Listing Directive.

company; and (b) for 'debt securities', i.e. securities representing a debt of the issuer – in other words bonds, rather than the share capital. There are conditions imposed on both the issuer and the securities issued by it, although the level of information required varies relative to whether the transferrable securities are equitable securities or debt securities – the former requiring a more extensive array of information than the latter.

Equity securities

As regards the guidelines (for the issuer) for equity securities, an initial requirement is that the 'legality' of the issuer is guaranteed. The issuer cannot be any entity, but rather must be an entity operating in conformity with 'the laws and regulations to which it is subject, as regards its formation and its operation under its statutes'.[38] Indirectly, given the tenor employed by the legislator, it can be inferred that an individual who wanted to issue securities to be listed would not have this venture admitted, as the sole eligible issuer is a corporation. Thus, it should be an entity having a legal personality, separate from that of its members (or owners); for instance, a partnership – in common law jurisdictions, a business organised collectively – would not fall within the ambit of 'entity' as it is bereft of a separate legal personality. Additionally, the Listing Directive requires, for the admission to listing, an adequate capitalisation of the issuer, of no less than Euro 1,000,000,[39] as well as the publication of its annual accounts for the three financial years preceding the application for official listing.[40]

The second category of requirements which must be satisfied to gain successful admission of shares relates to the shares themselves, rather than to the issuer. One of the requisites stipulates that shares shall be 'freely negotiable'. As a means of clarifying this requisite, it is worth noting that shares, in respect of which the respective bylaws of the issuer require authorisation from other shareholders or approval by the board of directors for the transfer to be valid, would be inconsistent with the public nature of the issue. Clauses of this nature would be apt for private companies but would be decidedly unsuitable for a company which harbours the ambition of issuing shares in a regulated market. The requisite of transferability shall be required, theoretically, also for shares which 'are not fully paid up as freely negotiable'.[41] However, in this case, the national legislation shall be permitted to treat these shares as freely negotiable, 'if arrangements have been made to ensure that the negotiability of such shares is not

38 See art. 42 Listing Directive.

39 Art. 43 Listing Directive. This figure is a 'floor'; a Member State or the stock exchange of that country may require a higher capitalisation. For instance, in Italy, the local stock exchange (Borsa Italiana), for the listing of shares, requires the issuer to have a minimal capital of Euro 5,000,000 (see Regolamento e Istruzioni dei Mercati Organizzati e Gestiti da Borsa Italiana S.p.A.). It is also stated that the company's 'capital and reserves, including profit or loss, from the last financial year, may be at least one million [Euros]'; however, according to the following art. 43(2), the requisite of the minimum capitalisation can be waived by the Member State, to the extent to which 'the competent authorities are satisfied that there will be an adequate market of the shares concerned.'

40 See art. 44 Listing Directive. However, according to the same provision, such a requisite can be derogated by the competent national authority, 'where such a derogation is desirable in the interests of the company or of investors and where the competent authorities are satisfied that investors have the necessary information available to be able to arrive at an informed judgement on the company and the shares for which admission to official listing is sought'.

41 Art. 45 Listing Directive. It is worth recalling that the concept of 'freely transferrable' securities reverberates with art. 40 of the MiFID I Directive too, as already discussed in section 2.2 of this chapter.

restricted and that dealing is made open and proper by providing the public with all appropriate information.'[42]

Debt securities

The requirements for debt securities relating to the issuer is decidedly laconic. The Listing Directive simply refers to only one – relating to the legality of the issuer: 'The legal position of the undertaking must be in conformity with the laws and regulations to which it is subject, as regards both its formation and its operation under its statutes.'[43] Nothing else is added in terms of requisites, markedly different from share securities, where the requirements relating to the issuer are significantly more extensive. The reason for this is an economic, rather than a legal one. The investment in shares carries with it a higher level of uncertainty; they represent the capital of the company and their value fluctuates, by definition, in proportion to the performance of the issuer. As a result, information relating to the issuer is fundamental in enabling the investor to assess the level of risk involved. Conversely, the debt security is a contractual obligation on the part of the company to return the capital invested by the investors, plus interest. Other than enabling the investor to assess his counterparty's risk of default, information relating to the issuer is deemed to be less essential.

In addition to the provision according to which '[t]he debt securities must be freely negotiable',[44] which also applies to shares, the Listing Directive requires that 'debt securities' comply 'with the laws and regulations to which they are subject'.[45] From a theoretical perspective, this norm is intended to create a harmonisation of the type of securities admissible. However, practically speaking, this would not necessarily transpire. In fact, there seem to be as many jurisdictions represented in the EU as there are variations of legislation, some of which may take a more loose approach to securities and their categorisation than others.

2.3.1.2 Listing and legal liabilities

Tort law, and, more generally, the law that governs liabilities in the context of the listing of securities, is still very much an affair of national law, as the Listing Directive has not ventured into this area. Specificities of such liability can therefore not be covered within the context of the present book, as this would require an arduous analysis of both the contract law and law of tort existing in each jurisdiction.

Nonetheless, it is possible to indicate the various potential legal actions: initiated by the issuer against the arranger (or arrangers) for responsibilities entailed to the mandate, for instance, or by the issuer against its legal advisors or financial advisors for negligence in the way the mandate has been carried out.[46] Additionally, investors too may be entitled to initiate legal proceedings against the issuer and the arranger(s) for any deceitful offer of the securities. In this respect, the range of possible scenarios which could generate such an outcome are numerous, albeit predominantly relating to the way the prospectus has been drafted, such as an incorrect description of the business of the issuer or of the securities, an incorrect reference to financial data,

42 Art. 46(2) Listing Directive.
43 Art. 42 Listing Directive.
44 Art. 54 Listing Directive.
45 Art. 53 Listing Directive.
46 The issuer may sue their lawyers for professional negligence for not correctly advising the issuer.

or an incorrect description of legal data within the prospectus. As a default response to all these potential cases, the arranger would either resist the relevant claim alone or, if contractually possible, raise an indemnity action against the accountants involved with the listing[47] or the relevant team of legal advisors.[48]

As stated above, the Listing Directive does not hint at any concept of responsibility; however, an attempt at harmonisation is made under an adjacent piece of legislation, the Prospectus Directive, as clarified below in section 2.3.2.2.

2.3.2 The offer of securities and the prospectus

If securities are offered, a general duty arises to inform the public of the kind of financial instruments which will thereafter be offered. Such securities may have the form of shares (i.e. representing equity) or bonds (i.e. representing debt). Irrespective of the form of securities issued (either equity or debt), these instruments, if offered to the public, must comply with certain rules so as to ensure that the beneficiary of the securities (the investor) is duly informed of the specific risk entailed to that investment.[49] This objective is achieved by way of the prospectus: a document that should contain the data the investor may reasonably be expected to rely on as regards both the issuer (the entity offering the securities) and the financial instruments being offered to the market.

The following subsections will address the prospectus and the modalities whereby this document is required to be drafted, under the relevant legal provisions. In addressing such provisions, emphasis shall be placed on the relevant EU Directives in this matter, as it is widely acknowledged that the Brussels regulator has been particularly productive in this area of financial law.

2.3.2.1 The rationale behind a prospectus

As alluded to above, the prospectus is legislated upon under the Prospectus Directive – a statute reflecting a legislative development which originated in 1980 and, ultimately, came to fruition roughly a decade ago. It still applies, although it has been amended in recent times.[50]

Historically, the concept of a prospectus does not have an EU genesis. Rather, its *ratio essendi* can be tracked back to experience across the Atlantic in the US securities markets, with its legislation enacted there since as early as the 1930s (particularly the Securities Exchange Act of 1934). The underpinning philosophy of

47 For instance, if the negligence is due to incorrect financial data provided to the arranger by the accountants involved with the listing.

48 The circumstances in this case could be several; for instance, negligence or omission in the way the legal advisors have liaised with the authority.

49 See the Prospectus Directive, particularly Recital 18:

> The provision of full information concerning securities and issuers of those securities promotes, together with rules on the conduct of business, the protection of investors. Moreover, such information provides an effective means of increasing confidence in securities and thus of contributing to the proper functioning and development of securities markets. The appropriate way to make this information available is to publish a prospectus.

50 See particularly Directive 2010/73/EU of the European Parliament and of the Council of 24 November 2010 amending Directives 2003/71/EC on the prospectus to be published when securities are offered to the public or admitted to trading and 2004/109/EC on the harmonisation of transparency requirements in relation to information about issuers whose securities are admitted to trading on a regulated market, OJ L 327.

the 1934 Securities Exchange Act, despite the highs and lows during its 80 years of lifespan, still remains basically the same; also in its adaptation within the EU financial markets during the 1980s: it is based on the idea that mandatory disclosure of the issuer and its instruments is necessary and that it improves standards of corporate governance of the company.[51] It is argued in the law and economics literature that the more information available, the closer to fairness the prices of securities are.[52]

However, the latest financial crisis engendered intriguing and, at the same time, dramatic questions as to whether the disclosure is actually effective. Nonetheless, the EU approach to the matter still remains the same: mandatory, instead of mere voluntary disclosure will still remain the architrave of the architecture in this area of law; although probably the real challenge in future will be the content of it and its effectiveness in terms of protection of the investor. Investor protection in connection with a specific financial instrument is considered one of the fundamental aims of the Prospectus Directive.[53] As indicated above, the risk attached to any investment is borne by the investor and any investment in securities is intrinsically insidious. The Prospectus Directive builds on this risk and notes, at Recital 19:

> Investment in securities, like any other form of investment, involves risk. Safeguards for the protection of the interests of actual and potential investors are required in all Member States in order to enable them to make an informed assessment of such risks and thus to take investment in full knowledge of the facts.

As a result, public companies, or those which aspire to become such, are under an obligation to provide the public (and, therefore, the potential investors) with a minimal level of disclosure to ensure that the risk entailed to the investment is not unknown. The information should be 'sufficient' (in terms of quantity of data provided), as well as 'objective' (in the way both the securities and the economic circumstances of the issuer are described).[54] Coupled with this is the principle that the information must be disclosed 'in an easily analysable and comprehensible form'.[55]

2.3.2.2 Prospectus Directive[56]

The object of the prospectus

The Prospectus Directive does not apply to all types of financial instruments, nor are its requirements mandatory for all issuers. As to financial instruments, the Directive applies to 'securities' defined as follows:

---

51 The unfettered reliance on the disclosure has been questioned by authors inclined to thinking that this disclosure is far from helpful. See G Benston, 'The Value of the SEC's Accounting Disclosure Requirement' (1969) 44 *Accounting Review* 515; G Benston, 'Required Disclosure and the Stock Market: An Evaluation of the Securities Exchange Act of 1934' (1973) 63 *American Economic Review* 132.

52 J Coffee, 'Market Failure and the Economic Case for a Mandatory Disclosure System' (1984) 70 *Virginia Law Review* 717.

53 Recital 16 Prospectus Directive. The Prospectus Directive has therefore also been defined as a 'product-driven' piece of legislation (see P Schammo, *EU Prospectus Directive* (Cambridge University Press, Cambridge 2010) 74).

54 Recital 20 Prospectus Directive.

55 Recital 20 Prospectus Directive.

56 In the literature, a brief description of the main aspects of the Prospectus Directive can be read in the following: HS Scott, *International Finance* (17th edn Foundation Press, New York 2010) 268, 273; PR Wood, *Regulation of International Finance* (Thomson/Sweet & Maxwell, London 2007) 117, 124.

> shares in companies and other securities equivalent to shares in companies, bonds and other forms of securities debt which are negotiable on the capital market and any other securities normally dealt in giving the right to acquire any such transferrable securities by subscription or exchange or giving rise to a cash settlement excluding instruments of payment.[57]

Pursuant to the same provision, this definition of securities may be expanded and supplemented at national level.

As far as issuers to which the Prospectus Directive applies are concerned, the exemptions (for specific issuers) contained in the Prospectus Directive are multifarious and shall be elaborated upon below. By means of a fleeting glimpse at the issue however, reference could be made to some types of issuers that, given their public nature, are exempted from the Prospectus Directive, such as the European Central Bank or any central bank of EU Member States.

A definition of the prospectus

The prospectus is a document that, as is the intention of the EU legislator, should ensure the achievement of, especially, investor protection. Despite its central role, the 'prospectus' is not defined in the legislation under discussion.[58] However, a clear description of its functions is provided under art. 5, where it is stipulated as follows:

> [T]he prospectus shall contain all information which, according to the particular nature of the issuer and of the securities offered to the public or admitted to trading on a regulated market, is necessary to enable investors to make an informed assessment of the assets and liabilities, financial position, profit and losses, and prospects of the issuer and of any guarantor, and of the rights attaching to such securities.

Under applicable national law of contract, the prospectus may qualify as a contract.[59]

The information contained in a prospectus

A prospectus consists of an analytical part, where emphasis is placed on both the issuer and the securities, and a summary.[60] The latter:

> in a brief manner and in non-technical language, convey[s] the essential characteristics and risks associated with the issuer, any guarantor and the securities, the language in which the prospectus was originally drawn up.

The summary shall also contain a series of cautions, such as an elucidation of the civil liabilities attached to those who have drafted the summary, including the translation.[61]

57 Art. 2(1)(a) Prospectus Directive.
58 There is no sign of if within the 'definitions' at art. 2.
59 Under English law, the 'prospectus constitutes a contractual document above all else' (A Hudson, *The Law of Finance* (1st edn Sweet & Maxwell, London 2009) 978 and, more recently, A Hudson, *The Law of Finance* (2nd edn Sweet & Maxwell, London 2013) 1078). And: 'It should not be forgotten, however, that a prospectus is a document which forms the representations on which initial subscribers for securities and purchasers in the after-market can be expected to rely when making their investment decisions. Therefore, these representations found contracts for the purchase of securities and may be actionable under contract law.'
60 Art. 5(2) Prospectus Directive.
61 Art. 5(2)(a) to (d) Prospectus Directive. On liabilities, see this section below.

The responsibility lies with the EU Commission, according to art. 7 of the Prospectus Directive, to provide requirements for the 'specific information' required for each type of security. In this respect, the Commission periodically publishes a list of model prospectuses which, in turn, are adopted at a national level within the prevailing legislation of each Member State.[62]

Although the power exercised by the Commission in establishing model prospectuses is quite discretionary, the Prospectus Directive does not refrain from shedding some light on a few of the main rules and principles. First, the principal distinction to be acknowledged is between equity securities and non-equity securities (such as debt securities).[63] In this respect, the information required is less for non-equity securities, seemingly on the assumption that the degree of risk carried by an equity investment is higher.[64]

Additionally, the various models available can be categorised with respect to retail offers and non-retail offers. The latter category, i.e. offers with a denomination per unit of at least Euro 100,000, typically requires less information as they are addressed to qualified investors in a better position to assess the risk.

A further distinction can be made in relation to the issuer, according to its size and its activities.[65] For small and medium enterprises, for instance, the EU Commission is permitted to impose a less stringent level of disclosure, for purposes of simplification. Furthermore, the nature of the issuer is usually taken into consideration by the Commission, so that qualified categories of issuers that are already supervised by a specific authority, are subject to less arduous models of prospectus.[66] The rationale behind this is that these entities are already supervised by a local authority, so that a simplified model of prospectus would avoid a potential duplication in the investigation on the issuer. In the same vein, a government issuing a bond shall be permitted to publish a simplified model of prospectus, on the assumption that a government is a reliable issuer and a secure paymaster.[67]

When is the publication of a prospectus required?

Not every offer of transferable securities gives rise to an obligation to publish a prospectus. Conversely, two circumstances trigger such an obligation: (1) the actual promotion of an offer of transferable securities to the public; and (2) the admission of transferable securities to an EEA regulated market.[68]

The first condition is more or less self-evident. In this respect, the Prospectus Directive stipulates, among its definitions, that a prospectus shall be qualified as 'a

---

62 The models 'created' by the EU Commission are contained in Commission Delegated Regulations issued on an annual basis. See http://ec.europa.eu/internal_market/securities/prospectus/index_en.htm, accessed 23 July 2014.

63 Art. 7(2)(a) Prospectus Directive.

64 In investing in debt securities, the simple question for the investor is to assess whether the issuer is in a position (or not) to honour the relevant payment upon maturity; conversely, in an equity investment, the investor's risk assessment impinges, also, on the way the company is managed and is in a position to undertake a profitable activity (R Panasar and P Boeckman, *European Securities Law* (Oxford University Press, Oxford 2010) 26).

65 Art. 7(2)(3) Prospectus Directive.

66 Art. 7(2)(d) Prospectus Directive.

67 Art. 7(2)(f)) Prospectus Directive.

68 It is correctly pointed out (P Schammo, *EU Prospectus Law* (Cambridge University Press, Cambridge 2011) 78) that, although the expression 'admission to trading of securities' does not have a specific meaning in EU law legislation, indeed 'regulated market' is an EU law notion, because defined by the MiFID I Directive. See also R Panasar and P Boeckman, *European Securities Law* (Oxford University Press, Oxford 2010) 19.

communication to persons in any form and by any means, presenting sufficient information in the terms of the offer and securities to be offered, so as to enable an investor to decide to purchase or subscribe to these securities.'[69] The definition of 'offer to the public', provided by the EU legislator, is clearly wider than the notion of 'contractual offer', which may have a specific meaning under the applicable national law of contract and may as such be binding on the offeror. The reason for this is that the EU legislator, so as to better safeguard the investor, has wished to further widen the ambit of the Prospectus Directive to also include mere invitations or enticements concerned with transferable securities (which under the applicable national law of contract may not be binding on the offeror).

The second condition to be met for the obligation to publish a prospectus is the admission of the relevant transferable securities to an EEA regulated market. In other words, the publication of the prospectus is not solely dependent on the communication of an offer to the public, but also on the circumstances in which the relevant securities actually 'enter' (i.e. are going to be listed in) a regulated market.

Some offers to the public fall within the scope of the Prospectus Directive, but are exempted from the obligation that a prospectus be published. Exemptions contrast with further situations that totally fall outside the scope of the Prospectus Directive; in these cases, the Prospectus Directive shall not apply at all.[70] As to the exemptions, their rationale usually is a trade-off between the aims of the Directive and the burden that an offeror can reasonably be charged with.

A first group of exemptions (i.e. technically defined cases where 'the obligation to publish a prospectus shall not apply') is contemplated under art. 3 of the Prospectus Directive and is as follows: (a) an offer of securities addressed solely to qualified investors;[71] (b) an offer of securities addressed to fewer than 150 natural or legal persons per Member State, other than qualified investors;[72] (c) an offer of securities addressed to investors who acquire securities for a total consideration of at least Euro

---

69 Art. 2(1)(d)) Prospectus Directive. Cf. also P Schammo, *EU Prospectus Law* (Cambridge University Press, Cambridge 2011) 80, for the purposes of the definition, 'the support or medium used to communicate an offer does not matter.'

70 Art. 1(2) of the Prospectus Directive refers to some cases of lack of applicability, such as, among others, 'units issued by collective investment undertakings other than the closed-end type' (a), the 'non-equity securities issued by a Member State or by one of a Member State's regional authorities, by public international bodies of which one or more Member States are members, by the European Central Bank or by the central banks of the Member States' (b).

71 'Qualified investors' are mainly 'seasoned investors whose level of expertise, experience and knowledge is such that this does not require the same level of protection as ordinary investors' (P Schammo, *EU Prospectus Law* (Cambridge University Press, Cambridge 2011) 126). In this area, the 2010 amendment of the Prospectus Directive has marked a turning point in the definition of 'qualified investor'. In its initial wording, the Prospectus Directive utilised is own definition and, therefore, qualified investors mainly as entities, and not individuals, with a presumable knowledge in financial products. Among these, there were banks and investment firms, but also governments and supranational institutions as well as corporations; the latter would have satisfied the definition so long as they employed 250 employees, they had a total balance sheet of over Euro 43,000,000 and an annual turnover exceeding Euro 50,000,000. This first category was automatically given the status of qualified investors; in the absence of the occurrence of the relevant requisites, the investor was not qualified, for purposes of the Prospectus Directive. Nowadays, the distinction in the Prospectus Directive reflects – and is connected to – the category of professional clients and retail clients, as traced in the MiFID I Directive (cf. P Schammo, *EU Prospectus Law* (Cambridge University Press, Cambridge 2011) 127) and, more recently, MiFID II. For details, see later Chapter 4.

72 This is called a 'private placement'; therefore an offer addressed to such a small number of investors, including individuals or 'small' enterprises, that the requirement of the publication of the prospectus would be overly burdensome.

100,000 per investor, for each separate offer;[73] (d) an offer of securities whose denomination per unit amounts to at least Euro 100,000;[74] and (e) an offer of securities with a total consideration of less than Euro 100,000 with the threshold calculated over a 12-month period.[75]

A further group of exemptions is contemplated in detail under art. 4(1) of the Prospectus Directive. Examples are an offer to the public of shares representing, over a period of 12 months, less than 10 per cent of the number of shares of the same class already admitted to trading on the same regulated market;[76] and shares issued in substitution for shares of the same class already admitted to trading on the same regulated market, should the issuing of such shares not involve any increase in the issued capital.[77]

The prospectus 'EU passport'

A further reason for an EU statute on prospectuses is that it allows for the achievement of synergies of scale in the offer of securities across the European Union. In fact, theoretically speaking, in the absence of common rules on the matter, each authority competent in every country should assume control over the approval of the prospectus in cases where the applicant decided to promote a cross-border offer of securities. To avoid any duplication of costs and legal burdens, the Prospectus Directive ensures that the prospectus is afforded an EU passport, thereby confirming that the approval of the prospectus by a competent national authority in an EU Member State suffices for purposes of further approvals by other authorities of the European countries where the securities are additionally offered.[78]

The tricky issue is to identify the 'competent authority'. Theoretically, a supranational legislator such as the EU could have adopted a liberal approach, where the issuer decides upon an authority from those operating in EEA countries (not necessarily coinciding with the corporate office of the issuer) for purposes of the approval of the prospectus. Following this line of reasoning, once the prospectus had been approved by this authority, the offer could proceed everywhere in the EEA without the need for any additional approval, while the offeror would benefit from a 'non-home passport'. However, if the system were as just described, the home-country authority of the issuer could feel that it is losing control over the activities and affairs of the issuer. To avoid this, the principle adopted by the Prospectus Directive is more

---

73 The required subscription, per each investor, of an amount of securities for a value of no less than Euros 100,000 means that, practically, exclusively major investors are concerned with the offer, rather than retail investors. Therefore, the reason for protecting the investor through the rules of the Prospectus Directive does not arise. The original threshold was Euro 50,000 per investor, in 2010 increased to the latest one. See art. 7(2)(b) and 19(4) of the Prospectus Directive, as amended respectively. Cf. P Schammo, *EU Prospectus Law* (Cambridge University Press, Cambridge 2011) 86.

74 The reason for the exclusion is similar to the previous one: a minimal amount of Euro 100,000 per unit means that, de facto, that offer is an off-limits area for retail investors, and conversely a hunting ground exclusively for major investors.

75 In this case, the reason for the exclusion is opposite: the offer is so small in value that it is presumed not to cause any possible financial harm to any investor.

76 For instance, a listed company with a share capital of Euro 100,000,000 which decided to increase its share capital by no more than Euro 9,000,000, with an offer of these shares to the public, would be exempt from the publication of the prospectus.

77 In this case, the exemption is necessary to avoid what, otherwise, would be a duplication of administrative encumbrances, where in reality there is no need for this, as the share capital remains the same.

78 See on the EU passport also extensively above, section 1.3.

rigorous: for transferable securities, the competent authority is the authority of the country where the issuer has its registered office.[79]

The exception to the norm arises in the case of an offer of non-equity securities with a denomination of at least Euro 1,000, or cash-settled warrants and exchangeable securities.[80] In these limited scenarios, the offeror shall be entitled to shop around before selecting, for approval of the prospectus, either the authority within the EEA of the country where the securities will be offered to the public or admitted to a regulated market, or the authority of the country of the issuer. A passported prospectus, approved in an EEA state according to the Prospectus Directive and used in a different EEA country, shall be provided with a certificate of approval of the competent authority, and a translation of the summary in the official language where it is going to be exported.

The approval of the prospectus

The prospectus must be approved in advance by the 'competent authority', before it can be published and the subsequent offer to the public commences. The request for approval is an administrative process whereby the prospectus is submitted to the authority which, after subjecting it to scrutiny, notifies the issuer that the publications can be released. The scrutiny undertaken by the authority does not pertain to the economic merit of the offeror; rather, it is a formal analysis of the compliance with the laws existing in the country of the authority, most notably the (implemented) Prospectus Directive.

The exact nature of the process is determined by the legislation of each respective EEA country; however, the EU legislator has codified some general guidelines, particularly in relation to the deadline for approval of the prospectus. In this respect, the time limit is 10 days from the submission of the draft prospectus by the offeror or the person requesting the admission (such as the arranger).[81] However, the time limit shall be extended to 20 days, 'if the public offer involves securities issued by an issuer which does not have any securities admitted to trading on a regulated market and who has not previously offered securities to the public.'[82] This time proviso, although ostensibly strict, is in reality mitigated by a provision, enforced by authorities to the point where it has become standard practice, allowing the authority to suspend, 'on reasonable grounds', the time permitted if 'the documents submitted . . . are incomplete' or 'supplementary information is needed.'[83] Finally, it is worth elucidating that should either deadline (10 or 20 days, respectively) lapse without the authority having granted the approval, this shall not be taken by the applicant as silent consent (art. 13(2)). Should such a scenario arise (i.e. lack of action on the part of the authority), the applicant, in accordance with the applicable national law, may have the option to sue the authority for damages. A likelier solution, however, would see the offeror (or arranger, on its behalf) set up amicable conversations so that the impasse may be clarified.

79 Art. 2(1)(m)(i) Prospectus Directive.
80 Art. 2(1)(m)(i) Prospectus Directive. As far as exchangeable securities are concerned, the additional condition is that the securities for which they can be exchanged are not those of the issuer or entity of its group.
81 Art. 13(2) Prospectus Directive.
82 Art. 13(3) Prospectus Directive.
83 Art. 13(4) Prospectus Directive.

Prospectus and liabilities

Tort law generally, and professional liability law in particular continue to remain largely a matter of national discretion,[84] although some recent attempts at harmonisation have been made within the body of EU legislation.[85] Yet the Prospectus Directive, in this area, does not aim to achieve a proper harmonisation of the civil liability regimes.[86]

More specifically, under art. 6(2) of the Prospectus Directive, each Member State is required to ensure that, in each jurisdiction, 'laws, regulation and administrative provisions on civil liability apply to those persons responsible for the information given in a prospectus.'[87] This provision seems vague enough to avoid any conflict with national laws, as it will probably suffice for each Member State to have its civil liability regime apply to the prospectus.[88] However, it is theoretically possible to infer that a Member State will be held to be in breach of the EU legislation, if it proved to have inadequate internal rules to tackle the issue of misleading information in the prospectus. Those who should be held responsible are at least the 'issuer' (and its management), the 'offeror',[89] and 'the person asking for the admission to trading on a regulated market' or 'the guarantor', as the case may be.[90] The role each of those persons plays in connection to the listing should be identified in the prospectus, so as to avoid any issues of transparency at a later point.[91]

---

84 As far as English law is concerned, any 'negligent misstatement' of a party to another usually falls within the sphere of tortious liability. So long as the defendant realises that the claimant may rely on the false representation, a common law liability will arise (*Shinhan Bank Ltd v Sea Containers Ltd* [2000] Lloyd's Rep. 406). However, the real issue remains as to whether a person, particularly an investor or categories of investor, is able to rely on that statement (see *Possfund Custodian Trustee Ltd v Diamond* [1996] 2 All E.R. 774; *Al-Nakib Investments (Jersey) Ltd v Longcroft* [1990] 3 All E.R. 321). Among scholars, see A Hudson, *Hudson: The Law of Finance* (2nd edn Sweet & Maxwell, London 2013) 720. Under the same English law, the offer of securities via a prospectus would give rise to a contract between the offeror and the subscriber; therefore, theoretically, an incorrect statement in a prospectus should be regarded as a breach of contract. However, the courts in Britain have been so far quite reluctant to hold such a liability, on the basis that the statement is not simply a term of a contract (R Panasar and P Boeckman, *European Securities Law* (Oxford University Press, Oxford 2010) 294).

85 Art. 35a(1) of Regulation (EC) No 1060/2009 of the European Parliament and of the Council of 16 September 2009 on credit rating agencies (the 'Credit Rating Agency Regulation') (as amended by Regulation (EC) No 462/2013) contains, for the first time, a direct ground for a liability claim against a credit rating agency.

86 The German proposal to introduce an effective common field of civil and tort liability in this area was abandoned in the final draft of the Prospectus Directive (P Schammo, *EU Prospectus Law* (Cambridge University Press, Cambridge 2011) 240, 241).

87 An example of implementation of this rule is the British legislation. Section 90 of the Financial Services and Markets Act 2000 cuts out the requirement, existing in the law of tort of that country, to prove breach of a duty of care, as the causation will suffice for purposes of a tortious liability. In this respect, the British statute transposes into the legislation the common law rule encapsulated in *Possfund Custodian Trustee Ltd v Diamond* [1996] 2 All E.R. 774.

Additionally, pursuant to s. 84(1)(d) of the same Financial Services and Markets Act 2000, para. 5.5.3R of the Prospectus Rules identifies some categories of professionals responsible for the prospectus: (a) the issuer; (b) directors and any other individual and/or professional giving the authorisation to be named as responsible for the prospectus; (c) any other individual and/or professional who has authorised the prospectus or part of it.

88 R Panasar and P Boeckman, *European Securities Law* (Oxford University Press 2010) 39. In this contribution, it is correctly emphasised that the mosaic of differing liability regimes, still inevitable in this phase of the EU integration, may still represent an impediment to the development of a pan-European market (ibid. 40).

89 Remarkably, according to the definitions of the Prospectus Directive (art. 2 (1)), the 'issuer' is 'a legal entity which issues or proposes to issue securities' (h); the 'offeror' (or 'person making an offer') means conversely, a 'legal entity or individual which offers securities to the public' (i).

90 Art. 6(1) Prospectus Directive.

91 Again, art. 6(1), part 2:

> The persons responsible shall be clearly identified in the prospectus by their names and functions or, in the case of legal persons, their names and registered offices, as well as declarations by them that, to the best of their knowledge, the information contained in the prospectus is in accordance with the facts and that the prospectus makes no omission likely to affect its import.

2.4 Further reading

Barnard, C, *The Substantive Law of the EU: The Four Freedoms* (4th edn Oxford University Press, Oxford 2013)

Blair, M, and Walker, G, *Financial Services Law* (Oxford University Press, Oxford 2006)

Coffee, J, 'Market Failure and the Economic Case for a Mandatory Disclosure System' (1984) 70 *Virginia Law Review* 717,753

Dashwood, A, Dougan, M, Rodger, B, Spaventa, E, and Wyatt, D, *Wyatt and Dashwood's European Union Law* (6th edn Hart Publishing, Oxford and Portland 2011)

Final Report of the Committee of the Wise Men in the Regulation of European Securities Markets, Brussels, 15 February 2001

French, D, Mayson, S, and Ryan, C, *Mayson, French and Ryan on Company Law* (30th edn Oxford University Press, Oxford 2013) 197, 224 (offering shares to the public) 352, 370 (market abuse) 225, 254 (transfer of shares)

Grundmann, S, *European Company Law Ius Communitatis, Volume* (2nd edn Intersentia, Cambridge, Antwerp and Portland 2012)

Gullifer, L, and Payne, J, *Corporate Finance Law* (Hart Publishing, Oxford and Portland 2011)

Hemetsberger, W, Schoppmann, H, Schwander, D, and Wengler, C, *European Banking and Financial Law* (2nd edn Kluwer Law International in association with European Association of Public Banks, Brussels 2006)

Hopt, KJ, and Wymeersch, E, *European Company and Financial Law: Text and Leading Cases* (3rd edn Oxford University Press, Oxford 2006)

Hudson, A, *The Law of Finance* (1st edn Sweet and Maxwell, London 2009)

Hudson, A, *The Law of Finance* (2nd edn Sweet & Maxwell, London 2013)

MacNeil, I, 'The Evolution of Regulatory Enforcement Action in the UK Capital Markets: A Case of Less is More?' (2007) 2 *Capital Markets Law Journal* 345, 369

MacNeil, IG, *An Introduction to the Law on Financial Investment* (2nd edn Hart Publishing, Oxford and Portland 2012)

Panasar, R, and Boeckman, P, *European Securities Law* (Oxford University Press, Oxford 2010)

Schammo, P, *EU Prospectus Law* (Cambridge University Press, Cambridge 2011)

Scott, HS, International Finance (17th edn Foundation Press, New York 2010)

Sfameni, P, and Giannelli, A, *Diritto degli Intermediari e dei Mercati Finanziari* (Egea, Milan 2013)

Soderquist, LD, and Gabaldon, TA, *Securities Law* (Foundation Press and Thomson West, New York 2004)

Wood, PR, *Regulation of International Finance* (Thomson/Sweet & Maxwell, London 2007)

Woods, L, and Watson, P, *Steiner and Woods EU Law* (11th edn Oxford University Press, Oxford 2012)

2.5 Questions

2.1 Historically, when were regulated markets established for the first time?

2.2 Is the operation of a stock exchange a reserved activity in the EU?

2.3 What kind of products do the regulated markets deal with?

2.4 What is the authority in charge of authorising a regulated market?

2.5 What is the difference between a regulated market and an MTF ('multilateral trading facility')?

2.6 What is the concept of 'EU passport', if applied to a prospectus?

2.7 Describe and analyse the legal concept of a 'prospectus' and the liabilities engendered by an untruthful prospectus.

2.8 What is the 'rationale behind' the existence of an EU Directive in relation to prospectuses?

Chapter 3

Market abuse

Chapter contents

3.1 The concept of 'secondary market'

From an economic point of view, the secondary market differs markedly from the primary market. The latter deals with the issuance of securities and possible admittance of those securities to the market for the first time, whereas the former is concerned with the trade of securities which have already been issued and may be traded in a regulated market. This distinction in definition is echoed in the legal framework. More specifically, the legislation addressed to the primary market deals with the way financial instruments must be introduced to the market for the first time (therefore, listing and/or prospectus topics discussed previously in Chapter 2). Conversely, legislation relating to the secondary market concerns the modalities whereby securities may be transferred, while also accounting for the legislator's interest in protection of the investor and the credibility of the market against any lack of transparency or general confusion which may befall it. Accordingly, the legislation at EU level in this area tackles two possible issues: first, the abusive nature by which securities once issued are dealt with from time to time, and second, the protection which investors must be afforded in cases where significant holdings in listed securities are transferred.

3.2 The Market Abuse Regulation

A regulated market of transferable securities must be based on principles of transparency, as the investor invests his money in a publicly traded company (either in its shares or bonds or in other securities) on the assumption that he can be informed of all relevant information relating to the securities (and the issuer). In contrast to a transparent market is an opaque market, where crucial information is withheld or even misleading.

If speculated upon from an ultra-liberal perspective, the market would ideally rule itself and would therefore not require any form of government regulation. Following this line of reasoning, the stock market should be self-governing. The prevailing approach nowadays is that the investor – and his legitimate expectations to be furnished with transparent information – cannot rely on the benevolent cooperation of the issuer, its management and his fellow investors. Therefore, it is generally believed that strict rules must be imposed on the issuer and, to a certain extent, on the market in which it operates. At EU level, this imposition is conveyed by way of legislation which, for more than a decade, has been adopted in order to protect the investor: principally embodied in European Parliament and Council Directive 2003/6/EC of 28 January 2003 on insider dealing and market manipulation (henceforth the 'Market Abuse Directive' or 'MA Directive'), and entered into force in April 2003 through Implementing Directive 2003/124.[1] More recently, the MA Directive and its ancillary

1 In full: Commission Directive 2003/124/EC of 22 December 2003 Implementing Directive 2003/6/EC of the European Parliament and of the Council as regards the definition and public disclosure of inside information and the definition of market manipulation, OJ C 161. The MA Regulation was published on 7 June 2014 and entered into force on the twentieth day following this application, i.e. on 28 June 2014. It will replace the current MA Directive no earlier than 3 July 2016 for its main body of provisions (art. 39 MA Regulation). However, for some specific legal provisions contemplated in the same art. 39, the applicability started on 2 July 2014.

legislation has been surpassed and overtaken by a new EU legislative structure mainly based on:

(a) Regulation (EU) No 596/2014 (henceforth the 'Market Abuse Regulation' or the 'MA Regulation');[2] and
(b) Directive 2014/57/EU of the European Parliament and of the Council of 16 April 2014 (henceforth the 'New Market Abuse Directive' or the 'New MA Directive').[3]

The underpinning philosophy of both the MA Directive and the MA Regulation still remains identical in substance. Recital 12 of the MA Directive stipulates as follows:

> The objective of legislation against insider dealing is the same as that of legislation against manipulation to ensure the integrity of Community financial markets and to enhance investor confidence in those markets. It is therefore advisable to adopt combined rules to combat both insider dealing and market manipulation. A single Directive will ensure throughout the Community the same framework for allocation of responsibilities, enforcement and cooperation.

The ultimate MA Regulation seems to adhere to the same line of reasoning, more specifically at Recital 2, which emphasises as follows:

> An integrated, efficient and transparent financial market requires market integrity. The smooth functioning of securities markets and public confidence in markets are prerequisites for economic growth and wealth. Market abuse harms the integrity of financial markets and public confidence in securities and derivatives.

Nonetheless, the MA Regulation marks a significant step forward for EU financial legislation; it reflects how significantly different the financial markets now are from those which, more than a decade ago, inspired the creation of Directive 2003/6. It is worth mentioning, among multifarious phenomena: (a) the emergence of new markets, platforms and over-the-counter ('OTC') markets trading in financial instruments; (b) inefficiencies in the way the previous legislation had regulated commodities and commodity derivatives; and (c) the lack of effective enforcement of the MA Directive by the authorities.

---

continued

The 'expiry date' for the MA Directive to be implemented in each Member State was 12 October 2004. Among the ancillary EU legislation following up on the MA Directive and Implementing Directive, it is worth highlighting the following: Commission Directive 2003/125/EC implementing Council Directive 2003/6/EC as regards the fair presentation of investment recommendations and the disclosure of conflicts of interest; Commission Directive 2004/72 implementing Directive 2003/6/EC as regards accepted market practices, the definition of inside information in relation to derivatives on commodities, the drawing up of lists of insiders, the notification of managers' transactions and the notification of suspicious transactions. See PR Wood, *Regulation of International Finance* (Thomson/Sweet & Maxwell, London 2007) 161, 172.

2 Regulation (EU) No 596/2014 of the European Parliament and of the Council of 16 April 2014 on market abuse (market abuse regulation) and repealing Directive 2003/6/EC of the European Parliament and of the Council and Commission Directives 2003/124/EC, 2003/125/EC and 2004/72/EC.

3 Directive 2014/57/EU of the European Parliament and of the Council of 16 April 2014 on criminal sanctions for market abuse.

Against the backdrop of this ever-changing and dynamic background, the EU legislator has developed an ambitious programme. It does not only focus, as already purported by the MA Directive, 'on financial instruments admitted to trading on a regulated market or for which a request for admission to trading on such a market has been made',[4] but also on 'any financial instruments traded on a regulated market, an MTF or an OTF, and any other conduct or action which can have an effect on such a financial instrument irrespective of whether it takes place on a trading venue.'[5]

In this new scenario, the principal activities subjected to the spotlight of the MA Regulation are, fundamentally, still those sanctioned by the previous statute, i.e. 'insider dealing', 'unlawful disclosure of inside information' and 'market manipulation'.[6] Accordingly, detailed explanation shall be provided later in this chapter, in respect to each. But first, it is worth clarifying the magnitude of the pertinent piece of legislation in this area, in terms of securities and markets involved, particularly in light of the MA Regulation recently passed in Brussels.

3.3 Market abuse: from Directive to Regulation

In regard to securities, the MA Directive adopted an already broad outlook, as inferable from the definition provided under its art. 1(3). Actually, when juxtaposed with other examples of EU legislation, including the Prospectus Directive, which exclusively deals with 'transferable securities',[7] the scope was rather large, given the fact that the wording of the MA Directive referred to 'financial instruments' and therefore also covered units in collective investment undertakings; money market instruments; financial-futures contracts; forward interest-rate agreements; interest-rate, currency and equity swaps; options to acquire or dispose of any instrument falling into these categories, including equivalent cash-settled instruments, derivatives on commodities; and any other instrument admitted to trading on a regulated market in a Member State or for which a request for admission to trading on such a market has been made.

The MA Regulation even enlarges and expands the magnitude of the previous legislation. Pursuant to art. 3(2) of the MA Regulation, this Regulation mainly relies on a dual layer: on the one hand, it covers 'securities' (a),[8] roughly corresponding to what was previously defined by the MA Directive; on the other hand, it also covers 'associated instruments' (b), including those which 'are not admitted to trading or traded on a trading venue, or for which a request for admission to trading on a trading venue has not been made.'[9] Remarkably, the MA Directive used to connect the

4 Recital 8 of the MA Regulation.
5 Ibid.
6 Recital 7 of the MA Regulation. In broader terms, market abuse is 'a concept that encompasses unlawful behaviour in the financial markets'.
7 See above, section 2.3.2 of this Chapter.
8 More specifically, according to art. 3(2)(a) of the MA Regulation, 'securities' are (i) 'shares and other securities equivalent to shares'; (ii) 'bonds and other forms of securities debt'; or (iii) 'securitised debt convertible or exchangeable into shares or into other securities equivalent to shares'.
9 The list of art. 3(2)(b) is multifarious: among the different 'associated instruments' mention can be made to (i) 'contracts or rights to subscribe for, acquire or dispose of securities' or (ii) 'financial derivatives of securities'. The MA Directive did not apply to this typology of financial instruments.

'financial instruments' to the 'regulated markets', and in this respect, it is thought the MA Regulation will improve the effectiveness of the past legislation. In other words, not every category of financial instrument used to fall within the previous legislation, rather exclusively those which, in every EEA country, resulted in being admitted to officially recognised markets and included in the list that the EU Commission, in cooperation with each national authority, used to keep updated.[10] For financial instruments not admitted to trading on a regulated market in a Member State, but whose values depended on financial instruments indeed admitted to trading in a EU, or better, in an EEA financial market, the main provisions of the MA Directive used to apply (arts 2, 3 and 4) but not the entire piece of legislation.

Pursuant to art. 2 of the new MA Regulation, it will apply not only to 'financial instruments admitted to trading on a regulated market' (as already prescribed under the MA Directive) but also to those 'for which a request for admission to trading on a regulated market has been made'. Additionally, and in a way significantly different from the past, the MA Regulation will apply also to 'financial instruments traded on an MTF, admitted to trading on an MTF or for which a request for admission to trading on an MTF has been made',[11] 'financial instruments traded on an OTF [organised trading facility]',[12] and 'financial instruments [different from the previous ones], the price or values of which depends on or has an effect on the price of a financial instrument referred to in those points, including, but not limited to, credit default swaps and contracts for difference.'[13] By way of interpretation of the new rules and their enlarged scope, well beyond the perimeter of the regulated markets, it can be affirmed that the EU legislator wants to ensure, in light of the exponential dimension of the market of OTC derivatives which many believe contributed to the last financial crisis, that the rigorous provisions on market abuse existing in the regulated markets are not circumvented through practices left unlegislated in the adjacent non-regulated markets. The outcome of this is that obligations and duties applicable to the operators in both markets are made symmetric.

3.3.1 Insider dealing

The first category of behaviour which falls within the scope of the MA Regulation is 'insider dealing'. Those in possession of inside information are prevented from using such knowledge to acquire or dispose of, or try to acquire or dispose of, for their own account or on behalf of others, either directly or indirectly, financial instruments to which that information relates.[14] In light of this brief description, insider dealing, as

10 In other words, the provisions found in the *corpus iuris* of the previous MA Directive were triggered by an important condition: that is to say, the financial instruments concerned be admitted to trading on a regulated market in at least one Member State, or at least a request of admission to trading in one of the EU regulated markets has been lodged. See art. 9(1) of the MA Directive.

11 Art. 2(1)(b) of the MA Regulation.

12 Art. 2(1)(c) of the MA Regulation.

13 Art. 2(1)(d) of the MA Regulation.

14 Art. 8(1) of the MA Regulation. To fulfil the intellectual curiosity of the reader, it may be recalled that the predecessor of such a norm was art. 2(1), sub-para. 1, of the MA Directive. Under the previous legislation, in a preliminary ruling, the ECJ ((Case C-45/08) *Spector Photo Group v Commissie voor het Bank – Financie and Assurantiewezen* [2010] BCC 827) held that, where a person is in possession of inside information, there is a rebuttable presumption that the information has been used.

described by the MA Regulation,[15] is centred on the concept of both 'insider' and 'inside information'. The insider, for purposes of the EU legislation under discussion, is the person possessing this information because he is, somehow, connected with the issuer and/or financial instruments. To elaborate, according to the terminology of the MA Regulation,[16] the insider is:

> any person who possesses that information as a result of (a) being a member of the administrative, management or supervisory bodies of the issuer . . .; (b) having a holding in the capital of the issuer . . .;[17] (c) having access to the information through the exercise of an employment, profession or duties; or (d) being involved in criminal activities.[18]

In other words, insiders are those engaged in a strategic endeavour within the confines of the issuer's business[19] or in connection with it[20] or, in any case, those who obtain the information by virtue of their criminal pursuits.

Inside information constitutes any information, 'of a precise nature',[21] 'which has not been made public' and that relates, 'directly or indirectly, to one or more issuers or to one or more financial instruments'.[22] Information, as articulated in this definition, if made public, should, in all likelihood, impart a telling blow (positive or negative) or, in the terminology of the MA Regulation, have 'a significant effect', 'on the prices of those financial instruments or on the price of related derivative financial instruments.'[23]

---

15 And the similar description in the previous MA Directive.

16 Art. 8(4) of the MA Regulation, previously art. 2(1), sub-para. 2, of the MA Directive.

17 The provisions under (a) and (b) are extended to the 'emission allowance market participant'. The latter, according to the 'definitions' of the MA Regulation (art. 3(1)(20)), is defined as 'any person who enters into transactions, including the placing of orders to trade, in emission allowances, auctioned products based thereon, or derivatives thereof.'

18 It is remarkable to note that any 'person' referred under art. 8(4), sub-para. 2, of the MA Regulation, must be extended, if a legal person, to the 'natural persons' taking part in the decision 'to carry out the acquisition, disposal, cancellation or amendment of an order for the account of the legal person concerned' (art. 8(5) of the MA Regulation, *mutatis mutandis* art. 2(2) of the MA Directive).

19 For instance, the management, the shareholders or those discharging professional duties within the issuer (any employee who had come across the inside information).

20 For instance, legal advisors, auditors or accountants.

21 Accordingly, information of a generic nature should be outwith the scope of the definition.

22 This is the tenor of art. 7(1) of the MA Regulation. Previously, the basic rules were, fundamentally, the same, albeit enshrined within art. 1(1) of the MA Directive.

In a preliminary ruling of the EUCJ ((Case C-19/11) *Markus Geltl v Daimler AG* [2012] 3 CMLR 32) the chairman of the multinational company Daimler informed the supervisory board that he was thinking of resigning, but actually he did not do so for another two months. At that time, the stock exchanges were notified and the share prices rose. Shareholders who had previously sold their shares sued for compensation. It was held that intermediate steps in a protracted process might have been tantamount to 'precise information'.

23 Art. 7(1)(a) of the MA Regulation, previously, *mutatis mutandis*, art. 1(1) of the MA Directive.

Remarkably, as a result of the MA Regulation, the concept of 'inside information', if relating to 'commodity derivatives', shall 'bask' in a larger perimeter of application. More specifically, as a result of art. 7(1)(b) of the MA Regulation, the 'inside information' relating to commodity derivatives is independent of the fact that the contract shall be listed in a market.

As far as persons in charge of the execution of orders concerning financial instruments, 'inside information' shall mean, additionally (art. 7(1)(d) of the MA Regulation, previously art. 1(1) of the MA Directive), 'information conveyed by a client and related to the client's pending orders, which is of a precise nature, relating, directly or indirectly, to one or more issuers or to one or more financial instruments, and which, if it were made public, would be likely to have a significant effect on the prices of those financial instruments, the price of related spot commodity contracts, or on the price of related derivative financial instruments.'

Finally, the MA Directive required each Member State to implement at national level administrative sanctions for violations of the principles, while it was left to the discretion of the local legislator what nature those sanctions would have (either criminal or civil).[24] In a significant move from the past, the new EU body of law by way of Directive 2014/57[25] establishes 'minimum rules for criminal sanctions for insider dealing', but also for the other two categories of conduct of unlawful disclosure and market manipulation, 'to ensure the integrity of financial markets in the Union and to enhance investor protection and confidence in those markets.'[26]

3.3.2 Unlawful disclosure of inside information

The underpinning philosophy of the MA Regulation is to prohibit the persons concerned (the 'insider', as defined in the same statute) to disclose inside information to any other person ('except where the disclosure is made in the normal exercise of an employment, a profession or duties'[27]), or to recommend or induce 'another person, on the basis of inside information, to acquire or dispose of financial instruments to which that information relates.'[28]

Interestingly, the EU legal provisions relating to insider dealing, when the MA Directive was still in force, used to set out 'minimum standards', from which each national legislator could derogate. Thus, an EU Member State which had decided to make more stringent the prohibitions of use of inside information, would not infringe the MA Directive, so long as the concept of 'inside information' remains correspondent to that forged in Brussels.[29]

Within the 'unlawful disclosure of inside information', the MA Regulation makes reference, for the first time, to a special conduct, that of 'market sounding'. This is basically, according to art. 11(1) of the MA Regulation:

> the communication of information, prior to the announcement of a transaction, in order to gauge the interest of potential investors in a possible transaction and the conditions

---

continued

Finally (and this provision does not have any bearing with the previous text of Directive 2003/6), it is stated (art. 7(1)(c) of the MA Regulation) that, as far as emission allowances (or auctioned products based on them) are concerned, 'inside information' is the 'information of a precise nature, which has not been made public, relating, directly or indirectly, to one or more such instruments, and which, if it were made public, would be likely to have a significant effect on the prices of such instruments or on the prices of related derivative financial instruments.'

24 This seems to be also the interpretation of scholars such as IG MacNeil, *An Introduction to the Law on Financial Investment* (2nd edn Hart Publishing, Oxford and Portland 2012) 416.

25 It is remarkable that in the new 'nomenclature' of the EU legislator, the Directive at stake is called the 'Market Abuse Directive'. To avoid confusion with what, historically, has been the Market Abuse Directive for more than a decade (Directive 2003/6), in this chapter the recent Directive 2014/57 shall be referred to exclusively by its number.

26 Art. 1(1) of Directive 2014/57. The purpose of the legislation is also to introduce and harmonise across the EU a criminal regime in this area, in light of the fact that some jurisdictions, in the past, did not cater for criminal sanctions.

27 Art. 10(1) of the MA Regulation, basically but not verbatim correspondent to art. 3(a) of the previous MA Directive.

28 Art. 10(1), second part, of the MA Regulation, previously art. 3(b) of the MA Directive.

29 Under the previous MA Directive, so was the *decisum* of the ECJ ((Case C-28/99) *Criminal proceedings against Jean Verdonck, Ronald Everaert and Edith de Baedts* [2001] ECR I-3399). On this assumption, see among scholars IG MacNeil, *An Introduction to the Law on Financial Investment* (2nd edn Hart Publishing, Oxford and Portland 2012) 416.

> relating to it such as its potential size or pricing, to one or more potential investors by . . . the issuer.[30]

Although conducting market soundings is a valuable tool to gauge the opinion of potential investors and therefore is quite beneficial to the financial markets (particularly when the latter either lack confidence or do not rely on a relevant benchmark or, anyway, are volatile[31]), they may require disclosure of inside information to potential investors. Market sounding, therefore, is not prohibited in principle. However, it requires a cautious approach by the disclosing market participant; the latter, according to art. 11(3) of the MA Regulation, 'shall specifically consider whether the market sounding will involve the disclosure of inside information', before the start of a market sounding. If this is the case, it shall make a written record of its conclusion and the reasons for it, with an obligation to provide the authority with these records, upon request of the latter.[32]

3.3.3 Market manipulation

A further category of behaviour prohibited under the MA Regulation is that of market manipulation.[33] According to art. 1(2) of the MA Directive, the general activity of market manipulation used to branch out into three subcategories: to mislead in terms of supply, demand or price of financial instruments; fictitious devices and deception; and dissemination of false information. Article 12 of the MA Regulation revamps the categories previously legislated, by adopting a quadripartite definition. In essence, a fourth conduct of market abuse makes its debut in the recently enacted EU statute under discussion, i.e. the dissemination of false information relating to benchmarks.[34] This further *genus* may address problems of speculation as emerged during the financial debt crisis, when it may have been incorrect information relating to the sovereign debt of some Euro-zone countries and their capacity to repay their debt, that played havoc across the financial markets.[35]

As to the first category of market manipulation, art. 12(1)(a) of the MA Regulation refers to a defined perimeter of activities; more specifically, transactions or orders to trade or any other behaviour which:

> – gives, or is likely to give, false or misleading signals as to the supply of, demand for, or price of, a financial instrument, a related spot commodity contract or an auctioned product based on emission allowances;

30 In addition to the 'issuer', the communication can originate, according to the same art. 11(1), also from a secondary offeror of a financial instrument, an emission allowance market participant or a third party acting on behalf of them.

31 See Recital 32 of the MA Regulation.

32 See, again, art. 11(3) of the MA Regulation.

33 In a very explicit way, art. 5 of the MA Directive stated that a 'Member State shall prohibit any person from engaging in market manipulation'.

34 Art. 12(1)(d).

35 The dissemination of false information relating to benchmarks is not an absolute novelty; in some EU countries such as Britain, the prohibition had already been introduced before the recently enacted MA Regulation, more specifically by the Financial Services Act 2012.

or

> – which secures, or is likely to secure, the price of one or several financial instruments, a related spot commodity contract or an auctioned product based on emission allowances at an abnormal or artificial level.

According to the same article of the MA Regulation, the person entering these orders or transactions or, more in general, engaging in such behaviour shall be exempt from sanctions, if it is established that his reason for so doing is 'legitimate' and that these transactions or orders to trade conform to 'accepted market practice'.[36]

The second area of market manipulation is concerned with a 'transaction, placing an order to trade or any other activity or behaviour . . . which employs a fictitious device or any other form of deception or contrivance'.[37]

The third conduct is defined, according to art. 12(1)(c) of the MA Regulation, as the dissemination of information:

> through the media, including the internet, or by any other means, which gives, or is likely to give, false or misleading signals as to the supply of, demand for, or price of, a financial instrument, a related spot commodity contract or an auctioned product based on emission allowances or secures, or is likely to secure, the price of one or several financial instruments, a related spot commodity contract or an auctioned product based on emission allowances at an abnormal or artificial level, including the dissemination or rumours.

Finally, and as already anticipated above, the last category of conduct, introduced by the MA Regulation and not contemplated in the previous legislation, is the transmission of 'false or misleading information' or the provision:

> of false or misleading inputs in relation to a benchmark where the person who made the transmission or provided the input knew or ought to have known that it was false or misleading, or any other behaviour which manipulates the calculation of a benchmark.[38]

In all of these four circumstances, the essential condition is that 'the person who made the dissemination knew, or ought to have known, that the information was false or misleading.'[39,40]

---

36 The 'accepted market practice' is better defined, in the MA Regulation, under art. 13. These 'accepted market practices' may be established also by the competent authority on the basis of criteria defined under art. 13(2).

37 Art. 12(1)(b) of the MA Regulation, previously, *mutatis mutandis*, art. 1(2)(b) of the MA Directive.

38 Art. 12(1)(d) of the MA Regulation.

39 Art. 12(1)(c) of the MA Regulation.

40 Art. 4 of the Implementing Directive 2003/124 used to provide details of such categories of conduct. As regards these misleading signals, mention used to be made to 'the extent to which orders to trade given or transactions undertaken represent a significant proportion of the daily volume of transactions in the relevant financial instrument on the regulated market concerned, in particular when these activities lead to a significant change in the price of a financial instrument.' As regards all the other signals provided under art. 4 of the Implementing Directive 2003/124, now repealed, see, among scholars, E Swan and J Virgo, *Market Abuse Regulation* (2nd edn Oxford University Press, Oxford 2010) 58. A more detailed elucidation of the concept of market manipulation was provided by an implementing document of the EU Commission published on 22 December 2003, Implementing Directive 2003/124/EC, where a non-exhaustive list of 'signals, which should not necessarily be deemed in themselves to constitute market manipulation', was provided.

3.4 Disclosure of inside information; insider lists; disclosure of own account transactions by persons discharging managerial responsibilities

As when the MA Directive was still in force, the MA Regulation continues to enjoin issuers to disclose inside information directly concerning them to the public as soon as possible.[41] Nonetheless, as far as the matter of disclosure is concerned, new notions previously missing, have been codified by the MA Regulation, i.e. the 'insider lists' and 'the disclosure of own account transactions by persons discharging managerial responsibilities'. A brief account of these will be provided in this section.

As to the first category (disclosure of inside information), the relevant rules are detailed in art. 17 of the Regulation under discussion.[42] The main purpose of these provisions is to ensure that one of the main values of the MA Regulation, i.e. market integrity, is not affected, nor prejudiced, in connection with an issuer. The MA Regulation requires the issuer to inform the public 'as soon as possible' of 'inside information which directly concerns that said issuer'.[43] As a result, the issuer shall guarantee that 'inside information is made public in a manner which enables fast access and complete, correct and timely assessment of the information by the public.'[44]

Therefore, the principle of transparency adopted would require the issuer to proceed immediately to the disclosure of the inside information relating to or concerned with the same issuer. Remarkably, art. 17(4) of the MA Regulation, in the same fashion as the previous MA Directive, allows a significant exception to the norm; the dissemination of the inside information may be delayed by the same issuer in three – alternative – circumstances: (a) the immediate disclosure is likely to prejudice the legitimate interests of the issuer;[45] (b) the delay of disclosure is not likely to mislead the public; or (c) the issuer[46] is in a position to keep the information confidential.[47]

As far as the 'insider lists' are concerned, this is a significant and remarkable novelty of the MA Regulation. It is legislated in its art. 18 that the issuer[48] is required to draw up a list of the persons who, on the one hand, 'have access to inside information', and on the other hand 'are working for them under a contract of employment', or 'performing tasks through which they have access to inside information, such as advisers, accountants or credit rating agencies'.[49] Such a list, the 'insider list', shall be updated 'promptly' by the issuer, according to the specific modalities of art. 18(4) of the MA Regulation.[50] The provision is made even more

41 See Linklaters, 'EU "Gets Tough" on Market Abuse', 20 October 2011, 4, www.linklaters.com/pdfs/mkt/london/Market_Abuse_briefing.pdf, accessed 15 July 2014.
42 Previously, art. 6 of the MA Directive.
43 Art. 17(1), first sub-para., of the MA Regulation.
44 Art. 17(1), second sub-para., of the MA Regulation.
45 Or the 'emission allowance market participant'.
46 Or the 'emission allowance market participant'.
47 Art. 17(4) of the MA Regulation.
48 The obligation applies also to the 'emission allowance market participant'.
49 Art. 18(1)(a) of the MA Regulation.
50 Art. 18(1)(b) of the MA Regulation.

persuasive and stringent due to art. 18(1)(c) requiring the issuer to provide the 'competent authority' with such a list.

Finally, as far as transactions by people discharging managerial responsibilities are concerned, the MA Regulation, more specifically art. 19,[51] requires them to notify the issuer[52] and the competent authority of 'every transaction conducted on their own account relating to the shares or debt instruments of that issuer or to derivatives or other financial instruments linked thereto'.

The notification at stake shall be made 'promptly' and, anyway, 'no later than three business days after the date of the transaction',[53] and the content of the notification shall comply with the requirements set out under art. 19(6).[54]

Two aspects, relating to the new concept of 'managers' transactions', are worthy of clarification. First, in terms of persons subject to the obligation at stake, the norm under comment is extended to 'persons closely associated' with the managers of the issuer. The relevant definition of 'persons closely associated' is given under art. 3(1)(26) of the MA Regulation, where, basically, reference is made to the 'spouse', 'a dependent child', 'a relative' and 'a legal person, trust or partnership the managerial responsibilities of which are discharged' by the same manager or by a person closely associated with the latter. Second, as far as the transaction to be communicated, not every transaction falls within the duty, but exclusively a transaction or a series of transactions exceeding a minimal threshold of Euro 5,000 'within a calendar year'[55] or the higher threshold fixed by the national authority, although in this latter case, despite the discretionary power, the threshold cannot be higher than Euro 20,000.[56]

3.5 Further reading

Alcock, A, 'Five Years of Market Abuse' (2007) 28(6) *Company Lawyer* 163, 171

Barnard, C, *The Substantive Law of the EU: The Four Freedoms* (4th edn Oxford University Press, Oxford 2013)

Benston, GJ, 'The Value of the SEC's Accounting Disclosure Requirement' (1969) 44 *Accounting Review* 515, 519

Benston, GJ, 'Required Disclosure and the Stock Market: An Evaluation of the Securities Exchange Act of 1934' (1973) 63 *American Economic Review* 132, 155

51 More specifically, art. 19(1).

52 Or, alternatively, any 'emission allowance market participant'. Additionally, the concept of issuer shall be that provided by the same MA Regulation, art. 3(1)(21): '[A] legal entity governed by private or public law, which issues or proposes to issue financial instruments, the issuer being, in case of depository receipts representing financial instruments, the issuer of the financial instruments represented.' Therefore, if the manager of the issuer decided to buy and sell securities issued by an entity different from the issuer, the legal provisions under discussion shall not apply.

53 Art. 19(1) of the MA Regulation.

54 Namely, the notification shall comprise of '(a) the name of the person; (b) the reason for the notification; (c) the name of the relevant issuer or emission allowance market participant; (d) a description and the identifier of the financial instrument; (e) the nature of the transaction(s) . . .; (f) the date and the place of the transaction(s); and (g) the price and volume of the transaction(s)'.

55 Art. 19(8) of the MA Regulation.

56 Art. 19(9) of the MA Regulation. If the national authority decided to exercise this power, the ESMA, the European Securities and Markets Authority, shall be informed of this.

Blair, M, and Walker, G, *Financial Services Law* (Oxford University Press, Oxford 2006)
Coffee, J, 'Market Failure and the Economic Case for a Mandatory Disclosure System' (1984) 70 *Virginia Law Review* 717, 753
Conceicao, C, 'The FSA's Approach to Taking Action against Market Abuse' (2007) 28(2) *Company Lawyer* 43, 45
Dashwood, A, Dougan, M, Rodger, B, Spaventa, E, and Wyatt, D, *Wyatt and Dashwood's European Union Law* (6th edn Hart Publishing, Oxford and Portland 2011)
Final Report of the Committee of the Wise Men in the Regulation of European Securities Markets, Brussels, 15 February 2001
French, D, Mayson, S, and Ryan, C, *Mayson, French and Ryan on Company Law* (30th edn Oxford University Press, Oxford 2013) 197, 224 (offering shares to the public) 352, 370 (market abuse) 225, 254 (Transfer of shares)
Gullifer, L, and Payne, J, *Corporate Finance Law* (Hart Publishing, Oxford and Portland 2011)
Grundmann, S, *European Company Law Ius Communitatis, Volume I* (2nd edn Intersentia, Cambridge, Antwerp and Portland 2012)
Hemetsberger, W, Schoppmann, H, Schwander, D and Wengler, C, *European Banking and Financial Law* (2nd edn Kluwer Law International in association with European Association of Public Banks, Brussels 2006)
Hopt, KJ, and Wymeersch, E, *European Company and Financial Law: Text and Leading Cases* (3rd Oxford University Press, Oxford 2006)
Hudson, A, *The Law of Finance* (1st edn Sweet & Maxwell, London 2009)
Hudson, A, *The Law of Finance* (2nd edn Sweet & Maxwell, London 2013)
Linklaters, 'EU "Gets Tough" on Market Abuse', 20 October 2011, www.linklaters.com/pdfs/mkt/london/Market_Abuse_briefing.pdf, accessed on 15 July 2014
MacNeil, I, 'The Evolution of Regulatory Enforcement Action in the UK Capital Markets: A Case of Less is More?' (2007) 2 *Capital Markets Law Journal* 345, 369
MacNeil, IG, *An Introduction to the Law on Financial Investment* (2nd edn Hart Publishing, Oxford and Portland 2012)
McVea, H, 'What's Wrong with Insider Trading?' (1995) 3(15) *Journal of Legal Studies* 390, 414
Panasar, R, and Boeckman, P, *European Securities Law* (Oxford University Press, Oxford 2010)
Schammo, P, *EU Prospectus Law* (Cambridge University Press, Cambridge 2011)
Scott, HS, *International Finance* (17th edn Foundation Press, New York 2010)
Sfameni, P, and Giannelli, A, *Diritto degli Intermediari e dei Mercati Finanziari* (Egea, Milan 2013)
Soderquist, LD, and Gabaldon, TA, *Securities Law* (Foundation Press and Thomson West, New York 2004)
Swan, E, and Virgo, J, *Market Abuse Regulation* (2nd edn Oxford University Press, Oxford 2010)
Wood, PR, *Regulation of International Finance* (Thomson/Sweet & Maxwell, London 2007)
Woods, L, and Watson, P, *Steiner and Woods EU Law* (11th edn Oxford University Press, Oxford 2012)

3.6 Questions

3.1 What is the rationale behind the EU Market Abuse Regulation and on what grounds can one say that insider dealing is morally wrong?

3.2 Can you describe the differences, from a legal point of view, between the Market Abuse Directive and the Market Abuse Regulation?

3.3 What is the concept of market sounding?

3.4 What is the 'insider list' and how does it work?

Chapter 4

Financial consumer protection

Chapter contents

4.1 From '*caveat emptor*' to consumer protection

Within the area of law typically referred to as contract law, it has traditionally been maintained that two contracting parties (e.g. in a sale: the seller and the purchaser), must be regarded, from a legal point of view, to be of equal standing in terms of conferred rights and obligations irrespective of their respective bargaining power, i.e. irrespective of their strength or weakness. As a consequence of such theoretical postulation and in light of the principle of party autonomy, i.e. the principle that each party must be free to choose what and with whom to contract, the law has generally refrained from meddling with the consumer/purchaser–provider/seller relationship as this area is traditionally deemed to be of a private nature. The Latin maxim '*caveat emptor*' (be aware, purchaser) typifies the paradigm of this liberal approach in that the onus rests on the purchaser, during the negotiations, to investigate the different terms and conditions of the prospective (sales) contract.

And yet, as the economic landscape has shifted, a proliferation of new technologies has accelerated the distribution of goods and a more egalitarian view has become commonplace; jurists have been faced with the task of developing forms of legislative protection for the consumer/purchaser to amend the basic principles manifested by the law of contract that were increasingly felt to be inadequate. This new scenario, coupled with a more prominent realisation of ideals of social justice, has facilitated a different awareness of the consumer's rights and, therefore, prompted a different approach to the private law and its sacrosanct principle of freedom of contract.[1]

From the perspective of this work, it is worth acknowledging from the outset that a more protective approach to the consumer/purchaser–provider/seller relationship has found fertile ground in the EU landscape. In EU terminology, as a rule of thumb, the consumer is defined as an individual – a physical person rather than an entity – who acquires goods or services; his counterparty being a seller or supplier acting in a professional capacity. The EU legislator assumes that the consumer has a relatively weak position and that, when acting for purposes outside his trade or business, the consumer must inherently tread on dangerous ground as he is exposed to the risk of abuse by the stronger party (i.e. the seller or supplier). Therefore, the legislator has moderated this position in respect to the consumer's rights against the counterparty.

The evolution of 'consumerist theory' in the EU is centred, at a legislative level, on a deeply ingrained piece of legislation: the Unfair Terms Directive.[2] This statute basically stipulates that, in any contract with a consumer (as defined in the Directive), disparities in the terms and conditions which are to the detriment of the weaker party shall not be binding on the consumer. Such scenarios are elaborated upon as the present chapter unfolds but for now, by way of an introduction, it is important to note that the Directive on unfair terms in consumer contracts applies to all such contracts between a seller or supplier and a consumer. Therefore, the entire range of financial contracts, from banking contracts (including investment contracts) to insurance contracts are

1 P Nebbia, *Unfair Contract Terms in European Law* (Hart Publishing, Oxford and Portland, Oregon 2007) 5.
2 In full: Council Directive 93/13/EEC of 5 April 1993 on unfair terms in consumer contracts, OJ L 95.

subject to its authority, in as far as they involve the sale or supply of goods and services.[3]

The means by which protection is afforded to the benefit of the consumer shall be the topic of analysis within the present chapter below.

Moreover, the commercialisation of services discharged remotely (in other words, outside the offices or premises of the supplier/seller), including those undertaken through the medium of techniques such as the telephone, the TV, email and internet, has given birth to the passing of specific legislation relating to 'distance contracts'. Also this body of law, more specifically where it has been crafted to regulate financial contracts, is discussed within the current chapter.[4]

Furthermore, in more recent times the level of protection afforded to a consumer acquiring services or goods in the financial sector has exceeded that provided by the framework of the Unfair Terms Directive by virtue of the development of a comprehensive body of legislation limited to the investment business. Remarkably, this body of legislation is not charged with protecting the banking/financial consumer in general, but is exclusively concerned with the consumer acquiring investment services. The relevant legal provisions have been enshrined within the Markets in Financial Instruments Directive II ('MiFID II')[5] and the Markets in Financial Instruments Regulation ('MiFIR').[6] Also this body of legislation shall be the subject matter of legal analysis below.

Finally, it is worthy of mention the power that, in this traditionally private law area, is increasingly bestowed upon EU authorities. An example of this is the ESMA, the European Securities and Markets Authority,[7] and its entitlement to exercise soft law powers in order to ensure that the financial markets for consumer products and services are consumer friendly.[8]

---

3 The exceptions are consumer credit contracts, subject to the Consumer Credit Directive (Directive 2008/48/EC) (M Furmston and J Chuah, *Commercial Law* (2nd edn Pearson, Harlow 2010), and see below, section 4.6).

4 General distance contracts are regulated in Directive 2011/83/EU of the European Parliament and of the Council of 25 October 2011 on consumer rights, amending Council Directive 93/13/EEC and Directive 1999/44/EC of the European Parliament and of the Council and repealing Council Directive 85/577/EEC and Directive 97/7/EC of the European Parliament and of the Council, OJ L 304, whereas financial distance contracts find their regulation in Directive 2002/65/EC of the European Parliament and of the Council of 23 September 2002 concerning the distance marketing of consumer financial services and amending Council Directive 90/619/EEC and Directives 97/7/EC and 98/27/EC, OJ L 271.

5 In full: Directive 2014/65/EU of the European Parliament and of the Council of 15 May 2014 on markets in financial instruments and amending Directive 2002/92/EC and Directive 2011/61/EU, OJ L 173.

6 In full: Regulation (EU) No 600/2014 of the European Parliament and of the Council of 15 May 2014 on markets in financial instruments and amending Regulation (EU) No 648/2012, OJ L 173.

7 Its creation, in replacement of the CESR (the Commission of European Securities Regulators), is the outcome of the so-called ESMA Regulation, i.e. Regulation (EU) No 1095/2010 of the European Union Parliament and of the Council of 24 November 2010 establishing a European Authority (European Securities and Markets Authority).

8 Art. 9 of the ESMA Regulation may be the paradigm for this. Art. 9(2), for instance, prescribes as follows:

> The Authority shall monitor new and existing financial activities ad may adopt guidelines and recommendations with a view to promoting the safety and soundness of markets and convergence of regulatory practice.

It is probably too early to speculate on an overwhelming influence of the EU authorities on the contractual area of financial contracts; however, it could be a step towards a future trend.

4.2 Unfair Terms Directive

4.2.1 Introduction

As mentioned at the outset of the present chapter, from a contract law perspective the existence of a bargaining power imbalance between two contracting parties (e.g. the seller or supplier on the one hand, and the acquirer of the goods or services on the other) was traditionally perceived to be legally irrelevant, both in respect to civil law traditions and, to an even greater extent, at common law. This may have changed, but discrepancies in the way the relationship between sellers/providers of services and consumers have subsequently been regulated at each national level may hamper the EU Treaty principles according to which goods, services and capital must move freely within the Union. Therefore, the European legislator has deemed it necessary to lay down harmonising rules with regard to the responsibility each country must bear in protecting consumers against unfair terms in the contracts they conclude with sellers and providers of services. In this respect, the Unfair Terms Directive[9] marks the emergence of a first set of European rules, and despite the differences existing in each country, aimed at harmonising 'the laws, regulations and administrative provisions of the Member States relating to unfair terms in contracts concluded between a seller or supplier and a consumer'.[10] The category of consumer which the Unfair Terms Directive tackles is defined as the 'natural person who . . . is acting for purposes that are outside his trade, business or profession'.[11]

A couple of observations are worth addressing in respect to the above definition of a consumer. First and foremost, the insertion of the adjective 'natural' prior to 'person' means that an entity (such as a company) is not consistent with the concept of a consumer, and therefore cannot be protected by the relevant provisions. It would appear that a consumer is confined to an individual. Furthermore, the 'consumer', albeit a natural person, will not benefit from any protection from the piece of legislation at stake, if he has acted for purposes connected with his professional or business activities. The reason for this seems to be that a person acquiring a good for use in the course of his business or profession (e.g. a lawyer buying a piece of furniture for his

9 In this respect, scholars (e.g. P Nebbia, *Unfair Contract Terms in European Law* (Hart Publishing, Oxford and Portland, Oregon 2007) 3) correctly emphasise that 'Directive 93/13 has therefore one peculiarity: it establishes a link between consumer protection and the internal market.'

10 Art. 1(1) of the Unfair Terms Directive. A brief description of the Directive under discussion can be found in W Hemetsberger, H Schoppmann, D Schwander and C Wengler, *European Banking and Financial Services Law* (Kluwer Law International in association with European Association of Public Banks, Alphen aan den Rijn 2006) 151; see also A Gkoutzinis, *Internet Banking and the Law in Europe* (Cambridge University Press, Cambridge 2006) 191, 193. For example, in the UK, Directive 93/13 has been transposed, originally, in the Unfair Terms in Consumer Contracts Regulations 1994, later replaced by the Unfair Terms in Consumer Contracts Regulations 1999. Among scholars, see for a more extensive explanation: Chitty on Contracts, *General Principles, Vol. I* (31st edn Sweet & Maxwell, London 2012) 1112; H Beale, B Fauvarque-Cosson, J Rutgers, D Tallon and S Vogenauer, *Cases, Materials and Text on Contract Law* (2nd edn Hart Publishing, Oxford and Portland 2010). It is worth noting that in the same jurisdiction (UK), the other pillar for the regulation of unfair contract terms, preceding the promulgation of Directive 1993/13, is the Unfair Contract Terms Act 1977. The latter statute, paradoxically, has a slightly larger scope than the 'Regulations 1999', first because it applies also to notices purporting to exclude or restrict the liability, second, for the reason that its perimeter of application also encompasses clauses that have been individually negotiated (E Peel, *Treitel: The Law of Contract* (30th edn Sweet & Maxwell, London 2010)).

11 Art. 2(b) of the Unfair Terms Directive. See R Cranston (ed.), *European Banking Law: The Banker-Customer Relationship* (2nd edn LLP, London and Hong Kong 1999).

office) is not to be considered a weak party, and acts as a professional or a businessman after all.[12]

Before undertaking a more detailed analysis of the main terms and rules of the Directive at stake, it is imperative to clarify that the provisions included within Directive 1993/13 apply to financial contracts, including banking/investment contracts and insurance policies. First, no exclusion for these kinds of transactions is contemplated within the Unfair Terms Directive.[13] Second, many financial contracts fall within the scope of 'contracts concluded between a seller or supplier and a consumer'; in fact, a bank, investment firm or insurance company can be conclusively viewed as a professional supplier or seller of, respectively, banking, investment and/or insurance services and products, in many cases to consumers.[14]

4.2.2 Main terms and provisions

The legal protection of the consumer afforded by the Unfair Terms Directive is predominantly achieved through the provisions of its art. 3. In this respect, the main concern of the EU legislator has been that a consumer (including a bank consumer) may be unduly and detrimentally affected, in the relevant contracts, by terms that have not been individually negotiated.[15] Put simply, these terms are not the outcome of a specific pre-contractual discussion with the seller or provider, but may be a consequence of the pressure which the party with greater bargaining power can exert on the other. Article 3(2) of the Directive under discussion clarifies the specific circumstances under which a term shall be regarded as 'not individually negotiated' and therefore possibly unfair: more specifically, this happens when such a term 'has been drafted in advance and the consumer has therefore not been able to influence the substance of the term, particularly in the context of a pre-formulated standard contract.'

A term is not binding upon the consumer provided the term has not been individually negotiated and it is 'contrary to the requirement of good faith' while, in its wake, 'it causes a significant imbalance in the parties' rights and obligations arising under the contract, to the detriment of the consumer.'[16]

These last two conditions, which must be met equally and therefore are cumulative rather than alternative avenues on which to dispute a contract,[17] are worthy of a brief analysis. First, the duty of good faith entails an obligation on the part of the seller or

12 It goes without saying that in contracts between two parties, both commercial (e.g. two legal entities or two individuals both acting for professional or business purposes), the EU legislation under discussion will not apply, on the assumption that such parties can look after themselves.

13 As already mentioned above under the previous section of this chapter, the Directive under discussion does not apply to consumer credit contracts, the latter being subject to the micro-system of legal provisions framed by Directive 2008/48/EC.

14 Remarkably, Directive 1993/13, albeit implemented in each country, still remains an important 'source' for each national court; to elaborate, the latter, following a *decisum* of the EUCJ (particularly Case C-106/89 *Marleasing SA v La Comercial Internacionale de Alimentacion SA* [1990] ECR I-4135), shall interpret the terms of the Directive under discussion to give effect also to the purposes of the Directive itself, not simply to the terms of the internal legislation.

15 Art. 3(1) of the Unfair Terms Directive.

16 Whether or not the Unfair Terms Directive introduces at EU level a general principle of good faith in consumer contracting is still debated. For a recent doctrinal analysis, see N Reich, *General Principles of EU Civil Law* (Intersentia, Cambridge, Antwerp, Portland 2014) 189, 212.

17 Indeed, a previous draft of the Directive referred to them as 'alternative' (E McKendrick, *Contract Law (Palgrave Macmillan Law Masters)* (10th edn Palgrave Macmillan, London 2013) 313).

supplier (in light of this work, the bank) to the consumer to ensure that from a substantial point of view, the supplier should not take advantage of the state of necessity or lack of experience of the consumer, while from a formal point of view, terms should be written in a legible and clear way and without traps. Second, for the term to be unfair, the lack of good faith must cause a 'significant imbalance', tipping the scales against the consumer. In this respect, the adjective 'significant' is, in itself, noteworthy as it could be construed very differently from two opposing viewpoints. On the one hand, in an interpretation that is more seller- and provider-friendly and, in all likelihood, more consistent with the common law tradition, the imbalance should be 'serious and exceptional', otherwise it will not be material. On the other hand, taken from a civil law perspective, the imbalance shall be deemed 'significant' so long as it is not trivial. Obviously, the latter interpretation is conducive to a broader scope of potential unfairness of terms and conditions within a consumer contract. The expression 'to the detriment of the consumer' is also worthy of further analysis. In some EU jurisdictions,[18] it was held that the expression does not add anything, as if it was a combination of 'words of description'.[19] Some scholars,[20] however, have voiced their contention that it has a meaning of itself and is not merely an explanation of 'significant imbalance'.

Furthermore, the consumer to be considered, in order to assess the detriment, is not the specific consumer affected but rather a general consumer in that position. In other words, the criterion adopted to assess the detriment is objective as opposed to subjective in nature.

Whether or not a contractual term is unfair, is ultimately a matter of interpretation. In particular, the nature of the goods and services at the time of the conclusion of the contract shall be taken into account. Furthermore, all the circumstances surrounding the conclusion of the contract, in addition to all the other terms that may have any bearing on the clause at stake, shall be duly assessed.[21] Nonetheless, the Unfair Terms Directive, in its Annex, provides a list of terms that are presumed to be 'unfair' (irrespective of whether they have been individually negotiated). Among the aforementioned terms, the following are worth highlighting: terms 'excluding or limiting the legal liability of a seller or supplier in the event of the death of a consumer or personal injury to the latter resulting from an act or omission of that seller or supplier' (a); terms 'requiring any consumer who fails to fulfil his obligation to pay a disproportionately high sum in compensation' (e). It would go beyond the scope of this work to delve into the full details of these terms.

Yet some other rules may deserve drawing attention to: if the terms of the contract are in writing for instance, the wording should be in plain, intelligible language, barring such and in case of doubt, 'the interpretation most favourable to the consumer shall prevail'.[22] A further important rule identified by the legislator is the legal consequence and impact of the unfair term on the contract as a whole; the term shall not bind the consumer, although the contract shall continue to exist minus

---

18 Reference can be made to the UK: *Director General of Fair Trading v First National Bank plc* [2001] UKHL 52, para. 36.
19 Ibid.
20 R Cranston, *Principles of Banking Law* (2nd edn Oxford University Press, Oxford 2002).
21 Art. 4(1) of the Unfair Terms Directive.
22 Art. 5 of the Unfair Terms Directive.

the unfair term.[23] This principle is embodied in the Latin maxim '*utile per inutile not vitiatur*', meaning that the validity of the contract as a whole cannot be affected by the invalidity of a specific clause.

4.2.3 Financial contracts

At the outset of this chapter, it was stated that the provisions under discussion apply to the entire range of financial contracts, in as far as they involve the sale or supply of goods and services to consumers. However, while the Annex to the Directive determines some terms always to be unfair, this does not apply to financial contracts. More specifically, although a term 'enabling the seller or supplier to terminate a contract of indeterminate duration without reasonable notice except where there are serious grounds for doing so' is considered an unfair term by definition,[24] a supplier of financial services reserving the 'right to terminate unilaterally a contract of indeterminate duration without notice where there is a valid reason' would not leave that supplier susceptible to the same outcome. In other words, the term in the latter case would not be unfair, so long as the 'supplier is required to inform the other contractual party or parties . . . immediately'.[25] Additionally, while on the one hand, a term 'enabling the seller or supplier to alter the terms of the contract unilaterally without a valid reason that is specified in the contract' is an unfair term,[26] on the other, this provision shall not apply in financial contracts where 'a supplier of financial services reserves the right to alter the rate of interest payable by the consumer or due to the latter, or the amount of other charges for financial services without notice'. This clause, if inserted in financial contracts, would therefore be binding although it will be subject to the condition that 'the supplier . . . inform[s] the other contracting party or parties . . . at the earliest opportunity' and that 'the latter are free to dissolve the contract immediately.'[27]

Finally, three terms listed in the Annex to the Directive are not determined unfair when used in certain derivative transactions, or more precisely, in transactions in transferable securities, financial instruments and other products or services where the price is linked to fluctuations in a stock exchange quotation or index or a financial market rate that the seller or supplier does not control.[28] This derivatives exception concerns the term:

> enabling the seller or supplier to terminate a contract of indeterminate duration without reasonable notice except where there are serious grounds for doing so;

the term:

> enabling the seller or supplier to alter the terms of the contract unilaterally without a valid reason that is specified in the contract;

---

23 Art. 6 of the Unfair Terms Directive.
24 Art. 1(g) of the Annex.
25 Art. 2(a) of the Annex.
26 Art. 1(j) of the Annex.
27 Art. 2(b) of the Annex.
28 Art. 2(c) of the Annex. See on derivatives more extensively below, Chapter 11.

and the term:

> providing for the price of goods to be determined at the time of delivery or allowing a seller of goods or supplier of services to increase their price without in both cases giving the consumer the corresponding right to cancel the contract if the final prices is too high in relation to the price agreed when the contract was concluded.[29]

The reason for these exclusions is that these terms represent the essence of derivatives contracts, which are, by definition, speculative transactions that may be terminated at any moment in time. Without the exceptions, these products could probably not be sold, with negative consequences for the various financial institutions and consumers who would wish to make use of these contracts for hedging purposes.

4.3 Distance contracts

4.3.1 Introduction

Ensuring the protection of the consumer in a contract which is negotiated at a place where the supplier or seller and consumer are physically present (e.g. at the branch of a bank), conjures up problematic aspects, some of which have already been identified and discussed in the present chapter. However, the consumer may be consigned to an even more delicate position in circumstances where the negotiation with the counterparty does not occur in the physical presence of the same, but at a distance. In practical terms, this could be the result of negotiations where the various mediums of modern distance communication are utilised. The telephone is one such well-established medium which, in recent times, has been largely surpassed by the internet and, particularly, by the advent of electronic mail, so allowing the supplier or seller and the consumer to reach an agreement on the conclusion of the contract without the requirement that both parties be physically present at the time. The use of these technologies, while certainly beneficial to the logistical aspect of contract negotiations, may add an increased risk to the consumer. Perhaps even more importantly from the perspective of the internal market, it has been argued that without European rules, consumers would not 'have access without discrimination to the widest possible range of financial services available'.[30]

---

29 Art. 1(g), (j) and (l) of the Annex, respectively.

30 Recital 3 of Directive 2002/65/EC of the European Parliament and of the Council of 23 September 2002 concerning the distance marketing of consumer financial services and amending Council Directive 90/619/EEC and Directives 97/7/EC and 98/27/EC, OJ L 271.

At the national level, the implementation of this piece of EU legislation has happened according to the internal rules. In England, for instance, the Consumer Protection (Distance Selling) Regulations 2000/2334, in force from 31 August 2000 (as amended by the Financial Services (Distance Marketing) Regulations 2004/2095, in force as from 31 October 2004, is the relevant statute. See, among others, JN Adams and H Macqueen, *Atiyah's Sale of Goods* (12th edn Pearson, Harlow 2010) 55, 60; E Peel, *Treitel: The Law of Contract* (30th edn Sweet & Maxwell, London 2011) 271. More recently, the Consumer Contracts (Information, Cancellation and Additional Rights) Regulations 2013, applicable to contracts made after 13 June 2014, superseded the Consumer Protection (Distant Selling) Regulations 2000/2334. However, for contracts made before 13 June 2014, the 2000 Regulations still apply.

In respect to primary sources concerning distance contracts, it is opportune to draw attention to two principal pieces of EU legislation: the Consumer Rights Directive,[31] in which distance contracts are considered in a more general way, and the Distance Financial Services Directive.[32] The latter Directive is more specifically concerned with the distance marketing of consumer financial services[33] save for credit cards and similar products more recently subject to a different EU legislative framework.[34] The Consumer Rights Directive excludes 'financial services',[35] so that the following will focus on the Distance Financial Services Directive. Similarly, a separate EU statute, outside the scope of this textbook, is the Directive on E-Commerce.[36]

4.3.2 Distance Financial Services Directive

First and foremost, it is worth highlighting the perimeter to which the application of the Distance Financial Services Directive is confined. The task of formulating a definition for a distance contract is anything but straightforward, given the multifarious possibilities that new technology continues to serve up to parties engaged in concluding contract negotiations. Despite this, the EU legislator offers a readily understandable definition of the phenomenon at stake: the 'distance contract' for financial services is:

> any contract concerning financial services concluded between a supplier and a consumer under an organised distance sales or service-provision scheme run by the supplier, who, for the purpose of that contract, makes exclusive use of one or more

---

31 In full: Directive 2011/83/EU of the European Parliament and of the Council of 25 October 2011 on consumer rights, amending Council Directive 93/13/EEC and Directive 1999/44/EC of the European Parliament and of the Council and repealing Council Directive 85/577/EEC and Directive 97/7/EC of the European Parliament and of the Council, OJ L 304.

This relatively recent Directive has repealed Directive 97/7/EC of 20 May 1997 on the protection of consumers of distance contracts. Directive 97/7 used to provide the consumer with the main protection on distance selling. Although Directive 97/7 applied to distance contracts, de facto it excluded a wide area of e-commerce, particularly B2B transactions. As regards the latter, Directive 2000/31 on electronic commerce would apply. This was due to the quite rigid definition of 'distance contract' under Directive 97/7, particularly art. 2(1): '[A]ny contract concerning goods or services concluded between a supplier and a consumer under an organised distance sales or service provision scheme run by the supplier who, for the purposes of the contract, makes exclusive use of one or more means of distance communication up to and including the moment at which the contract is concluded.'

For a commentary on this Directive, now abolished, see P Todd, *E-Commerce Law* (Routledge-Cavendish, Abingdon 2005).

32 European Parliament and Council Directive 2002/65/EC of 23 September 2002 concerning the distance marketing of consumer services and amending Council Directive 90/619/EEC and Directives 97/7/EC and 98/27/EC.

33 In the UK, among the different Member States, this piece of legislation has been transposed into the Financial Services (Distance Marketing) Regulations 2004/2095.

34 Notably, as far as credit cards are concerned, a specific framework has been forged by the EU legislator, i.e. Directive 2007/64 ('Payment Services Directive'). The latter, in the UK, among the different Member States, has been implemented though an amendment to the Financial Services (Distance Marketing) Regulations 2004. See, among scholars, EP Ellinger, E Lomnicka and CVM Hare, *Ellinger's Modern Banking Law* (5th edn Oxford University Press, Oxford 2011).

35 Art. 3(d) of the Consumer Rights Directive.

36 As far as commentaries on the Directive on Electronic Commerce (Directive 2000/31/EC of the European Parliament and of the Council of 8 June 2000 on certain legal aspects of information society services, in particular electronic commerce, in the Internal Market) are concerned, see QR Kroes (ed.), *E-Business Law of the European Union* (2nd edn Kluwer Law International, Alphen aan den Rijn 2010); L Edwards (ed.), *The New Legal Framework for E-Commerce in Europe* (Hart Publishing, Oxford and Portland 2005); P Todd, *E-Commerce* (Cavendish Publishing, London 2005); QR Kroes (ed.), *E-Business Law of the European Union* (Allen and Overy Legal Practice and Kluwer Law International, The Hague, London, New York 2003) 1, 6.

means of distance communication up to and including the time at which the contract is concluded.[37]

The terminology adopted refers to 'financial service', under art. 2(b), as 'any service of a banking, credit, insurance, personal pension, investment or payment nature'.[38] Thus, basically, the piece of legislation at stake covers a wide range of products; in fact all the products offered at distance by 'suppliers' operating in the financial industry (not only banks, but also insurers and investment firms) are accounted for. Also the concept of 'means of distance communication' is adapted relative to the nature of the products (financial in this case). In this respect, art. 2(e) refers to 'any means which, without the simultaneous physical presence of the supplier and the consumer, may be used for the distance marketing of a service between those parties.'

Substantively, the mechanism of consumer protection operated by the Directive concerns three pillars: (a) prior information; (b) written confirmation of information; and (c) right of withdrawal. First, in regard to the information which must be sent to the consumer in advance of the conclusion of the distance contract, the range of data to be provided is wide, and does not relate exclusively to the supplier and its characteristics, but includes also the financial service (main characteristics and risks) and the distance contract (particularly the right of withdrawal).[39]

The second pillar deals with the duty of the supplier to communicate to the consumer 'all the contractual terms and conditions and the information' connected with the contract and the relevant financial product, 'on paper or another durable medium available and accessible to the consumer in good time before the consumer is bound by any distance contract or offer.'[40]

Finally, the right of withdrawal is enshrined within the Distance Financial Services Directive; the time by which the consumer is entitled to exercise his withdrawal right is 14 calendar days. To further elaborate on this point, art. 6 of the Distance Financial Services Directive prescribes that Member States 'shall ensure that the consumer shall have a period of 14 calendar days to withdraw from the contract without penalty and without giving any reason.'[41] This period would appear to be a 'floor', rather than a mandatory period. In other words, a Member State is allowed, if it so wishes, to fix a longer period of withdrawal. Needless to say, in this case the local legislator is expected to duly consider two contrasting sides to the argument: on the one hand, the protection of the consumer (whereby a longer period – e.g. 30 days – would be consistent) and, on the other hand, lending support to the financial market and, particularly, to businesses operating within it. In this latter respect, to extend the cooling-off period beyond a 'reasonable' number of days could ultimately discourage operators, particularly those of foreign origin, from offering products at distance in that jurisdiction.

Given the specific characteristics of the financial market, the cooling-off period does not apply to derivatives or, to use the definition of the legislator, the 'financial

37 Art. 2(a) of the Distance Financial Services Directive.
38 'Financial service' is a concept unknown to the MiFID body of legislation. It might have helped if the legislator had adopted MiFID terminology so as to achieve consistency.
39 Art. 3 of the Distance Financial Services Directive.
40 Art. 5 of the Distance Financial Services Directive.
41 The period is extended to 30 calendar days for life insurance products and personal pension operation.

services whose price depends on fluctuations in the financial market outside the suppliers control, which may incur during the withdrawal period'.[42] Other exclusions are those relating to 'travel and baggage insurance policies or similar short-term insurance policies of less than one month's duration' and 'contracts whose performance has been fully completed by both parties at the consumer's express request before the consumer exercises his right of withdrawal'.[43]

4.4 Markets in financial instruments legislation

4.4.1 Introduction

As discussed earlier in this chapter, outwith the financial industry and by means of the Unfair Terms Directive, EU legislation has, for more than two decades, been fostering and promoting a legislative framework the purpose of which is to provide the consumer with a high degree of legal protection. This framework aims to ultimately ensure that, on the one hand, the consumer can be duly informed of the nature of the contract originating from (or potentially imposed by) his counterparty while, on the other hand, a specific mechanism of enforcement to the benefit of the consumer is permitted, i.e. the fact that a term may not be binding on the consumer should it not meet the expected standard of fairness.

As stated above, the financial industry and, particularly, the offering of banking and investment products to the public is an area that is not exempt from the general principles of the Unfair Terms Directive. However, the general protection afforded to a consumer at EU level, in the sale and provision of goods and services, is strengthened and enhanced in the area of the 'sale' and 'provision' of investment products; this specific protection is the outcome of ad hoc pieces of legislation that, over the past two decades, have moulded and forged the rules specifically governing the investment business.

The rationale behind this phenomenon is understandable. The crafting of investment products is characterised by a high level of complexity which calls for specific rules. Moreover, it is a relatively recent approach by the banking sector. Historically, the bank limited its business endeavours to the offer of typical bank products (bank accounts and savings accounts, on one hand, loans on the other), but the globalisation of world markets and the ensuing rise in competition fuelled by the presence of different players therein has radically altered the traditional landscape. It has given rise to a dual layer of products being offered by banks, i.e. the typical banking products, and the investment products. Thus, the latter is offered not only by investment firms, but also by banks, which must be specifically authorised by their supervisory authority to do so.[44]

42 Art. 6(2)(a) of the Distance Financial Services Directive.
43 Art. 6(2)(b) and (c) of the Distance Financial Services Directive, respectively.
44 See also extensively below, section 5.2.

From a historical point of view, the investor-oriented legislation initially hinged upon the Investment Services Directive 1993/22/EC ('ISD').[45] Upon its formulation, the ISD, although it expressly stated that investor protection must account for the differences between professional and non-professional investors, failed to administer specific rules on how the investor must be protected. Broadly speaking, generic rules of conduct were indeed laid down under art. 11 of the ISD: the loyalty principle (any investment firm must act honestly and fairly in catering to the best interests of its clients); informed consent (the investment firm must adequately disclose relevant material information on risks, costs, nature of the services, etc.); and know your customer (the investment firm must seek from its clients information regarding their financial situation, the investment experience and the objectives underpinning any financial services requested). However, the widely held belief was that the ISD did not succeed in creating a persuasive and convincing system of protection for the investor. The ISD has therefore been subsumed within the more comprehensive body of law consisting of the Markets in Financial Instruments Directive ('MiFID')[46] and the MiFID Implementing Directive.[47] In 2014, these two directives have been superseded, in turn, by MiFID II and MiFIR (together: 'MiFID legislation').[48]

4.4.2 MiFID legislation

Following in the footsteps of the ISD, but altogether more systematic and holistic in nature, the MiFID legislation draws a better demarcation line between the various counterparties to investment firms and banks offering financial products. The categorisation of clients is based on a tripartite approach: the professional clients, the retail clients, and finally, the elective client who, on its/his/her turn, can be the elective professional or the elective retail client.

The category of professional clients comprises the 'customers' who possess 'the experience, knowledge and expertise to make its own investment decisions and properly assess the risks that it incurs'.[49] This category includes among others: credit institutions, investment firms, pension funds, undertakings, central banks, but also 'large undertakings' not necessarily involved with financial business.[50] The reason being that the way the activities of these entities are carried out (businesses organised collectively) instils complete confidence in their ability to assess risk and any other relevant factors entailed to a financial product they commit to buy and/or order.[51]

45 In full: Council Directive 93/22/EEC of 11 May 1993 on the investment services in the securities field, OJ L 197 (6/8/1003).

46 In full: Directive 2004/39/EC of the European Parliament and of the Council of 21 April 2004 on markets in financial instruments amending Council Directives 85/611/EEC and 93/6/EEC and Directive 2000/12/EC of the European Parliament and of the Council and repealing Council Directive 93/22/EEC, OJ L 145.

47 In full: Commission Directive 2006/73/EC of 10 August 2006 implementing Directive 2004/39/EC of the European Parliament and of the Council as regards organisational requirements and operating conditions for investment firms and defined terms for the purposes of that Directive, OJ L 241.

48 A legal analysis relating to MiFID I can be read in PR Wood, *Regulation of International Finance* (Thomson/Sweet & Maxwell, London 2007) 125, 158.

49 Annex II of MiFID II.

50 In this case, according to Annex II(I)(2), the undertaking shall meet two of the following criteria: (a) a balance sheet total of at least Euro 20,000,000; (b) a net turnover of Euro 40,000,000; (c) own funds of at least Euro 2,000,000.

51 The actual category of 'professional clients' is detailed in Annex II of MiFID II ('Categories of client who are considered to be professionals').

Among the category of professional clients are also those who should be considered as retail clients, but who have opted out of the protection granted to the category of retails clients ('Clients who may be treated as professions on request') or, also, 'elective professional clients'.[52] The waiver of this protection means that they will be treated as professional clients, upon their own request, rather than as a result of any regulatory categorisation. Remarkably, although any retail client can opt out of the statutory protection and, therefore, be recategorised as 'professional', the onus lies with the investment firm to assess and judge the adequate expertise, experience, and knowledge of the investor beforehand. In the absence of an adequate judgement, the investor shall remain classified as a retail investor, despite having availed itself of the opportunity to opt out. Remarkably, according to the modalities recently set out by Annex II ('Procedure'), the waiver must be in writing, the investment firm shall give 'a clear written warning of the protections and investor compensation rights they may lose', the clients 'must state in writing, in a separate document from the contract, that they are aware of the consequences of losing such protections.'

Retail clients represent a class of clients who, being neither professional nor eligible counterparties, are deserving of the maximum level of protection available. Although the retail client is typically an individual, it can also include an entity which has failed to meet the definition of a 'professional client'. This specification is remarkable, if likened to the matter of the protection of the consumer, where conversely the customer worthy of protection must be exclusively an 'individual'. Retail clients shall also include those classified as 'elective', therefore those who, although considered to be professionals, have asked for the maximum protection (therefore, 'elective retail' counterparties).[53]

Finally, MiFID II contemplates the category of 'eligible counterparties'. An 'eligible counterparty' is a limited circle of entities, somehow connected with the financial and/or banking sector. More specifically, according to art. 30(2) of MiFID II, these are:

> investment firms, credit institutions, insurance companies, UCITS and their management companies, pension funds and their management companies, other financial institutions . . ., national governments and their corresponding offices including public bodies that deal with public debt at national level, central banks and supranational organisations.

In the case of investment services with an 'eligible counterparty', some rules of conduct under MiFID II shall not apply.[54] Nonetheless, in dealing with 'eligible counterparties', Member States shall ensure that 'basic' principles shall be complied with, such as honesty, fairness and professionalism in the way the investment firm

52 Annex II of MiFID II.

53 Remarkably, a client shall be treated as 'eligible' exclusively in relation to certain kinds of investment services, such as dealing for its own account, the execution of orders and certain other arrangements (see C Proctor, *The Law and Practice of International Banking* (Oxford University Press, Oxford 2010) 45).

54 Art. 30(1) of MiFID II. Among these exceptions are: (a) art. 24 ('General principles and information to clients') – with the exception of paras 4 and 5 of that article; (b) art. 25 ('Assessment of suitability and appropriateness and reporting to clients') – with the exception of para. 6; and art. 28(1) ('Client order handling rules').

liaises with the eligible counterparty. Additionally, there should be fairness, clarity and punctuality in the information provided.[55]

To summarise, the system of protection offered by the MiFID legislation, as far as the categories of counterparties are concerned, hinges upon two principal categories, although the opting-in and opting-out mechanism works, metaphorically speaking, akin to a lift or elevator allowing each category (retail and professional) to manoeuvre itself to a minimal or maximum level of protection, respectively, if specifically requested to do so by the investment firm or financial institution. Finally, 'eligible counterparties' constitute a further category, to a certain extent partly coinciding with 'professional clients', which, given the proximity of their business to that of the investment firm, do not require the application of the detailed rules of conduct of MiFID II, although MiFID II nonetheless requires a minimum compliance with basic rules of conduct.

Not only is the MiFID legislation concerned with a nuanced categorisation of the client, it also seeks to clearly define the principles by which the investment firm is bound when offering the products to its clientele. These rules of conduct are principally those relating to the duties of information, reporting and execution. In this respect, the first duty is to provide clear and faithful information, which is not misleading, to the client.

Irrespective of the categorisation of the client, the firm shall steadfastly act 'honestly, fairly and professionally in accordance with the best interest of its clients', in accordance with art. 24(1) of MiFID II.[56] Additionally, art. 24(3) of MiFID II grabs the attention where it states as follows:

> All information, including marketing communications, addressed by the investment firm to clients or potential clients shall be fair, clear and not misleading. Marketing communications shall be identifiable as such.

Furthermore, there is an additional duty owed on the part of the investment firm, according to art. 25, headed 'Assessment of suitability and appropriateness and reporting to clients'. This duty is, first and foremost, the duty to act with competence and knowledge; more specifically (art. 25(1)):

> Member States shall require investment firms to ensure and demonstrate to competent authorities on request that natural persons giving investment advice or information about financial instruments, investment services or ancillary services to clients on behalf of investment firms possess the necessary knowledge and competence to fulfil their obligations.

Within the duty to assess the suitability of offered investment services and financial instruments lies the additional duty to know the client (art. 25(2). According to this provision, the investment firm:

> shall obtain the necessary information regarding the client's or potential client's knowledge and experience in the investment field relevant to the specific type of product

55 Art. 30(1), para. 2, of MiFID II.

56 'Member States shall require that, when providing investment services and/or, where appropriate, ancillary services to clients, an investment firm act honestly, fairly and professionally in accordance with the best interests of its clients.'

> or service, that person's financial situation including his ability to bear losses, and his investment objectives including his risk tolerance so as to enable the investment firm to recommend to the client or potential client the investment services and financial instruments that are suitable for him and, in particular, are in accordance with his risk tolerance and ability to bear losses.

It stands to reason that any client who envisages a personal financial situation and personal investment objectives should furnish the investment firm with such information in advance, so allowing the investment firm to competently fulfil the duty owed to the client to carry out an adequate and suitable investment. The suitability of the investment for the client at hand is the parameter that the investment firm must comply with, founded on the knowledge of his/her profile. Ultimately, implied in this 'brief' is the concept that the client must understand the risks, the transaction must satisfy the investment objectives of the client and the client must be in a position to bear the financial risks implied in the transaction.

Third, there is a duty to ensure the 'best execution' of the client's instructions, in order that the interests of the client cannot be affected, principally in respect to costs, prices, timely execution, etc. As stated in art. 27(1) of MiFID II:

> Member States shall require that investment firms take all sufficient steps to obtain, when executing orders, the best possible result for their clients taking into account price, costs, speed, likelihood of execution and settlement, size, nature or any other consideration relevant to the execution of the order. Nevertheless, where there is a specific instruction from the client the investment firm shall execute the order following the specific instruction.

Finally, a general duty that investment firms must comply with, is the identification of conflicts of interest, according to art. 23 of MiFID II. Conflicts of interest may be of various kinds and do not lend themselves to an easy categorisation. Nonetheless, the provisions under the EU statute in discussion point to the potential relationship between the same investment firm (and its managers, employees and tied agents) and the clients, in so much as conflicts of interest 'arise in the course of providing any investment and ancillary services, or combination thereof, including those caused by the receipt of inducements from their parties or by the investment firm's own remuneration and other incentive structures' (art. 23(1) of MiFID II). In these circumstances, the investment firm should put in place, at organisational level, measures, detailed at art. 16(3) of MiFID II, aimed to prevent the adverse consequences of such conflicts.[57] Should these preventative measures not be effective, the unavoidable duty for the investment firm shall be, according to the precept of art. 23(2), the immediate disclosure to the client of such conflict of interest.[58]

57 The pillar of this organisational measure is that an investment firm 'shall maintain and operate effective organisational and administrative arrangements with a view to taking all reasonable steps designed to prevent conflicts of interest as defined in Article 23 from adversely affecting the interests of its clients' (art. 16(3), para. 1).

58 If, as a result of the conflict of interest, the client's interests are going to be damaged, then 'the investment firm shall clearly disclose to the client the general nature and/or sources of conflicts of interest and the steps taken to mitigate those risks undertaking business on its behalf.' (art. 23(2)). The modalities of such a disclosure are detailed under the following art. 23(3).

4.5 Consumer Credit Directive

As mentioned at the beginning of this chapter, credit agreements for consumers are now governed by a specific piece of legislation, which partly derogates, as far as credit contracts are concerned, from the general discipline of the Unfair Terms Directive. The body of provisions in this area is contained within Directive 2008/48 ('Consumer Credit Directive'),[59] which is the latest piece of legislation applicable to this area of law. Yet an even more specific statute has been adopted recently on consumer mortgage contracts, to be discussed in the following section.

First and foremost, the area of contracts to which this legislation applies relates to credit contracts with consumers. The definition of consumer does not differ from the general one provided under the Unfair Terms Directive. Thus, the consumer is 'the natural person who, in transactions covered by this Directive, is acting for purposes which are outside his trade, business or profession'.[60]

Second, the transaction falling under the micro-rules of the piece of legislation under discussion, is exclusively the 'credit agreement', i.e.:

> an agreement whereby a creditor grants or promises to grant to a consumer credit in the form of a deferred payment, loan or other similar financial accommodation, except for agreements for the provision on a continuing basis of services or for the supply of goods of the same kind, where the consumer pays for such services or goods for the duration of their provision by means of instalments.[61]

Thus, bank contracts that, technically speaking, are not based on a typical creditor/debtor relationship which involves a repayment through consecutive instalments of a certain amount of money,[62] do not fall within the Consumer Credit Directive; similarly, credit agreements guaranteed by mortgages are outside the scope of this EU statute.[63]

Additionally, as a result of a specific provision spelled out by the legislator, credit agreements 'involving a total amount of credit less than EUR 200 or more than EUR 75,000', are also outside the scope of the Consumer Credit Directive.

The main pillars on which the protection of the consumer in credit contracts lie, are: (a) detailed information that the creditor shall include while advertising these products;[64] (b) pre-contractual information to be provided to the consumer, before the credit contract can be concluded;[65] (c) the adequate assessment of the creditworthiness of the client;[66] and (d) the right of withdrawal.[67] The latter,

59 In full: Directive 2008/48/EC of the European Parliament and of the Council of 23 April 2008 on credit agreements for consumers and repealing Council Directive 87/102/EEC, OJ L 133.

60 Art. 3(a) of the Consumer Credit Directive.

61 Art. 3(c) of the Consumer Credit Directive.

62 For instance, a bank account.

63 'Mortgages' are now legislated by Directive 2014/17, detailed later under section 4.6 of this chapter.

64 Art. 4 of the Consumer Credit Directive.

65 Art. 5 of the Consumer Credit Directive.

66 Art. 8 of the Consumer Credit Directive. In essence: 'Member States shall ensure that, before the conclusion of the credit agreement, the creditor assesses the consumers creditworthiness on the basis of sufficient information, where appropriate obtained from the consumer and, where necessary, on the basis of a consultation of the relevant database' (art. 8(1)).

67 Art. 14 of the Consumer Credit Directive.

more specifically, shall be a period of 14 calendar days during which the consumer may withdraw from the credit agreement 'without giving any reason'[68] (art. 14(1), para. 1). According to the following paragraph of the same art. 14(1), it is stipulated, in more detail, that the period of withdrawal shall begin either 'from the day of the conclusion of the credit agreement' or 'from the day on which the consumer receives the contractual terms and conditions and information' required under art. 10 of the same Consumer Credit Directive, 'if that day is later than the date' of conclusion of the contract.

4.6 Mortgage Credit Directive

A further specified category of consumer, very recently acknowledged at EU level as a category worthy of specific protection, is that of the individual who enters into a credit agreement relating to residential immovable property. In practical terms, this is the person who, for himself or on behalf of his family, lodges an application with a credit institution (the lender) for a loan to buy a property and grants the lender a security interest on the property so acquired (a mortgage).

The financial sector has proved a particularly harsh domain over much of the last decade; until 2007, against the backdrop of a booming property market, many property buyers had nonchalantly availed themselves of readily available loans on the widely-held assumption that the underlying good (the property) would perpetually continue to rise in value. In reality, from 2008 the property market veered significantly in the opposite direction, with falling prices propelling property buyers inexorably towards 'negative equity'. Thus, property buyers who had purchased their property at the peak of the market, were forced to repay the lenders an amount that, in reality, did not reflect any longer the value of the property bought.

Aside from this economic consideration, a more legal concern arises in connection with the purchase of a property burdened by a mortgage. Although the borrower may have retained ownership of that property, if he proves not to be in a position to maintain the agreed repayment plan in the form of instalments which include both the principal and, unfortunately for the borrower, also a sometimes onerous level of interest, the lender is entitled, under virtually all national systems of property law, to execute the mortgage, i.e. to sell the property and take recourse on the proceeds.

In the context of this complex set of circumstances, the credulous consumer jumping unwittingly onto the property ladder has become a matter of grave concern; also from the perspective of the EU legislator. To that end, a piece of legislation, Directive 2014/17, was passed on 4 February 2014 ('Mortgage Credit Directive'),[69]

---

68 According to the following paragraph of the same art. 14(1), it is stipulated, in more detail, that the period of withdrawal shall begin either 'from the day of the conclusion of the credit agreement' or 'from the day on which the consumer receives the contractual terms and conditions and information' required under art. 10 of the same Directive, 'if that day is later than the date' of conclusion of the contract. Practically, these are the terms and conditions of the credit agreement detailing, among other aspects, 'the type of credit' and 'the duration of the credit agreement', 'the total amount of credit and the conditions governing the withdrawal.'

69 In full: Directive 2014/17/EU of the European Parliament and of the Council of 4 February 2014 on credit agreements for consumers relating to residential immovable property and amending Directives 2008/48/EC and 2013/36/EU and Regulation (EU) No 1093/2010, OJ L 60.

to react to and address the adverse consequences of 'irresponsible lending and borrowing by market-participants including credit intermediaries and non-credit institutions.'[70] Although the transposition of this Directive is not immediate,[71] the main principles enshrined therein are undoubtedly significant.

As to the merit of its specific provisions, the statute at stake stipulates that, although each Member State is not prevented 'from maintaining or introducing more stringent provisions in order to protect consumers',[72] an enhanced support platform shall be provided to the benefit of the consumer by each jurisdiction as a means of establishing a more responsible outlook to borrowing and debt management, in particular in relation to mortgage credit agreements.[73]

As inferable from the brief description above, the area of applicability of the Directive under discussion does not encompass the entire spectrum of bank contracts, but rather exclusively those concerned with the mortgage market and, more accurately, the 'residential' one.[74] To elaborate, the contractual frameworks affected by the new piece of legislation are, on the one hand and according to art. 3(1)(a), 'credit agreements which are secured by a mortgage or by another comparable security commonly used in a Member State on residential immovable property or secured by a right related to residential immovable property' and, on the other hand, pursuant to the following art. 3(1)(b), 'credit agreements the purpose of which is to acquire or retain property rights in land or in an existing or projected building.'

More stringent rules are imposed on lenders and on the way they conduct their business in this delicate market. In this respect, three main principles are highlighted by the EU legislator. First, the Mortgage Credit Directive relates to general information administered to the public, in cases where credit agreements were offered to the market. On the one hand, the manner in which credit agreements are advertised to the public is crucial. In this respect, any advertising concerning credit agreements of this kind shall refer, on a mandatory basis, to 'an interest rate or any figures relating to the cost of the credit'.[75] On the other hand, art. 13 of the Mortgage Credit Directive requires that each Member State shall ensure that any communication 'on paper or on another durable medium or in electronic form' is 'clear and comprehensible'. This obligation shall be complied with not simply by the creditors, but also by 'tied credit intermediaries' and their 'appointed representatives'.

An additional set of rules contained within the Mortgage Credit Directive is that relating to the contracts themselves. Although the arena of contract law is traditionally deemed a national one, ergo reserved to the discretion of each Member State as it is considered part of private or commercial law, the Directive does not refrain from dictating some remarkable provisions relating to the requirements for pre-contractual

---

continued

The Directive entered into force on 20 March 2014, on the twentieth day following its publication in the Official Gazette of the European Union; such publication occurred on 28 February 2014.

70 See Recital 4 of the Mortgage Credit Directive.

71 According to art. 42 of the Mortgage Credit Directive, Member States 'shall adopt and publish, by 21 March 2016, the law and regulations and administrative provisions necessary to comply with the Directive.'

72 Art. 2(1) of the Mortgage Credit Directive.

73 Art. 6(1) of the Mortgage Credit Directive.

74 The adjective 'residential' indirectly excludes from the applicability of the Mortgage Credit Directive mortgages for commercial properties, such as offices.

75 Art. 11(1) of the Mortgage Credit Directive.

information. According to art. 14, the creditor, regarding the specific legal provisions that each Member State shall set forth, is under an obligation to provide the consumer with 'personalised information needed to compare the credits available on the market, assess their implication and make an informed decision on whether to conclude a credit agreement'. This information is determined to be 'pre-contractual' as it shall precede the conclusion of the contract or, to use the terminology of the legislator, be made available 'in good time before the consumer is bound by any credit agreement or offer'. Similarly, the creditor, according to art. 16 of the Mortgage Credit Directive, shall provide 'adequate explanations' to the consumer 'on the proposed credit agreements and any ancillary services'. The concept of ancillary services is not clarified in terms of its boundaries, and this may lower any product, whether of a financial nature or not and irrespective of whether or not it was issued by the same lender, as long as a causal link can be established with the subscription of the credit agreement.[76] Regardless of the nature of the ancillary service, the general goal of the adequate explanation is to ensure that the credit agreement proposed to the client and the ancillary product is 'adapted to his needs and financial situation'.

The degree of creditworthiness demonstrated by the client is an additional matter of telling concern relative to the mortgage market and is specifically dealt with under art. 18 of the Directive under discussion. In this scenario, the creditworthiness of the borrower is a crucial barometer by which to assess whether the credit agreement can be entered into and, ultimately, the mortgage granted. More specifically, the assessment shall take into account 'factors relevant to verifying the prospect of the consumer to meet his obligations under the credit agreement'.[77] Consistent with this approach, 'the procedures and information on which the assessment is based are established, documented and maintained'.[78] Interestingly, with a provision – art. 18(3) – which constitutes a reprimand for much of the banking practices which spiralled out of control at the onset of the new millennium and where an assessment of the mortgage was superficially based on the value of the property to be purchased (and the accompanying assumption that it would increase), the correct criterion to establish creditworthiness shall be based, first and foremost, on the ability of the borrower to repay the instalments from his own income. The value of the property shall be a factor, but not the prevailing one. The provisions are completed with the obligation, borne by the creditor, to ensure that once the credit agreement is concluded the contract is not altered or cancelled 'on the grounds that the assessment of creditworthiness was incorrectly conducted'.[79]

---

76 A clear example is that of the British market of mortgages and the 'PPI scandal'. PPI (Payment Protection Insurance) is basically an insurance product which insures the repayment of the mortgage in case of major events affecting the borrower, such as death, illness or disability, or job loss. Although the PPI in itself is a legitimate product, it was unearthed in 2008 that this kind of policy had been sold to millions of UK borrowers, without the consumer being informed at all of its existence, or, if informed, with the consumers not needing or not being able to claim under the policy. The conundrum of the mis-selling of PPIs in Britain was solved by the Financial Services Authority (at that time, the competent authority) upon referral to the Financial Ombudsman Service (FSA, *The Assessment and Redress of Payment Protection Insurance Complaints* (August 2010)). Among scholars, see G Walker, 'UK Financial Services Reform', in G Walker and R Purves (eds), *Financial Services Law* (3rd edn Oxford University Press, Oxford 2014) 17.

77 Art. 18(1) of the Mortgage Credit Directive.

78 Art. 18(2) of the Mortgage Credit Directive.

79 Art. 18(4) of the Mortgage Credit Directive.

4.7 Further reading

Adams, JN, and Macqueen, H, *Atiyah's Sale of Goods* (12th edn Pearson, Harlow 2010)
Beale, H, Fauvarque-Cosson, B, Rutgers, J, Tallon, D, and Vogenauer, S, *Cases, Materials and Text on Contract Law* (2nd edn Hart Publishing, Oxford and Portland 2010)
Chitty on Contracts, *General Principles, Volume I* (31st edn Sweet and Maxwell, London 2012)
Cranston, R (ed.), *European Banking Law: The Banker-Customer Relationship* (2nd edn LLP, London and Hong Kong 1999)
Cranston, R, *Principles of Banking Law* (2nd edn Oxford University Press, Oxford 2002)
Edwards, L (ed.), *The New Legal Framework for E-Commerce in Europe* (Hart Publishing, Oxford and Portland 2005)
Ellinger, EP, Lomnicka, E, and Hare, CVM, *Ellinger's Modern Banking Law* (5th edn Oxford University Press, Oxford 2011)
FSA, *The Assessment and Redress of Payment Protection Insurance Complaints* (August 2010)
Furmston, M, and Chuah, J, *Commercial Law* (2nd edn Pearson, Harlow 2010)
Gkoutzinis, A, *Internet Banking and the Law in Europe* (Cambridge University Press, Cambridge 2006)
Hemetsberger, W, Schoppmann, H, Schwander, D, and Wengler, C, *European Banking and Financial Services Law* (Kluwer Law International in association with European Association of Public Banks, Alphen aan den Rijn 2006)
Kroes, QR (ed.), *E-Business Law of the European Union* (Allen & Overy Legal Practice and Kluwer Law International, The Hague, London, New York 2003)
Kroes, QR (ed.), *E-Business Law of the European Union* (2nd edn Kluwer Law International, Alphen aan den Rijn 2010)
McKendrick, E, *Contract Law (Palgrave Macmillan Law Masters)* (10th edn Palgrave Macmillan, London 2013)
Nebbia, P, *Unfair Contract Terms in European Law* (Hart Publishing, Oxford and Portland, Oregon 2007)
Peel, E, *Treitel: The Law of Contract* (30th edn Sweet & Maxwell, London 2011)
Reich, N, *General Principles of EU Civil Law* (Intersentia, Cambridge, Antwerp and Portland 2014)
Todd, P, *E-Commerce* (Cavendish Publishing Limited, London 2005)
Walker, G, 'UK Financial Services Reform', in G Walker and R Purves (eds), *Financial Services Law* (3rd edn Oxford University Press, Oxford 2014) 3, 56

4.8 Questions

4.1 Can you explain the *caveat emptor* principle?

4.2 Describe how European financial law has been part of the development that moves away from a strict adherence to the *caveat emptor* principle.

4.3 What is the notion of a 'consumer' from a legal point of view and according to the relevant EU statutes?

4.4 'The current European rules for investment services negate any responsibility for the consumer.' Discuss.

4.5 '(Very) small legal entities such as a one- or two-man company must fall under the EU law definition of "consumer".' Discuss.

4.6 What is the concept of 'unfair term' according to the relevant EU legislation?

4.7 Mr Johnson urgently wishes to borrow a substantial amount and calls Omega Bank. How has the European legislature sought to protect Mr Johnson?

4.8 Mr Johnson has inherited a sizeable amount of money from his late Aunt Petulia. He wishes to invest the money in stocks and bonds and calls Omega Bank. How has the European legislature sought to protect Mr Johnson?

4.9 According to the MiFID Directive, who is a 'professional client'? Who is an 'elective client'? And what about a 'retail client'?

4.10 As far as distance contracts are concerned, what is the main legal tool for the protection of the consumer?

4.11 Mr Johnson wants to take up a mortgage to buy a property. Can the bank lend him money without checking his income?

Part C

Financial institutions

Chapter 5

The bank and its organisation

Chapter contents

5.1 The banking business: history and current practice

Banks, as we know them today, have developed from moneychangers into deposit takers. This development took place in the late Middle Ages in the Italian city states. To be more precise, in Genoa this development may have taken place as early as around 1200, while in Venice, this development took place around 1300 AD.[1] Back in those earliest days, deposits were credited to a current account.

It is from this moment on that banks have fallen insolvent, as it was the case – and has been the case since – that bankers held only a tiny fraction of the sums received in deposit available for retrieval by depositors.[2] Moreover, it is since then that they have lent on longer terms than deposits could be retrieved.[3] Consequently, from their very inception on, the banks' business model has been inherently risky.

Also today, in essence, the banking business consists of obtaining deposits from customers, i.e. raising funds from the public, and lending money, i.e. giving credit to businesses, households and individuals. This is why a bank is, in EU law, sometimes technically referred to as a 'credit institution'. The bank's activity of obtaining funds and lending out the same can prove lucrative and profitable for the banker, so long as the bank is able to obtain, from the money lent to the businesses, households and individuals (e.g. loans), a higher remuneration than that which is returned to the customers for the money deposited by them (e.g. bank accounts). The remuneration which a banker receives is referred to as 'interest' and constitutes the variation of percentage on the amount of money lent from time to time. This interest is called 'active' if the money is lent by the bank while, if the money is borrowed by the bank, it is called 'passive', as that money is owed to the customer.

The margin between lending and borrowing is commonly referred to as the 'spread'. Thus, the degree of success demonstrated by a banker hinges upon his ability to procure from the money lent a sufficiently high margin of interest to allow the bank not only to cover its running costs, but also to secure a profit. There is another difference, already alluded to, between the money lent and borrowed by a bank which helps us understand why the business of banking is inherently risky: while the money deposited can, as a matter of principle, be retrieved at any time by the customers, the money borrowed is only due after a period of several years. This represents the 'transformation function' of a bank.[4] Should all customers run on the bank to retrieve their money at the same time, the bank will not be able to repay.

As discussed earlier in this textbook,[5] the banking business is generally a reserved activity. The established principle (certainly at EU level), although not a universal

---

1 R de Roover, 'New Interpretations of the History of Banking', in J Kirshner (ed.), *Business, Banking, and Economic Thought in Late Medieval and Early Modern Europe* (University of Chicago Press, Chicago 1974) 201 and RC Mueller, *The Venetian Money Market: Banks, Panics, and the Public Debt, 1200–1500* (Johns Hopkins University Press, London 1997) 8 respectively.

2 See RC Mueller, *The Venetian Money Market: Banks, Panics, and the Public Debt, 1200–1500* (Johns Hopkins University Press, London 1997) 16, 17.

3 Ibid. 12.

4 R Theissen, *EU Banking Supervision* (Eleven Publishers, The Hague 2013) 140.

5 Section 1.3 and also extensively below, Chapter 6.

stance,[6] is that typical banking activities (mainly, but not exclusively, the lending and borrowing functions) are regulated and such practices are therefore prohibited from use by non-authorised entities. Accordingly, an entity or individual engaged in the banking business, not duly endowed with the authorisation of the competent authority, would infringe the mandatory rules, which in some jurisdictions constitute a criminal offence. At EU level, this principle is administered by the Capital Requirements Directive IV ('CRD IV'), arts. 8(1) and 9(1),[7] which stipulate that each Member State, respectively, 'shall require credit institutions to obtain authorisation before commencing their activities' and 'shall prohibit persons or undertakings that are not credit institutions from carrying out the business of taking deposits or other repayable funds from the public.'[8]

While the regulatory framework has been introduced above, in section 1.3 and will be further dissected below in Chapter 6, the present chapter seeks to determine and analyse the various models of banking business, while paying due consideration to the way financial institutions are categorised accordingly (e.g. commercial banks; investment banks). Additionally, emphasis is placed on the organisational structure of financial institutions, particularly in respect to the subdivisions which emanate from them (e.g. branches and/or subsidiaries). Furthermore, a regulatory analysis is tendered in the matter of bank ownership and, specifically, the constraints currently prevailing within the EU as regards participations in banks held by commercial entities and/or businesses, and vice versa. Finally, the chapter contemplates the economic climate in assessing the legislative architecture of the bank as ultimately shaped within the EU, with a description of the various activities 'subject to mutual recognition' that a financial institution is entitled to discharge.

5.2 Categories of banks

Banks can be categorised in a variety of ways, relative to the different perspectives from which their activities can be observed and scrutinised.

5.2.1 Commercial banks and investment banks

First and foremost, a point of observation concerns the operational side of the bank. A bank often is a complex organisation with myriad levels of operation. The activities that a bank can carry out are numerous and range from the most basic offer of bank accounts and investment services (retail banking) to the most sophisticated services of corporate finance (investment banking), not to forget the spectrum of

---

6 The strict approach is certainly the EU one. However, there might be countries and/or jurisdictions where the pursuit of banking business is not reserved.

7 In full: Directive 2013/36/EU of the European Parliament and of the Council of 26 June 2013 on access to the activity of credit institutions and the prudential supervision of credit institutions and investment firms, amending Directive 2002/87/EC and repealing Directives 2006/48/EC and 2006/49/EC, OJ L 176. The latter Directives used to be referred to as the Capital Requirements Directive ('CRD') in conjunction with Directive 2006/49/EC of the European Parliament and of the Council of 14 June 2006 on the capital adequacy of investment firms and credit institutions, both published simultaneously on 14 June 2006.

8 The wording of art. 9 of CRD IV is identical to art. 5 of the previous Directive 2006/48.

banking products that can be offered to commercial business, such as leasing and factoring (commercial banking). Banks have also sought to offer clients of significant wealth tailor-made services, the purpose of which is to optimise their assets (private wealth).

In this respect, it is common to refer to commercial banks as institutions the main purpose of which is to deal with the vast array of retail customers, predominantly manifested in the offer of bank accounts to the general public and the lending of money to a commercial and business clientele (retail banking and commercial banking).

Investment banks are distinct from commercial banks in that they do not have, necessarily, a network of branches and do not liaise with retail clients. An investment bank operates with, and liaises with, corporations and/or other banks to offer them financial advice in transactions and activities of a certain level of complexity. The business we are referring to is principally advisory in nature, relating to corporate transactions such as mergers and acquisitions (usually referred to as M&A transactions) or admission of the shares of a company to the stock market (listing). These operations and transactions are typically carried out by a niche group of banks which are equipped to handle the required level of expertise. The investment bank can be a specialised autonomous bank operating as a boutique bank and not belonging to any group. However, with increasing regularity, major international banks are availing themselves of the opportunity to widen their portfolio to operate in the investment banking business also, either through specific 'arms' of their business (formally within the structure of the bank), or by way of subsidiaries belonging to the parent company of that major group.

5.2.2 Multifunctional groups vs. universal banks

An additional categorisation of banks stems from the corporate structure adopted. As regards to the range of activities a bank is engaged in, a recurring dilemma arises: how can a bank better organise that plurality of businesses from a corporate structure point of view? The answer and, therefore, solution to this question is two-fold and, to a certain extent, contradictory. On the one hand, the bank can be organised as a monolithic entity which, in practical terms, is in charge of, and responsible for everything. This form of credit institution channels the broad spectrum of activities through units and sections, each being specialised in one of the specific banking businesses such as commercial banking, investment banking, corporate finance and wealth management, but each belonging to the same corporate entity. In other words, the universal bank, as this model is commonly defined, performs the various banking activities through a unified structure, formally a single corporate entity rather than through several subsidiaries. The universal bank contrasts with the banking group model where, conversely, a parent company owns several corporate entities and, accordingly, each corporate entity operates the specific banking business concerned. Historically, it has been claimed that the universal model of bank organisation was of an Anglo-American nature, whereas the second model (the group) is traditionally associated with Germany. As the structure of a bank has recently become a topic of hot policy debate (see below), the pros and cons of these two models are worthy of further analysis within the context of this chapter.

First, the banking group may be a more flexible model of business. For instance, if the bank no longer wishes to perform one of the banking businesses, the obvious and relatively simple move would be to relinquish the holding in the subsidiary specialising in that business and find a purchaser who is both willing and available to step into the shoes of the current owner. Such an option is less practicable for a universal bank; in this case, the business is part of the broader structure of the bank and, therefore, any spin-off arising from the specific banking activity, no longer deemed strategically warranted, may not be executed without organisational burdens.

On the other hand, the universal bank may be a less expensive organisation; because the corporate structure does not involve entities, but rather embodies a unified corporation (with shared services), the running costs associated with the business may be, theoretically speaking, less onerous. For instance, the cost of maintaining a board of directors for each company within a group structure is a burden extraneous to the structure of a universal bank.

Perhaps even more importantly, further to the global financial crisis, legislatures in various parts of the world have contemplated structural reforms for the banking sector. Most of these initiatives have been prompted by the belief that retail banking is by definition less speculative and therefore less risky, as opposed to investment banking where transactions such as derivatives are concluded for the account and in the name of the bank itself, and which may be profitable in a positive trend of the market, but dangerously give rise to huge losses in an opposite scenario. Conversely, it has been argued that the universal banks are less risky, because they can better diversify their business. In the US (by means of the so-called Volcker Rule), in the UK (further to the Vicker Report) as well as on the EU level (further to the Liikanen Report), these considerations have led to legislative action.

More specifically, Section 619 of the Dodd Frank Act, known as the Volcker Rule, restricts deposit-taking banks from engaging in certain types of market-oriented activity (proprietary trading, i.e. trading for the account and in the name of the bank itself). The underlying intention of the rule is to safeguard the core of the banking system, i.e. commercial banks, and to prohibit them from engaging in more complex activities that are prone to conflicts of interest with the core objective of commercial banking (i.e. take deposits and make loans).[9] Conversely, the UK independent commission on banking chaired by Vickers recommended in 2011 that large UK banks should ring-fence their retail bank operations into separate legal subsidiaries with their own prudential safeguards.

On the European level, on 2 October 2012, a High-level Expert Group chaired by Erkki Liikanen – Governor of the Bank of Finland and a former member of the European Commission – presented its final report to the Commission. This report has now led to a draft regulation.[10] The Report advises that proprietary trading and other significant trading activities should be assigned to a separate legal entity if the activities to be separated amount to a significant share of a bank's business. This would ensure that trading activities beyond the threshold are carried out on a stand-alone basis and separate from the deposit bank. As a consequence, deposits would

9 High-level Expert Group on reforming the structure of the EU banking sector, Chaired by Erkki Liikanen, 2 October 2012 ('Liikanen Report') 84.

10 Proposal for a Regulation of the European Parliament and of the Council on structural measures improving the resilience of EU credit institutions, COM/2014/043 final.

no longer directly support risky trading activities. The Report argues, however, that the long-standing universal banking model in Europe would remain untouched, since the separated activities would be carried out in the same banking group. Hence, banks' ability to provide a wide range of financial services to their customers would be maintained.[11]

5.2.2.1 Branches

It is customary in the banking industry to refer to branches and subsidiaries as, respectively, the units and entities through which the structure of the bank is manifested. As alluded to above, the branch is the operating unit of the financial institution, usually located in close proximity to the area where that bank wishes to offer its products. Although branches – unlike subsidiaries – are not independent from a corporate point of view, they are usually organised according to a precise business model within which staff (e.g. cashiers) are supervised by a local, albeit 'light', management structure which, in turn, reports to the 'centre' (the headquarters of the financial institution). Similarly, the branch management is bestowed, in advance, with specific powers from headquarters so that, for the transactions they oversee, there is no need to receive an ad hoc authorisation from the 'central structure'. This is understandable as, otherwise, the decision-making process would be embroiled in bureaucracy to the point where it could virtually grind to a halt.[12] The branch, as an established phenomenon of the banking business, is a concept duly acknowledged at legislative level. To that end, art. 4(1) of the Capital Requirements Regulation 575/2013 ('CRR'),[13] particularly its point 17 defines the 'branch' as:

> a place of business which forms a legally dependent part of a credit institution and which carries out directly all or some of the transactions inherent in the business of institution.[14]

11 Liikanen Report, iii.

12 The limits could be of two kinds: 'qualitative' and 'quantitative'. As to the former, banks usually adopt an internal resolution whereby exclusively some specific transactions and/or activities can be authorised by the branch management; for instance, the opening of a bank account may be an ordinary activity delegated to the branch without previous authorisation of the central structure. Conversely, advice in the matter of M&A, which is quite complex, may fall within the exclusive competence of the central structure. As far as the 'quantitative' limits are concerned, they can be connected with the value of the transaction. To further elaborate, the opening of a bank account, which is an ordinary transaction usually delegated to the branch management, may require the previous authorisation of the headquarters, if the money concerned with the transaction exceeds a certain limit. According to this line of reasoning, for instance, a personal loan, which is usually an ordinary activity 'devolved' to the branch, may require the authorisation of the headquarters, if the amount of the commitment was above the threshold fixed in advance by the internal bylaws of the bank. Similarly, to authorise an overdraft on a bank account of a client, for an amount exceeding a certain amount (e.g. Euro 10,000), may be a matter well beyond the competence and power of a branch manager and, therefore, it is imaginable that an authorisation of the central function shall be required. The quantitative and qualitative limit of the transactions either devolved to the branch or reserved to the headquarters is a strategic choice of each financial institution and is adopted by a resolution of the board of directors of it. In this resolution, the powers delegated to the peripheral structures (therefore, the branches) are detailed as regards both the kinds of activities and applicable thresholds.

13 In full: Regulation (EU) No 575/2013 of the European Parliament and of the Council of 26 June 2013 on prudential requirements for credit institutions and investment firms and amending Regulation (EU) No 648/2012. As elucidated by Recital 5 of Regulation No 575/2013, such a Regulation, alongside Directive 2013/36/EU, 'should form the legal framework governing the access to the activity, the supervisory network and the prudential rules for credit institutions and investment firms'.

14 The definition corresponds to what previously used to be defined under Directive 2006/48, art. 4(3). However, it applies equally to both credit institutions and investment firms.

5.2.2.2 Subsidiaries

Subsidiaries are corporate entities owned, either directly or indirectly, by the parent company of a banking group. Within the constraints of shareholder control as required by the applicable national corporate law, they are autonomous and independent, from a corporate point of view, from the board of directors of the holding company.[15] Similarly, the directors of each subsidiary (in other words, those in charge of the business of that entity) reach their decisions autonomously, given that no hierarchical authorisation is required. However, this procedural blueprint does not translate into practice; de facto, the directors are usually appointed at the shareholders' meeting, where a significant percentage of the capital – or indeed the entire capital – is owned by the parent company and, therefore, they tend to constitute a reflection of the parent company, particularly in cases where 100 per cent of the share capital belongs to the parent company.[16] Although it would undoubtedly be too harsh to label the directors of the subsidiary of a credit institution as mere puppets,[17] nonetheless it must be acknowledged that their decisions tend to mirror the visions of the parent company, generally adopted within the power of management and coordination of that banking group.

In this respect, the most recent bank capital requirements legislation defines 'subsidiary' in art. 3 ('Definitions') (1)(15) of CRD IV by referring to point (16) of art. 4(1) of the CRR, which, in its turn, refers to Directive 83/349/EEC, and states that subsidiary means:

> (a) a subsidiary undertaking within the meaning of Articles 1 and 2 of Directive 83/349/EEC; (b) a subsidiary undertaking within the meaning of Article 1(1) of Directive 83/349/EEC and any undertaking over which a parent undertaking effectively exercises a dominant influence.[18]

Thus, in essence, the control exercised by a bank over a company as a shareholder or, failing this, a dominant influence on that company would suffice as the standard which, if met, would qualify that company as a 'subsidiary'.

---

15 Depending on the country or jurisdiction where they are located, they might have different forms.

16 It is likely that the directors of the subsidiary will be managers of the parent company or people well known to the parent company.

17 Usually, in any advanced jurisdiction, any director of a subsidiary may incur direct liability for any damage caused to third parties (including creditors) as a result of any decision adopted by the relevant board of directors. For example, in Britain see the Company Act 2006.

18 The previous Directive 2006/48, at art. 4(13)(a), used to refer, directly, to art. 1 and 2 of Directive 83/349/EEC for purposes of the definition of a 'subsidiary'. Seventh Council Directive 83/349/EEC of 13 June 1983 based on Article 54(3)(g) of the Treaty on consolidated accounts ('Consolidated Accounts Directive'). More specifically, according to art. 1 of the Consolidated Accounts Directive, a company shall be subject to drawing up consolidated accounts and a consolidated annual report if that undertaking (a parent undertaking) (a) 'has a majority of the shareholders' or members' voting rights in another undertaking (a subsidiary undertaking)' or (b) 'has the right to appoint or remove a majority of the members of the administrative, management or supervisory body of another undertaking (a subsidiary undertaking) and is at the same time a shareholder in or member of that undertaking' or, (c) 'has the right to exercise a dominant influence over an undertaking (a subsidiary undertaking) of which it is a shareholder or member, pursuant to a contract entered into with that undertaking or to a provision in its memorandum or articles of association, where the law governing that subsidiary undertaking permits its being subject to such contracts or provisions.'

5.2.2.3 Banking groups

The organisation of a bank through subsidiaries engenders the creation of a perimeter of companies, operating akin to planets orbiting within a solar system, where the planets represent the myriad subsidiaries and the sun the parent company. From a company law perspective, the group as such does not necessarily correspond to a legal concept and its categorisation will depend on the jurisdiction where (the parent company of) that group is incorporated.

In this respect, the paradigm in the common law system, particularly in England, is that tradition dictates that there is no such thing as a company group. Rather, English legislation identifies a company as a separate legal persona, set apart from the owners by way of the 'veil of incorporation', clearly defining the legal responsibilities of the body and those of the members.[19] In other EU Member States, however, the 'group' is expressly recognised as an autonomous legal concept in addition to the concept of the company, and therefore incurring, in some cases, specific responsibilities. An example is the case of Italy where the parent company,[20] based on a comparatively recent development of the national legislation, may be sued for the damages caused to third parties, particularly the shareholders of the subsidiary, in regard to the manner in which it has managed the group.

Banking legislation promoted at EU level and implemented in each Member State does not neglect the group, but rather reinforces its existence under certain conditions, particularly for purposes of supervision and accounting. In respect to the latter, art. 1 of the Consolidated Accounts Directive as evoked by the CRR (see above) for instance, requires any undertaking to draw up consolidated accounts and a consolidated annual report if that undertaking has 'a majority of the shareholders' or members' voting rights in another undertaking (a subsidiary undertaking)' (a) or, at least, it:

> has the right to appoint or remove a majority of the members of the administrative, management or supervisory body of another undertaking (a subsidiary undertaking) and is at the same time a shareholder in or member of that undertaking. (b).

5.2.3 Domestic banks and international banks

A further, albeit informal, categorisation of banks can be formed relative to the scope of their international or domestic operations. A financial institution with activities abroad is usually a major institution that, whether organised as a universal bank or as a group, is engaged in such a significant volume of activities that it may consider the market of its incorporation to be a strait jacket restricting its plans for expansion and growth. The *extra moenia* banking business, spurred on by the phenomenon of globalisation, may encapsulate not only the retailing sector, but also investment banking. Thus, a bank may directly control branches or own subsidiaries operating in the retail/commercial sector,[21] and may have operations in investment banking, manifested in sophisticated services of corporate finance offered in foreign markets.

---

19 For the English jurisdiction, see, among the others, D French, S Mayson and C Ryan, *Mayson, French and Ryan on Company Law* (29th edn Oxford University Press, Oxford 2013) 121, 166; PL Davies and S Worthington, *Gower and Davies: Principles of Modern Company Law* (9th edn Sweet & Maxwell, London 2012) 163, 250.

20 The norm is applicable whether or not the parent company is a bank. See art. 2497 of the Italian Civil Code ('Management and Coordination of Companies').

21 Leasing and factoring, for instance, but also pure retail banking such as the offer of bank accounts.

More recently, though, such internationalisation may be a declining trend in the banking industry. The financial crisis of 2007/08 has dealt a significant, and in some cases fatal blow to international institutions whose financial global activities often hinged upon speculative and risky transactions, thereby jeopardising the erstwhile stability and solidity of such financial institutions and in some cases even the stability of the entire financial system. Given that bank rescues by governments have not come without a cost,[22] it has been suggested (albeit not (yet?) prescribed under law) that major banks should relinquish their international business, particularly the financial one, and devote greater energy to the domestic market[23] and within the retail sector (see also above, under section 5.2.2). Financial institutions of this ilk can be more easily supervised as no strained cooperation is needed between supervisors of various countries that may have different constituencies with different interests. Moreover, the danger of contagion of a crisis in the case of a default by such an institution may thus be better controlled, possibly thereby contributing to the avoidance of exorbitant financial burdens on the tax payer.

5.3 Bank and 'industry'

The bank engages in a commercial business (it is obvious that lending money and raising funds in exchange for interest is not a charitable activity) and this, theoretically, would not prevent it from acquiring participations in commercial or industrial businesses. Similarly, under free market conditions, nothing would hinder a business from owning its own bank, because such a scenario could be perceived as a natural prerogative of any entrepreneur.

Beyond the theoretical permutations, a practical osmosis between industry and banks is traditionally perceived to be a contentious issue. A commercial company having a holding in a bank (and vice versa) conjures up a number of legitimate concerns: first and foremost of which is the risk of contagion. In view of the essential function a bank may have in the economy, the (in)solvency of a bank should not depend on the (in)insolvency of a business group entity. It would therefore be ideal to assure and guarantee the separation between the solvent business and the insolvent one.

A second concern, which, to some extent, overlaps with issues raised by the first, is the possibility of a conflict of interest: if a bank would be owned by a major commercial entity, a likely scenario would see it lend money preferably to its owners, as opposed to apportioning the credit risk among different borrowers with impartiality. It is generally believed, therefore, that a business should not buy its own bank and subsequently compel that credit institution to lend money to its group, as this would probably jeopardise a proper and impartial scrutiny of its creditworthiness. In the interests of transparency, an ideal scenario would require that a good entrepreneur

22 Britain seems to be the paradigm of this: in 2008, Royal Bank of Scotland, among other institutions, became insolvent as a result of too risky international activities in pure investment banking. The Government had to bail out the bank, by subscribing an increase of the share capital necessary to fill in the gigantic loss in the meantime accrued (approximately Euro 30 billion). De facto, the British taxpayer had to pay for the bail-out not for a domestic insolvency, but rather for the activities of the bank abroad.

23 The rationale behind this may also be that the competent authority may better assess the stability of the financial institution by focusing better on the domestic activities, whereas the international ones may lack intelligibility.

should provide a convincing argument to the counterparty (the credit institution) to deserve credit based on strong balance sheets and a strong financial position, rather than exploiting any competitive advantage of insiders.[24]

Third, the overly invasive presence of a bank in the share capital of industrial or commercial entities, and vice versa, could contribute to the profitability of the group in booming market conditions. However, set against an uncertain economic backdrop or worse, when the house of cards comes crashing down and businesses suffer losses or foreclosures become inevitable, this may prove an unmanageable obstacle for the bank, given the degree of proximity between the commercial entities and banks, with the latter struggling to recover their money from borrowers.

If the economic risks associated with an overly strict relationship between bankers and businesses are those described above, the legislation should not be, and indeed is not insensitive to dictating some specific and stringent rules in this area. As a general rule of good practice for a banker a 'Chinese Wall' has been erected, which is endorsed by legislation also at the EU level. This is deliberated over in the remainder of this chapter.

5.3.1 Bank owning an 'industry'

The reasons why a bank may wish to have a holding in a commercial entity or in industrial corporations are multifarious: aside from the hypothesis of the custodian (the bank as merely the intermediary holding the shares on behalf of its customers), the bank may purchase and sell holdings (i) to speculate on the equity of the corporation concerned[25] or, further, (ii) to convert into equity loans to the company that the borrower has not been able to honour.[26]

Irrespective of the reason for the bank being or becoming an 'industrialist' and regardless of specific local attitudes existing in this matter,[27] the relevant rules are quite strict and precise, at EU level. First and foremost, art. 89 of the CRR subjects to limits not any qualifying holding by a bank, but exclusively qualifying holdings of a credit institution outside the financial sector. In other words, the holdings that are allowed under art. 89(1) of the CRR are only those of a financial nature, such as (a) 'a financial sector entity' and (b):

24 R Cranston, *Principles of Banking Law* (2nd edn Oxford University Press, Oxford 2002) 26.

25 The credit institution may be totally disinterested in the specific business; however, it is confident that the value of the shares may increase and, as a result of a future sale, it can attain a significant capital gain.

26 For example, a 'corporate' borrower is not in a position to pay off its debts; the bank may believe that the option of the judicial enforcement of its credit – and therefore to cause the counterparty to default – could be detrimental to the same lender. In these circumstances, the two parties may reasonably decide to renegotiate a refinancing of their previous loan, whereby the credit of the bank is written off and the owner hives down to the lender significant shares of the capital. Usually, in these circumstances, the industrial holding will remain in the hands of the bank for a relatively short period, so long as the borrower concerned does not turn around and the relevant asset relocated in the market.

27 The model of long-term bank industry intersection is Germany; in this country, the investment of a bank in the share capital of a commercial entity can be a long-term one, accompanied also by the appointment of directors in the management body of the participated entity. This prolonged presence is viewed in a positive way by those who believe that the same commercial entity may benefit from this; a bank which is also a shareholder, would be less inclined to ask for an immediate foreclosure of the participated business, in case of temporary default. In this scenario, a milder option (e.g. a moratorium in the payment of the debts) would be the first option. On the other hand, a bank constantly acting as a 'watchdog' in the board of the directors, could end up 'bullying' the other shareholders, particularly the minority ones, through a dividend policy more informed to the short term than the long term. Ultimately, this would be detrimental to the minority shareholders and their expectation to own a solid company in the long term.

> an undertaking, that is not a financial sector entity, carrying on activities which the competent authority considers to be any of the following: (i) a direct extension of banking; (ii) ancillary to banking; (iii) leasing, factoring, the management of unit trusts, the management of data processing services or any other similar activity.

Additionally, under art. 89(1) of the CRR, the limits apply exclusively to holdings 'the amount of which exceeds 15 per cent of the eligible capital of the institution'. To elaborate, for holdings the amount of which is not particularly significant (again, below 15 per cent of the capital of the bank), that holding shall not be taken into account.

Now we have defined the perimeter of application of the norm, it is worth noting that the system of bank ownership in 'industrial' entities is envisaged by the CRR in a way considerably different from the past. In essence, according to art. 89(3) of the CRR, the global limit of industrial holdings by a credit institution must not exceed 60 per cent of the eligible capital of that bank.[28]

5.3.2 Commercial businesses or industries owning a bank

The intersection between bank and industry is mitigated also in the other – and to a certain extent opposite – direction whereby a commercial entity owns a participation in the share capital of a bank. In this case, however, there is no such thing as an ad hoc rule of the kind provided by art. 89 of the CRR.[29] The prescription is a more general one and relates to the requirements which the EU demands any bank to comply with for the taking up and pursuit of its business. More specifically, art. 22 of CRD IV[30] requires:

> any natural or legal person or such persons acting in concert (the 'proposed acquirer') who have taken a decision either to acquire, directly or indirectly, a qualifying holding in a credit institution or to further increase, directly or indirectly, such a qualifying holding in a credit institution

to inform, first and foremost, the competent authority. Pursuant to the same provision, 'qualifying holding' is regarded as the prospective acquisition or increase in the share capital of the credit institution so that the proportion of the voting rights or of the capital held 'would reach or exceed 20 per cent, 30 per cent, or 50 per cent or so that the credit institution would become its subsidiary.'[31]

---

28 Under the previous regime, Directive 2006/48 required each Member State to fix and impose by law (or soft legislation) a threshold of 15 per cent of the 'own funds' of a bank in respect to undertakings which were not credit institutions or financial institutions. This percentage (15 per cent) of its 'own funds' was a 'single' value, relating to each non-financial undertaking of a specific bank (art. 120(1) of Directive 2006/48). There was also a 'global' limit, equivalent to 60 per cent of the 'own funds' of the bank concerned; this limit corresponded to the entire portfolio of industrial holding belonging to a specific bank. In other words, not only could each bank's total holdings in non-financial undertakings not exceed 60 per cent of their 'own funds', but also the financial institution was required not to take part in a non-financial institution for more than 15 per cent of its own capital (art. 120(2) of Directive 2006/48, now repealed). See also below, Chapter 6.

29 Previously, art. 120 of the CRD.

30 Under the previous Directive 2006/48, this used to be legislated under art. 19.

31 It is worth highlighting that these thresholds cannot be derogated or altered by the national legislation.

In both cases (the acquisition of a 'qualifying holding' or its increase as a result of additional purchases), the competent authority is vested with the power to deny the authorisation (either to the acquisition of a 'qualifying holding' or an increase by one of the percentages), within 60 days if the prospective buyer is deemed unfit considering, as a result of that prospective acquisition, 'the sound and prudent management of the credit institution in which an acquisition is proposed'.[32] It is crucial to note that the provision just discussed (and other than art. 89 of the CRR, which is limited to banks holding interests in non-financials) is not limited to (the acquisition of) holdings in banks by non-financials, i.e. commercial entities and/or business corporations, but it applies also to acquisitions of shares or quotas of a credit institution by another bank or anyone else interested in owning a significant share of its capital. Remarkably, the acquisition of a bank by a non-financial institution is not prohibited, nor is the holding of a significant percentage and thus, theoretically, neither in respect to the entire capital.[33] Yet each competent authority is required to assess, before the acquisition comes into effect, whether the prospective purchaser (irrespective of whether its business is financial or industrial) is in a position to ensure the assessment criteria of art. 23 of CRD IV, including the 'sound and prudent management' of that financial institution.[34]

5.4 EU banking activities

Seen through the eyes of the EU legislator, the bank is an undertaking engaged in two main activities, being 'to take deposits or other repayable funds from the public and to grant credits for its own accounts'.[35] These two activities of accepting deposits and lending money would seem to represent the nuts and bolts of the banking business – in other words, the fundamental activities an entity must engage in for it to be defined as a 'credit institution'.

Additionally, the ambit of CRD IV extends 'banking activities' to include the operations listed in its Annex I, where the two core activities fuse with additional activities, the former and the latter thereby forming a 'list of activities subject to mutual recognition'.[36] As identified previously and to be discussed more extensively below

32 See art. 23 of CRD IV. The correspondent provision under the previous Directive 2006/48 was art. 19. CRD IV seems to leave to the authority more room in order to assess whether a credit institution can be authorised or not, given the fact that five assessment criteria are fixed by the legislator, including 'the reputation of the proposed acquirer' (art. 23 of CRD IV).

33 Conversely, in the opposite case of a holding in a commercial company by a bank, the limit highlighted in section 5.3.1 would be applicable.

34 This relative looseness of the discipline concerned with potential owners of a bank – whether 'financial' or 'industrial' – finds evidence in practice. In Britain, for instance, major retail groups, engaged in the pure commercial retail sector (Tesco; Sainsbury) may be sometimes the sole owners of their own bank. This does not infringe specific rules; it is obvious, though, that the local authority in Britain authorises in advance this significant non-financial holding in a credit institution and does not raise any objection; seemingly because the sound and prudent management of the bank has not been deemed so far affected by it.

35 Art. 4(1) of the CRR. Article 4(1) of Directive 2006/48 (now repealed) used to utilise similar language: '[T]o receive deposits or other repayable funds from the public and to grant credits for its own accounts.'

36 Directive 2006/48 had such a list in its Annex 1. The two lists are basically identical, but for the addition of 'issuing electronic money' (no 15), previously not a 'mutual recognition activity' under Directive 2006/48, and a linguistic variation in the definition of 'money transmission services' (see below following two footnotes).

(Chapter 6), these activities are qualified as 'subject to mutual recognition', because, once the bank has been authorised by its own competent authorities, such activities can be discharged through a specific regime of communication in any other EU Member State without the need for any additional authorisation.

Among the additional activities 'subject to mutual recognition', reference can be made to: 'financial leasing' (no 3 of Annex I); money transmission services, i.e., more technically, 'payment services'[37] (no 4); 'issuing and administering means of payment (e.g. travellers' cheques and bankers' drafts) insofar as such activity is not covered by point 4' (no 5); and 'guarantees and commitments' (no 6). Additionally, it is worth mentioning '[p]articipation in securities issues and the provision of services related to such issues' (no 8); '[a]dvice to undertakings on capital structure, industrial strategy and related questions and advice as well as services relating to mergers and the purchase of undertakings' (no 9); '[m]oney broking' (no 10); '[p]ortfolio management and advice' (no 11); '[s]afekeeping and administration of securities' (no 12);[38] '[c]redit reference services' (no 13); '[s]afe custody services' (no 14); and 'issuing electronic money' (no 15).

In respect to the activities catalogued above, it would appear that the range is both vast and comprehensive in its detailing of all the main businesses that a modern bank may seek to engage in: for instance, an investment bank typically offering advice in relation to M&A transactions and initial public offerings (IPOs) would fall within the activity described under number 9 of Annex 1, i.e. '[a]dvice to undertakings on capital structure, industrial strategy and related questions and advice as well as services relating to mergers and the purchase of undertakings.'

Among the activities 'subject to mutual recognition' is a small selection which a credit institution shares with other supervised entities, such as investment firms.[39] In this respect, it is worth referring to number 7 of Annex 1, which, particularly, mentions the trading for own account or for the account of customers in 'money market instruments . . .' (a), 'foreign exchange' (b), 'financial futures and options' (c), 'exchange and interest rate instruments' (d), 'transferrable securities' (e). Closely associated with this is the further activity, found under number 11, which relates to 'portfolio management and advice' and which is also permitted to investment firms. In these cases of overlap (ergo, activities reserved to banks but also permitted to investment firms), a bank, especially if of significant standing, may deem it opportune to organise its business within a group where the investment activities (particularly the trading on securities) are strategically delegated to a specialised entity, such as an investment firm which is totally or mainly held by a major commercial bank, the latter being the parent company. In this case, the parent company would typically not pursue the investment activities itself, but rather devolve them to the specialised company within the group, which has been specifically formed and organised for such a purpose.

37 As defined in art. 4(3) of Directive 2007/64/EC ('Payment Services Directive'), to be discussed below, Chapter 9.

38 See also further below, Chapter 9.

39 These activities are now governed by Directive 2004/39. In this respect, see further Chapter 8 below, concerned with investment firms, investment services and financial instruments, where these activities are explained in detail.

5.5 Further reading

Cranston, R, *Principles of Banking Law* (2nd edn Oxford University Press, Oxford 2002)

Davies, PL, and Worthington, S, *Gower and Davies: Principles of Modern Company Law* (9th edn Sweet & Maxwell, London 2012)

French, D, Mayson, S, and Ryan, C, *Mayson, French and Ryan on Company Law* (29th edn Oxford University Press, Oxford 2013)

Theissen, R, *EU Banking Supervision* (Eleven Publishers, The Hague 2013)

5.6 Questions

5.1 Can banking activities be feely exercised, i.e. without authorisation?

5.2 Explain the basic operations of a bank.

5.3 What is the difference between a commercial bank and an investment bank?

5.4 What is a bank 'subsidiary' under EU law?

5.5 'In the interest of financial stability, the universal banking model should be prohibited.' Discuss.

5.6 Is a bank allowed to own a commercial business under EU law?

5.7 Is a commercial business allowed to own a bank under EU law?

5.8 What are 'reserved activities' under EU banking law?

Chapter 6

Bank supervision

Chapter contents

6.1 The organisation of supervision

6.1.1 European banking supervision

6.1.1.1 Single Supervisory Mechanism (SSM)

Since the global financial crisis started in 2007, the European legislature has tried to create a safer and sounder financial sector for the European Union. One of the measures taken has been the creation of a European System of Financial Supervision under which three European Supervisory Authorities including the European Banking Authority ('EBA') have been established. But, as the crisis evolved and turned into the Eurozone debt crisis in 2010/11, it became clear that, for those countries which shared the Euro as a currency and were even more interdependent, more had to be done, in particular to break the vicious circle between banks and national finances. Consequently, in June 2012, Heads of State and Government agreed to create a banking union, completing the economic and monetary union, and allowing for centralised application of EU-wide rules for banks in the Euro area and any non-Euro Member States that would want to join.

A new regulatory framework with common rules for banks in all 28 Member States, set out in a 'single rulebook', is the foundation of the banking union. First and foremost, common rules must help to prevent bank crises. Centre stage is taken by the most recent capital requirements legislation package, i.e. the Capital Requirements Directive IV ('CRD IV') and the Capital Requirements Regulation ('CRR').[1] Should a bank suffer financial difficulties notwithstanding these rules of prudential supervision, a common framework has been set up to recover the bank or resolve it, i.e. to wind it down in an orderly way. This framework is mainly to be found in the Directive on Bank Recovery and Resolution ('BRRD').[2] Common rules will also ensure that all EU retail customers are guaranteed that their deposits up to Euro 100,000 per depositor (and per bank) are protected at all times and everywhere in the EU; notably, the details of these rules can be found in the Directive on Deposit Guarantee Schemes and its national implementation laws.[3]

For the Member States that use the Euro as their currency, the banking union will achieve uniform application of the common rules of prudential supervision by means of the so-called Single Supervisory Mechanism ('SSM').[4] Within this SSM, the European Central Bank ('ECB') has taken on the role as ultimate prudential supervisor of all 6,000 banks in the Euro area as of November 2014. Subsequently, it

---

1 In full: Directive 2013/36/EU of the European Parliament and of the Council of 26 June 2013 on access to the activity of credit institutions and the prudential supervision of credit institutions and investment firms, amending Directive 2002/87/EC and repealing Directives 2006/48/EC and 2006/49/EC, OJ L 176; and Regulation (EU) No 575/2013 of the European Parliament and of the Council of 26 June 2013 on prudential requirements for credit institutions and investment firms and amending Regulation (EU) No 648/2012, OJ L 176.

2 In full: Directive 2014/59/EU of the European Parliament and of the Council of 15 May 2014 establishing a framework for the recovery and resolution of credit institutions and investment firms and amending Council Directive 82/891/EEC, and Directives 2001/24/EC, 2002/47/EC, 2004/25/EC, 2005/56/EC, 2007/36/EC, 2011/35/EU, 2012/30/EU and 2013/36/EU, and Regulations (EU) No 1093/2010 and (EU) No 648/2012, of the European Parliament and of the Council, OJ L 173/190–348.

3 See, more extensively, below, Chapter 7.

4 The SSM has been created by virtue of Council Regulation (EU) No 1024/2013 of 15 October 2013 conferring specific tasks on the European Central Bank concerning policies relating to the prudential supervision of credit institutions, OJ L 287.

directly supervises, in short, the systemically important banks of the Eurozone, and is responsible indirectly, i.e. through the national supervisory authorities, for the prudential supervision of all other banks. Thus, it is hoped a truly European supervision mechanism will be achieved that will withstand the inclination to protect national interests, so that the link between banks and national finances will be broken.[5]

Together with the new EU-wide regulatory framework for the financial sector, the completed banking union represents a major milestone in the economic and monetary integration of the EU. It is hoped to restore financial stability and to create the right conditions for the financial sector to lend to the real economy, spurring economic recovery and job creation.

6.1.1.2 European Banking Authority (EBA)

Further to the De Larosière Report,[6] the EBA was established on 1 January 2011 as part of the European System of Financial Supervision ('ESFS').[7] It took over all existing responsibilities and tasks of the Committee of European Banking Supervisors. The EBA is an independent EU Authority which aims to ensure effective and consistent prudential regulation and supervision across the European banking sector. Its overall objectives are to maintain financial stability in the EU and to safeguard the integrity, efficiency and orderly functioning of the banking sector.

The main task of the EBA is to contribute to the creation of the European single rulebook in banking whose objective is to provide a single set of harmonised prudential rules for financial institutions throughout the EU. The EBA also plays a role in promoting convergence of supervisory practices and is mandated to assess risks and vulnerabilities in the EU banking sector.

6.1.1.3 European Central Bank (ECB)

The ECB is one of the seven institutions of the EU pursuant to the Treaty on European Union ('TEU'). The bank was established by the Treaty of Amsterdam in 1998, and is headquartered in Frankfurt, Germany.

The Maastricht Treaty of 1992, or TEU, mandated the creation of the European System of Central Banks ('ESCB'), of which the ECB and the 28 EU national central banks are a part. The ESCB is governed by the decision-making bodies of the ECB. Under the aegis of the ESCB sits the Eurosystem, composed of the ECB and the 18 national central banks of those EU Member States that use the Euro. The ECB is the central bank for the 'nineteen-nation' as of 1 January 2015 on which date Lithuania, too, has adopted the Euro as its currency. The ECB has a mandate to maintain price stability in countries that use the Euro, by setting key interest rates and controlling the money supply.

So as to fulfil the Maastricht Treaty's goal of creating a European Economic and Monetary Union ('EMU'), the ECB took over responsibility for monetary policy in the Euro area from the Member States in January 1999, two years prior to the

---

5 Please note that conduct supervision has not been unified within the Eurozone, although this is harmonised within the EU under the aegis of ESMA. On ESMA, see also section 1.3.5 above.

6 See above, section 1.3.5.

7 By virtue of Regulation (EU) No 1093/2010 of the European Parliament and of the Council of 24 November 2010 establishing a European Supervisory Authority (European Banking Authority), amending Decision No 716/2009/EC and repealing Commission Decision 2009/78/EC, OJ L 331.

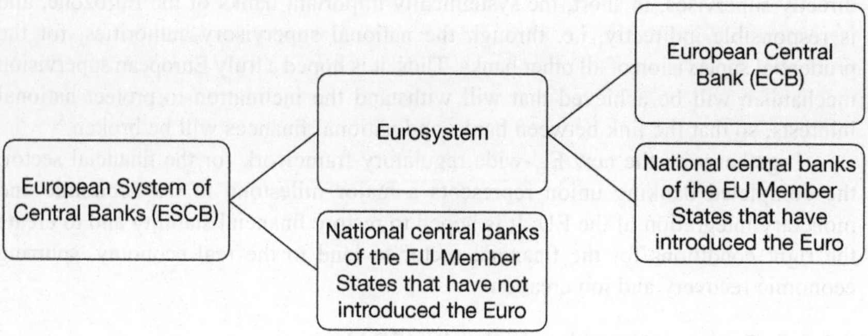

Figure 6.1 Schematic overview of the ESCB

circulation of the Euro currency. Since that moment the ECB has worked together with the countries' national central banks within the Eurozone. The aim of the single currency within the Eurozone is therefore to ensure price transparency, and an uncomplicated comparison of prices. This should improve competitiveness, by making it simpler to find the cheapest supplier for a product or service. It is also argued that the single currency eliminates the risk of currency fluctuations, making cross-border investments and trade within the Eurozone easier. Financial markets are possibly able to operate more effectively too, as the Euro facilitates their integration. So the single currency and its central bank are intended to be good for business, as well as for people who find it easier to travel, to shop or to work in other countries within the Eurozone.

6.1.2 National supervision

Most of the big decisions about the shape and content of the rules governing financial market activity in Europe are now taken at the EU level and the domestic laws of Member States have been relegated to an increasingly secondary role. Until the introduction of the ESFS and, especially, the SSM, this has not been matched by a simultaneous centralisation of supervisory responsibility. Instead, the tasks of day-to-day implementation and on-the-ground enforcement of this body of regulation largely fell to Member States' supervisory authorities, albeit with a layer of EU-wide structural coordination added on top. While under the new single supervisory regime the role of the EU will increase, the national authorities will continue to be the primary supervisors for many financial institutions.

One consequence of the lack of complete centralisation with respect to supervision is that the European financial market supervisory scene may continue to resemble a cluttered landscape. Many Member States divide supervisory responsibilities between several agencies, and also involve their central bank to a greater or lesser extent. The picture becomes even more crowded when the supervisory authorities from the EEA countries, the ECB and the European Commission are taken into account as well. All of these bodies participate in some way in one or more of the EU-wide coordinating structures.

Prior to the financial crisis, many countries located frontline responsibility for micro-prudential supervision of all sectors of financial market activity with a single regulatory authority that operated autonomously from the central bank. Countries in this group included Belgium, Denmark, Finland, Germany, Norway (EEA), Poland, Sweden and the United Kingdom. The Czech Republic and Slovakia also employed the integrated supervisor model but all of the relevant functions were performed by the central bank rather than by dedicated supervisory authorities. Some other countries divided responsibilities between the central bank (for banking supervision), a securities market supervisory authority, and one or more authorities that had responsibility for oversight in respect of insurance and pensions. This system is better known as sectorial supervision – Greece, Italy, Portugal and Spain were in this group.[8] Another model has been in operation in the Netherlands, whereby prudential supervision of banking, insurance and pensions were the responsibility of the central bank and another authority had responsibility for conduct of business regulation across all three sectors of financial market activity. The Dutch approach is sometimes dubbed a 'twin peaks' model, in which there is one supervisor for prudential matters and another one in respect of conduct of business.[9]

The global financial crisis triggered a fresh look at the above institutional arrangements and in particular a reappraisal of the role of central banks in financial supervision. Responsibility for macro-prudential supervision (i.e. systemic stability oversight) is a role that seems to have been reclaimed by central banks. The crisis demonstrated both that macro-prudential supervision had not been afforded sufficient priority in the preceding years, and that it is of critical importance to ensure that macro- and micro-prudential supervision are well aligned. In 2010, France reorganised its institutional structures along, broadly speaking, twin peaks lines, with a strong role for the Banque de France. The Irish legislature moved to put its central bank back at the centre of financial supervision and financial stability oversight. There have been discussions in Germany about putting the Bundesbank back at the centre of supervisory power. Belgium has also adjusted the relationship between its central bank and the financial market supervisor, and in 2010 passed a law to replace the Banking, Finance and Insurance Commission ('CBFA') with a new Financial Services and Markets Authority ('FSMA').

The diversity that currently exists in national institutional arrangements for the oversight of financial markets indicates that there is no foundation of common transnational assumptions about what financial market supervisory architecture should look like on which to build an overarching pan-European federal structure from the bottom up. Therefore, the Eurozone has chosen a top-down approach for unification of the oversight of financial markets.

As regards a non-Euro country, the British Government announced in June 2010 its intention to restructure the UK's financial services regulatory framework. Central to this restructuring is the replacement of the Financial Services Authority ('FSA') with a new twin peaks regulatory structure that combines oversight of the financial

8 In Italy, for instance, the Banca d'Italia is in charge of the supervision of credit institutions, the CONSOB (Commissione Nazionale per le Societa' e la Borsa) dedicated to the supervision of listed companies, the IVASS (Istituto per la Vigilanza sulle Assicurazioni), previously ISVAP, deputed to review the activity of insurers, and finally the COVIP (Commissone Vigilanza Fondi Pensione) for pension funds.

9 For a wide-ranging discussion on the concept of 'twin peaks' supervision, see M Brunnermeier, A Crockett, C Goodhart, AD Persaud and H Song Shin, *The Fundamental Principles of Financial Regulation* (International Center for Monetary and Banking Studies, Geneva 2009) *passim*.

system as a whole with firm-specific supervision. The Bank of England ('BoE') Financial Policy Committee has taken responsibility for macro-prudential regulation, focusing on the overarching stability of the financial system. Conduct of business regulation for all firms has become the responsibility of a new regulator, the Financial Conduct Authority ('FCA'), a BoE subsidiary. The FCA is also responsible for the prudential regulation of firms which fall outside the remit of the other new regulator, the Prudential Regulatory Authority ('PRA'). The PRA, also a BoE subsidiary, is responsible for micro-prudential regulation, with an objective of promoting the safety and soundness of regulated firms. Firms regulated by the PRA are therefore 'dual-regulated', with the PRA responsible for their prudential regulation and the FCA responsible for conduct of business supervision.[10]

6.2 Authorisation of the banking business

6.2.1 General

The TFEU sets out the basics for the right of establishment and cross-border service provision within the EU. However, the TFEU allows limitations to these freedoms for specific public health, public security and public order reasons, and provides the opportunity to harmonise both the effect of the freedoms and their limitations via Directives. The financial services area benefits from harmonisation. Before such harmonisation was achieved, domestic governments defined – each in different ways – what a bank was and under which conditions it would be allowed to enter their local market (both for home-grown banks and for EU or third country banks). In the absence of harmonisation Directives, domestic governments would be forced to set high fences around their territory and thus would invoke the right to limit the freedom of establishment and of services. The protection of the public, of the financial system and of the high standards in a Member State would allow Member States to act along this inclination. Conversely, the capital requirements legislation provides a commonly agreed framework on various types of cross-border market access methods within the EU. The framework intends to limit and/or eliminate such 'good reasons' to limit access, in order to stimulate the single market. Combined with minimum standards on prudential supervision, it allows banks that are authorised and supervised under those minimum standards, to operate across the EU, with limited and clearly defined intervention possibilities for host Member States.

Member States have to allow cross-border services to be provided and branches to be established by banks authorised and supervised by a supervisor of another Member State, if the licence of that bank as granted by its own supervisor includes the provision of those same services in its own Member State. However, this obligation to permit access is linked exclusively to the specific activities.

10 G Walker, 'UK Financial Services Reform', in G Walker and R Purves (eds), *Financial Services Law* (3rd edn Oxford University Press, Oxford 2014) 3, 56.

6.2.2 The EU 'passport'

The so-called 'European passport' was one of the first key achievements of harmonised banking supervision in the EU.[11] The EU created a European passport to enable a legal entity with a banking licence to set up branches and/or start selling services across borders in other Member States. It replaced the previous need to obtain a separate banking licence for each country where a bank wanted to do business, thus significantly reducing thresholds for banks to provide services in the single market. Under the European passport regime, a bank with a licence in its own Member State can opt to start providing services (cross-border or via a branch) in the territory of another Member State (the host state).

The passport process for prudential banking supervision is very low key indeed, in line with the freedoms of establishment and services of the Treaties. The procedure is as follows. For starting its activities through the branch, the home supervisory authority must have approved this intention.[12] Pursuant to art. 35(2) of CRD IV, the application for approval must contain the following data: (i) the Member State where the bank plans to set up the branch; (ii) a programme of operations setting out, *inter alia*, the types of business envisaged and the structural organisation of the branch; (iii) the address in the host Member State from which documents may be obtained; and (iv) the names of those to be responsible for the management of the branch.

Within three months after receipt of the application and the information required, the competent authority of the home Member State shall decide on the application.[13] The national supervisory authority shall approve the intention, unless the credit institution's operations or financial position are inadequate in view of its intention.[14] The competent authority shall also notify the host regulator.[15] Such notification contains information regarding the volume of own funds, the solvency ratio and, where applicable, information on the deposit guarantee scheme applicable to the particular branch.[16] The credit institution will be informed accordingly.[17]

The vast bulk of prudential supervision remains with the home supervisor of the legal entity, with some limited rights (more for branches, less for cross-border services) for the host supervisor of the legal entity. The process for cross-border services has been reduced to a formal process; for branches it contains minor but relatively more cumbersome material aspects. A branch is a permanent physical extension of the licensed legal entity into another Member State,[18] while cross-border services should not have such a presence in the host market (and are thus less 'material' to host Member State markets). The borderline between branches and services (and activities that do not require a notification at all, e.g. a visit of a bank official to another bank in the other Member State), is not always clear, even though it has consequences both for the type of notification to be sent and – after the bank starts its

11 On the European passport, see also above, section 1.3.3.
12 See also above, section 5.4 for the list of authorised activities.
13 This precept can be inferred from art. 35(3), para. 1, of CRD IV.
14 Ibid.
15 Ibid.
16 Art. 35(1), para. 2, of CRD IV.
17 This is inferable from the expression 'and shall inform the credit institution accordingly' within art. 35(3), para. 1, of CRD IV.
18 As regards the concept of 'branch' in the banking industry, see Chapter 5, above.

activities – for the role of host supervisors regarding the cross-border presence of the foreign bank.

Banks from the European Economic Area ('EEA') are treated as if they are banks from an EU Member State for the purpose of market access. This follows from the EEA Treaty, which reciprocally allows access to and from all the EEA states, including all EU states. This is conditional upon the non-EU EEA states taking over all prudential supervision Directives. Banks from other third countries do not benefit from a European passport, unless they have a fully licensed subsidiary in one of the EU Member States. Such a subsidiary is an EU entity and – once it has passed all the hurdles of the licensing process – has the same rights and obligations as any other bank with an EU authorisation to passport within the EU.

6.2.3 Non-compliance

If a credit institution conducting its business in another Member State, either by the establishment of a branch or by way of the cross-border provision of services, has received an instruction relating to its operations or its financial situation, and the credit institution has not, or not sufficiently, complied with that instruction,[19] the home state regulator may adopt 'appropriate measures',[20] including, seemingly, the suspension of that credit institution from conducting its business through either a branch or the cross-border provision of services in the other Member State. The home state authority shall notify the host regulator(s) involved with this decision. From the time of this notification, the credit institution may no longer conduct its business from the branch or as a cross-border service provider in the other Member State.

If a bank which conducts its business from a branch in another Member State fails to comply with statutory regulations applicable in the host Member State, the home state regulator, having received a notification to that effect from the host state regulator, shall, without delay, issue an instruction to the bank to adhere to the line of conduct set out in the instruction order within a reasonable term specified, in order to put an end to the violation of the statutory regulations applicable in the host Member State. If the bank has not, or not sufficiently, complied with the instruction, the national regulator, having informed the host state regulator, may prevent the bank from concluding new contracts in the host Member State. The host state regulator will be informed of the measures taken.[21]

In conclusion, if the banking licence of a bank is withdrawn by the national supervisory authority, this authority must also inform the regulators of the Member State(s) in which the bank has a branch or to which it provides services.

19 The specific hypotheses contemplated within CRD IV, particularly art. 41(1), para. 1, are the following: '(a) the credit institution does not comply with the national provision transposing [Directive 2013/36] or with [Regulation 575/2013]; '(b) there is material risk that the credit institution will not comply with the national provisions transposing [Directive 2013/36] or with [Regulation 575/2013]'.

20 This is the expression utilised by CRD IV, art. 41(1), para. 2.

21 Art. 41(2) of CRD IV.

6.3 Prudential supervision

6.3.1 The stability of the bank

One of the main reasons to institute supervision on individual banks and banking groups is the interconnectivity of the financial system and the important role banks play in it. If a bank or banking group fails, there are risks to financial stability, as its bankruptcy could lead to the bankruptcy of its contracting parties and clients, including other banks, and so on. Moreover, a distrust of a bank may easily spill over to other banks: if one of them is not trusted anymore, other banks and their services may also become suspect. Prudential supervision should therefore aim to strengthen financial stability.

Financial stability as such is not a defined concept in the CRD legislation or in other EU legislation. Several economists have proposed definitions, but there does not appear to be any real consensus.[22] Common elements are a safe and well-functioning financial environment and the absence of shocks and 'negative externalities' (i.e. the absence of financial instability). In this sense, anything that helps to make financial structures safer and less prone to shocks is geared towards financial stability.

When a shock to financial stability occurs, this is called a financial crisis. Financial crises are of all times and places and can be caused by any source of instability. Financial instability may lead to damage to the general economy if shocks to it are not resolved quickly. Banks are inherently instable due to their short-term borrowing and long-term lending business,[23] with additional instability and contagion sources added by procyclical valuation standards, investments, cross-border business and size, as well as the use of their business to stimulate risky lending to enterprises and governments. Financial stability instruments aim to prevent or resolve this financial instability of banks (and other financial institutions).

However, the effectiveness of financial stability instruments should not be overstated as financial stability can never be guaranteed, for the business of borrowing against lending is inherently risky. To take away that risk would render lending impossible and therefore limit the possibility of growth. Nonetheless, they may contribute to the prevention of avoidable negative shocks, to dampen the negative effects of financial instability when it occurs, while attempting not to inhibit growth too much. Some negative shocks can be prevented by, for example, monitoring traders to avoid fraud and ensuring liquidity, each of which has caused crises in the past and for which we are thus forewarned. Financial stability can be strived for by a wide range of instruments, mainly geared towards not rocking the boat or shock absorbers once the boat starts rocking in any case, and allowing economic growth and wellbeing to develop (still but also only) at a measured pace. The remainder of this chapter will pay attention to the capital adequacy requirements of the CRD legislation as a financial stability instrument, but also to the CRD's provisions on liquidity risk, large exposures, corporate governance and remuneration.

---

22 Some commentators refer to it as a 'public good' ('S Griffith-Jones, 'International Financial Stability and Market Efficiency as a Global Public Good', in I Kaul et al. (eds), *Providing Global Public Goods* (Oxford University Press, Oxford 2003) 435, 436.

23 See above, section 5.1.

6.3.2 Solvability and capital buffers

Thanks to the work of the Basel Committee on Banking Supervision (BCBS of the Bank for International Settlements), the basic formula of a mandatory solvency ratio has been rolled out in a reasonably harmonised fashion across the globe, including the EU. In the EU, the latest Basel Accord (the so-called Basel III Accord) has been implemented as CRD IV and CRR.[24] Under these statutes, banks are required to have capital buffers. Capital buffers of specific quality types are required, calculated in relation to the risk the bank runs, in addition to sufficient capital for company law and licensing purposes. Subject to the availability of these capital buffers of at least the amount required for its calculated risk, the bank is allowed to attract money from companies and from consumers, and to subsequently use that money for its own account by lending or investing it.

Capital buffers aim to ensure that – even if losses are made from onwards lending or investment – the money attracted from depositors and regular bondholders can be repaid. Thus, capital buffers consist of instruments on the liability side of the balance sheet that are available to absorb losses, both in a going concern, as well as in a gone concern scenario. If there is not sufficient money to pay both creditors and shareholders back, first losses are borne by the shareholders. Only if their claim has been fully written down, can creditors face losses on their claims. Shareholders are therefore considered 'risk investors' under company/bankruptcy law. This makes equity for banks rather expensive as the premium for that risk needs to be substantial (either in substantial dividends or share price rises). The attempt to reduce those costs leads to a search for other capital buffer components that are cheaper but still provide safety – a buffer – for creditors. Subordinated loans and hybrids – e.g. loans that have some characteristics of shares – may be accepted as a buffer for capital adequacy purposes, such as the solvency ratio. However, the 2007–13 subprime crisis showed that some of these components did not serve as an actual financial buffer in a going concern situation, let alone in liquidation. In sum, the intended goal of financial stability was not achieved, leading to a reassessment of several capital buffer components.

It is generally accepted that capital buffers need to have two characteristics: the buffers need to be of sufficient size, and of sufficient quality. Whereas the desirability of high quality buffers has been the starting point, the BCBS and the CRD legislation still also accept lower quality capital buffers, such as subordinated loans. These lower quality buffers can supplement – up to certain limits – high quality capital buffers, such as issued and fully paid up shares. In the latest Basel III Accord, the amount of lower quality capital buffer types is slightly reduced, while the definition of high quality characteristics has been slightly enhanced, with some further improvements on the overall quality of capital buffers made during the decades-long transitional period. The percentage of the solvency ratio that is covered by capital buffers that must conform to the highest set of quality requirements formulated is gradually increased. Basel III also makes explicit that such capital buffers are useful in a going concern situation, while some other financial buffers may only avail creditors in a liquidation or gone concern scenario.

24 On the transposition of soft law into hard law, see S De Vido, 'The FRB and Other New Modes of Governance', in M Waibel and G Burdeau (eds), *The Legal Implications of Global Financial Crises / Les implications juridiques des crises financières de caractère mondial* (Martinus Nijhoff, Leiden, forthcoming 2015).

The gradual enhancement just discussed is the result of a compromise between on the one hand the need to improve the safety of the banking system, and on the other hand certain difficulties many banks would have encountered if the new capital requirements had been implemented too abruptly. It has been argued that banks' lending capacity would have been significantly reduced if banks had to increase their capital buffers too quickly and this argument has prevented a 'big bang' approach.

Capital can be defined in various ways. The accounting definition of capital is not identical to the definition used for regulatory capital adequacy purposes. Regulatory capital is more conservative than accounting capital. For the purposes of regulatory capital adequacy for banks, capital is not defined simply by deducting the value of an institution's liabilities (what it owes) from its assets (what it owns). Only capital that is at all times freely available to absorb losses qualifies as regulatory capital. Additional conservatism is added by adjusting this measure of capital further by, for example, deducting assets that may not have a stable value in stressed market circumstances (e.g. goodwill) and not recognising gains that have not yet been realised.

The capital adequacy requirement is the amount of capital an institution is required to hold to cover unexpected losses, relative to its total amount of assets. In the CRR, this is called the 'own funds requirement' and is expressed as a percentage of risk-weighted assets. The purpose of this capital is to absorb the losses on its assets that a bank does not expect to make in the normal course of business (unexpected losses). The more capital a bank has, the more losses it can suffer before it defaults.

In order to calculate the capital an institution needs to hold against its assets, the CRR defines how to weigh an institution's assets relative to their risk. This phenomenon is known as risk-weighted assets or RWAs. Safe assets such as cash are disregarded, other assets such as loans to other institutions are considered more risky and get a higher weight. The more risky assets an institution holds, the more capital it has to maintain. This risk weighing of assets is done not only as regards assets on a bank's balance sheet, but banks must also maintain capital against risks related to off-balance sheet exposures such as loan and credit card commitments, which are also risk weighed.

Capital comes in different forms that serve different purposes. In essence and as alluded to above, there are two types of capital:

- *Going concern capital:* this is the type of capital that has a loss absorbing capacity so that an institution can continue its activities and prevents insolvency. This type of capital is called 'Tier 1 capital'. Pursuant to art. 26 of the CRR, Tier 1 capital of an institution consists of the sum of the Common Equity Tier 1 capital ('CET 1') and Additional Tier 1 capital ('AT 1'). In short, CET 1 can be capital instruments, share premium accounts related to these capital instruments and retained earnings. CRR does not define 'capital instruments', but lists its conditions in art. 28 and 29. In short, most common equity will qualify. Also AT 1 capital is not defined in the CRR, but capital instruments must comply with the list of conditions of art. 52(1) of the CRR in order to qualify as AT 1 capital. In short, certain subordinated loans, hybrids and convertibles, i.e. loans that are paid only after 'senior' loans have been paid, loans which resemble common equity and loans that may be converted into shares, may qualify.
- *Gone concern capital:* this is the type of capital that helps ensure that depositors and senior creditors can be repaid if the institution fails. This type of capital is called

'Tier 2 capital'. Also this category of capital may include hybrid capital and subordinated debt, but the conditions to qualify as Tier 2 capital – which are to be found in art. 63 of the CRR – are less stringent than the conditions for AT 1.

Under the previous capital adequacy rules, banks and investment firms needed to have a total amount of capital buffer equal to at least 8 per cent of risk weighted assets, i.e. a capital ratio of 8 per cent. Under CRD IV and the CRR the total capital an institution will need to hold as a capital buffer remains at 8 per cent, but within that 8 per cent, 4.5 per cent (instead of 2 per cent) has to be of the highest quality: CET1.

The criteria for capital instruments to qualify as either CET 1, AT 1 or Tier 2 have also become more stringent. Furthermore, the latest CRD legislation significantly increases the effective level of regulatory capital that institutions are required to have by the introduction of five new categories of buffers: the capital conservation buffer, the counter-cyclical buffer, the systemic risk buffer, the global systemic institutions buffer and the other systemic institutions buffer. Thus, the new legislation does more than only increasing the quality of capital. In addition, on top of all these own funds requirements, supervisors may demand extra capital to cover for other risks following a supervisory review and institutions may also decide to hold an additional amount of capital on their own initiative.

Institutions can increase their capital adequacy in (at least) the following two ways:

- *Increase capital:* An institution can increase its capital by issuing new instruments that qualify as regulatory capital (Tier 1 or Tier 2) or not pay dividends to its

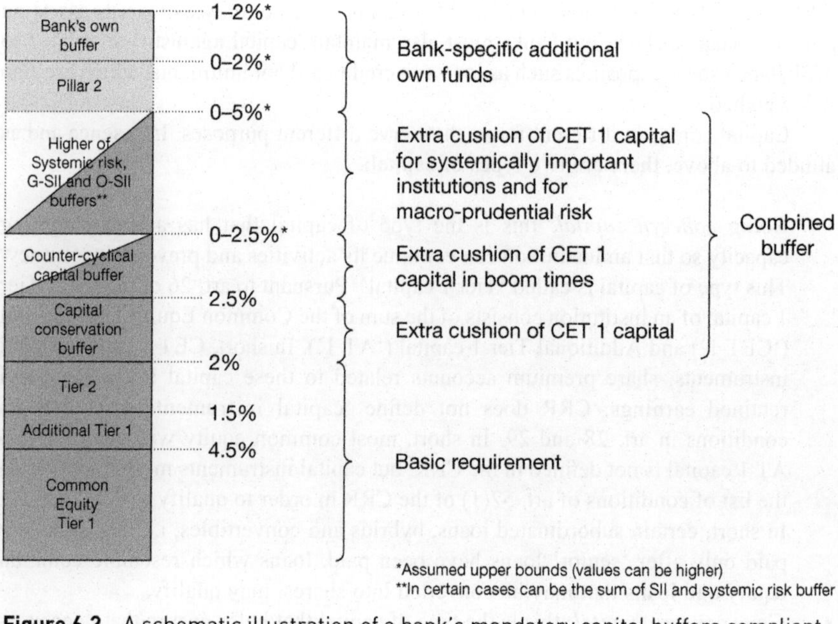

Figure 6.2 A schematic illustration of a bank's mandatory capital buffers compliant with the current capital requirement rules

shareholders, i.e. to retain profits, so that these new instruments and retained profits become included in its capital base. Provided the amount of RWAs is not increased, such new instruments and retained profits increase the capital ratio;
- *Reduce risk-weighted assets:* An institution can also cut back on lending, sell loan portfolios and/or make less risky loans and investments, thereby reducing its RWAs, which has the effect of – for a given amount of capital – increasing its capital ratio.

6.3.3 Liquidity, large exposures and leverage

Liquidity risk is the inability of a bank to meet its obligations when they become due, because of a lack of available cash. This may be the case notwithstanding other assets the bank may hold. In other words, a bank may be solvent but nonetheless illiquid, for instance when its other assets, such as holdings in companies and/or properties, cannot be quickly sold. Liquidity risk, together with leverage (explained below), has been a major issue in the past and, probably, a contributory factor to the global financial crisis. To avoid unwanted relapses, the recent legislation of CRD IV requires the competent authorities to ensure that 'institutions have robust strategies, policies, processes and systems for the identification, measurement, management and monitoring of liquidity risk over an appropriate set of time horizons'.[25] The ultimate purpose of this is to guarantee that 'institutions maintain adequate levels of liquidity buffers.'[26]

Furthermore, the CRD legislation contains new provisions on a bank's leverage. While, generally speaking, leverage is the ratio between total debt and equity, leverage, as defined by the CRR at art. 4(93), is the 'relative size of an institution's assets, off-balance sheet obligations and contingent obligations to pay or to deliver or to provide collateral . . . compared to that institution's own funds'. What the Directive aims to tackle is 'excessive leverage', i.e. the 'risk resulting from an institution's vulnerability due to leverage or contingent leverage that may require immediate corrective measures to its business plan'.[27] In this respect, CRD IV requires the competent authorities existing in each Member State to ensure that 'institutions have policies and processes in place for the identification, management and monitoring of the risk of excessive leverage.'[28] Moreover, the same authorities must ensure that not only the leverage risk is identified by each credit institution, but also that the institutions address, 'in a precautionary manner',[29] 'the potential increases in the risk of excessive leverage'.[30] More practically, the increase of risk may arise, among the several circumstances, from the reduction of the own funds of the bank due to expected or realised losses.

Finally, the large exposure regime aims to limit the maximum damage the failure of one client can do to the bank. Some banks become overly dependent on one client to the extent that if the client fails, the banks automatically fail as a result of this. For this purpose, the large exposure regime was introduced in addition to the risk-weighted approach. In its most basic form, it obliges a bank to:

25 Art. 86(1).
26 Art. 86(1).
27 Art. 4(94) of the CRR.
28 Art. 87(1) of CRD IV.
29 Art. 87(2) of CRD IV.
30 Ibid.

- add up all exposures to one client plus all exposures to other clients which are so interconnected with that one client that should the latter fail, all these other clients can be expected to fail with it;
- to monitor all substantial ('large') exposures, meaning all exposures to a client or group of interconnected clients that exceed 10 per cent of the bank's own funds (art. 392 of the CRR);
- not to allow any such large exposure to exceed a quarter of the banks own funds (art. 395 of the CRR).

The thinking behind the large exposures regime is quite simple. Select all exposures which are large in comparison with your own funds, and do not let an exposure become too large towards a single client (or group of clients), as that would expose the bank to failure if the client fails (or moves to another bank). Unlike the approaches to other categories of risk, the large exposures regime does not primarily rely on capital requirements to limit/manage risk. In this sense it is the odd one out of the quantitative requirements. The large exposures regime works on the premise that even if capital requirements would cover the other risk categories, it is still not a good idea to put all the eggs of the bank into one basket. The large exposures regime complements the capital requirements by providing barriers to overinvestment (e.g. by lending) in any specific counterparty or group of connected clients, except where the risk is limited by protection measures or where it is part of normal trading policies for a limited time. In the area of the trading book, the limits set may be exceeded if capital is maintained for the excess.

It is intended that the hard wiring of absolute limits does not hamper the banks too much (as they still allow sizable loans to be made), while it attempts to limit the potential damage resulting from concentration risk to a client. Though this basic thinking is simple, and attempts have been made to implement or make the regime in such a straightforward manner and reduce the number of national discretions, it remains riddled with exceptions, discretions and supervisory decisions, reducing its usefulness as a risk reducing factor. By way of example, exposures to a Member State are exempted from the regime (cf. art. 400 of the CRR), which caused serious problems in the 2007–13 subprime crisis for a wide range of banks that had excessively large exposures to their own Member State or other Member States.

6.3.4 Corporate governance and remuneration

The available systems of corporate governance of banks across the EU are multifarious even when discounting the differences in legal systems. Some jurisdictions lean toward a unitary management structure,[31] others prefer a dual one,[32] in some cases even both are possible options according to the strategy of the company concerned.[33] Yet the global financial crisis and the collapse of some major financial institutions

---

31 The UK Companies Act 2006 epitomises this. Among many, see D French, S Mayson and C Rayn, *Mayson, French and Ryan on Company Law* (31st edn Oxford University Press, Oxford 2014) 418, 465.

32 This is the case in Germany. See M Siems and D Cabrelli, *Comparative Company Law: A Case-Based Approach* (Oxford University Press, Oxford 2013) *passim*.

33 Italy, in a creative way, has adopted a system of corporate governance that, according to the articles of association of each business entity, can be either unitary or dual.

have cast serious doubts on systems of governance based on voluntary codes of conduct, rather than on binding rules.[34] It has shown that loose corporate governance may drive a coach and horses through the canons of sound and prudent management of a credit institution: accordingly, the underpinning philosophy of the EU, in the aftermath of the widespread bank failures, is based on principles and standards, to be implemented in each Member State, the purpose of which is:

> to ensure effective oversight by the management body, promote a sound risk culture at all levels of credit institutions and investment firms and enable competent authorities to monitor the adequacy of internal governance arrangements.[35]

Against this background lie the main novelties of the rules within the CRD in the area of corporate governance. First and foremost, all the members of the management body 'shall commit sufficient time to perform their functions in the institution'.[36] In this respect, it may be inferred that the EU legislator seems to regard as non-eligible casual directors, those bank directors dedicating a very limited time to their managerial role.[37]

Additionally, the piece of legislation at stake does not allow an individual to hold, as far as major banking institutions are concerned,[38] more than one of the following combinations of directorships at the same time: (a) 'one executive directorship with two non-executive directorships'; (b) 'four non-executive directorships',[39] although some mechanisms of ponderation are in place which make specific directorships held within the same banking group weighted as one directorship.[40] In a nutshell, thc phenomenon of the Jack-of-all-trades-and-master-of-none director, sitting on numerous boards of different banking groups but in reality not seriously dedicated to any of them, should be prevented in light of rules where, de facto, the quality of the directorship rather the quantity is required to make sure that banks are managed properly and without unreasonable risks.

The remuneration, the second topic treated in this section, is yet another area of intervention of the EU legislator. Also in this case, the financial crisis which unfolded

---

34 Recital 53 of CRD IV. At doctrinal level and with regard to the loose British system of corporate governance, see P de Gioia-Carabellese, 'Non-executive Directors and Auditors in the Context of the UK Corporate Governance: Two (or Too Many?) "Pirandellian" characters Still in the Search of an Author?' (2011) 22 *European Business Law Review* 759, 789. See also, as regards the British scandals in the area of corporate governance, P de Gioia-Carabellese, 'Corporate Governance of British Banks and Duties of Directors: Practical Implications of the Royal Bank of Scotland's Demise' (2014) 2 *Law and Economics Yearly Review* 134, 165. For a broader analysis of the British system of corporate governance and its traditional voluntary approach based on 'Codes' (the UK Corporate Governance Code) and reports (recently, the Walker Report), see IG MacNeil, *An Introduction to the Law on Financial Investment* (2nd edn Hart Publishing, Oxford and Portland 2012) 335, 351.

35 Recital 54 of CRD IV.

36 Art. 91 of CRD IV.

37 Again, see P de Gioia-Carabellese, 'Non-executive Directors and Auditors in the Context of the UK Corporate Governance: Two (or Too Many?) "Pirandellian" characters Still in the Search of an Author?' (2011) 22 *European Business Law Review* 759, 789. It may be predicted that the recent piece of EU legislation has given the 'last rite' to this controversial category, already criticised by scholars.

38 The adjective 'major' is connected with 'size, internal organisation and the nature, the scope and the complexity of its activities' and is defined by each Member State (Art. 91(3) of CRD IV).

39 Art. 91(3) of CRD IV.

40 More specifically, pursuant to art. 91(4), some multiple directorships shall count as a single directorship: '(a) executive or non-executive directorship held within the same group'; '(b) executive or non-executive directorships held within: (i) institutions which are members of the same institutional protection scheme . . .; (ii) undertakings (including non-financial entities) in which the institution holds a qualifying holding'.

in 2008 seems to be one of the reasons for the hitherto unknown detailed precepts promulgated in Brussels. Briefly, a remuneration of the top management too generously inclined to reward the short-term choices rather than the long-term ones, may put in danger the stability of the bank. In fact, it is now generally believed that short-term high remuneration may be an opportunity for the top manager to engage in (too) risky transactions and operations. In light of this scenario, the entire structure of remuneration, traditionally an area left to the discretion of each institution, has been the subject of decisive intervention. The new principles that, on a mandatory basis, the competent authorities have to comply with, fix the remuneration for the staff and, in general terms, for any employee, as detailed under art. 92(2). Among the most important ones:

> (a) the remuneration policy [shall] be consistent with and promotes sound and effective risk management and [shall] not encourage risk-taking that exceeds the level of tolerated risk of the institution; (b) the remuneration policy is in line with the business strategy, objectives, values and long-term interests of the institution, and incorporates measures to avoid conflicts of interest; (c) the institution's management body in its supervisory function adopts and periodically reviews the general principles of the remuneration policy and is responsible for overseeing its implementation; (d) the implementation of the remuneration policy is, at least annually, subject to central and independent internal review for compliance with policies and procedures for remuneration adopted by the management body in its supervisory function.

6.4 Further reading

Alexander, K, and Dhumale, R, *Research Handbook on International Financial Regulation* (Edward Elgar, Cheltenham 2012)

Brunnermeier, M, Crockett, A, Goodhart, C, Persaud, AD, and Song Shin, H, *The Fundamental Principles of Financial Regulation* (International Center for Monetary and Banking Studies, Geneva 2009)

de Gioia-Carabellese, P, 'Non-executive Directors and Auditors in the context of the UK Corporate Governance: Two (or Too Many?) "Pirandellian" characters Still in the Search of an Author?' (2011) 22 *European Business Law Review* 759, 789

de Gioia-Carabellese, P, 'Corporate Governance of British Banks and Duties of Directors: Practical Implications of the Royal Bank of Scotland's Demise' (2014) 2 *Law and Economics Yearly Review* 134, 165

De Vido, S, 'The FRB and Other New Modes of Governance', in M Waibel and G Burdeau (eds), *The Legal Implications of Global Financial Crises / Les implications juridiques des crises financières de caractère mondial* (Martinus Nijhoff, Leiden, forthcoming 2015)

French, D, Mayson, S, and Ryan, C, *Mayson, French and Ryan on Company Law* (31st edn Oxford University Press, Oxford 2014)

Gersten, C, Klein, G, Schopmann, H, Schwander, D, and Wengler, C, *European Banking and Financial Services Law* (Kluwer Law International, Deventer 2004)

Gleeson, S, *International Regulation of Banking. Basel II: Capital and Risk Requirements* (Oxford University Press, Oxford 2010)

Griffith-Jones, S, 'International Financial Stability and Market Efficiency as a Global Public Good', in I Kaul et al. (eds), *Providing Global Public Goods* (Oxford University Press, Oxford 2003) 435, 454

MacNeil, IG, *An Introduction to the Law on Financial Investment* (2nd edn Hart Publishing, Oxford and Portland 2012)
Proctor, C, *The Law and Practice of International Banking* (Oxford University Press, Oxford 2010)
Scott, HS, and Gelpern, A, *International Finance: Transactions, Policy and Regulation* (Thomson Reuters/Foundation Press, New York 2012)
Siems, M, and Cabrelli, D, *Comparative Company Law: A Case-Based Approach* (Oxford University Press, Oxford 2013)
Theissen, R, *EU Banking Supervision* (Eleven International Publishing, The Hague 2013)
Walker, G, 'UK Financial Services Reform', in G Walker and R Purves (eds), *Financial Services Law* (3rd edn Oxford University Press, Oxford 2014) 3, 56
Wood, PR, *Regulation of International Finance* (Sweet & Maxwell, London 2007)
Wood, PR, *Law and Practice of International Finance* (Sweet & Maxwell, London 2008)
Wymeersch, E, Hopt, KJ, and Ferrarini, G, *Financial Regulation and Supervision: A Post-crisis Analysis* (Oxford University Press, Oxford 2012)

6.5 Questions

6.1 Which problem(s) does the banking union aim to solve?

6.2 What is the relationship between the EBA and the ECB?

6.3 What is a 'twin peak' model of supervision and how does it differ from other models?

6.4 'The European passporting regime is a cause of, rather than a solution to, the financial crisis.' Discuss.

6.5 To what extent do the Basel III and CRD IV capital adequacy requirements differ from the previous ones?

6.6 'The new capital adequacy requirements of Basel III and the CRD legislation will not be able to prevent the next financial crisis.' Discuss.

Chapter 7

The bank and its insolvency

Chapter contents

7.1 Bank insolvency and the law

Some have claimed that banks are not susceptible to failure, as such institutions are deemed the paymaster par excellence in financial and international transactions.[1] However, in truth, and as dramatically brought to light by the recent global financial crisis of 2007/08, banks may be illiquid or, even worse, become fully insolvent.[2] This should not have come as a surprise – although in reality it did – for the business of a bank is inherently risky (as explained above, section 5.1). In fact, bank failures have occurred since banks have existed in the form as we know them today, i.e. since the thirteenth century. Moreover, the word 'bankrupt', which can be found in practically all languages of the world to mean insolvency, even derives from the failure of a bank. Bankruptcy (English), *bankroet* (Dutch), *Bankrott* (German), *bancarota* (Portuguese) and *банкротство* (Russian) all find their origin in the Italian *banca rotta*. The ritual act of breaking a banker's table or *banco*,[3] behind which he conducted his business, used to signify that banker's insolvency.[4]

The legal approach to bank insolvencies can differ significantly depending on the respective jurisdictions, legal traditions and economic scenarios existing in each case. In some countries,[5] specific proceedings for the liquidation of banks have been put in place that derogate from the normal reorganisation and winding up proceedings which apply to commercial businesses. This usually implies that a judicial decision affecting a financial institution such as a declaration of insolvency, cannot be adopted without a form of cooperation with the supervisory authority. Moreover, the practical reality of this regime is that in some cases, proceedings can be adopted directly by the administrative authority,[6] independently from any competent judicial body.

A pertinent example of the above regime can be found in the US where, as early as the nineteenth century, special rules were designed to govern the liquidation process or, in general terms, any measure of reorganisation applicable to financial institutions. The underlying rationale behind this is that, by its very nature, any insolvency within the banking industry may give rise to a systemic risk. More specifically, a special insolvency regime has been justified because of the interconnectedness of the banking

---

1 See F Capriglione, *Crisi a Confronto (1929 e 2009): Il Caso Italiano* (CEDAM 2009).

2 Although the definition of insolvency and illiquidity varies per jurisdiction, from an accounting perspective, 'insolvency' occurs when a company (or a financial institution) does not have adequate liquid assets (cash, or easily converted into cash), to pay its debts when they fall due. The entity may be otherwise profitable and have a healthy balance sheet, but may fall into insolvency if too many of its assets are difficult to convert quickly into cash (i.e. they are illiquid assets). Companies can, therefore, often recover from insolvency if they can persuade their creditors to give them long enough to convert less liquid assets into cash. PM Collier, *Accounting for Managers* (4th edn, Wiley 2012).

3 In Italian, the masculine '*banco*', rather than '*banca*', corresponds to the English 'desk'. However, the original term '*banco*' (the masculine form) has more recently been usurped by the feminine '*banca*', which is also the name defining a bank in contemporary Italian. Interestingly, the medieval term '*banco*' (again, literally a desk) is a synonym of the more recent '*banca*' (bank), albeit an archaic one, nowadays basically in desuetude.

4 M Haentjens, 'Bank Recovery and Resolution: An Overview of International Initiatives' (2014) *International Insolvency Law Review* 255 et seq.

5 An example is Italy and its statutory legal provisions dedicated to the insolvency of credit institutions, found within Legislative Decree No 185/1993 (*Testo Unico delle leggi in material bancaria e creditizia*). More specifically: art. 70, concerned with the *amministrazione straordinaria* and art. 80 et seq., dealing with the *liquidazione coatta amministrativa*. Other, more recent examples include the UK and Germany. See also below.

6 By 'administrative authority' it is meant a supervisory authority, government authority, a central authority or any public authority that, in that specific country, is designated to deal with an administrative procedure.

sector and the critical functions it performs. Consequently, it is argued a disorderly bank failure should be staved off by an active role of the administrative authority (i.e. the supervisor), as such authority is supposed to be able to achieve more efficiency and speed than court proceedings can.[7]

Standing in stark contrast to the aforementioned procedure is the approach adopted by countries, which included, until recently, the UK,[8] where the insolvency of banks is treated in a similar manner to that of commercial businesses. Thus, insolvency rules apply uniformly to commercial businesses and financial institutions and, in theory, the procedural rules governing commercial businesses apply likewise to financial ones.

An important issue that may arise when dealing with the insolvency of banks is the cross-border magnitude of the insolvency proceeding; the globalisation of the markets and the transnational activity of banks mean that international groups may operate across a wide spectrum of jurisdictions, with subsidiaries and/or branches established in each respective country.[9] In this scenario, the declaration of insolvency of the entire group, or of specific subsidiaries in a specific country, may give rise to delicate legal issues regarding the way in which the assets of the group, scattered across a diverse range of jurisdictions, must be treated. The seminal case epitomising the 'mayhem' caused by a cross-border bank insolvency is the BCCI one, a financial institution with headquarters in London, Luxemburg and the Cayman Islands. In 1992, at the onset of its crisis, insolvency procedures were initiated in the three aforementioned countries. As a matter of course, the three competent local courts within each of the three respective jurisdictions ruled that the assets relating or pertaining to the operations of BCCI should be distributed. However, these rulings appeared to be influenced by the different approach taken by some courts in further countries (that is to say, countries other than those where the headquarters were located), where BCCI had branches. Notably, a US court held that the assets of the BCCI branch located in New York should be ring-fenced and distributed preferentially to US creditors. These rulings, though, were inconsistent with the reality of BCCI's operations in New York; in fact, the branch located there did not have these assets on its own account, but rather exclusively on behalf of the three headquarters for purposes of payment obligations in US dollars. An alternative course of action would have seen the relevant money deemed by the US courts as assets belonging to the three headquarters, rather than pertaining solely to the US branch.

The BCCI case is an example of the inherent difficulties which the operational activities of a bank at international level may present for the organisation of insolvency proceedings. These proceedings, in more recent times, have been the subject matter

7 M Haentjens, 'National Insolvency in International Bank Insolvencies', in B Santen and D Offeren (eds), *Perspectives on International Insolvency Law: A Tribute to Bob Wessels* (Leiden Law School 2014) 8, notes, in commenting on the BRRD, that the main objective of a bank insolvency proceeding is to be fast and efficient; in this scenario, the protection of creditors is subordinated.

8 In reality, in the UK, as a result of the financial crisis of 2007/08, specific legislation relating to the insolvency of banks has been enacted through the Banking Act 2009. According to this piece of legislation, there is a 'Special Resolution Regime', applicable to distressed banks. This regime is based on, first and foremost, pre-insolvency sterilisation; second, on banking insolvency and administration. See EP Ellinger, E Lomincka and CVM Hare, *Ellinger's Modern Banking Law* (Oxford University Press, Oxford 2011) 28, 29.

9 See also above, section 5.2.2.

of intervention in the form of a host of EU legislation. First, the Winding-up Directive[10] sets out harmonised private international law rules about the insolvency of credit institutions throughout the EU. This Directive takes on board the legal dilemmas which came to prominence in the BCCI case and the inextricable difficulties originating from that; essentially, this piece of legislation dictates a general rule – the details of which are explained as the present chapter unfolds – according to which insolvency proceedings initiated against a bank in their home country must be recognised across the EU, while separate proceedings against branches located in further EU countries are precluded.[11]

Fresh in our memories is a more recent example of an international bank insolvency: that of Lehman Brothers.[12] It is generally believed that the insolvency of this investment bank on 15 September 2008 sparked the global financial crisis. In this ensuing crisis, numerous banks found themselves in trouble and a tremendous amount of government money was injected into failing banks. Several banks appeared to be too big to fail: their failure would have caused a disruption of the entire financial system. Between October 2008 and October 2011 in Europe alone, the European Commission approved Euro 4.5 trillion of state aid measures to financial institutions.[13]

To address the too-big-to-fail problem and to prevent future bail-outs with public money, legislators on all levels have proposed legislative action. On the global level, organisations such as the Financial Stability Board, the Bank for International Settlements, the International Monetary Fund and the World Bank have all drafted principles and guidelines for the modernisation of, in short, bank insolvency law. On the national level, as already alluded to above, various legislatures enacted specialist bank insolvency regimes. All these principles and specialist regimes have in common that they aim to minimise costs for taxpayers and allow banks to fail.

On the European level, a common recovery and resolution regime for banks has been accomplished through the Bank Recovery and Resolution Directive ('BRRD')[14] that will have to be implemented in all Member States, and the Single Resolution Mechanism ('SRM') that will apply to the Eurozone countries. The BRRD mainly aims to prevent, through the harmonisation of substantive bank insolvency law rules, the disorderly resolution of credit institutions or, at least, to defuse the negative

10 In full: Directive 2001/24/EC of the European Parliament and of the Council of 4 April 2001 on the reorganisation and winding up of credit institutions, OJ L 125. See further below section 7.1.1.

11 Ultimately, these rules aim to prevent any attempt, in a jurisdiction where the bank has got branches, to ring-fence the assets located there, to the benefit of the local creditors; all the assets of the bank, wherever located in the EU, must be deemed part of the global assets of the bank incorporated in its home country and, therefore, to be apprehended to be distributed among the creditors of the bank. The corollary of this rule is that the jurisdiction of the incorporation of the bank must treat all the creditors according to their rights.

12 It is noted (see C Mooney and G Morton, 'Harmonizing Insolvency Law for Intermediated Securities: The Way Forward', in T Keijser (ed), *Transnational Securities Law* (Oxford University Press, Oxford 2014) 215) that, in the Lehman Brothers International Europe case, there was an absence of 'any procedure enabling the administrators to make distributions of client assets based on claims received by a specified "bar date" on a basis that would be binding on subsequent claimants.' Although the administrators tried to address this issue by the application of the scheme of arrangement procedure (a well-established scheme under English law, now found in the Companies Act 2006, section 895 et seq.), 'the courts held that they lacked jurisdiction to sanction such an extension' (ibid.).

13 'New crisis management measures to avoid future bank bail-outs', Commission press release of 6 June 2012.

14 In full: Directive 2014/59/EU of the European Parliament and of the Council of 15 May 2014 establishing a framework for the recovery and resolution of credit institutions and investment firms and amending Council Directive 82/891/EEC, and Directives 2001/24/EC, 2002/47/EC, 2004/25/EC, 2005/56/EC, 2007/36/EC, 2011/35/EU, 2012/30/EU and 2013/36/EU, and Regulations (EU) No 1093/2010 and (EU) No 648/2012, of the European Parliament and of the Council, OJ L 173.

consequences originating from them so that the likely contagion of other institutions and the expensive and onerous financial support by the governments involved could be avoided in the future.

The SRM is built on a Regulation and an intergovernmental agreement.[15] As the disorderly failure of the Fortis group has shown, cooperation between the relevant national authorities is critical and fraught with conflicts, as the same authorities are expected to protect different (national) interests. The Regulation therefore brings about, for the Member States that use the Euro as their currency and any other country that wishes to accede, the unified application of the BRRD by a new European resolution authority, i.e. the Single Resolution Board ('SRB'). Thus, this SRB rather than any national authority will be responsible for any and all resolution measures taken as regards cross-border and significant banks in the Eurozone.

Finally, and partly as a result of the banking crisis, EU legislation aims to further harmonise or even unify the deposit guarantee schemes, i.e. the schemes that aim to protect the depositor of the bank in circumstances where his deposits are not available for retrieval, by requiring each country to implement a scheme guaranteeing depositors a coverage of a designated amount of money. The most recent legislative framework in this area is the recast Deposit Guarantee Scheme Directive of 16 April 2014 ('DGS Directive').[16]

7.1.1 European bank insolvency law

7.1.1.1 Winding-up Directive

Within the domain of banking law, the insolvency of banks has been legislated upon for more than a decade; the seminal case which instigated legislative intervention (the BCCI case) and the controversial manner in which transnational insolvency was treated at judicial level, have already been alluded to at the outset of the current chapter. It is important to reiterate at this point that private international law or conflict of laws regarding the matter of insolvency, to which reference is made in this section, relates exclusively to bank insolvency, which is included within the Winding-up Directive. For insurance companies, a separate European statute has been enacted that is similar to the Winding-up Directive.[17] Juxtaposed with this is insolvency concerning commercial business, the *sedes materiae* of which, at EU level, is the regulation on insolvency proceedings.[18]

15 In full: Regulation (EU) No 806/2014 of the European Parliament and of the Council of 15 July 2014 establishing uniform rules and a uniform procedure for the resolution of credit institutions and certain investment firms in the framework of a Single Resolution Mechanism and a Single Resolution Fund and amending Regulation (EU) No 1093/2010, OJ L 225; and Agreement on the transfer and mutualisation of contributions to the Single Resolution Fund of 14 May 2014 (8457/14).

16 In full: Directive 2014/49/EU of the European Parliament and of the Council of 16 April 2014 on deposit guarantee schemes (recast), OJ L 173.

17 See B Wessels and G Moss, *EU Banking and Insurance Insolvency* (Oxford University Press, 2006).

18 Council Regulation (EC) No 1346/2000 of 29 May 2000 on insolvency proceedings (henceforth the 'European Insolvency Regulation'). Article 1(2) of the European Insolvency Regulation clearly states that the 'Regulation shall not apply to insolvency proceedings concerning insurance undertakings, credit institutions, investment undertakings which provide services involving the holding of funds or securities to third parties, or to collective investment undertakings.' For commentaries on the Insolvency Regulation, see WW McBryde, A Flessner and SCJJ Kortmann, *Principles of European Insolvency Law, Vol. 4* (Kluwer Legal Publishers, Deventer 2003). For the state of the art of the prospective reforms, see B Hess, P Oberhammer and T Pfeiffer, *European Insolvency Law: The Heidelberg-Luxemburg-Vienna Report* (CH Beck, Hart and Nomos, Munich 2013).

Conceptually, the alignment of insolvency law is one of the most arduous legal feats a supranational law-maker may face. Insolvency law is a national matter by definition, traditionally left to the discretion of each local legislator. The reason for this is that the distribution of assets among creditors, set in motion by a case of insolvency, is very much a reflection of national political and policy choices, which do not naturally lend themselves to a homogeneous alignment of legislation. Moreover, from a private international law perspective, bankruptcy law is regarded as mandatory rules of a jurisdiction, therefore applicable irrespective of any party agreement.

Despite these objective difficulties, a convergence of EU private international law regarding the insolvency of credit institutions has been achieved, through a succession of principles and statutory provisions to be henceforth explained and discussed. First and foremost, the principle adopted within the EU is the home country one.[19] Fundamentally, the insolvency of a credit institution operating across the EU or, at least, in another Member State than its own (i.e. the country of incorporation of the bank) is an event falling within the competence of the home 'administrative or judicial authorities', irrespective of whether other branches of that bank are located outwith the home country or indeed whether or not that bank provides transnational services beyond its own jurisdiction of incorporation.

In referring to the 'administrative or judicial authorities', the EU legislature demonstrates expert adeptness in giving a wide berth to the insidious waters of the differences existing among the respective national jurisdictions and the multitude of ways in which insolvency is initiated, either overseen by a judicial authority or by an administrative one. As established by the definition provided under art. 2 of the Winding-up Directive, the administrative or judicial authorities are 'such administrative or judicial authorities of the Member States as are competent for the purposes of reorganisation measures or winding-up procedures.' Against the backdrop of this rather ambiguous definition, the ensuing art. 3 prescribes that the judicial or administrative authorities of the home Member State 'shall alone be empowered to decide on the implementation of one or more reorganisation measures in a credit institution, including branches established in other Member States.' To elaborate upon this point, the provision entails that the resolution of a winding-up of a bank incorporated in a given Member State belongs exclusively to the administrative authority of that country (or to the bankruptcy court located there) and that resolution by the competent authority is deemed effective across the broad spectrum of EU countries wherein that bank had opened branches.

The EU legislator has acknowledged the need to provide a definition of the insolvency procedures to which the Winding-up Directive applies.[20] In this respect, two such procedures are identified: (a) 'reorganisation measures'; and (b) 'winding-up'. The former shall be applicable to financial institutions where the recovery of the financial institution is still within the realms of possibility. Should this be the case, the measures are intended 'to preserve or restore the financial situation of a credit institution' although they could affect 'third parties' pre-existing rights'. Within this

19 See on this principle also above, section 1.3.

20 For the purposes of comparison, the European Insolvency Regulation, for commercial insolvencies, seems to be more explicit as it spells out the principle that the 'Regulation shall apply to collective insolvency proceedings which entail the partial or total divestment of a debtor and the appointment of a liquidator.'

rather extensive category, defined under art. 2 (headed 'Definition'), are to be included measures involving 'the possibility of a suspension of payments, suspension of enforcement measures or reduction of claims.'

The Winding-up Directive elaborates a second kind of 'crisis': the winding-up, referred to as a collective proceeding:

> opened and monitored by the administrative or judicial authorities of a Member State *with the aim of realising assets* under the supervision of those authorities, including where the proceedings are terminated by a composition or other, similar measure. [emphasis added]

Whichever procedure is adopted (either the 'reorganisation measure' or the 'winding-up'), the Directive is resolute in specifying that any decision to initiate a procedure rests with the administrative or judicial authorities of the home Member State; the relevant decision, once adopted, shall be applicable to all branches established in other Member States.[21] The other EU country (or countries) wherein the bank has opened branches shall have no grounds on which to object to the opening of the procedure as the procedure adopted by the home authorities shall be effective across all other Member States where the bank carries out activities through its branches.[22] Critically, this principle applies to 'branches', but not to 'subsidiaries'; it follows then that independent entities of a group will be subject to the insolvency law of that local jurisdiction, unless they themselves have branch offices.

In order to obtain the full cooperation of the authorities representing the relevant EU countries, the Winding-up Directive, at art. 9(2), requires that the administrative or judicial authority that initiates the procedure in the country of incorporation of the bank concerned communicates the decision to the authorities of any other affected countries as a matter of urgency, accompanied by a description of the practical effects which the relevant proceeding may precipitate.

It is worth noting that the cardinal principle which permeates the Winding-up Directive and, more specifically, the winding-up proceeding is, as spelled out under art. 10(1), that, save for specific exceptions, the credit institution shall be wound up 'in accordance with the laws, regulations and procedures applicable in its home Member State'. To elaborate, paragraph 2 of the same article stipulates that the legislation in force in the home Member State shall determine 'the goods subject to administration and the treatment of goods acquired by the credit institution after the opening of winding-up proceedings' (a) and 'the claims which are to be lodged against the credit institution and the treatment of claims after the opening of winding-up proceedings' (f).

---

21 This system applicable to the banking system contrasts with that set forth under the Insolvency Regulation. In this case, the norm is that 'the courts of the Member State within the territory of which the centre of a debtor's main interests is situated shall have jurisdiction to open insolvency proceedings' (art. 3(1)), whereas 'the courts of another Member State shall have jurisdiction to open insolvency proceedings against that debtor only if he possesses an establishment within the territory of that other Member State' (art. 3(2)).

22 For non-banking insolvency, the rule is the opposite: if the debtor has got establishments in other Member States, the courts of the latter shall open additional and separate proceedings (art. 3(2) of the European Insolvency Regulation).

The claims that the creditor is entitled to lodge is certainly a hot potato when viewed from the legal perspective of the EU legislator. The EU market represents a favourable arena for consumers, wherein they can benefit from goods and/or services offered and/or provided by enterprises and banks incorporated in another EU country. It stands to reason that, in times of high competition, the free right of establishment theoretically allows the consumer to benefit from the best prices and the best conditions. However, this scenario could throw up an inextricable conundrum and an onerous predicament, were the EU bank to default on its debts, leaving its EU customers to raise claims against a foreign entity and before a foreign court and/or administrative authority. To cater for such an eventuality, art. 16(1) of the Winding-up Directive bestows upon any creditor with domicile, head office or residence in a Member State different from the home Member State, 'the right to lodge claims or to submit written observations relating to the claims'.

The subsequent paragraph 2 has augmented this principle with a series of practical suggestions and prescriptions. Particularly remarkable is the stipulation that any claims 'shall be treated in the same way and accorded the same ranking as claims of an equivalent nature which may be lodged by creditors of the home Member State.'[23]

The Directive under discussion refrains from tackling, with a properly harmonised set of rules, the issues of substantive law typically connected with cross-border insolvency. The matter is unquestionably the set-off and the possibility for a counterparty (A) of an insolvent institution (B) to compensate its debt towards B by means of its credit vis-à-vis the same entity B. In such a scenario, the Winding-up Directive recognises such a right, so long as it is permitted by the law applicable to the credit institution's claim (art. 23). Similarly, in the case of netting agreements,[24] the matter is entrusted to the law of contract governing such agreements (art. 25).[25]

To conclude, the Directive on the reorganisation and winding-up of credit institutions represents a framework addressing bank failures. The degree of alignment it exhibits, however, is limited, aside from the principle of the competence of the country of incorporation of the bank for decisions relating to the commencement of the state of insolvency. Beyond the DGS Directive, the broader and more important aspects of a bank's insolvency remain reserved to the legislation of each respective Member State wherein the bank operates by way of its own branches. This is now regulated and harmonised by the BRRD and SRM to be discussed below.

23 Art. 16(1)(2) of the Insolvency Directive. Any information relating to measures adopted against an institution shall be disseminated using the official language/languages of the home Member State (art. 17 of the Winding-up Directive). According to art. 17(2), any creditor that has established a domicile or head office in a country other than the home Member State shall lodge a claim in the official language of his/its Member State. However, in a slightly incongruous conclusion, the creditor 'may be required to provide a translation into that language of the lodgement of the claim'. There is no doubt, though, that this ideal option would have caused remarkable organisational issues for the liquidators.

24 Netting agreements are clauses whereby the parties arrange in advance that the different credit and debit transactions occurring with each other every day are not executed on an individual basis, but on a net basis, i.e. converted to a net sum or balance. On its turn, the balance, if positive, is given to one party by the other, if negative given by the former to the latter. There are some jurisdictions, such as Italy, where judicial courts at the beginning did not recognise the validity of the netting agreements. See also Chapter 11 below.

25 It is the Collateral Directive (see also below, Chapter 12) that brings about substantive law harmonisation on these two topics. The Collateral Directive requires each Member State to ensure that (a) any sum owed under a transaction, or (b) any cash collateral 'by sale or appropriation' of the collateral property, shall be 'fit' to be set off. In other words, provisions previously existing in a country not permitting netting or set-off, are henceforth prohibited as the matter is harmonised.

7.1.1.2 BRRD and SRM

The next legislative steps towards a more harmonised approach to the insolvency of credit institutions and investment firms transpired in the BRRD[26] and, for the Eurozone Member States, in the SRM. The BRRD has been in force since 1 July 2014 and must have been implemented into national laws as of 1 January 2015.[27] The SRM Regulation becomes operational on 1 January 2016. The scope of the BRRD extends to acting both as a preventative measure and as a means of managing a bank failure. As a result of the BRRD, national authorities (and, in the case of the SRM, the SRB) are empowered to intervene both by taking proactive action in respect to the credit institution, and by reacting when the actual failure occurs.[28]

The rationale behind the BRRD is to stave off any future likelihood that banks will fail in a disorderly manner, by providing a (mandatory) alternative to ordinary national insolvency rules, as such failures 'not only pose risks, but could also result in a significant disruption of essential banking functions to citizens, businesses and the wider economy.'[29] Additionally, the BRRD, as a bank insolvency proceeding, is aimed to safeguard the essential services and protect certain shareholders, whereas in a normal proceeding, not addressed to banks, the main interest is to maximise creditor value. Stemming from this ontological difference of the two proceedings is the consideration that normal insolvency proceedings can be too lengthy as they involve complex negotiations with creditors, whereas, as far as the BRRD is concerned, the relevant rules are geared towards efficiency rather than fairness to creditors. Of equal importance, normal insolvency proceedings usually take place under objective judicial supervision, according to a timescale that can be time consuming depending on the

---

26 The first draft of the BRRD was published by the European Commission (EC) on 6 June 2012. In full: Proposal for a Directive of the European Parliament and of the Council establishing a framework for the recovery and resolution of credit institutions and investment firms and amending Council Directives 77/91/EEC and 82/891/EC, Directives 2001/24/EC, 2002/47/EC, 2004/25/EC, 2005/56/EC, 2007/36/EC and 2011/35/EC and Regulation (EU) No 1093/2010, 2012/0150 (COD). A first commentary on the BRRD proposal can be read in M Haentjens, 'Bank Recovery and Resolution: An Overview of International Initiatives', in M Haentjens and B Wessels (eds), *Bank Recovery and Resolution: A Conference Book* (Eleven Publishers, The Hague 2014) 3, 22; T Verdoes, J Adriaanse and A Verweij, 'Bank Recovery Plans: Strengths and Weaknesses – How to Make a Boiling Banker Frog Jump', in M Haentjens and B Wessels (eds), *Bank Recovery and Resolution: A Conference Book* (Eleven Publishers, The Hague 2014) 25, 47; S Madaus, 'Bank Failure and Pre-emptive Planning', in M Haentjens and B Wessels (eds), *Bank Recovery and Resolution: A Conference Book* (Eleven Publishers, The Hague 2014) 49, 76; S Mezzacapo, 'Towards a New Regulatory Framework for Banking Recovery and Resolution in the EU' (2013) 2 *Law and Economics Yearly Review* (part 1) 213, 241. See also European Commission, 'EU Bank Recovery and Resolution Directive (BRRD): Frequently Asked Questions', MEMO/14/297, 15 April 2014, http://europa.eu/rapid/press-release_MEMO-14-297_en.htm, accessed 3 July 2014.

27 As regards the timing of the transposition of the BRRD in the laws, regulations and administrative provisions of each Member State, the deadline was established, for the vast majority of its provisions, for 31 December 2014. Each Member State has been permitted to apply the relevant measures starting from 1 January 2015 of Directive 2014/59 (art. 130(1) of the BRRD). The exception to this is the bail-in provisions, for which application can be delayed by the Member States until January 2016.

28 Both the BRRD and the SRM build on global recommendations: the Financial Stability Board's 'Key Attributes of Effective Resolution Regimes for Financial Institutions', published in October 2011, and the recommendations on the resolution of a cross-border bank of the Basel Committee on Banking Supervision of March 2010.

As regards the possible friction between bail-out plans and EU state aid rules, see CA Russo, 'The New Course of EU State Aid rules during the 2007–09 Financial Crisis', in K Alexander and R Dhumale (eds), *Research Handbook on International Financial Regulation* (Edward Elgar, Cheltenham (UK) and Northampton (MA – USA) 2012) 171, 192.

29 M Hoban, MP, Letter to HM Secretary, 26 June 2012, 1, 2.

jurisdiction, whereas the resolution measures under the BRRD are taken by the resolution authority only.[30]

Importantly, the BRRD shall apply to a wide range of institutions: essentially, all credit institutions and investment firms subject to the Capital Requirements legislation (CRD IV and CRR[31]) in addition to financial holding companies.[32] Therefore, the net of potential applicants has been cast relatively wide by the EU legislator. Remarkably, the BRRD does not only apply to the EU Member States, but to the entire European Economic Area (EEA). This is particularly noteworthy as its scope thus includes non-Eurozone Member States such as the UK and Sweden, whereas the SSM (Single Supervisory Mechanism) and the SRM are conversely restricted to the Eurozone (and countries that wish to accede to the SSM).[33]

In essence, the BRRD mainly rests on the following three pillars.

Recovery and resolution plans

First and foremost, the initial preventive instrument provided under the BRRD is recovery planning. More specifically, in each Member State, each financial institution concerned (again, not only credit institutions but also investment firms) must be obliged by law to formulate and maintain 'a recovery plan'.[34] This plan, to be drawn and maintained by each institution, shall set out measures that the institution may take to improve and, therefore, restore its financial situation, should it suffer a significant deterioration. Although the recovery plan is a document adopted by each financial institution independently, it shall be submitted to the competent authority for review.[35] The recovery plan shall be scrutinised by the competent authority within six months of the submission by the financial institution; the authority shall grant approval of to the recovery plan, so long as, mainly, two requisites are met, more specifically: thanks to the implementation of the arrangements proposed in the plan, the 'viability and financial position of the institution or of the group' can be maintained or restored;[36] and 'the plan and specific options within the plan are reasonably likely to be implemented quickly and effectively in situations of financial stress and avoiding to the maximum extent possible any significant adverse effect on the financial system.'[37]

30 M Haentjens, 'National Insolvency in International Bank Insolvencies', in B Santen and D Offeren (eds), *Perspectives on International Insolvency Law: A Tribute to Bob Wessels* (Leiden Law School 2014) 8.

31 See above, Chapter 6.

32 Art. 1(1) of the BRRD, i.e. (a) 'institutions that are established in the Union'; (b) 'financial institutions that are established in the Union when the financial institution is a subsidiary of a credit institution or investment firm, . . . and is covered by the supervision of the parent undertaking on a consolidated basis . . .'; (c) 'financial holding companies, mixed financial holding companies and mixed-activity holding companies that are established in the Union'; (d) 'parent financial holding companies in a Member State, Union parent financial holding companies, parent mixed financial holding companies and a member State, Union parent mixed financial holding companies'; (e) 'branches of institutions that are established outside the Union in accordance with the specific conditions laid down [in the same Directive]'.

33 The SSM and SRM have been created in order to safeguard the financial stability in the Banking Union as a whole or in one or more of its Member States, concerned, after the so-called Eurozone crisis and the risk, particularly acute in 2013, that the banking system of some EU countries could have collapsed under the public debt crisis of their respective countries.

34 Art. 5 of the BRRD.

35 Art. 6(1) of the BRRD.

36 Art. 6(2)(a) of the BRRD.

37 Art. 6(2)(b) of the BRRD.

The BRRD contains specific provisions for groups. In this respect, the BRRD[38] requires each Member State to ensure that the relevant parent undertaking is in charge of drawing up and maintaining a recovery plan relating to the group, rather than the single bank. The group recovery plan shall be scrutinised by the competent authority after an assessment about its feasibility, according to rules that, *mutatis mutandis*, are those applicable to the recovery plan of the single bank.[39]

Coupled with the recovery plan is the resolution planning, adopted through a process of collaboration and consultation by the 'resolution authority' (all Member States need to appoint a resolution authority, i.e. an independent public authority which performs the resolution tasks and manages the resolution process[40]).[41] The resolution plan is embraced in so far as the institution in question is, in the eyes of the resolution authority, 'resolvable' in the case of a crisis, i.e. either the financial institution may be liquidated 'under normal insolvency proceedings',[42] without the use of public money,[43] or the crisis can be resolved 'by applying the different resolution tools and powers to the institution'[44] (these 'resolution tools' will be discussed below).

Early intervention measures

Second, 'early intervention measures' must be made available to the resolution authorities operating in each Member State.[45] Any contemplation of deploying such measures implies that the financial position of the institution in question has 'significantly deteriorated'.[46] The specific measures made available in such a scenario are, among others,[47] to require the management body to implement one or more of the measures set out in the recovery plan and, probably the harshest one, the possible replacement, on the recommendation of the supervisor, of the management of the financial institution concerned with a 'temporary administrator' appointed to such an end.

---

38 Art. 7 of the BRRD.

39 Art. 8 of the BRRD defines 'Assessment of group recovery plans'.

40 Art. 3 of the BRRD.

41 Art. 10 of the BRRD.

42 See specifically art. 15(1), second part, of the BRRD.

43 This is a very important condition: the recovery plan implies that there is no 'extraordinary financial support beside the use of financial arrangements', nor any 'central bank emergency liquidity assistance', nor 'any central bank liquidity provided under non-standard collateralisation, tenor and interest rate terms' (art. 15(1) of the BRRD).

44 See again art. 15(1), second part, of the BRRD.

45 Art. 27 ff of the BRRD.

46 More specifically, according to art. 27(1) of the BRRD, when the institution infringes or deteriorates the main parameters set out under the CRR.

47 In this scenario, according to the detailed precepts of art. 27 of the BRRD, measures can be:

(a) To require the management body to implement one or more of the measures set out in the recovery plan.

(b) To require the management body of the institution 'to examine the situation, identify measures to overcome any problems identified and draw up an action programme to overcome those problems and a timetable for its implementation'.

(c) To require the management body to convene a meeting of the shareholders, or, alternatively, to convene the meeting ex officio, if the management body failed to comply with the request of the authority.

(d) To require one member of the management body or senior management to be removed if that person or those persons are found 'unfit to perform their duties'.

Resolution and resolution tools

Should the aforementioned measures prove ineffective, the powers vested in the resolution authority shall extend to consider even more extreme measures, represented as a group under the third pillar of the BRRD termed 'resolution'.[48]

Conditions for the resolution or, better, for the adoption of one of the 'resolution tools' are threefold: first, the relevant authority must assess whether 'the institution [is] failing or [is] likely to fail'; second, 'there is no reasonable prospect that any alternative private sector measures . . . would prevent the failure of the institution within a reasonable timeframe'; and third, 'a resolution action is necessary in the public interest'.[49]

In this scenario, the resolution authorities shall be entitled to use the following five resolution tools:[50] (1) the appointment of a 'special manager' taking over the failing institution's management; (2) the sale of the business or the shares of the institution concerned, without the prior approval of the board of directors or the shareholders, to a private sector purchaser;[51] (3) a measure whereby the assets and/or liabilities of the institution at stake are transferred to an alternative entity owned, wholly or partly, by the resolution authority (such an entity is referred to as a 'bridge institution');[52] (4) a similar transfer may be effectuated with non-viable assets to a vehicle that is commonly denoted as a 'bad bank' (in a process defined as 'asset separation');[53] and (5) the final measure – and probably the most controversial[54] contemplated within the BRRD – is the 'bail-in tool',[55] which can mean both the whole or partial conversion of the unsecured claims against the financial institution (i.e. in short, debt instruments) into shares, and the write-off, in whole or in part, of existing unsecured claims.[56] Also, the bank may be recapitalised by write-off, in whole or in part, of the shares in order 'to restore its ability to comply with the conditions for authorisation . . . and to continue to carry out the activities for which it is authorised'.[57] Nonetheless, the rights of the creditors protected under the DGS Directive to be discussed below will remain unaffected. Ultimately, the underpinning philosophy of the resolution tools is that 'no financial institution shall be unconditionally protected from an orderly market exit'.[58]

---

48 Art. 31 ff of the BRRD.

49 Art. 32 of the BRRD.

50 The 'resolution tools' are detailed under art. 37 ff of the BRRD.

51 Art. 37(3)(a) of the BRRD. The specific modalities of this tool are detailed under arts 38 and 39 of the BRRD.

52 Art. 37(1)(b). Arts 40 and 41 of the BRRD contain the details of this procedure.
See, commenting on the draft Directive rather than the final statute, S Madaus, 'Bank Failure and Pre-emptive Planning', in M Haentjens and B Wessels, *Bank Recovery and Resolution* (Eleven Publishers, The Hague 2004) 61, 62.

53 Art. 37(1)(c) of the BRRD. For the details of this resolution tool, see art. 42 of the BRRD.

54 The definition is utilised by S Madaus, 'Bank Failure and Pre-emptive Planning', in M Haentjens and B Wessels (eds), *Bank Recovery and Resolution* (Eleven Publishers, The Hague 2004) 63.

55 The terminology is reminiscent of the opposite mechanism of the bail-out, which conversely implied the use of taxpayer money to bail out a credit institution.

56 On possible frictions of the Directive under discussion with the European Convention on Human Rights, particularly its art. 1, the right to peaceful enjoyment of possessions, see A Schild, 'Does the Directive on the Recovery and Resolution of Credit Institutions Provide Sufficient Fundamental Rights Protection?' in M Haentjens and B Wessels (eds), *Bank Recovery and Resolution* (Eleven Publishers, The Hague 2004) 77, 85. The conclusion seems to be the following one (A Schild, ibid. 85): 'As long as the member states will dutifully implement the safeguards as set forth in the relevant provisions of the RRD, it is difficult to envisage a situation in which either Article 1 Protocol No. 1 or Article 13 of the Convention will be violated.'

57 Art. 43(1)(a) of the BRRD. Pursuant to art. 43(2)(b) of the BRRD, such recapitalisation can also be used for the bridge institution and asset management vehicle.

58 S Mezzacapo, 'Towards a New Regulatory Framework for Banking Recovery and Resolution in the EU' (2013) 2 *Law and Economics Yearly Review* (part 1) 211.

Having dissected the main pillars of the statute under discussion, it is worth mentioning that the BRRD renders mandatory in each Member State the set-up of a fund (or more than one), called 'resolution financial arrangements', to be financed by way of contributions from all the banks belonging to the system of the country.[59] Fundamentally, the set-up of resolution financial arrangements is aimed to finance the application by the resolution authority of the 'resolution tools and powers'.[60] On its part, each Member State shall ensure that, by a target date (31 December 2024), the 'available financial means' of all the funds (or 'financial arrangements', to use the jargon of the Brussels legislator) existing in that country are tantamount to at least 1 per cent of the 'covered deposits' of all institutions in that specific Member State. In the intention of the EU legislator, the financial arrangements existing in each Member State are not separate from each other, rather they can borrow from each other.[61] The circumstances under which the financial arrangements are entitled to put forward a request of liquidity are exceptional, such as (art. 106(1)) (a) the inability of the amounts raised with the 'ex ante contributions' to 'cover the losses, costs or other expenses' of that financial arrangement; (b) if the 'extraordinary ex-post contributions . . . are not immediately accessible'; and (c) 'the alternative funding means . . . are not immediately accessible on reasonable terms.'

For the Eurozone countries, the financial arrangements just discussed will be used to form a Single Resolution Fund that is created pursuant to the SRM Regulation.[62] As stated above, the same Regulation creates an SRB that will act as the European resolution authority and thus be empowered to take the resolution decisions just discussed as regards all cross-border credit institutions and the institutions comprised in the SSM. The national resolution authorities assist the SRB by preparing and implementing the resolution decisions, as instructed by the SRB, and take the decisions about the resolution of less significant credit institutions.[63]

To conclude this section, the legislative 'bazookas' recently conceived and implemented to cope with bank failures are aimed to prevent a bank insolvency or, if the insolvency actually materialises, to minimise the negative repercussions of it.[64]

---

59 Arts 100 and 103 of the BRRD. The latter provision refers to 'ex-ante contributions', as 'contributions . . . raised at least annually from the institutions authorised in their territory including Union branches'. These contributions shall be proportionate to the amount of the liabilities of the institution concerned, excluding the own funds, minus the 'covered deposits', 'with respect to the aggregate liabilities (excluding own funds) less covered deposits of all the institutions authorised in the territory of the Member State' (art. 103(2) of the BRRD).

In addition to the 'ex-ante contributions', the BRRD (more specifically art. 104) refers to the 'ex-post contributions', which are additional contributions that the credit institutions taking part in a financial arrangement may be asked to pay, if the available financial means 'are not sufficient to cover the losses, costs or other expenses incurred by the use of the financial arrangements.'

Finally, art. 105 of the BRRD refers to 'alternative funding means', as a mechanism whereby financial arrangements in each country shall be allowed to 'contract borrowings or other forms of support from institutions, financial institutions or other third parties' in cases where both the ex-ante contributions and the ex-post contributions were not adequate 'to cover losses, costs or other expenses' incurred by the use of that specific financial arrangement.

60 Art. 100(1) of the BRRD.

61 Art. 99, in terms of principle, and art. 106, as to the specific legal provision. More specifically, on the one hand, financial arrangements existing under a specific jurisdiction are entitled to make a request to borrow from other financial arrangements and (art. 106(1)), on the other hand, financial arrangements shall have the power to lend to other financial arrangements (art. 106(2)).

62 Art. 67(1) of the SRM Regulation.

63 Art. 96 of the SRM Regulation.

64 Recital 1 of the BRRD.

Without these measures, mainly preventive rather than remedial, the insolvency of the bank would require the Government to 'step up to the plate' through an onerous deployment of public money. As a result of the BRRD and SRM, the authorities are now provided with a serious set of weapons, allowing them to intervene 'early and quickly' in relation to the unsound or failing institution.[65] It is hoped that these tools, briefly described above in this section, from the softer one ('recovery and resolution planning') to the harshest one ('resolution tools'), will mean that the continuity of the critical financial and economic functions of the institution in question should be unaffected; perhaps even more importantly, the impact of the failure of that institution on the financial system and, more in general, the economy, should be minimised.

7.2 Protection of the depositor

7.2.1 Introduction

There are two fundamental reasons for protecting the customer of a credit institution or of an investment firm, those being: (a) to guarantee to the depositor or investor, respectively, the restitution of the amount of money deposited with a credit institution[66] or invested in financial instruments in cases where the credit institution or investment firm is insolvent or, in general terms, not in a position to repay its obligations towards these depositors and investors; and (b) pertinent to the previous reason, to ensure that a crisis engulfing a specific financial institution does not precipitate a domino effect with the capacity to consume the entire financial industry. Particularly, with regard to this second aspect, any lack of protection afforded to the depositor and investor could prompt them to withdraw their savings and/or investments, not only from their own financial institution but also from other financial institutions, in fear that the dominoes may imminently fall in their direction and detrimentally affect the ability of their financial counterparty to honour its payment obligations.

Ultimately, and of more significance, the existence or non-existence of an adequate level of protection to safeguard the depositor impinges on the same credibility of the financial industry of a country. On the one hand, to provide the customers with the requisite level of protection, should an individual bank be unable to repay the money deposited, may encourage them to deposit money in its accounts, thereby increasing the bank's liquidity.[67] On the other hand, an excessive level of protection afforded to the bank customer to offset the insolvency of a financial institution, could be counter-productive in terms of the sound and prudent management of that enterprise, as this could result in an overly confident approach of the bank's clientele towards their bank, while inducing risky and reckless conduct on the part of the management of that financial institution.

65 Recital 5 of the BRRD.
66 Deposits here may include (positive balances on) bank accounts and savings accounts.
67 The liquidity of a bank is directly proportional to the ability of the same financial institution to lend money to businesses and individuals. The higher the amount of money deposited with a bank, the higher the liquidity to be lent to the market.

The balance between inviting risk, at one end of the spectrum, and safeguarding the credibility of the financial system in case of insolvency of a bank, on the other, is typically and essentially a task fulfilled by the legislator of each respective country. In each jurisdiction, it is the law-maker that usually decides, by means of a general policy, what the best approach to safeguarding the depositor should be. In the specific case of the Member States of the European Union and, more specifically, those countries belonging to the EEA, this matter has been the subject of a harmonisation process which has been in motion since 1994. In other words, the EU legislator has deemed an adequate protection of the depositor to be one of the cardinal principles of the EU banking system. Therefore, the formation in each country of at least one scheme designed to safeguard bank depositors is not an optional measure left to the discretion of the Member State, but a mandatory process and, ultimately, a condition precedent for the authorisation of a bank.[68]

The present chapter considers both the protection of the depositor of a credit institution (section 7.2.2) and the protection afforded to the investor, i.e. the customer of an investment firm (section 7.3). The investment firm and business (investment services in financial instruments) is explored in greater detail in the next chapter.

7.2.2 Deposit Guarantee Scheme Directives

In this section, a description is provided of the safety net existing at EU level and its role in safeguarding depositors. A need for the bank customer to be adequately protected at EU level, is a comparatively recent development. Merely two decades ago, Directive 94/19 of 1994[69] ushered in the principle of an EU mandatory level of protective cover to the benefit of the holder of a deposit held by a bank, in cases where the deposit became 'unavailable'.[70]

This piece of legislation, amended on one occasion since,[71] was *ius positum* for about two decades. However, as a result of an intense review of the matter,[72]

68 An EU bank asking a central authority to be authorised to exercise banking business would not be allowed to if it did not demonstrate to be part of a depositors' protection scheme.

69 In full: Directive 94/19/EC of the European Parliament and of the Council of 30 May 1994 on deposit-guarantee schemes as regards the coverage level and the payout delay, EJ L 68/3 (henceforth also 'Directive 94/19').

70 According to Directive 94/19, Recital 9, 'the deposit-guarantee schemes must intervene as soon as deposits become unavailable'.

71 As emphasised later, the amendment occurred as late as 2009 by means of Directive 2009/14. In full: Directive 2009/14/EC of the European Parliament and of the Council of 11 March 2009 amending Directive 94/19/EC on deposit-guarantee schemes as regards the coverage level and the pay-out delay, OJ L 68/3.

72 As well as within the EU legislation, an important role, in the legislation aimed to protect depositors, has also been played for a while by further supra national organisations. This is the case with the G20 or 'The Group of Twenty', the forum for the governments and central bank governors from 20 major economies in the world. The body called the Financial Stability Forum ('FSF'), originally created by the G20 in the wake of the Asian financial crisis, was succeeded, at the London Summit of 2 April 2009, by an additional one, the Financial Stability Board ('FSB'), the latter having a more extended membership (G20, *Declaration on Strengthening the Financial System* (2 April 2009)). The FSB includes representatives from the heads of the national treasuries, central banks and financial authorities as well as representatives from the principal financial institutions, other technical committees and observers such as the EU.

For the purposes of the topic at stake, worthy of mention is a document by the FSF (*FSF, Principles for Sound Compensation Practices* (April 2009) at www.financialstabilityboard.org/publications/r_0904b.pdf, accessed 3 July 2014) where nine Principles for Sound Compensation Practices have been spelled out (particularly, effective governance of compensation and effective alignment of compensation with prudent risk-taking and effective supervisory oversight and engagement by stakeholders). The FSB followed up on these, by issuing a series of implementation standards in September 2009 dealing with governance, compensation and a new piece of legislation has been recently passed, that being the so-called DGS Directive,[73] the purpose of which is to create a more harmonised pan-European system of protection for depositors.

An assessment of the new legislation represents the focal point of this section, although any discernible similarities and differences between past and future statute will be addressed also.

7.2.2.1 From 'minimum' to 'maximum' harmonisation

Under the previous piece of legislation (Directive 1994/19), a requisite level of protection to be afforded to the depositor was not imposed on each country by way of a fixed figure; rather, 'harmonisation' represented, merely, a *minimum* sum of money that the depositor was entitled to claim from the national scheme in cases where the funds held by the relevant bank were unavailable. In such a scenario, each Member State was obligated to comply with this 'nominal' minimum figure.[74] Therefore, the limit functioned as a 'floor', while a country was fully entitled to afford to its depositors a higher level of protection than that required under the Directive.

There are historically two opposing traditions: the laissez-faire approach, with its reluctance to sanction any form of protection scheme;[75] and the rigid approach, with its traditional concern for the customer affected by the insolvency of the bank.[76] In finding some middle ground, the level of protection had leaned towards the former camp, being, as it was, initially fixed in the original version of Directive 94/19, art. 7(1) at ECU 20,000 (later Euro 20,000).[77] More recently, in the aftermath of the financial crisis of 2007/08, the EU legislator elected to increase the minimum limit of protection. More specifically, Directive 2009/14 stipulates that the minimum limit is now Euro 100,000.[78]

---

continued

capital, pay structure and risk alignment, disclosure and supervisory oversight (Financial Stability Board, *FSB Principles for Sound Compensation Practices – Implementation Standards* (September 2009), www.financialstabilityboard.org/publications/r_090925c.pdf, accessed 3 July 2014).

73 Pursuant to art. 22 of Directive 2014/49, this piece of legislation has been in force since 1 July 2014, although some specific provisions (e.g. art. 6(1) on the amount of the coverage for each depositor) were delayed until 4 July 2015. Finally, as far as the transposition in each country is concerned, art. 20 stipulates that the relevant laws, regulations and administrative provisions shall be brought into force by 3 July 2015, although for some specific provisions (e.g. art. 8(4) of the DGS Directive) the compliance is postponed until 31 May 2016.

74 For a commentary on Directive 1994/19, see, e.g. C Proctor, *The Law and Practice of International Banking* (Oxford University Press, Oxford 2010) 265, 268.

75 To simplify this school of thought, and also to avoid any moral hazard on the part of both the depositors and the bank directors, the customers should take the brunt of the money deposited with the bank, as it is their responsibility to check in advance the reliability of the financial institution.

76 This approach seems to reflect the legal tradition of civil law jurisdictions and their more accentuated and developed attitude to consumer protection.

77 An additional stipulation (in accordance with art. 7(4)) provided that the Member State may be liable to guarantee a sum constituting no less than 90 per cent of the minimum amount of Euro 20,000. In other words, the depositor may experience his minimum cover watered down by an additional 10 per cent if the legislation of that EU country had chosen to be less generous towards the rights of the depositors. An opportunity that, for instance, Britain did not miss taking, in its first national provisions.

78 Art. 1 of the DGS Directive carried a significant amendment of para. 1 of art. 7 of Directive 1994/19, by prescribing that '[b]y 31 December 2010, Member States shall ensure that the coverage for the aggregate deposits of each depositor shall be set at Euro 100 000 in the event of deposits being unavailable.' Moreover, the previously optional final 10 per cent of the minimum limit has been removed. For countries such as Britain, not adopting the Euro, albeit part of the EU, 'the amounts of national currencies effectively paid to depositors are equivalent to those set out in the Directive' (art. 1(1)(b) of the DGS Directive).

Bearing the above in mind, the DGS Directive has recently advanced a different approach to tackling the protection of the depositor; rather than striving for 'minimum harmonisation', 'a uniform level of protection', i.e. maximum harmonisation is promoted.[79] To elaborate, in a clear departure from past arrangements, no country shall be permitted to increase the 'floor' of protection (currently Euro 100,000) although, for 'certain transactions, or serving certain social or other purposes', a Member State shall be entitled to increase the protection.[80]

The reason for this radical shift of direction was the observation that the previous system of minimum harmonisation had created, at the time of the financial crisis in 2008, a number of significant distortions. Among these, of particular significance was the movement of depositors from countries where the level of protection was low to others where a greater deal of protection was offered.[81]

7.2.2.2 From the local to the pan-European scheme

Pursuant to the previous statute, but also in light of the new DGS Directive, each Member State must ensure, first, that a deposit protection scheme is in place in that country and, second, that the scheme guarantees the depositors of the bank not only in the country of authorisation (the 'home country') but also in any other EU and EEA country ('host country') where that bank carries out operations either through branches or by way of a mutual recognition regime. In theoretical terms, but also in practice in some countries, more than a single scheme may be in place in the same jurisdiction,[82] so long as it has been authorised by the local authority.[83]

Quite interestingly, under the previous legislation, the scheme itself, i.e. the banking sector funding the scheme, and not the local central bank where the failed credit institution has been authorised, was the final 'paymaster' of any claims lodged by the depositors.[84] Conversely, the new DGS Directive aspires to form a more mutual

79 Recital 6 of the DGS Directive.

80 Recital 26 of the DGS Directive. More specifically, according to art. 6(2) of the DGS Directive, some deposits are protected above Euro 100,000 for at least three months and up to 12 months: '(a) deposits resulting from real estate transactions relating to private residential properties; (b) deposits that serve social purposes laid down in national law and are linked to particular life events of a depositor such as marriage, divorce, retirement, dismissal, redundancy, invalidity or death; (c) deposits that serve purposes laid down in national law and are based on the payment of insurance benefits or compensation for criminal injuries or wrongful conviction.'

81 In light of the DGS Directive, as the level of protection is now fully harmonised, the topping-up process and export ban have been rendered obsolete; as the Euro 100,000 sum represents a uniform level of coverage across Europe and no potential extortion may thus arise, these two concepts are no longer applicable. Notwithstanding this, the DGS Directive establishes a transitional regime applicable to countries that, on 1 January 2008, provided a level of coverage in excess of Euro 100,000; in such cases, these countries 'may reapply that higher coverage level until 31 December 2018' (art. 19(4) of the DGS Directive) although in the intervening period the limit would be capped at Euro 300,000, regardless of whether the coverage had been previously higher.

Based on Directive 1994/19, the coverage level adopted by a specific country could have been unlimited, notwithstanding the floor of Euro 100,000.

82 See, e.g. Italy, where cooperative banks adhere to a specific scheme, organised under the aegis of the cooperative network.

83 According to the DGS Directive, art. 1, the piece of legislation applies to '(a) statutory DGSs; (b) contractual DGSs that are officially recognised as DGSs . . .; (c) institutional protection schemes that are officially recognised as DGSs . . .; (d) credit institutions affiliated to the schemes'.

84 More practically, the central bank (or, as far as the Eurozone countries are concerned, the European Central Bank) was the 'entity' which, ultimately, would guarantee, in some shape or form, the repayment of the obligations of the depositors, in cases where the same scheme of that country was not in a position to keep up with repayment of the claims.

and solidary system of deposit guarantee schemes. More specifically, art. 12 heralds the concept of a link between deposit guarantee schemes, through the mechanism of mutual borrowing between DGSs, so that any lack of liquidity inhibiting the schemes in a country can be compensated by support from schemes operating in other countries.[85]

7.2.2.3 The beneficiary

The beneficiary of the scheme, from the EU legislator's perspective, does not involve any bank costumer, but rather the holder of a 'deposit', i.e. a deposit shall mean:

> a credit balance which results from funds left in an account or from temporary situations deriving from normal banking transactions and which a credit institution is required to repay under the legal and contractual conditions applicable, including a fixed term deposit and a savings deposit.[86]

Not every depositor is expected – or indeed entitled – to be protected in accordance with the principles underpinning the EU Directives, rather exclusively 'eligible deposits', i.e. 'deposits that are not excluded from protection pursuant to Article 5' of the DGS Directive. The underlying philosophy renders the coverage applicable exclusively to the retail depositor who may subsequently lodge a claim with the scheme in place. As a result, categories of depositors such as 'financial institutions', 'insurance undertakings' or central and local authorities are 'excluded' from the safety net of EU legislation and, therefore, are unprotected by national statute also.[87]

Finally, the coverage threshold of Euro 100,000 relates to 'aggregate deposits' for each depositor, rather than for an individual deposit.[88] The obvious consequence being that the depositor will be unable to cherry-pick from two (or more) different deposits, amounting to as much as Euro 100,000 with the same financial institution. If a depositor really intended to minimise the risk, he would spread the risk among a range of institutions, rather than employing multiple deposits with a single bank. The

85 More specifically, for the borrowing to take place, some conditions must be met (art. 12(1)): (a) 'the borrowing DGS is not able to fulfil its obligations . . . because of a lack of available financial means'; (b) 'the borrowing DGS has made recourse to extraordinary contributions'; (c) 'the borrowing DGS undertakes the legal commitment that the borrowing funds will be used in order to pay [the claims of the depositors]'; (d) 'the borrowing DGS is not currently subject to an obligations to repay a loan to other DGSs'; (e) 'the borrowing DGS states the amount of money requested'; (f) 'the total amount lent does not exceed 0.5 per cent of covered deposits of the borrowing DGS'; (g) 'the borrowing DGS informs EBA without delay and states the reasons why the conditions [required under legislation] are fulfilled and the amount of money requested.'

86 Art. 2(1)(3) of the DGS Directive. The concept of 'deposit' was contained in the previous Directive 1994/19, under its Art. 1. The bond-holder used to be excluded from the cover (Directive 1994/19, art. 1(3)), although technically speaking a bond is a bank debt, albeit payable upon expiry rather than upon demand. Now, in the new legislative scenario, the exclusion can be inferred from art. 5(1)(k) of the DGS Directive ('debt securities issued by a credit institution and liabilities arising out of own acceptances and promissory notes' are 'excluded' from the repayment).

87 Originally, under Directive 1994/19, this used to be legislated under its Annex I, deposits by 'financial institutions' (art. 1), 'insurance undertakings' (art. 2), 'government and central administrative authorities' (art. 3), 'provincial, regional, local and municipal authorities' (art. 4), 'collective investment undertakings' (art. 5), 'pension and retirement funds' (art. 6). Now, the DGS Directive, at art. 5, seems to (in essence) confirm these exclusions, albeit in different language among others, 'deposits made by other credit institutions on their own behalf and for their own account' (a), 'deposits by financial institutions' (c), 'deposits by investment firms' (e), deposits by insurance companies (f), 'deposits by collective investment undertakings' (h), 'deposits by pension and retirement funds' (i), 'deposits by public authorities' (j).

88 Art. 6(1) of the DGS Directive.

tenor of the DGS Directive remains unclear, however, over whether the limit applies to each bank or each banking group. As the EU legislation specifically refers to credit institutions, it is possible to infer that the protection level remains intact irrespective of the existence of a banking group.[89]

The actual modalities, whereby the depositor may reclaim his money, are subject to the details of the scheme existing in that country. Usually, at national level, all authorised schemes are hinged on bylaws and regulations stipulating the detailed guidelines to be adopted. Despite this, the EU legislator takes pains to spell out the general principles which, as a matter of course, every scheme must comply with.

The reliability of a 'protection scheme' is also dependent on the speed with which the depositor's claim is settled, subsequent to the default of a financial institution. It is no coincidence that the DGS Directive, in this respect, has been increasingly generous to the depositor. Most recently, the DGS Directive has reduced the time limit even further to 'seven working days of the date on which a relevant administrative authority makes a determination . . . or a judicial authority makes a ruling' in respect of that specific credit institution.[90] Furthermore, under the new DGS Directive, a postponement, which shall not exceed three months, is granted exclusively in regard to depositors 'not absolutely entitled to the sums held in an account'.[91]

7.3 Protection of the investor

7.3.1 Introduction

The investor is a person who, in the simplest terms, extends money or financial instruments to an investment firm for the purpose of investment in financial instruments. Therefore, the investor is conceptually distinct from a depositor; the latter deposits money with the bank, which is, in turn, typically obligated to return the money immediately if requested to do so. Conversely, the investor transfers money or securities to the investment firm, which will subsequently engage in a speculative activity, i.e. the investment. Despite these conceptual distinctions between investor

89 For example, if a depositor was the holder of two bank accounts, of Euro 100,000, with two credit institutions belonging to the same group, in the case of insolvency of the group, it is possible to affirm, based on the black letter of the legislation, that he can claim from the competent scheme Euro 100,000 for each deposit.

90 Art. 8 of the DGS Directive. Nevertheless, for this new accelerated deadline, a transitional period until 31 December 2023 shall be in force (art. 8(2)), allowing each Member State to derogate from the new strict deadline. More specifically, instead of the fast payment by seven working days, a Member State may establish repayment periods of no longer than '20 working days until 31 December 2018' (art. 8(2)(a)), or '15 working days from 1 January 2023 until 31 December 2020' (art. 8(2)(b)) or '10 working days from 1 January 2021 until 31 December 2023' (art. 8(2)(c)). In its original version, Directive 1994/19 prescribed, at art. 10, that any claims should be settled 'within three months' of the date the supervisory authority had declared the institution 'unable to repay its depositors' or, alternatively, the date on which the same judicial authority had likewise arrived at the same conclusion. As a result of the amendments carried out by Directive 2009/19, the time limit was dramatically curtailed to 20 working days, with the added clarification that this time limit should include also 'the collection and transmission of the accurate data on depositors and deposits, which are necessary for the verification of the claims.' It is worth noting that, during this transitional period, in circumstances where the DGSs were not in a position to make the repayable amount available within seven working days, 'they shall ensure that depositors have access to an appropriate amount of their covered deposits to cover the cost of living within five working days of a request' (art. 8(4) of the DGS Directive).

91 See combined reading of arts 8(3) and 7(3) of the DGS Directive.

and depositor, the investment business is nonetheless afforded a form of protection, in accordance with principles and criteria addressed earlier in this chapter and similar to the depositor protection just discussed. In brief, the rationale behind the legislative intervention of the EU in this area is the overarching principle that any protection of investors is instrumental in maintaining public confidence in the financial system, and to secure both these elements (protection and confidence) would ensure a proper functioning of the market in this area of the financial industry.

7.3.2 Directive on Investor Compensation Schemes

First and foremost, in terms of primary sources, it is worth noting that the leading piece of legislation in this area is Directive 97/9/EC ('Compensation Scheme Directive').[92] As required by this statute, in each Member State one or more investor compensation schemes must be 'introduced and officially recognised'.[93] The corollary of this principle is that 'no investment firm authorized in that Member State may carry on investment business unless it belongs to such a scheme.'[94] Albeit indirectly, it can be inferred that participation or non-participation in at least one scheme will be sufficient to ensure the investment firm is authorised or, in cases where that firm was excluded from the scheme, a reason for it to be struck off respectively.[95]

The conceptual distinction between investor and depositor is echoed in the level of protection afforded to each at a legislative level.[96] The EU legislator has afforded both categories a degree of protection, although the way in which each is implemented differs significantly.

The cover afforded to the investor is triggered by two scenarios: the inability of the investment firm either to 'repay money owed to or belonging to investors and held on their behalf in connection with investment business' or to 'return to investors any instruments belonging to them and held, administered or managed on their behalf in connection with investment business.'[97] This contrasts sharply with the sole scenario contemplated by the DGS Directive on depositors, where only the inability to repay money to the depositor triggers the DGS. It is possible to affirm that this can be attributed to the fact that investment business is more articulated and complex than banking business, the latter operating exclusively on money given to the bank rather than involving financial instruments.

92 In full: Directive 97/0/EC of the European Parliament and of the Council of 3 March 1997 on investor-compensation schemes, OJ L 084, 26/03/1997.
93 Art. 2(1) of the Compensation Scheme Directive.
94 Art. 2(1), part 2, of the Compensation Scheme Directive.
95 For a discussion on the Italian scheme of protection for investors, see P de Gioia-Carabellese, 'Commentary to Artt. 59, 60 and 72', in G Alpa and F Capriglione (eds), *Commentario al Testo Unico delle Disposizioni in Materia di Intermediazione Finanziaria* (CEDAM, Padua 1998) 563, 575, 582–692, 700.
96 The 'investor' is defined as 'any person who has entrusted money with or instruments to an investment firm in connection with investment business' (art. 1(4) of the Compensation Scheme Directive). Within the Compensation Scheme Directive, the 'depositor' is not defined; however, as already mentioned above in this chapter, 'deposit' is 'any credit balance which results from funds left in an account or from temporary situations deriving from normal banking transactions and which a credit institution must repay under the legal and contractual conditions applicable, and any debt evidenced by a certificate issued by a credit institution.'
97 Art. 2(2), part 2, of the Compensation Scheme Directive.

In terms of level of cover, each Member State is entitled to fix a specific figure, deemed as sufficient to protect the investor in cases where the investment firm is unable to honour its obligations. The harmonisation process, however, ensures that this sum cannot drop below a minimum amount fixed by the EU legislator, currently corresponding to Euro 20,000.[98] The less generous sum allocated for the investor, when compared to that for the depositor, can be attributed to the fact that, as alluded to above, the investment business is by definition a more speculative activity than the deposit of money with a bank. The Directive, in this respect, is adamant that investors should 'take due care in their choice of investment firms.'[99] Accordingly, an exclusive group of investors (or, more specifically, investors involved with a small sum of money and/or instruments) fall within the safety net of the EU legislator. Nonetheless, a Member State could decide to increase the level of protection for investors to a sum well beyond what is required.

The cover shall constitute an aggregate of the claims of that investor against the insolvent investment firm so that, should an investor hold several accounts with that firm where each is slightly below the limit of cover in that Member State, he cannot (unfairly) benefit from the full restitution of each, if the aggregate sum of all the accounts belonging to him is exceeded.

Practically, the means by which investors are informed and paid their claim vis-à-vis the investment firm, is established by the compensation scheme stepping into the shoes of the insolvent investment firm. In this respect, the Compensation Scheme Directive is concise and simply stipulates that the 'compensation scheme shall take appropriate measures to inform investors of the determination or ruling' which may have affected the investment firm (i.e. the decision of either an administrative authority or a judicial one).[100] The compensation scheme 'may fix a period during which investors shall be required to submit their claims', although the EU legislator goes on to clarify that this period cannot be less than five months from the date when the 'determination or ruling' of the administrative or judicial authority has been issued or, at any rate, has been made public.[101] Obviously, this minimum period of time has been implemented to protect investors who may ignore or be unaware of any default on the part of their counterparty; an overly restricted time period would, de facto, deprive them of their legal entitlement to lodge their claims.

Following the same line of reasoning, the EU legislator wishes to ensure that, in safeguarding the credibility of the financial market, claims are paid 'as soon as possible and at the latest within three months of the establishment of the eligibility and the amount of the claim.' In this respect, any delay in repayment to the investors must be exclusively attributed to 'wholly exceptional circumstances and in special cases' and, in any case, must be authorised by the competent authority. If utilised, this extension cannot exceed a period of three months.[102]

98 Art. 4 of the Compensation Scheme Directive.
99 Recital 13 of the Compensation Scheme Directive.
100 See art. 9(1) of the Compensation Scheme Directive.
101 Art. 9(1) of the Compensation Scheme Directive.
102 Art. 9(2) of the Compensation Scheme Directive.

Finally, the overlap that potentially may arise between the two Directives in regard to the protection of depositors and investors, in cases where a bank offering both deposits and authorised to carry out investment services became insolvent, should be acknowledged. In such a scenario, that credit institution would be under the stewardship of two schemes: the investor scheme, for customers who have engaged in investment services; the depositor scheme, for customers who, conversely, have deposited funds with the bank. The customer can lodge a claim under both the schemes, if he was both a depositor and an investor. The sum of cover available to that customer would be the limit prescribed for the applicable investor protection scheme, as far as his investment activities are concerned; additionally, it would be the (typically higher) limit with regard to the sum of money deposited with that same counterparty.

7.4 Further reading

Capriglione, F, 'Financial Crisis and Sovereign Debt: The European Union between Risks and Opportunities' (2012) 1 *Law and Economics Yearly Review* 4, 76

Collier, PM, *Accounting for Managers* (4th edn Wiley, 2012)

Cranston, R, *Principles of Banking Law* (2nd edn Oxford University Press, Oxford 2002)

de Gioia-Carabellese, P, 'Commentary to artt. 59, 60 and 72', in G Alpa and F Capriglione (eds), *Commentario al Testo Unico delle Disposizioni in Materia di Intermediazione Finanziaria* (CEDAM, Padua 1998) 563, 575, 582–692, 700

Ellinger, EP, Lomnicka, E, and Hare, CVM, *Ellingers' Modern Banking Law* (Oxford University Press, Oxford 2011)

Financial Stability Board, *Principles for Sound Compensation Practices – Implementation Standards* (September 2009), www.financialstabilityboard.org/publications/r_090925c.pdf, accessed 3 July 2014

Haentjens, M, 'Bank Recovery and Resolution: An Overview of International Initiatives' (2014) *International Insolvency Law Review* 255, 270

Haentjens, M, and Wessels, B, (eds), *Bank Recovery and Resolution: A Conference Book* (Eleven Publishers, The Hague 2014)

Hess, B, Oberhammer, P, and Pfeiffer, T, *European Insolvency Law The Heidelberg-Luxemburg-Vienna Report* (CH Beck, Hart and Nomos, Munich 2013)

Hudson, A, *Hudson: The Law of Finance* (2nd edn Sweet & Maxwell, London 2013)

McBryde, WW, Flessner, A, and Kortmann, SCJJ, *Principles of European Insolvency Law, Volume 4* (Kluwer Legal Publishers, Deventer 2003)

Mezzacapo, S, 'Towards a New Regulatory Framework for banking Recovery and Resolution in the EU' (2013) 2 *Law and Economics Yearly Review* (part 1) 213, 241

Mooney, C, and Morton, G, 'Harmonizing Insolvency Law for Intermediated Securities: The Way Forward', in T Keijser (ed), *Transnational Securities Law* (Oxford University Press, Oxford 2014) 193, 239

Proctor, C, *The Law and Practice of International Banking* (Oxford University Press, Oxford 2010)

Russo, CA, 'The New Course of EU State Aid Rules during the 2007–09 Financial Crisis', in K Alexander and R Dhumale (eds), *Research Handbook on International Financial Regulation* (Edward Elgar, Cheltenham (UK) and Northampton (MA – USA) 2012)

Wessels, B, and Moss, G, *EU Banking and Insurance Insolvency* (Oxford University Press, Oxford 2006)

7.5 Questions

7.1 What is the main difference between a 'reorganisation measure' and a 'winding-up procedure' under the Winding-up Directive (Directive 2001/24)?

7.2 'Under the Winding-up Directive, the authority in charge of a bank insolvency procedure is exclusively an administrative one, i.e. a government authority, rather than a judicial one.' Discuss.

7.3 In the case of the winding-up procedure of a bank, is it true that the authority in charge of that procedure is each and every one of the authorities where that 'insolvent' EU bank operates through either subsidiaries or branches?

7.4 Discuss the underlying philosophy of the Bank Recovery and Resolution Directive (Directive 2014/59).

7.5 Discuss the scope of both the BRRD and the SRM, and the reason for the difference.

7.6 What is the 'bail-in tool' according to the Bank Recovery and Resolution Directive?

7.7 'The Deposit Guarantee Scheme Directive (Directive 2014/49) has unified European law as regards the level of protection of depositors'. Discuss.

7.8 What is the rationale behind the protection of the depositor and investor?

7.9 What would be the difference (if any) between depositor protection and investor protection?

Chapter 8

The investment firm and fund

Chapter contents

8.1 Investment firm versus bank

Alongside banks, insurance companies and pension funds, the investment firm is traditionally considered one of the key players in the financial industry. By definition, investment firms are the operators of investment services and investment activities relating to financial instruments.[1] Thus, the investment firm is to the capital markets what the bank is to the banking sector and, finally, what the insurance company is to the insurance market. For instance, the execution of an order to sell or buy securities listed on a stock market is a typical example of activity reserved to investment firms. However, while three of the aforementioned four sectors (banking, insurance and pension funds) have maintained a well-established constitution and adhere to clearly defined boundaries, the same cannot be said of investment business.

Capital markets have been swept up in a three-decade-long wave of intensification triggered by the globalisation of economies and the burgeoning role played by stock markets; the shift from small, 'boutique' brokerage firms to modern investment firms and the direct involvement of banks in investment activities. As a result of this last development, the once prominent demarcation line between investment firms and banks has steadily been whittled away, with investment banks (i.e. banks operating principally in the capital markets) fulfilling an increasingly important role on the stage dominated by investment businesses and traditional investment firms (or brokerage houses). Thus, investment firms have been progressively integrated within major banking groups in accordance with the composition of a universal bank.[2] Where in this chapter we refer to 'investment firms', we therefore mean both investment firms per se, i.e. traditional boutique firms, and banks acting in the capacity of investment firms, i.e. banks performing investment services and activities.

The investment business, in its own right, has grown enormously quantitatively speaking, which is due in part to the emergence of new channels of marketing and selling of the relevant products, i.e. door-to-door and online activities. Accordingly, from a legal perspective, the business at stake is governed by detailed legal provisions and rules, the discussion of which forms the basis of this chapter.

Furthermore, the evolution of the markets and incorporation of new technologies has equipped investment businesses with an array of new financial products and innovative forms of organisation. Besides investment firms, the investment business is dominated by investment funds. Where investment firms, in essence, facilitate the sale and purchase of financial instruments, investment funds form financial instruments themselves. This is certainly the case when it comes to the undertakings in collective investment, and the specific securities – the units – representing the participation of the investor in the common fund. So as to leave no stone unturned, this form of investment business, as well as the alternative investment funds, will also be discussed in the present chapter.

---

1 For the demarcation line between investment services and investment activities, see below, section 8.2.

2 See Chapter 5 above.

8.2 The investment firm under MiFID

8.2.1 Reserved activities

The investment firm, as an entity operating in the financial sector, is legislated upon by the EU; the relevant pieces of legislation in this case are Regulation (EU) No 600/2014 on markets in financial instruments ('MiFIR')[3] and Directive 2014/65 on markets in financial instruments ('MiFID II').[4] According to art. 4 of the latter statute, the investment firm is defined as 'any legal person whose regular occupation or business is the provision of one or more investment services to third parties and/or the performance of one or more investment activities on a professional basis.' This definition encapsulates the economic reality of modern capital markets where boutique investment firms together with banks are the main operators in the stock markets to accommodate the pursuit of investment activities.

In turn, 'investment services and investment activities'[5] – in other words, the subjects of the investment contracts that the investment firm (and the bank) enters into with its customers[6] – are elaborated upon under Annex I of MiFID II, Section A of which specifies nine 'undertakings'[7] to include the '[r]eception and transmission of orders in relation to one of more financial instruments', the '[e]xecution of orders on behalf of clients', '[d]ealing on own account', '[p]ortfolio management', '[i]nvestment advice', '[u]nderwriting of financial instruments and/or placing of financial instruments on a firm commitment basis', '[p]lacing of financial instruments without a firm commitment basis',[8] '[o]peration of an MTF [multilateral trading

3 In full: Regulation (EU) No 600/2014 of the European Parliament and of the Council of 15 May 2014 on markets in financial instruments and amending Regulation (EU) No 648/2012 [on OTC derivatives, central counterparties and trade repositories], OJ L 173.

4 In full: Directive 2014/65/EU of the European Parliament and of the Council of 15 May 2014 on markets in financial instruments and amending directive 2002/92/EC and Directive 2011/61/EU, OJ L 173. MiFID II was published in the Official Journal of the European Union on 12 June 2014 and, according to its art. 93, its transposition in each Member State shall take place for the nearly totality of its provisions, by 3 July 2016. The previous Directive governing this area, Directive 2004/39 or MiFID I, should be phased out by 3 January 2017, according to art. 94 of MiFID II. We have indicated some similarities and differences between MiFID I and II in Chapter 4.

5 From a legal point of view, investment services and investment activities are different: 'investment services' are services carried out by the investment firm *in the interests of the client*, even though under its own name, while investment activities are carried out by the investment firm *in its own interest*. A typical example of the latter is the activity of organisation of Multilateral Trading Facilities ('MTFs').

6 The definition of 'investment contract' is commonly adopted in the US, where the legislation misses a concept of investment services and investment activities. See, among others, LD Soderquist and TA Gabaldon, *Securities Law* (2nd ed Foundation Press and Thomson/West, New York 2004) 3. From a comparative analysis between the EU and the US, it is also worth noting that the comprehensive category of 'investment activity' carried out by an investment firm would correspond, basically, to the following categories of professionals: (a) the 'broker', as 'the person engaged in the business of effecting transactions in securities for the account of others'; (b) the 'dealer' as 'the person engaged in the business of buying and selling securities for his own account'; (c) the 'investment adviser' as 'the person who, for compensation, engages in the business of advising others . . . as to the advisability of investing in, purchasing or selling securities' (see TL Hazen, *Securities Regulation in a Nutshell* (10th edn West Publishing/Thomson Reuters, St Paul (MN) 2009) 196, 197).

7 In MiFID I the investment activities and investment services used to be eight; this is because the OTF, recently introduced by MiFID II (see later), was not part of the definition.

8 An EU definition of underwriting and placement is not provided, although an interpretation of them can be inferred (P Sfameni and A Giannelli, *Diritto degli Intermediari e dei Mercati Finanziari* (EGEA, Milan 2013) 85, 86). More specifically, underwriting and/or placing, if relating to financial instruments, are agreements between the issuer (or the offeror) and the investment firm in charge of the placement. Under the relevant terms and conditions, the latter undertakes to offer to the public the financial instruments issued, at a specific price and, in some cases, in previously defined slots of time.

facility]',[9] '[o]peration of an OTF [organised trading facility].'[10] Of these nine investment services and investment activities, portfolio management might be worthy of a brief clarification. Individual portfolio management refers to the contractual relationship existing between a customer and a professional (the investment firm), where the latter uses its expertise as an investment advisor for the investment of securities and money of an individual customer. It is different from collective portfolio management, where the investment firm is an advisor to a fund, the units of which belong to a plurality of investors, rather than a single investor.[11]

Pursuant to Annex 1 of MiFID II, Section C,[12] the investment services and investment activities just referred to must relate to 'financial instruments', which are, in essence, distinguished between 'transferrable securities', such as shares, bonds and derivatives.[13] In respect to the latter, art. 4 of Section C of Annex 1 contemplates:

> [o]ptions, futures, swaps, forward rate agreements and any other derivative contracts relating to securities, currencies, interest rates or yields, emission allowances or other derivatives instruments, financial indices or financial measures which may be settled physically or in cash.

Additionally, financial instruments are also, *inter alia*, 'money-market instruments' (such as covered bonds), and 'units in collective investment undertakings'.[14]

Finally, MiFID II also addresses the category of 'ancillary services', which cannot be defined as reserved services; theoretically, they could be discharged by non-investment firms also. However, the EU legislator does not allow an investment firm to carry out exclusively one or more ancillary services, if at least one 'main' investment service or investment activity has not been authorised. The definition of these ancillary services is furnished under Annex 1 of MiFID II, particularly within Section B.[15] Among these activities, reference can be made to:

---

continued

The placement 'on a firm commitment basis' entails a full responsibility of the investment firm to buy the residual financial instruments that were not offered; it is quite obvious that this placement, differently from the other one ('without a firm commitment basis') will be more onerous for the offeror/issuer as the specific commitment of the investment firm is usually 'priced'.

9 A 'multilateral trading facility' is 'a multilateral system, operated by an investment firm or a market operator, which brings together multiple third-party buying and selling interests in financial instruments – in the system and in accordance with non-discretionary rules – in a way that results in an [investment contract]' (art. 4(1)(22) of MiFID II).

10 An 'organised trading facility' is 'a multilateral system which is not a regulated market or an MTF and in which multiple third-party buying and selling interests in bonds, structured finance products, emission allowances or derivatives are able to interact in the system in a way that results in an [investment contract]' (art. 4(1)(23) of MiFID II). This specific investment activity did not used to be included in the previous Directive 2004/39, MiFID I, and therefore it is a novelty of MiFID II.

11 See D Busch and DA De Mott, *Liability of Asset Managers* (Oxford University Press, Oxford 2012) 3. For the concept of collective fund or mutual fund see below, section 8.3.

12 Also in MiFID I, the 'financial instruments' used to be defined under Annex I, Section C.

13 'Security', rather than 'financial instrument', is the terminology adopted in the US. See s. 2(a) of the Securities Act (1933) (see LD Soderquist and TA Gabaldon, *Securities Law* (2nd edn Foundation Press and Thomson/West, New York 2004) 2).

14 See also Chapter 11.

15 It is worth noting that the 'ancillary activities' contemplated under Annex I, Section B, of MiFID II are basically similar to those previously mentioned in MiFID I, and contained in the same Annex I, Section B.

1 Safekeeping and administration of financial instruments for the account of clients, including custodianship and related services such as cash/collateral management and excluding maintaining securities accounts at the top tier level;
2 Granting credits or loans to an investor to allow him to carry out a transaction in one or more financial instruments, where the firm granting the credit or loan is involved in the transaction;
3 Advice to undertakings on capital structure, industrial strategy and related matters and advice and services relating to mergers and the purchase of undertakings;
4 Foreign exchange services where these are connected to the provision of investment services;
5 Investment research and financial analysis or other forms of general recommendation relating to transactions in financial instruments;
6 Services related to underwriting.

8.2.2 Initial capital and authorisation process

Similarly to what is required for credit institutions, an investment firm must be endowed with a minimal capital so as to ensure that the business has a financial buffer to accommodate losses, and is carried out seriously and with a certain degree of commitment. In this respect, the EU legislator established floors for the Member States, also connected with the kind of services provided. The relevant provisions, initially codified in a specific piece of legislation (i.e. Directive 2006/49, specifically concerned with the capital adequacy of investment firms and credit institutions), have now been transposed into the recent CRD IV legislation, which concerns, among others, 'prudential supervision of credit institutions and investment firms'.[16] Apart from the cosmetic variation of the pertinent legislative instrument, the substance of the provisions has remained basically the same: (a) the initial capital of an investment firm shall be of at least Euro 730,000;[17] however, (b) such minimum capital may be reduced to Euro 125,000 for investment firms having a more limited activity;[18] and finally, (c) the floor may, at the discretion of the relevant Member State, be further reduced to Euro 50,000[19] for an investment firm that 'is not authorised to hold client money or securities, to deal for its own account, to underwrite issues on a firm commitment basis.'

As a result of the definitions provided by Annex I of MiFID II, any undertaking of investment services and investment activities on financial instruments is a reserved activity, permissible solely to those individuals or entities securing prior authorisation from the competent authority, as established in each Member State. In this respect, art. 5 of MiFID II[20] stipulates that:

16 See, more extensively, Chapter 5.
17 Art. 28(1) of CRD IV.
18 More specifically, according to art. 29(1) of CRD IV, an investment firm not dealing 'in any financial instruments for its own account or [not underwriting] issues of financial instruments on a firm commitment basis, but which holds client money or securities and which offers one or more of the following services . . .: a) the reception and transmission of investors' orders for financial instruments; (b) the execution of investors' orders for financial instruments; (c) the management of individual portfolios of investment in financial instruments.'
19 Art. 29(3) of CRD IV.
20 This provision basically mirrors art. 5 of MiFID I.

> Each Member State shall require that the provision of investment services and/or the performance of investment activities as a regular occupation or business on a professional basis be subject to prior authorisation in accordance with this Chapter. Such authorisation shall be granted by the home Member State competent authority designated in accordance with Article 67.[21]

The competent authority grants the authorisation, to the benefit of the investment firm, for one or more investment services and/or investment activities[22] required by the applicant. As already stated, the reserved investment services and investment activities can be exercised by an authorised EU bank also. In this case, however, no specific authorisation under MiFID II is prescribed, which means that, de facto, the authority overseeing a bank (e.g. the Bundesbank in Germany, the Banca d'Italia in Italy) will authorise the pursuit and undertaking of investment services by EU banks.[23]

It can be inferred from art. 6 of MiFID II[24] that a request lodged with the home country authority may relate to the full spectrum of investment services and activities, but also just one investment service may be requested and allowed. Any initial authorisation(s) granted for one or more of the activities does not prohibit the investment firm concerned from making a further request, at a later stage, for an extension of the authorisation, so that additional activities can be included.

The principle of an EU passport, firmly entrenched in the operations undertaken by banks,[25] is *mutatis mutandis* adopted by MiFID II in order to define the kinds of cross-border activities that the authorised entity can perform, either through the establishment of branches or in the cross-border provision of services.[26]

---

21 Chapter I, Title II.

22 Remarkably, the authorisation may also cover one or more of the ancillary activities/services, although the principle is spelled out (art. 6(1)) that authorisation 'shall in no case be granted solely for the provision of ancillary services.'

23 See Recital 38 of MiFID II, basically mirroring Recital 18 of Directive 2004/39.

'Credit institutions . . . should not need another authorisation under this Directive in order to provide investment services or perform investment activities. When a credit institution decides to provide investment services or perform investment activities the competent authorities, before granting an authorisation under Directive 2013/36/EU, should verify that it complies with the relevant provisions of this Directive.' (see CM Grundmann-van de Krol, 'The Markets in Financial Instruments Directive and Asset Management', in D Busch and A De Mott (eds), *Liability of Asset Managers* (Oxford University Press, Oxford 2012) 31).

24 'The home Member State shall ensure that the authorisation specifies the investment services or activities which the investment firm is authorised to provide. The authorisation may cover one or more of the ancillary services set out in Section B of Annex 1. Authorisation shall in no case be granted solely for the provision of ancillary services.'

25 See above, sections 1.3 and 6.2.

26 Art. 6(3) of MiFID II. The details of this cross-border activity and the relevant modalities are contained in the same MiFID II, art. 34, as far as the freedom to provide cross-border investment services and activities is concerned, and art. 35, as regards the freedom to establish a branch. Basically, without entering into the minutiae of the specific provisions, the rules are, *mutatis mutandis*, those provided for credit institutions (see Chapter 6 above).

Therefore, the competent authority of the home Member State, within one month of receiving the information of the investment firm to provide services in a further EU country, will 'forward it to the competent authority of the host Member State' and the 'investment firm may then start to provide the investment services and activities concerned in the host Member State' (art. 34 of MiFID II).

Also, as regards the freedom to establish branches, communication by the investment firm to its home country authority of its intention to open branches in a different Member State (art. 35(2) of MiFID II); as such, 'unless the competent authority of the home Member State has reason to doubt the adequacy of the administrative structure or the financial situation of an investment firm, taking into account the activities envisaged', the home authority shall provide, within three months, this communication to both the authority of the designated host country and the investment firm concerned (art. 35(3) of MiFID II). Eventually, according to art. 35(6) of

From a practical point of view, the request, and subsequent wait, for authorisation from the home country authority may be a time-consuming process. This is indicative of the legal complexity inhibiting the administrative procedure, where the supervisor shall be thorough to the point that he 'is fully satisfied that the applicant complies with all requirements under the provisions adopted pursuant to this Directive.'[27] However, the time allocated to the relevant authority is not without restriction. Art. 7(3) of MiFID II suggests an allotted time period for each Member State of six months in which the process must be completed, and the approval or rejection of the application disclosed. It is a prerequisite of any application that the information provided be extensive, and must include 'a programme of operations setting out inter alia the types of business envisaged and the organisational structure'.[28]

8.2.3 Fitness of the directors, notification of qualifying shareholders

The investment firm business, and the delicate area in which it operates, is acknowledged by the EU legislator. In art. 9(3) of MiFID II, it is prescribed that each Member State shall be required to ensure that:

> the management body of an investment firm defines, oversees and is accountable for the implementation of the governance arrangements that ensure effective and prudent management of the investment firm including the segregation of duties in the investment firm and the prevention of conflicts of interest, and in a manner that promotes the integrity of the market and the interest of clients.[29]

Coupled with this is the provision, comparable with that applicable to banks under the corresponding legislation, stipulating that the national legislations ensure the management of the investment firms be undertaken by at least two persons meeting the requirements laid down above.

The identity of persons having, directly or indirectly, a qualifying holding in an investment firm must be communicated to the relevant supervisory authority, typically as an essential part of the application.[30] As for investment firms (and similar to banks),

---

continued

MiFID II, the branch shall be established and shall be able to commence its business, once it has received such a communication from the competent authority of the host Member State or, if this was not communicated, 'at the latest after two months from the date of transmission of the communication by the competent authority of the home Member State.' It is worth noting that, according to art. 35(5), where 'the competent authority of the home Member State refuses to communicate the information to the competent authority of the host Member State, it shall give reasons for its refusal to the investment firm concerned within three months of receiving all the information.'

27 Art. 7(1) of MiFID II.

28 Art. 7(2) of MiFID II.

29 The previous correspondent provision of MiFID I, at art. 9, used to be less rigorous: the EU used to require each respective Member State to ensure that the person who effectively directs the business of an investment firm is 'of sufficiently good repute and sufficiently experienced'; these requisites, to be detailed at national level, should be conducive to effecting 'the sound and prudent management of the investment firm.'

30 This is not clearly prescribed, although it is indirectly inferable from the tenor of art. 10 of MiFID II:

> The competent authorities shall not authorise the provision of investment services or performance of investment activities by an investment firm until they have been informed of the identities of the shareholders or members, whether direct or indirect, natural or legal persons, that have qualifying holdings and the amounts of those holdings.

the EU approach turns out to be more rigorous than for a company carrying out its business in a non-reserved sector. More specifically, the relevant supervisory authority assesses the identities of persons wishing to obtain, directly or indirectly, a qualifying holding in an investment firm, whereupon each Member State, according to the prescriptions set out in art. 10(1), paragraph 2, of MiFID II,[31] shall refuse authorisation if the identities of the shareholders are deemed likely to jeopardise 'the sound and prudent management of the investment firm.'[32]

The communication, to the supervisory authority, of the identity of the persons having a qualifying holding in the investment firm at the time of the application underlines the urgency with which each EU Member State must request notification of any variation of the ownership structure of the firm; also for sale and purchase of qualifying holdings.[33] Such communication must precede the conclusion of the relevant sale and purchase agreement, although it would seem to be allowed if a contract has been concluded but is made subject to the conveyance of further communication to the competent authority and its subsequent approval.[34]

The same rationale behind the sale and purchase of a qualifying holding in the investment firm applies to the increase of holding by the same person; any rise or fall above and below certain thresholds (i.e. 20 per cent, 33 per cent and 50 per cent, or the acquisition or cessation of control of the firm) shall be conveyed to the competent authority and encounter the possibility of objection, should the supervisor deem the variation prejudicial to the 'sound and prudent management' of the investment firm.[35]

8.2.4 The financial salesman

In the contemporary format of investment business, the conclusion of the investment contract is increasingly conducted beyond the physical confines of a traditional branch of the investment firm, or bank offering the same contract. The relatively recent phenomenon of online banking for instance, can no longer be deemed a new phenomenon given the degree to which it has become fully entrenched in banking operations.

A further avenue along which investment services relating to financial instruments can be offered is through the medium of door-to-door sales discharged by individuals who are not necessarily employed by the investment firm. Door-to-door sales basically constitute a promotion and sale of investment services beyond the premises of the principal, i.e. the headquarters or branches of the investment firm or bank. This activity is discharged by people who are not necessarily employees of the principal but rather agents, i.e. a self-employed category earning their living by charging a percentage based on the volume of deals they conclude on behalf of the investment

31 Basically corresponding to art. 10 of MiFID I.

32 Likewise, according to art. 10(3) of MiFID II, in cases where the influence exercised by qualifying shareholders is 'likely to be prejudicial to the sound and prudent management of an investment firm, the competent authority [shall] take appropriate measures to put an end to that situation.'

33 Therefore, the notification of the relevant ownership structure is not simply coincidental with the authorisation but also later in connection with future variations of it.

34 Art. 10(3), subpara. 2, of MiFID II; more specifically: '[T]he competent authority shall have up to three months from the date of the notification of a proposed acquisition . . . to oppose such a plan if, in view of the need to ensure sound and prudent management of the investment firm, it is not satisfied as to the suitability of the persons [having a qualifying holding].'

35 Art. 11 of MiFID II, corresponding to 10(3)(2) of MiFID I.

firm. In both cases (either employees or agents connected with the principal), the local legislation usually requires that these categories of professionals be enrolled on a special register,[36] while the enrolment is subject to the prior successful completion of a training course organised by the local authority or of a relevant exam.

It is worth stressing that not all jurisdictions acknowledge the category of the agent engaged in promoting and selling investment services of the investment firm (or bank). Nonetheless, the EU legislator requires that for those Member States adopting the 'financial agent', adequate rules are in place in order to safeguard investors. The relevant provisions worthy of a closer look are those of art. 29 of MiFID II.[37] More specifically, art. 29(1) of the same Directive stipulates that it is to the discretion of the Member State 'to allow an investment firm to appoint tied agents for the purposes of promoting the services of the investment firm'. The mandate of such a tied agent usually includes:

> soliciting business or receiving orders from clients or potential clients and transmitting them, placing financial instruments and providing advice in respect of such financial instruments and services offered by that investment firm.

It can be deduced from the above that, in other words, the tied agent is not a mandatory figure given that a Member State may decide not to contemplate them. However, if the local legislature did decide to opt in, the principles to comply with are those to be found under art. 29 of MiFID II. In this respect, the first discernible principle is clarified where art. 29(2) concerns the concept of vicarious liability of the tied agents. If the tied agent has been appointed by an investment firm, the principal shall remain 'fully and unconditionally responsible for any action or omission on the part of the tied agent when acting on behalf of the investment firm.' Linked to this is the relevant provision (again, art. 29(2)), requiring any state permitting this category of persons to ensure they disclose 'the capacity in which [they are] acting and the firm which [they are] representing when contracting or before dealing with any client or potential client.'

Not only is the investment firm vicariously liable for acts and omissions of the tied agent, but it is further required, under the auspices of each applicable local legislation, to monitor the activities of their agents in order to ensure full compliance with the EU statute.[38]

The tied agent is not an ordinary agent working for a principal, but rather is a qualified professional discharging a delicate activity with the potential to influence investors. As a result of this special statute, an EU Member State choosing to recognise tied agents must ensure that a public register (as defined in MiFID II) is formulated.[39] Enrolment is subject to, on the one hand, the 'good repute' of the prospective tied agent and, on the other, an 'appropriate general, commercial and professional knowledge' of the activity he will discharge.[40]

36 PR Wood, *Regulation of International Finance* (Thomson/Sweet and Maxwell, London 2007) 149.
37 Corresponding, with some differences, to art. 23 of MiFID I.
38 Art. 29(2), para. 3, of MiFID II.
39 Art. 29(3), para. 1, of MiFID II.
40 Art. 29(3), para., 2 of MiFID II.

The tied agent, if contemplated for use by an EU Member State, is a reserved category of professionals whose licence to operate is conditional on enrolment with the public register. The firm shall take full responsibility, when appointing these tied agents, in ensuring that exclusively those enrolled are appointed. This onus on the investment firms can be inferred, indirectly, from art. 29(5) of MiFID II.

The monitoring process undertaken by the investment firm operates not simply at the outset of the activity (when the mandate is delivered to the tied agent by the investment firm), but stretches throughout the tenure of the mandate. In this respect, the provisions existing in each Member State must ensure that:

> investment firms appointing tied agents take adequate measures in order to avoid any negative impact that the activities of the tied agent . . . could have on the activities carried out by the tied agent on behalf of the investment firm.[41]

All in all, the tied agent is an optional category engaged in the promotion and sale of investment services beyond the premises of the investment firm, through the medium of door-do-door sales. In so far as an EU Member State has chosen to create a register of tied agents, the rules to be complied with shall be those of art. 29 of MiFID II. Of these, the most significant is probably the principle of vicarious liability on the part of the principal for any act and/or omission the tied agent should incur in discharging the activity.

8.3 The investment fund

8.3.1 Introduction

This paragraph is dedicated to the discussion and analysis of one of the most sophisticated financial instruments: the units in collective investment undertakings.

By way of an introduction, it is worth emphasising that the units at stake are 'financial instruments', as MiFID II explicitly includes the units in collective investment undertakings within Section C of Annex 1. Although the units in collective investment undertakings fall within the category of financial instruments, a specific ad hoc legislation has been in place for a number of years at EU level, due to the complexity of these financial products. In fact, the units do not, in themselves, represent securities, but rather quotas or shares in an investment fund.[42] The fund is fed by the (cash) contributions of a number of investors, undertaking one or more quotas or shares. Subsequently, the fund invests this cash in securities (but possibly not exclusively securities), in accordance with the investment strategy tailored to each fund and laid down in its investment programme. From a legislative perspective, funds may be distinguished between those that qualify as undertakings for collective investment in transferable securities ('UCITS') and are covered as such by Directive

41 Art. 29(4), para. 1, of MiFID II.

42 In some countries, the fund is called an 'investment fund,' in other ones, a 'mutual fund'. Entailed to the adjective 'mutual' is the fact that the relevant units can be underwritten by any investor.

2009/65/EC ('UCITS Directive'),[43] and collective investment undertakings that are not covered by the same Directive. These latter investment undertakings, i.e. alternative funds, are covered by Directive 2011/61/EU on Alternative Investment Fund Managers ('AIFMD') and the Alternative Investment Fund Managers Regulations (AIFMD and the latter Regulations together: 'AIFMD legislation').[44] As a gross generalisation, it could be stated that these alternative investment funds use investment strategies more innovative than a traditional fund, and may have a limited number of investors providing significant amounts of money. These alternative funds include hedge funds and private equity funds. A legal analysis specifically addressing alternative investment funds and the comparatively recent piece of EU legislation is provided under section 8.3.4 below.

8.3.2 UCITS V

The specific nature of the units in collective investment undertakings (or 'mutual funds', to use the American terminology) is the justification underlying the need for detailed EU legislation in this matter, originally administered by Directive 85/611/EEC.[45] This Directive has been recast by several subsequent amendments and replaced by the above mentioned UCITS Directive. In its turn, this UCITS Directive has been amended most recently by Directive 2014/91/EU ('UCITS V Directive'; UCITS Directive and UCITS V Directive together: 'UCITS V'). The rationale behind these pieces of legislation is to harmonise, as far as possible, the prevailing rules in each respective Member State on this matter so as to ensure that a better circulation of the units can be realised, together with a strong protection of the unit-holder.[46] Additionally, the harmonisation process provides UCITS with an EU passport; once UCITS are initially authorised in one Member State, that shall suffice for purposes of authorisation in any other Member State where the units are to be marketed.

UCITS V clarifies, from the outset, the concept of undertakings for collective investment in transferable securities. Pursuant to art. 1(2) of UCITS V, 'UCITS' are 'undertakings',

---

43 Directive 2009/65/EC of the European Parliament and of the Council of 13 July 2009 on the coordination of laws, regulations and administrative provisions relating to undertakings for collective investment in transferable securities (UCITS) (recast). Most recently, this Directive has been recast by Directive 2014/91/EU of the European Parliament and of the Council of 23 July 2014 amending Directive 2009/65/EC on the coordination of laws, regulations and administrative provisions relating to undertakings for collective investment in transferable securities (UCITS) as regards depositary functions, remuneration policies and sanctions, OJ L 257.

44 Directive 2011/61/EU of the European Parliament and of the Council of 8 June 2011 on Alternative Investment Fund Managers and amending Directives 2003/41/EC and 2009/65/EC and Regulations (EC) No 1060/2009 and (EU) No 1095/2010; Commission Delegated Regulation (EU) No 694/2014 of 17 December 2013 supplementing Directive 2011/61/EU of the European Parliament and of the Council with regard to regulatory technical standards determining types of alternative investment fund managers, OJ L 183; Commission Implementing Regulation (EU) No 447/2013; and Commission Implementing Regulation (EU) No 448/2013.

45 In full: Council Directive 85/611/EEC of 20 December 1985 on the coordination of laws, regulations and administrative provisions relating to undertakings for collective investments in transferrable securities, OJ L 375/3.

For literature concerned with Directive 85/611, see PR Wood, *Regulation of International Finance* (Thomson/Sweet & Maxwell, London 2007) 158, 160.

46 HS Scott and A Gelpern, *International Finance: Transactions, Policy, and Regulation* (19th edn Foundation Press and Thomson Reuters, New York 2012) 380, 381.

> with the sole object of collective investment in transferable securities or in other liquid financial assets referred to in Article 50(1) of capital raised from the public and which operate on the principle of risk-spreading

and

> with units which are, at the request of holders, repurchased or redeemed, directly or indirectly, out of those undertakings' assets. Action taken by a UCITS to ensure that the stock exchange value of its units does not significantly vary from their net asset value shall be regarded as equivalent to such repurchase or redemption.

Thus, UCITS covered by UCITS V are exclusively of an open-ended nature, meaning that their units can be redeemed or repurchased by the fund at the request of the investor. Closed-end UCITS are outwith the scope of UCITS V,[47] likewise are, for instance, UCITS which raise capital without promoting the sale of these units to the public within the EU.[48]

Looked at from a practical point of view, investing in UCITS can be considerably advantageous to an investor: when subscribing to one or more units (i.e. when paying for one or more participation rights in UCITS), the investor relies on the ability of the management company to optimise his capital through an investment policy bound by the principles of risk-spreading. The more the management company invests money of the fund in profitable securities, the greater the likelihood that the unit-holder will see the value of his units rise. Any profits realised by the unit-holder are therefore dependent upon a future increase in the values of the units, together with the distribution of 'dividends' at the discretion of the management company.

From the above it follows that UCITS are inexorably linked with a management company (a concept defined in UCITS V) tasked with overseeing and managing the investment of the fund. Metaphorically speaking, the management company constitutes the head of operations while its apparatus (directors and managers) is in charge of professionally investing the funds raised from the public. The fund, then, is the body, i.e., the volume of money that, once raised from the public, must be invested in securities with a favourable outcome dependent on the ability of the management company to exercise the correct choice of investment. The activity at stake is speculative: the investor will have to put faith in an increase in the future value of the unit so that, as a result of the sale or redemption of the unit, he can realise a profit.[49] Conversely, he cannot be offered any guarantee on the profitability of this activity. The investment in the fund may turn out to be unprofitable; in this case, the investor forgoes any right to claim back the sum of money given at the time of the subscription. The difference between the higher value of the units at the time of the subscription

47 Closed-end funds are collective investment funds the units of which cannot be disinvested upon request of the investor but during a specific period of time. Conversely, in the open-end fund, the investor is always entitled to ask for – and obtain – the redemption of his units by the same fund, according to the modalities indicated by the fund itself.

48 Art. 3(a) and (b) of UCITS V, respectively. Conversely, closed-end funds may fall under the scope of the AIFMD Regulation; see art. 1 of the Commission Delegated Regulation (EU) No 694/2014 of 17 December 2013.

49 A partial way out for the investor – but this applies exclusively to open-end funds – is to ask for the redemption of the unit; however, in closed-end funds, the investor relinquishes any right to claim back that sum of money.

and the lower value, when the unit is sold or redeemed, constitutes the loss reported by the investor.

The limited possibilities to reclaim any money invested as just discussed do not include potential proceedings, under the applicable national private or commercial law, against the management company for a mismanagement of funds if it could be demonstrated that the maladministration had been instrumental in furthering the loss beyond what might be expected of a professional entity operating in that sector. From a private law point of view, although in various EU jurisdictions there is no such thing as a legal concept of asset manager, scholars tend to characterise the relationship between investor and management company as agency, where the investor, as principal, has given a mandate to the management company as agent to invest.[50]

Because of the delicate nature of the activity tasked to the management company, it must be authorised in advance in the country where it is established, so long as the home authority has ascertained that the specific requisites are in place; more specifically: (a) an initial capital of, in principle, Euro 125,000; (b) the names of the directors, who shall manifest the necessary good repute and experience; (c) a programme of activity; and (d) information on the close ties which may exist between the directors and natural or legal persons owning the entity. In this respect, it is important to ensure that these ties do not prevent the effective exercise of supervisory functions by the competent authorities.[51]

In the execution of its business activities, the management company is supported by a depositary responsible for the safe keeping of the assets of the mutual fund. The depositary (usually an authorised bank) is an entity which establishes a close working relationship with the management company but which remains independent of it. Actually, art. 25(1) of UCITS V expressly prescribes that '[n]o single company shall act as both investment company and depositary'. The reason for this is that, in discharging its safe keeping role, the depositary acts 'solely in the interests of the unit-holders'.[52] It is important to note that the mutual fund is one thing, but the capital and own funds of the management company itself are quite another. Therefore, the borderline etched to separate the assets of the two entities is rigorously marshalled.

8.3.3 Investment funds and rules of transparency

At the outset of this section, it was alluded to that UCITS may invest in securities in accordance with the programme of each specific fund. This programme must be made public to the prospective investors from the start. In this respect, two aspects should be emphasised.

First and foremost, any opportunity for the management company to invest the fund in securities and cash is constrained by specific mandatory rules set forth under the UCITS Directive. In the context of this book, it is not feasible to enter into the details of these regulations given their exhaustive nature. The fundamental underlying

---

50 In a pure common law jurisdiction, the paradigm of this is England and Wales. See L Van Setten and T Plews, 'England and Wales', in D Busch and DA De Mott (eds), *Liability of Asset Managers* (Oxford University Press, Oxford 2012) 331, 368. From the perspective of a mixed legal system, see D Cabrelli, 'Scotland', in D Busch and DA De Mott (eds), *Liability of Asset Managers* (Oxford University Press, Oxford 2012) 507, 533.

51 Art. 7(1)(a), (b), (c) and (2) of UCITS V, respectively.

52 Art. 25(2) of UCITS V.

principle is that UCITS will spread the risk, rather than concentrating it within a single pursuit. In adhering to this line of reasoning, a UCITS fund 'may invest no more than 5 per cent of its assets in transferrable securities issued by the same body'.[53] To allow for a higher percentage would overexpose the fund to the same issuer. Similarly, some UCITS V rules reflect the underpinning philosophy of an investment fund, i.e. an investment fund is not so much concerned with the management of the company it invests in as it is not an entrepreneur but rather an investor holding a financial interest in the profitability of the shares in which it has invested its money. In this vein, UCITS V clearly prohibits that the management company acquire, to the benefit of the fund, 'shares carrying voting rights which would enable it to exercise significant influence over the management of the issuing body'.[54]

That said, in the adjacent area of the rules of transparency, the UCITS Directive prescribes that essential documents connected to the fund be published, i.e. the prospectus, an annual report for each financial year and a half-yearly report covering the first six months of the financial year.[55] Of these documents, the greatest significance can be attached to the prospectus. In a similar vein to the general prospectus,[56] it contains the 'information necessary for investors to be able to make an informed judgement of the investment proposed to them'.[57] The prospectus relating to UCITS shall comply with the standards provided in Schedule A of Annex I of the Directive under discussion. This standard represents a 'floor' of information which the management company cannot fall short of while it is, of course, fully entitled to exceed the minimal level of data required under the statute.

8.3.4 Alternative investment funds

As has previously been alluded to in this chapter,[58] alternative investment funds are funds which are less traditional than UCITS. They are more speculative, in the sense that their investment strategy can be more innovative and the single investor may invest a larger amount of money.[59] Yet legislation, at least at EU level, was absent prior to the introduction of the AIFMD in 2011. The purpose of this comparatively recent legislation was, fundamentally, to 'provide for an internal market for AIFMs and a harmonised and stringent regulatory and supervisory framework for the activities within the Union of all AIFMs'.[60] The rationale behind the legislation at stake is practical in nature and its pertinence to the recent financial crises is clear: a number of AIFM strategies are 'vulnerable to some or several important risks in relation to investors, other market participants and markets'.[61] As a result of this, the legislator has envisaged the need to establish 'a framework capable of addressing those risks

53 Art. 52(1) of UCITS V.
54 Art. 56 of UCITS V.
55 Art. 68 of UCITS V.
56 See also above, Chapter 2.
57 Art. 69 of UCITS V.
58 Section 8.3.1.
59 An analysis of the AIFMD can be found in E Wymeersch, *Alternative Investment Fund Regulation* (Wolters Kluwer, Alphen aan den Rijn 2012); D Zetzsche (ed), *The Alternative Investment Fund Managers Directive* (Worters Kluwer, Alphen aan den Rijn 2012).
60 Recital 4 of Directive 2011/61/EU.
61 Recital 3 of Directive 2011/61.

taking into account the diverse range of investment strategies and techniques employed by AIFMs'.[62]

Interestingly, the AIFM Directive, which prescribes specific rules relating to the manager of the fund (the 'AIFM'), does not lay down specific rules for the fund itself. Accordingly, the fund will be subject to the legislation existing in each country. Nevertheless, it might be helpful to discuss the main provisions of this Directive.

8.3.4.1 Authorisation

First and foremost, the AIFM, i.e. the manager directly responsible for an alternative investment fund ('AIF'), shall have secured prior authorisation from the relevant home country authority. Remarkably, subsequent to being granted such authority, the AIFM shall be permitted to carry out only limited activities, specifically those detailed under Annex I of the Directive under discussion, including portfolio management and risk management. Accordingly, the full spectrum of investment activities and investment services pertaining to financial instruments, usually granted to investment firms, are precluded from the ambit of authority exercised by AIF managers.

The conditions to be satisfied prior to granting the authorisation just mentioned are those detailed under art. 8, where one of the most important requirements is an initial capital of Euro 300,000.[63] Also, in cases where the value of the portfolios managed by the AIFM exceeds Euro 250 million, the AIF's own funds must constitute 0.02 per cent of the amount by which the value of the portfolios of the AIFM exceeds Euro 250 million.[64] The authorisation shall be regarded as withdrawn by the competent authority should one of the circumstances detailed under art. 11 transpire, the most important of which are, seemingly, the obtainment of the authorisation 'by making false statements or by any other irregular means' or in cases where the AIFM 'no longer meets the conditions under which authorisation was granted'.

Once the AIFM has acquired authorisation in its own (i.e. home) Member State, by way of the EU passport the authorisation shall be immediately valid in each Member State[65] and the AIFM shall have the capacity to both manage and commercialise funds to professional investors[66] within the Union, without the need for any further authorisation by the authority of the other Member State where the funds are either managed or commercialised.[67] But if the units of the AIF were offered to the public, then the decision will rest with the authority of the other Member States as to whether or not the commercialisation of the AIF is granted authorisation.[68]

62 Ibid.
63 However, the minimum capital shall be reduced to Euro 125,000 if the AIFM was appointed exclusively as 'external manager'.
64 Art. 9(3) of the AIFMD.
65 Art. 8 of the AIFMD.
66 P Sfafemi and A Giannelli, *Diritto degli Intermediari e dei Mercati Finanziari* (EGEA, Milan 2013) 194.
67 Arts 31–33 of the AIMFD.
68 Art. 43 of the AIFMD. See also P Sfafemi and A Giannelli, *Diritto degli Intermediari e dei Mercati Finanziari* (EGEA, Milan 2013) 194.

8.3.4.2 Organisational requirements

In light of the speculative nature of the AIF, clear guidelines have been installed to ensure that their managers, i.e. the AIFMs, use 'at all times, adequate and appropriate human and technical resources that are necessary for the proper management of AIFs'.[69] In this scenario, according to the precepts of the EU legislator, the competent authorities of the home Member State of the AIFM shall require that 'the AIFM has sound administrative and accounting procedures, control and safeguard arrangements for electronic data processing and adequate internal control mechanisms'.[70] In perusing the details of the organisational requirements, it is worth acknowledging that the legislation under discussion expressly requires that the AIFM puts in place 'appropriate and consistent procedures' to ensure that 'a proper and independent valuation of the assets of the AIF can be performed'.[71]

The delegation of the functions of a fund manager opens the door to a number of possible risks: the investor typically relies on the credibility and reliability of the delegated manager, the entity formally in charge of the management of the fund. Conversely, a delegation of functions to third parties may in turn jeopardise the principles of transparency and affect the same credibility of the management functions. This concern, already relevant across the spectrum of mutual funds, is magnified when dealing with a fund (AIF) which is more speculative in nature. In light of this, the EU legislator ensures that the delegation of functions, albeit permitted, is subject to a control of the authority of the competent Member State. Thus, when delegating to third parties, the entity planning to carry out the management of an AIF must be notified to the authority.[72] Also, the effectiveness of the agreement must comply with several conditions, among which a special mention can be made of the following:

> the alternative investment fund manager must be able to justify its entire delegation structure on objective reasons;[73]

> the delegate must dispose of sufficient resources to perform the respective tasks and the persons who effectively conduct the business of the delegate must be of sufficiently good repute and sufficiently experienced;[74]

> where the delegation concerns portfolio management or risk management, it must be conferred only on undertakings which are authorised or registered for the purposes of asset management and subject to supervision.[75]

The AIFM delegating these functions:

> must be able to demonstrate that the delegate is qualified and capable of undertaking the functions in question, that it was selected with all due care and that the AIFM is in

69 Art. 18(1) of the AIFMD.
70 Ibid.
71 Art. 19(1) of the AIFMD.
72 Art. 20(1) of the AIFMD.
73 Art. 20(1)(a) of the AIFMD.
74 Art. 20(1)(b) of the AIFMD.
75 Art. 20(1)(c) of the AIFMD.

a position to monitor effectively at any time the delegated activity, to give at any time further instructions to the delegate and to withdraw the delegation with immediate effect when this is in the interest of investors.[76]

In other words, the delegation is – and cannot be – an opportunity for the authorised intermediary (the AIFM), on the one hand, to eschew its responsibilities and, on the other, to expose the investor to a risk that is considerably more than originally envisaged.

Finally, the AIFM shall engage the services of an authorised institution to act as a depositary, by definition a bank,[77] and the appointment of this depositary, which is mandatory, shall be documented by virtue of a written contract.[78]

8.4 Further reading

Busch, D, and De Mott, DA (eds), *Liability of Asset Managers* (Oxford University Press, Oxford 2012)
Hazen, TL, *Securities Regulation in a Nutshell* (10th edn West Publishing/Thomson Reuters, St Paul (MN) 2009)
Hudson, A, *Hudson: The Law of Finance* (2nd edn Sweet & Maxwell, London 2013)
Scott, HS, and Gelpern, A, *International Finance: Transactions, Policy, and Regulation* (19th edn Foundation Press and Thomson Reuters, New York 2012)
Soderquist, LD, and Gabaldon, TA, *Securities Law* (2nd edn Foundation Press and Thomson/West, New York 2004)
Wood, PR, *Regulation of International Finance* (Thomson/Sweet & Maxwell, London 2007)
Wymeersch, E, *Alternative Investment Fund Regulation* (Wolters Kluwer, Alphen aan den Rijn 2012)
Zetzsche, D (ed), *The Alternative Investment Fund Managers Directive* (Worters Kluwer, Alphen aan den Rijn 2012)

8.5 Questions

8.1 What is an investment firm and what is the difference between an investment firm and a credit institution (or bank)?

8.2 From a legal point of view, can you summarise the kind of activities that an investment bank can carry out?

---

76 Art. 20(1)(f) of the AIFMD.
77 Art. 21(1) of the AIFMD.
78 Although the terms and conditions of this contract are left to the discretion of the contracting parties, the legislation under discussion takes pains to highlight (art. 21(2) of the AIFMD) the main aspects of the agreement that shall be necessarily indicated in the contract; particularly, 'the flow of information deemed necessary to allow the depositary to perform its functions for the AIF for which it has been appointed as depositary, as set out [in the AIFMD] and in other relevant laws, regulations or administrative provisions'.

8.3 What would you need for starting an investment firm business?

8.4 What would a bank need for conducting investment services and activities?

8.5 Is the minimum capital for an investment firm the same as that required for a bank?

8.6 What is an investment fund, and what is the difference between an investment fund and an investment firm?

8.7 What is the difference between UCITS and an AIF?

8.8 Can an alternative investment fund be managed by an investment firm?

Part D

Financial contracts

Chapter 9

Custody and transfer of money and securities

Chapter contents

9.1 Introduction

As stated in an earlier chapter,[1] banks as we know them today have developed from their original role as moneychangers to include within their contemporary scope of activities the business of deposit taking, i.e. the accepting of monies from the public for purposes of custody. Historically, in the Italian city states of the thirteenth century, people brought their coins to a banker primarily for the safe keeping of these monies, but also so that the banker could facilitate, upon a transfer order by his client(s), cross-border[2] transfers of this cash. Even at this pioneering stage of the banking business, deposits were already credited to accounts and the banker could effectuate a cross-border transfer order simply by orchestrating the relevant credit and debit entries in the accounts he maintained in his books or, to use more technical terminology, by making the relevant book-entries in his ledgers.[3] It is not difficult to envisage how this system of book-entry transfers was instrumental in minimising the multitude of risks that would stem from a physical cross-border transfer of monies. This system was thus conceived and put in practice for dealings with money, and has subsequently been refined over the ensuing centuries. It was only over the course of the last century that the invention of accounts and book-entry transfers has also been generally applied to the custody of securities. As a result of the technological advancements which have materialised at a seemingly perpetual rate over the latter half of the last century, the accounts maintained on (physical) books just referred to, both in relation to money and securities, have been replaced by electronic accounts. Thus, the bulk of monies and securities in contemporary banking are held and transferred through the medium of electronic book-entries in electronic accounts.

As a matter of principle, from the thirteenth century onwards, virtually the full spectrum of jurisdictions have embarked on the adoption of a system whereby claims of money depositors rank *pari passu*, i.e. *pro rata parte*, with claims of the bank's other creditors. Back in those formative years, deposits for safe keeping were classified as *depositum regulare* ('regular deposit'), while deposits into a current account were distinguished as *depositum irregulare* ('irregular deposit'). Under the Roman law concept of *depositum* (*regulare*), a depositor has a property right in individual deposited assets.[4] In practice, this obligated the custodian bank to register the individual assets held for each individual depositor. This concept applied both to monies and, later, also to securities. However, as the practice of individual custody involved increasingly burdensome administrative costs, assets became merged in the custodian's coffers and administered on a collective basis. Moreover, as its assets were essentially fungible and, therefore, interchangeable, the banker could only return equivalent properties, i.e. not the very same assets that the client had deposited, but synonymous with the

---

1 Section 5.1.

2 In the medieval context the term 'cross-border' should be contextualised as referring to a transaction aimed to be executed between two different city states sometimes not far from each other, yet formally under a different sovereignty.

3 R De Roover, 'New Interpretations of the History of Banking', in J Kirshner (ed.), *Business, Banking, and Economic Thought in Late Medieval and Early Modern Europe* (University of Chicago Press, Chicago 1974) 201 and RC Mueller, *The Venetian Money Market: Banks, Panics, and the Public Debt, 1200–1500* (Johns Hopkins University Press, London 1997) 8.

4 P Du Plessis, *Borkowski's Textbook on Roman Law* (4th edn Oxford University Press, Oxford 2010) 300, 302.

original assets in terms of both quality and quantity.[5] Consequently, in most legal systems, such a commingling implies the loss of ownership, which leaves the investor with a *pari passu* claim against his custodian, and provides little or no protection in the case of the custodian's insolvency.[6] This form of custody, under which the depositor essentially loses ownership and the custodian is obligated to return equivalent assets, has been coined *depositum irregulare*.[7]

This chapter deals with the custody and transfer of money, i.e. cash, and securities. From a private or commercial law perspective,[8] the custody of money and securities has not been the subject of much European harmonisation. However, in the immediate aftermath of the recent global financial crisis, the issue of the custody of money and securities and, specifically segregation, i.e. the segregation of client assets from the bank's own assets and from the assets between clients, has caught the eye of many advisory groups and legislators across the globe. In the following, the rules of segregation that follow from the MiFID II legislation[9] and the recent Central Securities Deposits ('CSD') Regulation[10] will be discussed. Also, attention will be drawn to the various solutions which, in the private law field, the relevant jurisdictions have developed for securities custody, in order to deal with and, ultimately, minimise the issue of loss of ownership under the *depositum irregulare* concept.

Subsequently, consideration will be given to the transfer of money and securities by way of book-entries (or 'giro-transfer', as it is more commonly referred to in many continental European jurisdictions). It should be noted that this area, which forms such a critical aspect of daily life, has not been the subject of much European private law harmonisation. Nevertheless, the transfer of money is currently governed by an ambitious European project, i.e. the Single European Payments Area ('SEPA'), which consists of the EEA in addition to Switzerland and the principality of Monaco. Under the SEPA Regulation,[11] banks or, more broadly and accurately, payment services providers, must implement certain technical requirements for credit and debit transactions in Euro within the EU. Furthermore, a crucial aspect of SEPA is the Payment Services Directive,[12] which aims to harmonise the regulatory framework regarding payment services providers, i.e. credit institutions and, in short, the range

5 Cf. M Haentjens, *Harmonisation of Securities Law* (Kluwer Law International, Alphen aan den Rijn 2007) 29 et seq.

6 For depositor protection under deposit guarantee schemes, see section 7.3.

7 C Bernasconi, *The Law Applicable to Dispositions of Securities Held through Indirect Holding Systems* (November 2000) (Preliminary Document no 1 to the Hague Conference on Private International Law) 19.

8 As with the following chapters, this chapter takes a transactional perspective, and is therefore more concerned with private or commercial law aspects than with regulatory elements.

9 Most importantly: Directive 2014/65/EU of the European Parliament and of the Council of 15 May 2014 on markets in financial instruments and amending Directive 2002/92/EC and Directive 2011/61/EU, OJ L 173 ('MiFID II'); and Regulation (EU) No 600/2014 of the European Parliament and of the Council of 15 May 2014 on markets in financial instruments and amending Regulation (EU) No 648/2012, OJ L 173 ('MiFIR'). See also above, section 8.2.

10 In full: Regulation (EU) No 909/2014 of the European Parliament and of the Council of 23 July 2014 on improving securities settlement in the European Union and on central securities depositories and amending Directives 98/26/EC and 2014/65/EU and Regulation (EU) No 236/2012, OJ L 257/1.

11 In full: Regulation (EU) No 260/2012 of the European Parliament and of the Council of 14 March 2012 establishing technical and business requirements for credit transfers and direct debits in euro and amending Regulation (EC) No 924/2009, OJ L 94.

12 In full: Directive 2007/64/EC of the European Parliament and of the Council of 13 November 2007 on payment services in the internal market amending Directives 97/7/EC, 2002/65/EC, 2005/60/EC and 2006/48/EC and repealing Directive 97/5/EC, OJ L 319.

of institutions which manage payment transactions in Euro.[13] Thus, it introduces an authorisation requirement for the pursuit of payment services business. These technical and regulatory guidelines put in place via SEPA and the Payment Services Directive will not be subject to an extensive discussion in the present chapter. Rather, as this chapter takes a private or commercial law perspective, greater attention will be given to the Settlement Finality Directive,[14] which deals with transfer (orders) of both money and securities and which aims to reduce the systemic risk associated with participation in payment and securities settlement systems, and, more specifically, the risk that materialises when a participant in such a system becomes insolvent.[15]

9.2 Custody of money and securities[16]

9.2.1 General

As stated above, depositors nowadays hold the greatest part of their money and securities in electronic accounts with their bank. This type of custody can commonly be qualified as *depositum irregulare* and is complicated by two factors. First and foremost, in today's financial system, cash and securities are virtually always centrally stored: cash with a central bank and securities with a central securities depository ('CSD'). Practically, clients, particularly retail clients, never hold their assets (cash and securities) with these central depository institutions, as these are held on an account with a financial institution. In its turn, the latter, which is often a bank, may hold these assets on an account with the central depositories. On the account with the central depository, duly registered in the financial institution's name, the aggregate of all client assets of this institution is credited. This account is therefore commonly denoted as an 'omnibus' account. Thus, this omnibus account does not distinguish (either legally or operationally) between the underlying retail clients and may or may not include the financial institution's own assets. Moreover, between the retail client and the central depository, multiple financial institutions may be interposed; in this scenario, several omnibus accounts will exist between the retail client and the central depository, as the financial institution in our example may hold an omnibus account with a second institution, and so on.

Second, today's multi-tiered system is only rarely purely domestic. Financial institutions holding (omnibus) accounts with each other may be located in different

13 Scholars (C Proctor, *The Law and Practice of International Banking* (Oxford University Press, Oxford 2010) 76) point out the main objectives of Directive 2007/64: first and foremost, 'to allow a wider range of participants (including non-banks) in the market for payment services'; additionally, to strengthen consumer protection, 'with rules requiring clarity and transparency of charging structures'.

14 In full: Directive 98/26/EC of the European Parliament and of the Council of 19 May 1998 on settlement finality in payment and securities settlement systems, OJ L 166.

15 For a brief commentary on the Settlement Finality Directive, see C Proctor, *The Law and Practice of International Banking* (Oxford University Press, Oxford 2010) 591, 601.

16 The following draws on M Haentjens and WAK Rank, 'Legal and Operational Asset Segregation', in M Haentjens and B Wessels (eds), *Crisis Management in the Banking Sector* (Edward Elgar, Cheltenham, forthcoming 2015).

jurisdictions, and only rarely will a client's securities portfolio consist of securities issued by issuers located in only one jurisdiction. These different jurisdictions may treat the holding and protection of client assets differently, while under the conflict of laws rule that was introduced into European Union law by the Settlement Finality Directive and the Collateral Directive,[17] the law of the place applies where the 'relevant' securities account is located, i.e. the account on which the securities in question are credited. This means that in a securities custody chain where multiple financial intermediaries are interposed between client and central securities depository, multiple laws may apply which may have different (substantive) rules on the holding and protection of the same client assets.

9.2.2 Custody of money

Cash is the most fungible thing, by definition. As stated above, from the thirteenth century onwards, depositors of cash money rank *pari passu* with other depositors and, more generally, with other creditors of the bank. In most continental European legal systems, client money forms part of a bank's property and segregation (again, the separation of client assets from the bank's own assets and from the assets between clients) is therefore usually accomplished by operational rules only. Under English law, however, client money does not form part of the property of a bank that has accepted client funds. Upon receipt, those funds form part of a statutory trust and thus take free of the bank's own creditors' claims. In the insolvency of Lehman Brothers International (Europe), the UK Supreme Court decided, in short, that even where funds have not been operationally segregated from the firm's own accounts, these funds take free of the firm's own creditors. This also means that if losses occur within the trust formed by client funds, these losses must be shared among the clients, whether or not they have been operationally segregated.[18]

In the Lehman Brothers case just discussed, the Court also considered the Markets in Financial Instruments Directive I ('MiFID I'[19]). MiFID I gave the principal and most general European rule regarding segregation both for cash (i.e. 'funds' in MiFID I terminology) and for securities: 'An investment firm shall, when holding funds belonging to clients, make adequate arrangements to safeguard the clients' rights.'[20] Just as was the case for securities (see also further below), this rule was further

17 Art. 9(2) of the Settlement Finality Directive (to be discussed below); and art. 9 of Directive 2002/47/EC of the European Parliament and of the Council of 6 June 2002 on financial collateral arrangements, OJ L 168/43. On this Directive, see more extensively below, Chapter 12. The same rule can be discerned in § 8–110 (1994) of the US Uniform Commercial Code enacted in all US States, and in the (not yet enacted) Convention on the law applicable to certain rights in respect of securities held with an intermediary, although these latter two instruments give primacy to party autonomy. These rules show that there is not even a global uniform conflict of laws rule to determine which (substantive) rules apply to the holding and protection of client assets.

18 *Re Lehman Brothers International (Europe) (In Administration)* [2012] UKSC 6 (SC). See, among many, e.g. D Gruyaert and S van Loock, 'UK Supreme Court Decision on Lehman Brothers Client Money: Equity or Lottery' (2014) 2 *European Review of Private Law* 217–250.

19 In full: European Parliament and Council Directive 2004/39/EC of 21 April 2004 on markets in financial instruments amending Council Directives 85/611/EEC and 93/6/EEC and Directive 2000/12/EC of the European Parliament and of the Council and repealing Council Directive 93/22/EEC, OJ L 145.

20 Art. 13(8) of MiFID I.

substantiated for cash in the MiFID Implementing Directive.[21] This general rule for cash will be retained under MiFID II and MiFIR, albeit under a different article number. MiFID II now states in its art. 16(9):

> An investment firm shall, when holding funds belonging to clients, make adequate arrangements to safeguard the rights of clients and, except in the case of credit institutions, prevent the use of client funds for its own account.

What applies to cash applies to securities also: pursuant to Implementing Directive, art. 16, the Member States shall require that, for the purpose of safeguarding clients' rights in relation to funds belonging to them, investment firms comply with the requirement that they must keep such records and accounts as necessary to enable them at any time and without delay to distinguish assets held for one client from assets held for any other client, and from their own assets. If, for reasons of the applicable law, including in particular the law relating to property or insolvency, the arrangements made by investment firms in compliance with the above requirement are not sufficient to satisfy the requirement of art. 13(8) of MiFID I, Member States shall prescribe the measures that investment firms must take in order to comply with those obligations.

The MiFID rules just discussed apply to investment firms, but they have a far wider scope as they also apply to banks,[22] as well as to:

> market operators, data reporting services providers, and third-country firms providing investment services or performing investment activities through the establishment of a branch in the Union.[23]

They may apply not only to legal persons, but also to natural persons.[24] Remarkably, in most European jurisdictions, investment firms[25] will not be allowed to hold cash on behalf of clients other than cash in connection with the providsion of investment services, because they are not allowed to act as a bank without being licensed as such.[26] Payment institutions are under a separate obligation to safeguard their clients' funds. Interestingly, under the Payment Services Directive, Member States are offered the choice to accomplish this either through property law segregation or insurance.[27] As a matter of principle, property law regulation is left to the discretion of the Member States.[28]

21 Art. 16 of Commission Directive 2006/73/EC of 10 August 2006 implementing Directive 2004/39/EC of the European Parliament and of the Council as regards organisational requirements and operating conditions for investment firms and defined terms for the purposes of that Directive, OJ L 241.

22 In cases where these entities also provided investment services (art. 1(3) and (4) of MiFID II).

23 Art. 1(1) of MiFID II.

24 Art. 4 caput and (1) of MiFID I, now Art. 2(1)(1) MiFIR.

25 On investment firms, see above, Chapter 8.

26 Pursuant to art. 4(1) under (1) of the Capital Requirements Regulation ('CRR'), a bank is an undertaking, the business of which is to take deposits or other repayable funds from the public and to grant credits for its own account. Similarly, it may be prohibited from attracting repayable funds from the public without an exemption or a dispensation from a prudential regulatory authority.

27 Art. 9(1)(a)–(c) of the Payment Services Directive.

28 Cf. art. 16(2) MiFID Implementing Directive, cited above.

9.2.3 Securities custody

9.2.3.1 General

If a bank or investment firm does not record the individual numbers of the securities it holds for each client separately, or, more generally, if these securities are not in any way identifiable as a specific client's property, most civil law jurisdictions will deem these securities to form part of that bank's or investment firm's (own) property. As stated above, this phenomenon is commonly denoted as *depositum irregulare* and involves the commingling of the assets of various depositors held collectively by one financial institution. It has dramatic consequences: without specific legislation having been enacted or special measures having been taken, the commingling of securities to which multiple clients are entitled would mean that those securities are deemed to be part of the bankruptcy estate in the event the bank or the investment firm that holds those securities falls bankrupt.[29] Civil law jurisdictions therefore need both legal and operational rules to accomplish asset segregation and client protection.

In common law jurisdictions, as a general rule, client securities do not form part of the property of a bank or an investment firm, at least in as far as the bank's or the investment firm's administration holds the securities for the benefit of clients. Such securities form part of a statutory trust and thus take free of the bank's or the investment firm's own creditors' claims. Common law jurisdictions therefore need operational rules to achieve asset segregation and client protection.

9.2.3.2 MiFID

What has been stated above in the context of custody of cash also applies to securities custody; MiFID I gave the principal and most general European rule in this regard:

> An investment firm shall, when holding financial instruments belonging to clients, make adequate arrangements so as to safeguard clients' ownership rights, especially in the event of the investment firm's insolvency.[30]

This rule was further specified and substantiated in art. 16 of the MiFID Implementing Directive.[31] Recently, MiFID II and MiFIR, i.e. the recast of MiFID I, have been enacted. In these instruments, the above rule is retained albeit under different article numbers.[32] MiFID II now states in its art. 16(8):

> An investment firm shall, when holding financial instruments belonging to clients, make adequate arrangements so as to safeguard the ownership rights of clients, especially in the event of the investment firm's insolvency, and to prevent the use of a client's financial instruments on own account except with the client's express consent.

---

29 Cf. M Haentjens, *Harmonisation of Securities Law* (Kluwer Law International, Alphen aan den Rijn 2007) 33, 35.

30 Art. 13(7) of MiFID I.

31 See also above, section 9.2.2.

32 Art. 16(8) and (9) of MiFID II and 2 caput and (1) of the MiFIR, respectively.

The above cited provisions pertain to 'financial instruments' and provide for two rules: a general requirement for investment firms to 'make adequate arrangements so as to safeguard the ownership rights of clients', and, additionally, a prohibition on investment firms using a client's financial instruments 'on own account'. This second rule means that an investment firm is not allowed to use the financial instruments it holds for its clients for its own purposes if and when the client has not expressly consented.[33] The first rule has been further explained in Implementing Directive, art. 16(1), which is still in force and reads as follows:

> Member States shall require that, for the purposes of safeguarding clients' rights in relation to financial instruments belonging to them, investment firms comply with the following requirements: (a) they must keep such records and accounts as are necessary to enable them at any time and without delay to distinguish assets held for one client from assets held for any other client, and from their own assets.

Art. 16(1), thus, is mainly an operational rule. However, the European legislator realised that operational segregation may not be sufficient to accomplish client protection. Article 16(2) of the MiFID Implementing Directive therefore reads:

> If, for reasons of the applicable law, including in particular the law relating to property or insolvency, the arrangements made by investment firms in compliance with paragraph 1 to safeguard clients' rights are not sufficient to satisfy the requirements of Article 13(7) and (8) of Directive 2004/39/EC, Member States shall prescribe the measures that investment firms must take in order to comply with those obligations.

Indirectly, the MiFID rules also apply to investment funds. More specifically, the recent Alternative Investment Fund Managers Directive ('AIFMD')[34] as well as the amended Undertakings for Collective Investment in Transferable Securities Directive[35] require that fund assets are held with a depositary, and that such depositary must segregate these fund assets from its own assets under the MiFID rules just referred to. More specifically, art. 21(8)(a) of the AIFMD reads:

> The assets of the AIF or the AIFM acting on behalf of the AIF shall be entrusted to the depositary for safe-keeping, as follows: (a) for financial instruments that can be held in custody: (i) the depositary shall hold in custody all financial instruments that can be registered in a financial instruments account opened in the depositary's books and all financial instruments that can be physically delivered to the depositary; (ii) for that purpose, the depositary shall ensure that all those financial instruments that can be registered in a financial instruments account opened in the depositary's books are registered in the depositary's books within segregated accounts in accordance with the

33 The investment firm might wish, for instance, to enter into securities lending transactions and thus make a profit on the portfolios held. On securities lending transactions, see extensively below, Chapter 12.

34 See above, section 8.3.4.

35 See also above, section 8.3.2.

principles set out in Article 16 of Directive 2006/73/EC, opened in the name of the AIF or the AIFM acting on behalf of the AIF, so that they can be clearly identified as belonging to the AIF in accordance with the applicable law at all times.[36]

9.2.3.3 Private/commercial law

It has just been discussed how MiFID I and the MiFID Implementing Directive introduced, on the European level, statutory operational standards for the custody of securities. However, international harmonisation (let alone unification) of private or commercial law rules for securities custody seems to be a mere utopia, as different jurisdictions have developed different legal regimes of securities custody. Nevertheless, there have been attempts and initiatives of harmonisation, which we will discuss further below.

The principal distinction between the current regimes of securities custody is between jurisdictions that confer clients some kind of co-property interest in their securities and jurisdictions that have developed other views. Co-property interests are known in civil law jurisdictions such as Germany, Spain and the Netherlands, where it is based on the *Depotgesetz*, the *Ley del Mercado de Valores* and the *Wet giraal effectenverkeer*, respectively. Fungible custody in Belgium and Luxembourg is based on *Koninklijk Besluit* (Royal Decree) *no 62* and several *Règlements grand-ducal* (Grand-ducal Decrees) respectively, which establish co-ownership in notional pools of securities.[37]

To give an example of a system that confers clients some kind of co-property interest in their securities in order to eliminate the consequences of commingling, the *Wet giraal effectenverkeer* – the Dutch Act for securities custody and transfer – makes securities that are subject to this specific statute and which are deposited on behalf of a client with an 'intermediary' form part of a collective deposit (or 'pool') of securities of the same kind, i.e. securities that are mutually interchangeable, deposited with that institution on behalf of clients. By virtue of the Dutch piece of legislation under comment, clients who have deposited their securities with an intermediary, give up their individual ownership of the securities deposited and become joint owners of the relevant collective deposit, pro rata to the quantity of securities deposited. Since a collective deposit does not form part of the assets of the intermediary, the securities are not available to the intermediary's liquidator if the intermediary becomes insolvent, and are therefore protected. Each joint owner of a collective deposit has a claim *in rem* against the intermediary. On the same basis as the collective deposits are established with intermediaries, so-called 'giro deposits' are established with the CSD. Just as a collective deposit is a pool consisting of securities of a particular kind deposited with an intermediary by its clients and administered by the intermediary, a giro deposit is a pool consisting of securities of a particular kind deposited by intermediaries with the CSD and administered by the CSD.

---

36 Art. 22(5)(a) of UCITS V is identical, *mutatis mutandis*. See also art. 22a(3), added by the European Parliament, on specific requirements when the depositary delegates its tasks to a third party.

37 Of 17 February 1971, of 8 June 1994, of 7 June 1996, of 16 August 2000 and a statute of 3 September 1996. See also the EU Clearing and Settlement Legal Certainty Group Questionnaire (2007), 130 ('EU Questionnaire').

The 'other views' just referred to can be distinguished in the Anglo-American models and so-called 'transparent' models. Under UK and US law, investors enjoy a bundle of rights *in rem* as well as *in personam* against their intermediary. In the UK, account holders' contractual rights follow from their contract with the custodian, while their property law rights classify as co-ownership rights, which may follow from the concept of a trust.[38] In the US, the Uniform Commercial Code ('UCC'), art. 8, provides investors with proprietary and contractual rights in respect of the securities to which they are entitled.

Brazilian and Chinese law represent examples of jurisdictions where client accounts are segregated on all levels of the custody chain. Thus, these systems qualify financial intermediaries as mere account operators and (fictionally) regard securities custody as *depositum*, i.e. the administration of individual assets per individual client.

It requires little imagination to realise that the above differences in legal regimes 'may give rise to legal disputes as to ownership and entitlement to the assets, and complicate transfers or the rapid return of the assets to clients' as the Basel Committee on Banking Supervision warned.[39] Consequently, securities custody has been the subject of various international harmonisation initiatives, many of which have not yet been enacted. On the European level, the European Commission has been working on harmonisation of securities custody law since the so-called Giovannini Reports of 2001 and 2003, but at the time of writing, no draft proposal has yet been published.

Recently adopted is the Central Securities Depository Regulation ('CSD Regulation').[40] This Regulation is primarily directed at financial market infrastructures, of which CSD are of relevance in the present context. It mirrors the MiFID Implementing Directive and provides that a CSD shall segregate the accounts held by financial intermediaries with the CSD (in this Regulation, 'participants') from those of other participants and its own assets. It also provides that a CSD must enable its participants to segregate the securities of that participant's clients from those of the participant's own. Also, CSDs and participants must give participants and their clients, respectively, the choice to either register omnibus accounts or accounts per individual client.[41]

---

38 See EU Questionnaire (2007), 143–4. Among British scholars (A Hudson, *Hudson: The Law of Finance* (2nd edn Sweet & Maxwell, London 2013) 636) it is emphasised that a proprietary right 'means a right over property, whether in the form of "absolute title" . . ., or title recognized by common law (such as the rights of a trustee under a trust), or equitable rights (such as the rights of a beneficiary under a trust).' It is added (ibid.) that a proprietary right 'is important because the holder of a right can enforce that proprietary right against any third party even if some other person who is using or who has possession of the property goes into insolvency, or purports to transfer that property to a third party, or something of that sort.'

Of equal important, in the common law jurisdictions, is the concept of tracing, i.e. 'the process by which a claimant seeks to establish title to property taken from her or to establish title to property which has been substituted for that original property' (A Hudson, *Hudson: The Law of Finance* (2nd edn Sweet & Maxwell, London 2013) 692). What the tracing does, at common law, differently from the civil law systems, is 'to begin with the claimant's property rights through the succession of accounts, funds and mixtures into which that money or substitutes for that money have passed. If this tracing process is successful, the claimant is then able to establish one of a number of potential remedies against any funds which can be shown to contain any traceable residue of the original property' (ibid. 693).

39 See the BCBS Report.

40 In full: Regulation (EU) No 909/2014 of the European Parliament and of the Council of 23 July 2014 on improving securities settlement in the European Union and on central securities depositories and amending Directives 98/26/EC and 2014/65/EU and Regulation (EU) No 236/2012, OJ L 257/1.

41 Art. 38 of the CSD Regulation.

9.3 Transfer of money and securities

9.3.1 Settlement and clearing

In the preceding sections, we have discussed the multi-tiered model in which cash and securities are held through financial institutions, with an emphasis on the legal position of the client/account holder in that model. In this section, we will focus less on the static situation in which cash and securities are held in accounts with a financial institution, but rather on the dynamic scenario in which the same assets are transferred, or, as commonly referred to, 'settled'.

So as to introduce the topic, let us consider the following two, simplified examples of a securities transfer or 'settlement'. First, assume transferor A and transferee B are clients of the same bank X, and bank X maintains omnibus accounts with the local central securities depository. Upon A's order, this bank debits A's securities account and credits B's account with the same amount. The bank's omnibus account with the CSD remains unchanged, as the transfer can be perfected solely on the books of the bank.

Now assume transferor A and transferee C are not clients of the same bank. A remains a client of bank X, while C is a client of bank Y. Also in this instance, A orders his bank, X, to debit his securities account. Bank X then debits A's account and the local CSD consequently debits X's omnibus account. Assuming C's bank, Y, is located in the same jurisdiction and therefore also maintains omnibus accounts with the CSD, the CSD then credits bank Y's account. Finally, bank Y credits C's securities account, by which the transfer is completed.[42]

A transfer of money largely follows the same pattern as the two examples of a securities transfer just given. For a money transfer, one only needs to substitute 'payor' for transferor and 'payee' for transferee, and 'central bank' for CSD.

It is important to note that the relationships between A and his bank, as well as between B/C and their bank must be considered separately, as these relationships are legally to be distinguished from the relationship between A and B/C – which relationship may nonetheless have given the cause for the securities transfer. In the case of securities transfers that have been concluded on a stock exchange, transferor and transferee are normally even unaware of each other's identity and merely order their respective financial institutions to buy or sell securities of a certain type.

Also important to note is that, for most cash and securities transfers, the financial institutions that effectuate these transfers for their clients and themselves make use of a 'clearing house' or a 'central counterparty' (the latter is also referred to as 'CCP'). Such clearing house or CCP have in common that they calculate the aggregate of the obligations of all transactions that the participants, i.e. the financial institutions that participate in the system managed by the clearing house or CCP, conclude between themselves on a given day. While the actual delivery or transfer of assets is called 'settlement', this calculation process is called 'clearing'.

42 See Giovannini Group, 2001 Report, 11, for a schematic overview of settlement in a domestic context. In practice, however, Y often credits C's securities account before Y's account with the CSD is correspondingly credited.

Whereas trade-for-trade settlement systems, i.e. systems wherein payment and transfer of every single transaction is calculated individually and no netting or set-off takes place, might provide a high level of transparency, they are costly and technically difficult to realise.[43] Moreover, netting or set-off of securities and payment transfers reduces the risks associated with individual transfers and thus result in a cost reduction. In most systems, both delivery and payment obligations are therefore netted, which is performed by a CCP or a clearing house.

In a clearing house system, the clearing house calculates the net positions of all its participants' obligations or all their transfer orders.[44] At the end of the trading cycle, the clearing house typically submits the netted orders to the CSD and central bank, and the CSD and central bank credit and debit the participants' accounts accordingly. Where the clearing house does not become a (central) counterparty to its participants, a CCP is interposed between the participants' transactions and in that capacity takes over their obligations by novation.[45] Thus, for all transactions, the financial institution of the transferor (in the case of a securities transfer) or payor (in the case of a cash transfer) has to deliver (or pay, in the latter case) to the CCP instead of to the financial institution of the transferee/payee. The CCP consequently also takes over all the risks attached to non-performance by a defaulting party, and the use of a CCP therefore results in a considerable reduction of settlement risk. Then, i.e. after a trading day, the CCP usually nets all the obligations, thereby reducing 'all outstanding residuals to a single debit/credit between itself and each member (rather than a multiplicity of bilateral exposures between members).'[46]

Although similar, the netting by a CCP and a clearing house must be distinguished, as in a CCP system, the net balance has to be paid/delivered to or by the CCP, whereas in a clearing house system, the net balance is paid/delivered between the participants themselves through accounts with the CSD and the central bank. For that purpose, the CCP's participants maintain so-called clearing member accounts with the CCP, and consequently hold both a clearing member account with the CCP and a securities and cash account with the CSD and central bank.

9.3.2 Settlement Finality Directive[47]

Other than for reasons of (operational) mistakes by the financial institutions that maintain cash and securities accounts, the reversal of entries in cash and securities accounts is mainly prompted by the insolvency of one of the parties involved. The European legislature addressed the reversal of transfers relatively early. Based on this legislative framework, it is acknowledged that legal uncertainty should be minimised, particularly in the context of such a vital element of modern economies, and recognised that in payment and securities settlement systems, an enormous amount

43 M Haentjens, *Harmonisation of Securities Law* (Kluwer International Law, Alphen aan den Rijn 2007) 44, 46.

44 Cf. art. 2(e) of the Settlement Finality Directive, to be discussed below, section 9.3.2, and see L Van Setten in M Vereecken and A Nijenhuis (eds), *Settlement Finality in the European Union: The EU Directive and Its Implementation in Selected Jurisdictions* (Kluwer, Deventer 2003) 267.

45 Cf. art. 2(c) of the Settlement Finality Directive, to be discussed below, section 9.3.2.

46 L Van Setten in M Vereecken and A Nijenhuis (eds), *Settlement Finality in the European Union: The EU Directive and Its Implementation in Selected Jurisdictions* (Kluwer, Deventer 2003), 269. See also Giovannini Group, 2001 Report.

47 The following is based on M Haentjens, *Harmonisation of Securities Law* (Kluwer International Law, Alphen aan den Rijn 2007) 237 et seq.

of transactions between numerous participants is multilaterally effectuated on a daily basis, while the reversal of settlements in that context is cumbersome and often impossible.

Consequently, the Settlement Finality Directive was adopted on 19 May 1998.[48] Its main purpose has been to reduce the systemic risk associated with participation in payment and securities settlement systems, and, more specifically, the risk that materialises when a participant in such a system becomes insolvent.[49] Therefore, the Settlement Finality Directive, first and foremost, determines that transfer orders and payment netting be final and non-revocable in nature; it determines which insolvency rules are applicable to claims and obligations in a payment/securities settlement system; and it insulates (the enforcement of) collateral, i.e. the assets that are used to secure an obligation,[50] from insolvency proceedings. Moreover, the Settlement Finality Directive provides for a conflict of laws rule regarding some proprietary issues of securities custody and transfer law. As a general matter, the Settlement Finality Directive constitutes a departure from traditional European financial law legislation where the focus lies on mutual recognition of home-country supervision; the Settlement Finality Directive gives primacy to the law and the rules of the settlement and payment systems.

Article 3 is the Settlement Finality Directive's pivotal provision of substantive law. It requires national laws to ensure that transfer orders and netting are enforceable once entered into a payment or securities settlement system. Enforceability is to be ensured regardless of the commencement of insolvency proceedings against a participant of the system after that entry, while art. 3 further states that the moment of entry should be defined by the rules of the system itself. From which moment onwards a transfer order cannot be revoked is also to be defined by the rules of the system: art. 5 of the Settlement Finality Directive.

Article 7 determines that the insolvency of a participant in a payment or securities settlement system has no retroactive effects with regard to this and other participants' rights and obligations towards the system. This provision is complemented by art. 9(1), requiring the EU Member States to implement legislation that insulates (the enforcement of) collateral from the effects of insolvency proceedings commenced against a participant in a system.

Conflict of laws rules are found in arts 8 and 9. The rationale behind both provisions is that neither the operator of a payment or securities settlement system, nor its participants should have to take into account the national law of the participants, particularly those of an insolvency nature, for purposes of determining their rights and obligations against the system. Article 8 provides that the effects of one of the participant's insolvency be determined by the law designated by the operator of the settlement system, thus deviating from the general rule under which the law of the jurisdiction where insolvency proceedings commenced will apply (*lex concursus*).[51]

48 In the UK, Directive 98/26 was transposed by means of the Financial Markets and Insolvency (Settlement Finality) Regulations 1999. See C Proctor, *The Law and Practice of International Banking* (Oxford University Press, Oxford 2010) 592.

49 See Recitals 2, 4 and 9 of the Settlement Finality Directive.

50 On collateral, see extensively below, Chapter 12.

51 See M Ooi, *Shares and Other Securities in the Conflict of Laws* (Oxford University Press, Oxford 2003) 250. Cf. art. 9 of the EU Insolvency Regulation (Council Regulation 1346/2000/EC of 29 May 2000 on insolvency proceedings, OJ L 160/1).

Where a participant has obtained collateral in the form of securities, art. 9(2) refers to the law of the EU jurisdiction where this participant's/collateral taker's rights are registered to determine their nature.[52] The Settlement Finality Directive has been implemented in all Member States with no significant deviations.[53]

9.4 Further reading

Benjamin, J, *Financial Law* (Oxford University Press, Oxford 2007)

Bernasconi, C, *The Law Applicable to Dispositions of Securities Held Through Indirect Holding Systems* (November 2000) (Preliminary Document no 1 to the Hague Conference on Private International Law), available at www.hcch.net

De Roover, R, 'New Interpretations of the History of Banking', in J Kirshner (ed.), *Business, Banking, and Economic Thought in Late Medieval and Early Modern Europe* (University of Chicago Press, Chicago 1974)

Du Plessis, P, *Borkowski's Textbook on Roman Law* (4th edn Oxford University Press, Oxford 2010)

Giovannini Group, *Cross-Border Clearing and Settlement Arrangements in the European Union* (November 2001), available at http://ec.europa.eu/internal_market/financial-markets/

Giovannini Group, *Second Report on EU Clearing and Settlement Arrangements* (April 2003), available at http://ec.europa.eu/internal_market/financial-markets/

Goode, R, 'The Nature and Transfer of Rights in Dematerialised and Immobilised Securities' (1996) 4 *Journal of International Banking and Financial Law* 167–76

Gruyaert, D, and van Loock, S, 'UK Supreme Court Decision on Lehman Brothers Client Money: Equity or Lottery' (2014) 2 *European Review of Private Law* 217–50

Haentjens, M, *Harmonisation of Securities Law* (Kluwer Law International, Alphen aan den Rijn 2007)

Hudson, A, *Hudson: The Law of Finance* (2nd edn Sweet & Maxwell, London 2013)

Keijser, T (ed.), *Transnational Securities Law* (Oxford University Press, Oxford 2014)

Mueller, RC, *The Venetian Money Market: Banks, Panics, and the Public Debt, 1200–1500* (Johns Hopkins University Press, London 1997)

Ooi, M, *Shares and Other Securities in the Conflict of Laws* (Oxford University Press, Oxford 2003)

Paech, P, *Cross-Border Issues of Securities Law: European Efforts to Support Securities Markets with a Coherent Legal Framework* (European Parliament briefing note 2011)

Proctor, C, *The Law and Practice of International Banking* (Oxford University Press, Oxford 2010)

Proctor, C, *Mann on the Legal Aspect of Money* (Oxford University Press, Oxford 2012)

Vereecken, M, and Nijenhuis, A, (eds), *Settlement Finality in the European Union: The EU Directive and Its Implementation in Selected Jurisdictions* (Kluwer, Deventer 2003)

---

52 Cf., in slightly different wording, the Winding-up Directive, art. 25; see above, Chapter 7.

53 Report from the Commission, Evaluation report on the Settlement Finality Directive 98/26/EC (EU 25), COM(2005), 657 final/2, 9.

9.5 Questions

9.1 What is the difference between *depositum regulare* and *depositum irregulare*?

9.2 Describe how MiFID aims to protect money depositors.

9.3 Describe how various systems of civil/commercial law aim to protect securities depositors.

9.4 Why would multilateral netting reduce risk?

9.5 What is the difference between clearing and settlement?

9.6 Describe three ways the Settlement Finality Directive aims to reduce risk.

Chapter 10

Loan finance

Chapter contents

10.1 What is loan finance?

10.1.1 Introduction

This chapter relates to loan finance. A loan contract constitutes one of the simplest forms of commercial contracts: in essence, a lender advances money to a borrower who is then obligated to pay it back, usually with the addition of interest. Within the context of loan finance, loans may be distinguished in various ways. First, a demarcation line can be drawn between term loans and overdrafts. Term loans are loans which are extended for a fixed term, cancellable only if certain conditions are satisfied and repayable prematurely only in the event of default or the occurrence of certain other predefined events. This form of finance is very predictable and starkly contrasts with overdrafts. Overdrafts are loans that can be extended, but also cancelled and repaid at any time. Loans may also be distinguished by the parties involved. For example, a bilateral loan may be entered into between a borrower and a single bank, while a syndicated loan may occur by way of the involvement of multiple banks or other financial institutions. The group of lenders may be relatively small in number, sometimes referred to as a 'club loan' or conversely, may be more heavily populated and, in exceptional cases, the number may run into hundreds of lenders. In regard to the borrower, a distinction can be made in accordance with the size of the company or group. Bank loans can be granted to corporate and governmental borrowers, but can also be extended to small or medium-sized private companies and, as a matter of course, to private individuals. This chapter will deal primarily with loans advanced by several banks (typically referred to as 'syndicated loans') to large enterprises and governmental bodies.

Loan finance has not been subject to much statutory European private law harmonisation. Loans, therefore, largely remain governed by the applicable national law of contract, which may vary considerably from one country to another. However, when it comes to large bank loans the standard documentation of the Loan Market Association ('LMA') is habitually used (see also further below on the LMA). In accordance with the LMA documentation, parties typically opt for English law but other applicable laws may also be selected and relevant versions of the LMA documentation are available for each respective option provided. Nonetheless, the LMA documentation has brought about a significant degree of harmonisation and this chapter will therefore pay considerable attention to it.

In a typical loan document, the financial terms form the core element of the agreement between the parties. Yet, of at least equivalent importance are the non-financial (i.e. 'legal') terms such as the covenants and events of default. In establishing these conditions, to be discussed below, the bank wishes to generate as much certainty as possible that the loan will eventually be repaid by the borrower. The borrower, for his part, has a vested interest in securing as much flexibility on the repayment of the loan as possible.

10.1.2 Purposes of loan finance

Companies typically use a mix of sources of funding, i.e. capital, to finance their growth and business development. In essence, sources of capital can be distinguished between equity capital and debt capital. Equity capital is self-funded from retained cash and equity share capital. Debt capital may include long- and short-term bank loans, syndicated loans by a syndicate of banks and perhaps institutional investors, transaction specific finance and short-term (less than one year) capital market debt.

With every finance transaction the company has to determine which type of finance is most suitable. Sometimes, especially in larger finance transactions, more than one source will be used. Both equity capital and debt capital have their own characteristics which influence the choice to use, either one of them or both for the financing of the company. In contrast with equity capital, debt capital can be characterised as follows: (i) debt capital providers, i.e. lenders, bear less risk than equity capital providers in that they rank *pari passu* with other creditors while equity providers are subordinated to debt providers (which is particularly relevant in the company's insolvency); (ii) in Europe, debt capital is most commonly provided as a loan; (iii) debt capital creates a repayment right, i.e. claim, for the lender/creditor; (iv) the return on the loan is provided as interest (which may be tax deductible for the company) and does not depend on the company's profit or reserves; and (v) the relation between lenders and the company is to a large extent laid down in the credit documentation and applicable contract law.

10.1.3 Syndication of bank loans

The essence of syndication is that two or more banks agree to make loans to a borrower on common terms governed by a single agreement between all parties.[1] The syndication is generally initiated by the grant of a mandate by the borrower to an arranging bank or group of arranging banks setting out the financial terms of the proposed loan, and authorising the arranging bank(s) or 'arrangers' to arrange syndication, i.e. find other banks to participate in the loan. The actual terms of the mandate naturally depend upon the type of borrower and its credit standing. Nevertheless, there is a core market practice. Investment grade borrowers (rated BBB or above) can typically obtain better terms than borrowers rated speculative. The financial terms are set out in a 'term sheet', which states the amount, term, repayment schedule, interest margin, fees, any special terms and a general statement that the loan will contain representations and warranties, covenants, events of default and other usual clauses.

The arranging bank: (a) assists the borrower in preparing an information memorandum about the borrower and setting out the terms of the loan for despatch to potential bank participants; (b) solicits expressions of interest from these potential participants; and (c) negotiates the loan documentation. Once the loan documentation is agreed, then all of the banks sign up the syndicated loan agreement with the borrower and in the agreement appoint one of their number, usually the lead arranging bank, as their agent to administer the loan. It is for convenience of administration that

---

1 It is correctly highlighted (C Proctor, *The Law and Practice of International Banking* (Oxford University Press, Oxford 2010) 387) that some transactions may 'be of such a size that, in the interests of prudence, a single bank would not wish to make available on its own'. See also EP Ellinger, E Lomnicka and CVM Hare, *Ellinger's Modern Banking Law* (5th edn Oxford University Press, Oxford 2011) 781, 787. Moreover, banks may be deterred from doing so under the 'excessive leverage' and 'large exposures' rules of the CRD legislation discussed above, in section 6.3

one of the banks is appointed agent of the syndicate through whom payment and communications are channelled.[2]

In the syndicated market it is common that each bank will make loans up to its specified commitment and that each bank's obligations are not meant to be joint and several, as syndications are not intended to be a partnership. Therefore, banks do not underwrite each other or guarantee to the borrower that other banks in the syndicate will remain solvent. At the same time, the participating banks do have to cooperate because certain decisions have to be made as a group during the term of the loan. The banks may agree between themselves to delegate certain decisions to majority control, e.g. certain waivers of non-payment obligations and the right to accelerate the loan on an event of default. But most commonly, the more important decisions are subject to all lenders' consent.

Under the usual method of syndication, all banks sign the loan agreement. But at a later stage, a bank may wish to transfer its claim under the loan for multiple reasons. For example, the original bank might transfer its claim to make a profit out of this trading, to remove the claim from its balance sheet as it would cause an undesired capital adequacy requirement,[3] or to securitise the claim.[4] For all these reasons, the marketability of the claims arising from a loan is essential. The main methods of transferring the claims, or, more specifically, the participations in a syndicated loan are: (i) by assignment, in which the original bank assigns (a portion of) the loan to the new bank; (ii) by sub-participation, in which the original bank agrees to pay to the new bank amounts equal to the new bank's share of payments received by the original bank from the borrower; or (iii) by novation, in which the original bank, the new bank and the borrower all agree to novate (a portion of) the loan agreement to the new bank.

10.1.4 Loan Market Association

The Loan Market Association is an association of international banks active in the London market.[5] One of its key objectives is to harmonise certain provisions of the documentation for syndicated credits, i.e. claims arising from loans that are made available by a group or syndication of banks. The harmonisation is primarily with a view to enhancing the tradeability of these credits and reducing the time and cost of negotiations, and therefore improving liquidity, efficiency and transparency in the syndicated loan markets in Europe, the Middle East and Africa. The LMA does not seek to standardise deal-specific terms, which depend upon the circumstances of the credit, but the commercially less important areas of the documents so as to allow lenders and borrowers to focus on the more important commercial aspects of individual transactions.

---

2 A Hudson, *Hudson: The Law of Finance* (2nd edn Sweet & Maxwell, London 2013) 1006, 1007. It is emphasised that the 'lead bank will ordinarily act as the agent of the lenders in collecting all payments of interest from the borrower'.

3 On capital adequacy rules, see above, Chapter 6.

4 On securitisation, see below, Chapter 13.

5 Since the establishment of the LMA in 1996, its membership has grown steadily and now in 2015 stands at 576 organisations covering 56 nationalities, comprising commercial and investment banks, institutional investors, law firms, service providers and rating agencies.

10.2 Documentation structure and facilities

10.2.1 Structure of the documentation

In current standard LMA documentation, broadly speaking, the agreement can be divided into three sections. The first section consists of the core provisions of the loan, such as the facilities to be provided (to be discussed below), the principal amounts, the repayment instalments and repayment dates, the interest rates and periods, the fees and the specifics of payment such as the currency, time and place. Also a provision is included regarding tax and other unforeseeable additional costs.

The second section contains the conditions precedent. Only if these conditions are satisfied is the bank obliged to lend the agreed amount under the loan agreement. First, there are conditions precedent to all loans. These are to ensure that all legal matters, including the required security, are in order. The conditions precedent in this second section provide in outline that the bank is not obliged to make any loans until the bank has received such items as constitutional documents of the borrower and its authorisations, e.g. board resolutions, process agency appointment under a forum selection clause, and legal opinions as to the validity of the documentation and other matters. Second, there are conditions precedent to each loan separately. These clauses provide in outline that the bank is not obliged to make a loan unless, at the time of the request for the loan and the borrowing of the loan, and immediately after the loan is made, the representations and warranties are true and up to date, no event of default has occurred (or will occur in the near future) and there has been no material adverse change in the borrower's financial conditions. In addition to the conditions precedent, the second section also consists of the covenants, the representations and warranties, as well as the events of default. The events of default are events that give the banks the expressed permission to accelerate outstanding loans, suspend further loans and cancel its obligations. Finally, this section determines which security has to be granted to the lenders.

The third section deals with various (operational) issues regarding the syndicated nature of the loan, such as the role of the agent and the transfer of loan participations. This section also contains the 'boiler plate' clauses such as the choice of law and forum clause.

10.2.2 The facilities

Most commonly, the lenders offer different kinds of facilities in the loan agreement. Regardless of the type of facility, the agreement always concerns a lender providing a loan to a borrower who has to repay the principal amount and an additional amount as interest. When the bank provides a loan facility, it will commit itself to provide the borrower with a fixed amount of money that can be drawn in a lump sum or in parts. Loan facilities can be categorised in different ways, of which the most important ones will be discussed below. However, one has to keep in mind that the classifications below are merely meant as an illustration of existing possibilities. New types can be developed and existing types might become obsolete.

10.2.2.1 Availability

Term loan – A term loan is a loan that is made available to the borrower on the basis that it will be repaid in specified instalments over a set period of time or at once (which is then called a 'bullet loan'). Generally the drawdown of a term loan by the borrower is only possible within a short time after closing, i.e. conclusion, of the agreement. This is called the availability period or commitment period. Once repaid, a term loan cannot be redrawn. If parties agree on a fixed interest rate, the term loan is called a fixed rate term loan, but in most cases the rate is floating instead of fixed so that the loan is called a floating rate term loan. From an economic point of view, the floating rate term loan is almost similar to the rollover term loan. A rollover term loan is a loan that has to be repaid at the end of an interest period, but will then be redrawn for a new period. This makes it possible to agree on a long-term loan with a short-term interest rate. Term loans are generally used for a specific financing requirement such as an asset purchase. It is a long-term debt on the borrower's balance sheet.

Revolving credit – A revolving loan is a term loan which can be drawn at any moment during the term of the loan and can be redrawn after a (partial) repayment. Such a facility is most commonly used for credit needs that increase in a specific season.

Demand loan – A demand loan is a facility that the lenders make available but which the lenders are able to cancel or require repayment of at any time (or 'on demand'), although sometimes a notice period has to be taken into account. Therefore, the facility might also be called an 'uncommitted facility'. Facilities of this type do not require lengthy documentation as there is no need for undertakings or events of default, the lender being free to terminate the facility at will. The lack of a commitment by the lender is a significant disadvantage to a borrower. On the other hand, the capital adequacy treatment of such facilities may result in them being cheaper for a borrower than committed facilities of a longer duration.

Stand-by loan – When a borrower desires to have more flexibility, he can choose a stand-by loan facility. In this scenario the banks commit themselves to provide a loan at the request of the borrower. Because the banks enter into this commitment, they have to reserve the amount during the term of the loan. For this commitment a commitment fee will be charged to the borrower, calculated on the non-drawn part of the stand-by facility.

Overdraft facility – Another possibility is that the borrower has fluctuating financing requirements, e.g. for working capital. For this situation the overdraft facility was invented. An overdraft facility is a facility that the borrower may draw down, repay and then draw again. This is different from a term loan, which, once the borrower has repaid, cannot be reborrowed. By having the ability to repay and reborrow, the borrower is able to ensure that levels of borrowing at any time do not exceed his financial requirements at that time. An overdraft facility may be committed or uncommitted. In a committed facility, the lenders would commit to lend up to a specified sum for a given period, for example 12 months. The borrower could draw up to the limit at any time, repay as it wishes and have the comfort of being able to draw again, up to the limit, at any time within the committed period. However, the borrower will need to pay a commitment fee to the lenders for any part of the facility that the borrower is not using at any time, and that the lenders remain committed to lend. If the facility is uncommitted or if the period of the commitment is short then the facility usually will be a current liability on the borrower's balance sheet. Sometimes an overdraft facility contains a clause to make sure the facility is used only for predefined temporarily increased credit needs. Thus, the overdraft facility slightly differs from a revolving credit, as a revolving credit is used for specific foreseeable credit needs while the overdraft facility commonly is used as a working capital facility, meaning it might be used for temporarily increased credit needs.

Contingent liability facility – Another – albeit atypical – type of facility is the contingent liability facility. Under this facility the bank takes on the obligation to pay a certain amount of money to a creditor of the borrower, instead of to the borrower itself. Thus, this facility makes it possible for a borrower to guarantee the payment of a debt, since the bank has to fulfil the borrower's payment obligations. Important examples of such a facility are the bank guarantee or a letter of credit, which are both quite similar.

10.2.2.2 Lenders' credit decision

Corporate finance – A corporate finance transaction is one in which there is neither a specific asset nor a specific stream of income on which the lenders' credit decision is based, but rather they are relying on the general financial position of the borrower. This is also known as 'balance sheet lending'.

Asset finance – An asset finance transaction is one in which the future value of a certain asset is a key factor in the lenders' credit risk assessment. This, of course, has major implications for the security required and the documentation.

Project finance – A project finance transaction is one in which the income generated by the project is a key factor in the lenders' credit decision. In the context of asset and project financing, it should be noted that the lenders are often taking a mixture of asset risk, project risk, and corporate risk. For example, lenders providing ship finance (which is regarded as asset finance) will not only assess the future value of the ship; they will often also look at the operator's balance sheet and financial ratios and at the likely income that the ship will generate. In other words, the lenders will take asset, project, and corporate risk into account when they consider making available a facility that is traditionally regarded as an asset finance transaction.

Limited recourse financing – Some transactions (most commonly project finance) are put together on a 'limited recourse' basis. This means that the lenders accept that they will only be repaid out of prespecified assets. This may be done by having a contractual limitation on recourse. Alternatively, it may be done structurally, by establishing a special purpose entity that will own only the assets (e.g. project assets and income) to which the lenders are intended to have recourse, with the lender lending to that entity.

10.2.2.3 Purpose of the loan

Acquisition finance – Acquisition finance is finance used to acquire something, usually a company.

Bridge finance – Bridge finance is finance made available to bridge a funding gap. For example, when a company requires financing for a corporate acquisition, it may intend to raise the bulk of that finance through issuing bonds on the capital markets, but it may need interim finance to cover the period during which the bonds have not yet been issued and paid up, etc. A bridge loan is also often used in acquisition finance when there is not enough time to negotiate complete finance documentation including the security, before the take over has to take place. Therefore, banks have created the possibility of a simpler bridge loan with only little security (most commonly a pledge over shares of the target company) for a short period of time, with the objective to negotiate the actual finance documentation prior to the maturity date of the temporary bridge loan. To speed up the negotiations for the take-out loan, i.e. the full-fledged loan, the bridge loan quite often consists of a step-up clause which determines that the interest rate will increase after a certain lapse of time. A bridge finance loan is usually high interest, short-term debt provided by the house bank of the borrower.

Mezzanine finance or venture capital – Mezzanine finance or venture capital is finance used where traditional finance is not available in sufficient amounts to meet the borrower's needs. Generally companies meet their financing requirements by a mixture of debt and equity (see also above, section 10.1.2). Where the level of debt is high compared to the amount of equity, the company is described as 'highly leveraged' or 'highly geared'. When equity plus the amounts available from traditional lenders is insufficient to meet the needs, borrowers may approach mezzanine financiers to make up the difference. The claims that arise from the finance they provide will be subordinate to the claims that arise from a traditional loan. Thus, it will carry more risk and therefore the interest will be higher. Generally the mezzanine financier will also require some form of 'equity kicker' – i.e. in addition to the margin they will require a share in any profits from the transaction.

Refinancing – Refinancing is finance made available to repay existing debt. This may be done to achieve less onerous covenants or more favourable margins, to reflect new corporate structures, to increase leverage, as part of a restructuring following a default, or for other reasons.

Mismatch facilities – These are facilities that seek to match the difference between what is available to a borrower from a given source and what the borrower needs. For example, in a securitisation a borrower may require a mismatch facility to bridge the gap between the dates when the payments on receivables come in, and the dates on which the issued bonds have to be paid.[6]

6 See further below, Chapter 13.

10.3 Documentation clauses

In the following, we will discuss some of the most common and important clauses in finance documentation, with a specific focus on LMA documentation.

10.3.1 Purpose and conditions of utilisation

Under the purpose clause, the borrower undertakes to use the loan for a specified purpose. This does not, in itself, provide a great deal of protection for the lenders for three reasons. First, the borrower may disregard the clause, using money for other, unauthorised purposes (and thus putting the lenders in the position of, at best, having assumed a different credit risk from the one intended). Additionally, the loan may be used for the intended purpose, but its availability may result in other moneys being able to be diverted to a purpose that the lenders would not have funded. Third, the purpose stated is often quite vague, for example 'general corporate purposes', leaving a lot room for interpretation.

Nevertheless, the purpose clause is of some value. It may assist in good faith arguments by the lenders (e.g. to demonstrate their lack of awareness of any illegal use or use in contravention of a regulation). It will, in most cases, be likely to trigger discussions about intended use of the facility, which may then become more specifically detailed. It can, in the worst cases, assist in establishing a claim in fraud if the borrower uses the funds for any unauthorised purpose.

10.3.2 Payment, repayment and prepayment

One of the essential elements of the credit agreement, at least from the lender's perspective, is the repayment of the loan, including the accrued interest. The repayment clause is therefore an important clause in the contract. Repayment may be made in instalments or in a single amount ('bullet'). Instalments must often be made in equal semi-annual amounts, commencing after a 'grace period'. The jargon for a larger final instalment is a 'balloon'.

Prepayments, i.e. payments made prior to the agreed moment(s), are generally discouraged. If the borrower would like to repay the loan any earlier than agreed upon, so-called 'break costs' will be calculated. The reason behind these additional costs in case of an early prepayment is that the bank is assumed to fund the loan by matching deposits in the (interbank) market, which it on-lends to the borrower. In the case of an early prepayment the bank wants to be compensated for the costs it has made in the interbank market for the availability of sufficient funds, since these costs will now no longer be compensated by the interest payments of the borrower.

Also, the way a repayment or prepayment has been made is determined by the payments clause. This clause provides in outline that the borrower and the bank will make all payments in the specified currency, in immediately available funds, to the specified bank account in the country of currency, without set-off or counterclaim. Both bank and borrower are invariably required to make payments in the financial centre of the country of the currency (e.g. US dollars in New York City, sterling in London, Yen in Tokyo and Euros in the principal financial centre of a Member State or London). Although, technically, payments could be made by other means, large payments are always made through a clearing system of the country of the currency.[7]

In syndicated loans, the borrower makes payments to the agent bank who distributes them to the banks pro rata to their participation in the loan. Under English law, the borrower is discharged after paying the agent even if the agent of the banks fails to pay the banks. This is because the agent is the agent of the banks and payment to an agent is deemed to represent payment to the principal.

The prohibition of set-off would prevent, for example, a set-off by the borrower of its debt following from the loan against its claim following from a deposit with the lender. The lenders' arguments for the prohibition on set-off and counterclaims by the borrower are commonly: (1) the maxim 'pay now, litigate later';[8] (2) the cash flow principle (the bank uses payments to repay the underlying interbank loan); and (3) the clause improves the transferability of loans, as the transferee bank thus will not have to run the risk that the borrower might invoke a set-off right it had against the transferor bank.

10.3.3 Interest, margin, costs and fees

10.3.3.1 Interest and margin

The interest calculated by the bank usually consists of three elements: (1) compensation for the costs the bank incurs; (2) a risk element that depends on the creditworthiness of the borrower; and (3) a profit mark-up for the bank. All of these elements are generally expressed as 'basis points'. One basis point is one-hundredth of 1 per cent, so that 50 basis points is 0.5 or 1/2 per cent. The borrower commonly pays interest at a percentage that is calculated as a 'margin' or 'spread' in basis points, e.g. 100 basis points, above the Euro Interbank Offered Rate (EURIBOR) or the London Interbank Offered Rate (LIBOR). This is the rate at which the bank is offered deposits matching as to currency and maturity in the European, respectively London, interbank market as shown on a market provider's screen service – usually at 11.00 a.m. local time in the funding market two business days before the interest period concerned.

In floating rate loans, the interest rate changes periodically. The borrower may choose interest periods of (generally) one, three or six months (and sometimes even nine or twelve months) during which the interest rate is fixed. A longer interest period gives more security but at the same time will be relatively more expensive. Interest is calculated on a 360-day-a-year or 365-day-a-year basis and interest is payable at the end of an interest period or at least six-monthly. In the case of a default the borrower will have to pay default interest at about 100 to 200 basis points higher than the regular interest rate.

10.3.3.2 Costs and fees

Several clauses have been designed to protect the margin or spread payable to the bank. First, under the tax grossing-up clause, if the borrower must deduct taxes, it has to pay extra so that the bank receives the full amount. Second, under the increased costs

7 On payment and clearing, see above, Chapter 9.

8 Or *solve et repete* clause, to put it in Latin terminology.

clause, if any law or official directive increases the bank's underlying costs, the borrower must compensate those costs. Central bank reserve requirements, special taxes, capital adequacy rules and liquidity requirements may impose costs on the bank which are attributable to the loan but which are not reflected in the costs of funding deposits. The weakness of this clause is the practical difficulty of allocating certain costs to particular loans and also the commercial acceptability of passing on some costs. Probably because of this an increased cost claim is highly unusual in international loans. Additionally, the borrower usually is obliged to bear all costs in connection with the negotiation, drafting and amending of the credit documentation.

Besides the different cost provisions just discussed there are also some arrangements with regard to the fees. First, the borrower has to pay an 'arrangement fee' to the lead manager of the arranging banks, which is commonly stipulated in a confidential fee letter. In the case of a stand-by loan facility (see above, section 10.2.2.1), also a commitment fee will be payable by the borrower. Generally this commitment fee is a percentage of the stand-by amount.

10.3.4 Guarantees, representations and undertakings

Next to the conditions precedent, it is the guarantees, representations, undertakings and events of default that form the second part of the loan agreement. This part regulates the working relationship between the lenders and the borrower, and hence is often the most heavily negotiated part of the document.

10.3.4.1 Guarantees

A bank will consider security for repayment of the loan of utmost importance. Therefore, it is commonly agreed that the borrower has to grant different types of security. Not only property law or real security interests such as pledges and mortgages are granted, but also personal security rights. A prime example of such a personal security right can be found in the guarantee clause. Under the so-called 'all moneys' guarantee, for instance, a third party guarantor guarantees whatever monies the borrower owes the lenders from time to time. In the context of major financings, 'all moneys' guarantees are unusual. In typical major financings loan documentation such as LMA documentation, the guarantee clause constitutes a primary obligation on a guarantor to pay sums under the loan agreement if these sums remain unpaid by the borrower. The intention is to ensure that any difficulties with the underlying debt do not affect the guarantor's liability. Therefore, the LMA documentation also contains an indemnity for losses resulting from unpaid sums because of invalidity, illegality, or unenforceability. Furthermore, the guarantee is a continuing guarantee. This means that the guarantee relates not only to the original loan (which may well have been repaid) but also to the readvanced loans from time to time. This is especially important in a revolving credit.

10.3.4.2 Representations

Representations and warranties are typical English law inspired statements inserted into the contract that list the basic assumptions that encouraged each side to agree to the deal.[9] The idea is for one side to put the other side on notice that it is relying on

9 PR Wood, *International Loans, Bonds, Guarantees, Legal Opinions (The Law and Practice of International Finance Series, Vol. 3)* (2nd edn Thomson/Sweet & Maxwell, London 2007) 64, 68.

certain facts, both past and present, and that it expects those facts to survive into the future. Technically speaking, representations and warranties are distinct legal concepts. Each gives rise to a different legal remedy if a deal goes sour and ends up in court. Representations are past and present facts that spell out why each side was brought into the deal. A misrepresentation claim, if proved, gives rise to damages and a remedy called rescission, which is the unwinding or undoing of the deal. Warranties are inserted to protect a party if losses arise because the future does not unfold in the way that was represented by those facts. A breach of warranty gives rise to damages. However, for most practical purposes, if any of the statements (whether a representation or a warranty) transpires to be untrue, the lenders will rely on their contractual rights (not to lend and/or to accelerate) which arise as a result. These rights are the same for a misrepresentation as for a breach of warranty.

Credit agreements contain an elaborate series of mainly standardised representations by the borrower. Banking practice distinguishes between legal representations and commercial representations. The former basically deal with the legal validity of the agreement,[10] while the latter deal with the borrower's financial condition and credit standing. In practice, the representations are investigatory and therefore, (hopefully) flush out problems in advance because they trigger disclosure of information, which is especially useful under English law because there is no general duty to negotiate in good faith.[11]

A frequently used representation is the one regarding the *pari passu* ranking of the debt.[12] Together with the negative pledge and cross-default clauses this clause is important for, especially, unsecured lenders to ensure that they are and remain on an equal footing with other lenders to the borrower.[13] The intention is to ensure that the syndicate of lenders for this loan is at least equal with all other unsecured creditors, or, if not, that they know what creditors have priority. The *pari passu* clause requires the loan to be of at least equal ranking with other unsecured debts. In other words, it requires that the borrower confirms that on the borrower's insolvency, the lenders will share the borrower's assets that are available to unsecured creditors pro rata with other unsecured creditors. However, the clause does not prevent the borrower from paying other debts before making payment on the loan, giving security for other debts[14] and agreeing different, more favourable, terms in any loan agreements with other creditors.

10.3.4.3 Undertakings

The purposes of the undertakings are to ensure the lenders have the information they need; to ensure good housekeeping by the borrower; to give the lenders leverage; and

10 Legal representations include such matters as legal status of the borrower (e.g. duly incorporated company, powers and authorisations of the borrower and the legal validity and enforceability of the borrower's obligations). Commercial representations include such matters as no litigation, actual or known to be threatened (material on group basis); borrower's last (group) accounts are materially correct; the information memorandum is materially correct and not misleading, projections reasonably based, no material omissions (to best knowledge and belief of the borrower); no material adverse change in (group) financial condition since date of last accounts; and no (material) default on contracts or other debt.

11 Actually, in English law there is no such thing as a good faith principle as a whole. See E McKendrick, *Contract Law. Text, Cases, and Materials* (5th edn Oxford University Press, Oxford 2012) 494, 518.

12 Sometimes, the *pari passu* clause is also a warranty and even sometimes a covenant as well.

13 R Cranston, *Principles of Banking Law* (2nd edn Oxford University Press, Oxford 2002) 321.

14 This is something the negative pledge clause tries to avoid; see on negative pledge the section immediately below.

to protect the borrower's assets. Usually the undertakings cover: (1) provisions of information; (2) financial covenants; and (3) positive and negative covenants relating to protection of assets.

Provision of information – The most important information undertakings relate to the financials of the borrowing company or group. Therefore, generally, the parent company has to supply to the lenders, via the agent, its audited financial statements. Both consolidated statements, and statements of each member of the group who is a party to the finance documents separately, are commonly required. A consolidated statement concerns the highest level in the group to which the lenders have recourse, which thus gives financial information for the whole of the group below that company. Together with the audited annual statements the lenders might require an auditor's certificate confirming compliance with the financial ratios.

Furthermore, the company commonly has to provide to the lenders all documents dispatched by the company to its shareholders or its creditors. This is intended to ensure that those events that are significant enough to be notified to shareholders and/or creditors are, at the same time, notified to the lenders. However, in the case of private companies, it may be appropriate to limit this requirement since the shareholders of private companies are often immediately involved in day-to-day management and may receive more information than would be appropriate for a lender.

In the same vein, the borrower may have to supply to the lenders all details of a litigation, arbitration or administrative procedure, as soon as the company becomes aware of it (and if it might, if adversely determined, have a material adverse effect).

Financial covenants – The financial covenants relate to the financial ratios that are agreed upon in connection with the monitoring of the borrower. More specifically, these covenants determine which aspects of the borrower's financial condition will be monitored and tested by the lenders, at which level of the group the tests are run; in respect of what periods the tests are run; and what the consequences of breach of a ratio are.

Positive and negative covenants relating to protection of assets – The general positive covenants are minimal; the most important positive covenant is to comply with laws affecting the loan. The negative covenants usually consist of the negative pledge clause, a no disposal clause, and a clause prohibiting mergers or change of business.

The negative pledge is especially important from a legal point of view. The clause prohibits the borrower from giving security to a third party[15] unless that security falls within one of the exceptions to the clause.[16] There are many different reasons for inclusion of a negative pledge and its significance varies from transaction to transaction, but first of all, its role is to preserve equality among the lenders and it protects the borrower's pool of assets from being dissipated. In a secured transaction, lenders may

---

15 R Cranston, *Principles of Banking Law* (2nd edn Oxford University Press, Oxford 2002) 315, 321.

16 Generally, only few exceptions as to the negative pledge undertaking are permitted. Exceptions might concern (among others): existing security, netting or set-off in the course of ordinary banking arrangements, operation of law, after acquired property/companies and security entered into pursuant to the finance documents themselves.

also want to have the negative pledge in place so as to facilitate the lenders' control of the company, enable the lenders to easily sell the company as a going concern should an event of default occur, and reduce the likelihood of other creditors taking action against the company.

The consequence of a breach of the negative pledge is not entirely clear from a legal point of view, and somehow problematic from a practical point of observation. The clause aims to ensure that if the lenders need to enforce their rights against the borrower, all of the borrower's assets will be shared equally. If the borrower breaches the clause, the lenders may be contractually allowed to accelerate (i.e. to demand immediate repayment of the loan in advance of its normal due date). Yet if they do so, they will then be in the situation which the clause was intended to avoid – i.e. of having to enforce but not having equal access to the borrowers' assets. In other words, the clause does not in fact protect the lenders against a borrower which breaches the clause. The position may be different if the person taking security knew, or should have known, that that security was given in breach of the negative pledge.[17]

10.3.5 Events of default

10.3.5.1 Effects and classification of defaults

An event of default is a predefined event which allows the lender to demand immediate repayment of the loan in advance of its normal due date ('acceleration').[18] Especially in revolving credit facilities, the occurrence of an event of default normally also allows the lender to cancel any obligations to make further loan advances. The events of default are not concerned with fault, but only of risk as they set out the circumstances on which parties have agreed that the level of risk has changed. Calling a default is a last resort and will usually lead to the immediate demise of the borrower. Thus, the ability to call a default is primarily to provide a sanction and to strengthen the hand of the bank in restructuring negotiations unless the case is hopeless. The existence of these rights gives the lenders leverage to negotiate adjustments to the transaction (such as a change in security or interest) if any of the specified events occurs.

An (actual) default such as a breach of an undertaking is something which may or may not mature into an 'event of default' as defined in the agreement. Both a default and an event of default automatically result in the release of the lenders from their obligation to lend new money unless the majority of the lenders waive the default. However, some defaults are also automatically considered events of default. An example is a breach of financial ratio, which is automatically an event of default in most loan agreements. Many defaults become events of default only after a period of time ('grace period') and/or the giving of notice. Once a default occurs, the borrower is obliged to notify the lenders. Failure to do so results in a separate (usually automatic)

---

17 Under English common law, in these exceptional circumstances, the beneficiary of the promise would be entitled to sue the third party and successfully ask for the invalidation of the security granted in breach of the negative pledge. This is referred to as the 'rule of De Mattos', named after the *decisum De Mattos v Gibson* (1858) 4 De G & J 276. Among scholars, see R Cranston, *Principles of Banking Law* (2nd edn Oxford University Press, Oxford 2002) 319.

18 Ibid. 321, 322.

event of default. Once an event of default has occurred, the lenders have the right to accelerate the loan. Acceleration does not happen automatically. The lenders can elect whether or not to exercise that right and the loan will only become repayable early if the lenders make a demand for such payment. The lenders' right to accelerate the loan, or not to lend additional monies will cease to be exercisable in certain circumstances if the loan document states that those rights are only exercisable while the event of default is 'continuing'.

Roughly, there are two types of events of default: actual events of default (such as the failure to pay principal or interest when it falls due for payment) and prospective events of default (such as when payment is not yet due, but it is clear that it will not be capable of being paid when it does fall due). Events of default commonly have four main effects by the express terms of the loan contract. First, an event of default expressly permits the bank to accelerate outstanding loans. Second, an event of default permits the bank to cancel its obligations to extend further loans. Third, it enables the bank to suspend further loans under the 'conditions precedent' clause. Last, an event may constitute a default under other (credit) agreements of the borrower under a cross-default clause (see further the section immediately below).

Below, three commonly used events of default in loan documentation are discussed in more detail. It concerns the cross-default clause, the material adverse change clause and the change of control clause.[19] All three are important from a legal point of view because of their use or effect.

10.3.5.2 Cross-default

Cross-default means that the borrower fails to pay another financial debt outside of the loan agreement when due, or other financial debt is accelerated, or a commitment to lend other financial debt is cancelled, an event of default or pending event of default occurs in relation to any other financial debt, or collateral security for financial debt becomes enforceable or is enforced.[20] This clause is of critical importance because a default under any other financial indebtedness of any group member constitutes an event of default under the facilities agreement itself. This clause constitutes a phase in the negotiations on which borrowers usually spend some time in striking an acceptable deal with lenders.

The aim of the cross-default clause from the lenders' point of view is to ensure that they are on an equal footing with all the other creditors of the group. If another lender is not paid and accelerates, demanding repayment at once, or if another lender has the right to accelerate, the lenders also wish to be able to accelerate repayment of the facilities themselves (even if the borrower has not otherwise defaulted under the facilities agreement).[21] The borrower will wish to restrict the circumstances in which

---

19 To be more complete: the main events of default are non-payment; non-compliance with other terms, such as covenants; breach of representation and warranty; cross-default; actual or declared insolvency; creditor executions; change of control; and material adverse change. Materiality tests and grace periods may be agreed, especially if the borrower has a strong bargaining position.

20 PR Wood, *International Loans, Bonds, Guarantees, Legal Opinions (The Law and Practice of International Finance Series, Vol. 3)* (2nd edn Thomson/Sweet & Maxwell, London 2007) 103, 104.

21 As the bank thus has the sanction of acceleration to bring the house down, it gives the bank the ability to be present at the table in debt restructuring negotiations. In practice however, the cross-default has an 'inertia effect'. If everybody can accelerate, then nobody can, since this inevitably leads to bankruptcy, which might not be to the lenders' benefit. (Ibid. 103.)

the lenders can demand repayment under the facilities agreement on the basis of defaults under other financing arrangements. Express limitations on the clause may include the scope of 'debt' that is relevant for the cross-default clause. For instance, debt may be limited to borrowing and guarantees of borrowing and exclude operational debt such as trade debt, because otherwise many borrowers would often be in default. Another way of limiting the scope can be reached by agreeing on a threshold amount. Thresholds may be different for principal and interest. Sometimes the default is limited to actual acceleration of other loans, rather than the potential occurrence of either a pending default or an event whereby the debt is capable of being accelerated. This is often called cross-acceleration, as opposed to cross-default.

10.3.5.3 Material adverse change

Under the material adverse change clause, an event of default shall be deemed to have occurred if any circumstances arise which, in the (reasonable) opinion of the majority banks, might be/is likely to/will have a material adverse effect on the financial conditions of the borrower or on the ability of the borrower to comply with its obligations under the loan agreement.[22]

Generally, an adverse change in financial conditions would be 'material' if the circumstance, if known at the time of the conclusion of the contract, would have caused the bank not to lend at all or to lend on significantly more onerous terms, e.g. as to interest, maturity or security. Consideration could be given also to the criteria used by recognised rating agencies in posting significant credit downgrades. Often there is a double test: any 'material adverse change' must also affect 'the ability of the borrower to perform.[23] From a lender's point of view, the clause should apply only to significant deteriorations whereas a precise financial test would confer greater predictability for both sides.

The material adverse change clause is important in practice for the lender, as it allows the bank to exercise a suasion and pressure on the counterparty. Although the bargaining power balance between lender and borrower varies significantly depending on the practical circumstances, the inclusion of this clause is fairly standard. Nevertheless, sometimes borrowers can successfully argue that lenders are adequately protected by all the other representations, covenants and events of default, and do not need, in addition to the latter, to embed in the contract the ability to accelerate or stop a drawing on the grounds that there has been a material adverse change.

10.3.5.4 Change of control

Change of control means that it constitutes an event of default if a single person (or persons acting in concert) acquires control of the borrower and/or existing controllers of the borrower lose control. Especially where the borrower is a public company and

---

22 See, under English common law, *BNP Paribas v Yukos Oil* [2005] EWHC 1321. In this case the controversy was centred on whether two events subsequent to the conclusion of the facility (i.e. the imprisonment of the directors of the borrower and an unexpected US$3 billion tax bill charged on the borrower itself) could constitute a 'material adverse change'. It is reminded by Hudson (A Hudson, *Hudson The Law of Finance* (2nd edn Sweet & Maxwell, London 2013) 1010) that, in a scenario where the borrower reported a fall of 20 per cent in its net assets, it was held (*Levison v Farin* [1978] 2 All ER 1149) that this was tantamount to a 'material adverse change'.

23 PR Wood, *International Loans, Bonds, Guarantees, Legal Opinions (The Law and Practice of International Finance Series, Vol. 3)* (2nd edn Thomson/Sweet & Maxwell, London 2007) 106, 107.

becomes controlled by a single shareholder, for instance as a result of a takeover, it is easier for the new shareholder to manipulate the assets than if the borrower had remained a public company.[24]

10.3.6 Boilerplate

The provisions in the third and last part of a typical loan agreement are commonly referred to as boilerplate. The boilerplate contains clauses relating to issues such as loan transfers, the agency role, notices and jurisdiction. Usually, various schedules are also attached to the loan agreement. These are used to attach additional documents and lists, such as the drawdown notice, confidentiality letter and list of conditions precedent.

10.3.6.1 Changes to parties

One of the most important boilerplate clauses concerns changes to the parties of the agreement. Usually, the loan agreement foresees a possibility for the lenders to transfer their part of the loan to another financial institution. There are multiple methods by which a new lender can acquire an interest in the loan. For the agreement itself the most important possibilities under English law are a transfer of rights and obligations (classically, by novation) or an assignment of rights.[25] Other options (such as subparticipation or credit derivatives) do not involve the borrower, and therefore do not have to be stipulated in the agreement.

Transferring secured loans gives rise to specific problems. Therefore, syndicated credits generally contain largely standardised and detailed provisions whereby a lender may novate its rights and obligations to another bank or financial institution. The novation may amount to a complete substitution of the new lender, or rather as an assignment of the rights of the old lender and the assumption by the new lender of obligations under the loan agreement plus the release of the old lender.[26] The difference between the two is that a novation cancels old loans completely (which might have adverse effects on any security for the loan unless held by a trustee or agent for the lenders), whereas an assignment and assumption preserves the old loan and their security.

Not only the lenders, also borrowers or guarantors might change during the term of the loan. As a general rule, the loan agreement prohibits the borrowers and guarantors from transferring their rights or obligations under the agreement. However, most commonly it is allowed that new additional group members become entitled to

---

24 Ibid. 108, 109.

25 Under English common law, 'assignment' is not technically possible, although rights can be assigned under the equity theory and, as regards properties, under s. 136(1) of the Law of Property Act 1925 (see E McKendrick, *Contract Law* (10th edn Palgrave Macmillan Law Masters, London 2013) 136). In the neighbouring jurisdiction of the British Isles (Scotland), the English assignment is referred to as 'assignation': a different term defining a similar phenomenon (see HL MacQueen and J Thomson, *Contract Law in Scotland* (3rd edn Bloomsbury Professional Edinburgh) 2012 90.

26 The assignment could be prohibited under the terms of the loan, particularly in cases where the borrower prefers to control who the lender is. A lender with a too aggressive policy on acceleration clauses, for instance, would not be a comfortable counterparty for the lender. A Hudson, *Hudson: The Law of Finance* (2nd edn Sweet and Maxwell, London 2012) 1013.

make drawings under the facility. However, this will only be allowed if the new party is approved by the lenders, signs an accession letter, and delivers certain conditions precedent.[27]

10.3.6.2 The agent

The boilerplate clauses re the agent reflect the intention of a syndicated loan that the agent should have an administrative role only and should not be obliged to look after the interests of syndicate members nor to exercise any discretions on their behalf.[28] Instead, it is intended that the agent should merely act as a conduit for receipt of money and information. The extent to which (other) lenders are relying on the agent, therefore, is limited as far as possible. The loan agreement does, in certain cases, allow the agent to take decisions on behalf of the syndicate (as opposed to requiring it to do so). In exercising these rights, and in the relationship with the borrower(s) generally, the agent should be aware that, if in practice it takes decisions on behalf of the syndicate (such as the decision to approve conditions precedent, or to approve a legal opinion for the purpose of accepting a new obligor), it may expose itself to liability to the syndicate.[29]

10.3.6.3 Waivers

In the loan agreement the issue of waivers and (especially under English law) estoppel have to be addressed.[30] The main concern in relation to a loan is that, following a default, the lenders may lead the borrower to believe that they do not intend to exercise their rights and, ultimately, they may be held to have waived the rights or be estopped from exercising them. As a matter of course, the lenders wish to make sure this will not happen. Furthermore, if the borrower defaults and the lenders do not plan to exercise their rights immediately, the lenders might write to the borrower advising that they are reserving their rights to be exercised as they see fit in the future.

10.3.6.4 Governing law

Lenders commonly require loan agreements for large sums of money to be governed by English or New York law. The reasons for this are, first and foremost, historical: Britain, until WW1, and America until now, have been the largest economies in the world. Additionally, banks prefer their 'own home' law by definition, and because so

---

27 Conversely, it is possible that a borrower or guarantor resigns from the credit agreement. That party will then have to request such resignation by delivering a resignation letter to the agent. The agent will only accept such letter and notify the other parties, if the borrower or guarantor has repaid its loans and other moneys due from it under the agreement, provided there is no default at that time.

28 The agent should be distinguished from the arranger. The latter's role comes to an end with the signing of the facility agreement, whereas the former's one continues, with the main purposes of the agent being the administering of the agreed facility. See C Proctor, *The Law and Practice of International Banking* (Oxford University Press, Oxford 2010) 393, 398.

29 For example, as regards the rights of the syndicate agent to enforce the obligations of the loan vis-à-vis the borrower, it was held in *British Energy Power v Credit Suisse* [2008] EWCA Civ 53, that the agent would act as 'principal' if this was inferable from the terms of the loan.

30 In English law, the doctrine of estoppel is based on an entrenched court decision, *Hughes v Metropolitan Ry* (1877) 2 App. Cas 439. E Peel, *Treitel: The Law of Contract* (30th edn Sweet & Maxwell, London 2010) 109, 121. Among the different estoppels (promissory, proprietary, by convention, contractual) the estoppel by representation would be, *mutatis mutandis*, applicable to the parties to a loan contract: it will occur when 'a person who makes a representation of existing fact which induces the other party to act to his detriment in reliance on the representation will not be permitted subsequently to act inconsistently with that representation' (see E McKendrick, *Contract Law* (10th edn Palgrave Macmillan Law Masters, London 2013) 92, 93).

many major financial institutions are still located either in London or New York, they tend to feel safe with a choice for either of those two laws.[31] Irrespective of the rationale behind this trend, the convergence worldwide towards two main legal systems (either the English or the New York one) generally makes syndication of very large sums of money easier. Lenders also commonly argue that these laws respect freedom of contract to a large extent and are reluctant to interfere in negotiated agreements, making for a fair degree of certainty in relation to the effect of the agreement.[32]

10.3.6.5 Conditions precedent

The borrowers usually require mainly corporate documents and legal documents as conditions precedent to be submitted. For the lenders it is normal to require copies of the constitutional documents and of board resolutions of the borrowers, as lenders do not want to be involved in unauthorised transactions. The resolutions will, of course, need to have been made in accordance with the company's constitution, including such matters as quorum, notice of meeting and declaration of directors' interests. Sometimes a shareholders' resolution will also be required.

Quite often legal opinions are also required as a condition precedent. Those opinions have to be obtained from lawyers from the governing law jurisdiction of the agreement and from lawyers from the countries in which the borrowers are incorporated. Because under the conflict of laws rules of many jurisdictions, the law where these are incorporated will govern issues such as how the documents are authorised and, assuming that the place of incorporation is also the main place of business of the companies, will also govern issues relating to winding up and enforcement of judgment against the borrower. Yet lenders need to consider all countries which may have an impact on the enforceability of the borrower's obligations to repay the loan and of any security given, to decide whether to obtain legal opinions in those countries.

10.4 Security

10.4.1 Purposes of security

From the lenders' perspective, the primary purpose of security is to reduce the credit risk, i.e. the risk that the loan is not repaid, and to obtain priority over other creditors in the event of the debtor's bankruptcy or liquidation. A security interest gives a creditor a property right over an asset (in this context also called 'collateral') which enables the creditor to realise the collateral in case the debtor defaults on his repayment obligation(s). In other words, it enables the creditor to sell the collateral and satisfy

31 PR Wood, *Conflict of Laws and International Finance (The Law and Practice of International Finance Series, Vol. 6)* (Thomson/Sweet & Maxwell, London 2007) 12.

32 Ibid. 13. A further aspect is the predictability and the attitude of English courts to 'enforce the bargain of the parties strictly' and not to acknowledge civil law principles, such as good faith. In other words, less discretion is given to the court in English law. See, e.g., *Shepherd & Cooper Ltd v TSB Bank plc* [1996] 2 All ER 654.

his claims on the debtor. Importantly, a security interest is a protection against the insolvency of the debtor, as the secured creditor takes free of any claims of the debtor's unsecured creditors.

A secondary but important consideration may be that security gives the creditor a certain measure of influence or control. This is particularly true if a creditor holds a general security interest such as a floating charge, which covers substantially the entirety of a debtor company's assets.[33] The priority enjoyed by the security taker is likely to deter unsecured creditors from enforcement actions and thus may contribute to the orderly reorganisation of the company, the sale of it as a going concern or the effective realisation of its assets.

There may also be other reasons for taking security.[34] The holding of a security may allow the beneficiary (the bank) to reduce the weight given to its counterparty risk under the applicable capital adequacy rules; ultimately, this reduction of weighted risk may result in being extremely useful for the purposes of capital adequacy of the credit institution itself.

From the viewpoint of the borrower, the ability to furnish security may reduce the lenders' credit risk assessment, so that they may be willing to advance funds which might not otherwise be available, or so that they may offer them on less onerous terms.

10.4.2 Security trustee and parallel debt

Where security is to be given to more than one secured creditor, e.g. a syndicate of banks, it is useful for a trustee to hold the security for the common benefit of the creditors. In the case of syndicated bank loans, the trustee usually is the agent bank. In essence, a trust is an arrangement whereby the trustee holds title to an asset (in the present context, the secured claims plus the security interest) for beneficiaries (in the present context, the syndicate participants) so that the asset is immune from the personal creditors of the trustee (the agent bank).

One of the main advantages of a security trustee is that it would be impracticable to grant security interests to each individual creditor when numerous creditors are involved. Also, the use of a trustee makes easier and more practical both the common monitoring of covenants and control over the collateral. Moreover, because the trustee holds the security interest(s) and hence can be authorised to deal with the collateral without involving the (sometimes numerous) syndicate participants, the trustee can facilitate and control the distribution of the realisation proceeds and other payments among the creditors. Another advantage of the trustee materialises in the context of a large syndicated loan; in particular, because of the use of a trustee, creditors can transfer their claims by novation so that their part of the loan is transferred, while new creditors can be added without the need to grant new security in their favour. As the

33 The floating charge is a security historically tied with Britain and the jurisdictions existing in the British Isles. In the latest Companies Act 2006, the relevant legal provisions are in Part 25, sections 859A–894. Among scholars, see AJ Boyle, *Boyle and Birds Company Law* (9th edn Jordan, Bristol 2014) Chapter 32 ('Debentures, Charges and Registration'); P Davies and S Worthington, *Gower and Davies Principles of Modern Company Law* (9th edn Sweet & Maxwell, London 2012) Chapter 31 ('Debentures') and 32 ('Company Charges'); A Dignam and J Lowry, *Company Law* (7th edn Oxford University Press, Oxford 2012) 104, 115.

34 For a general overview on guarantees and securities in the banking and financial sector, from a British perspective, see C Proctor, *The Law and Practice of International Banking* (Oxford University Press, Oxford 2010) 477, 621.

trustee is the holder of the security, the trustee essentially only needs to determine the creditors' identities when the time comes to distribute the trust property. Under common law, the trustee itself may be changed without recreating the security in favour of the new trustee – a simple vesting declaration would suffice.

However, a trust cannot be created under all legal systems. First, a trust is a typical common law concept[35] and is not possible under many civil law jurisdictions, although some European countries have ratified the Hague Trust Convention so that a common law trust may be recognised there. Furthermore, some civil law jurisdictions require that the holders of a security interest should also be the creditors of the secured claim(s). In a syndicated loan, this is usually not the case, as the (non-lending) trustee or agent holds security for all lenders.

In transactions governed by Dutch law this has often been solved by the creation of a so-called 'parallel debt'. As it has been developed in the Netherlands, in a parallel debt structure, the borrower acknowledges an additional debt to the agent, which debt equals the aggregate of the borrower's obligations to the lenders under the syndicated loan. Also, it is contractually agreed that a payment to the agent of an amount under the parallel debt discharges the borrower from the corresponding obligations to the lenders. Thus, the parallel debt never exceeds the borrower's combined obligations towards the lenders and a parallel, but independent, separate debt has been created

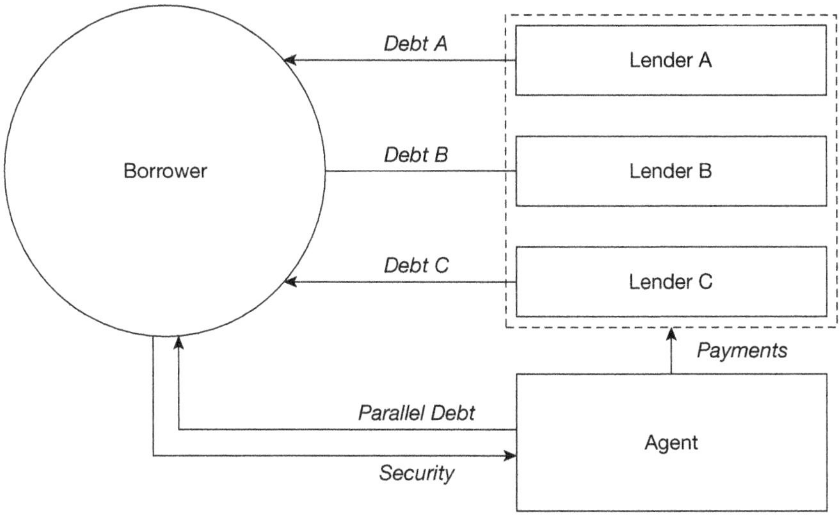

Figure 10.1 A simplified structure chart of a parallel debt

35 From an English perspective, see G Moffat, *Trusts Law: Texts and Materials* (4th edn Cambridge University Press, Cambridge 2005) *passim*; S Gardner, *An Introduction to the Law of Trusts* (3rd edn Oxford University Press, Oxford 2011) *passim*. The latter scholar provides the following definition of trust:

> A trust is a situation in which property is vested in someone (a trustee), who is under legally recognised obligations, at least some of which are of a proprietary kind, to handle it in a certain way, and to the exclusion of any personal interest. The obligations may arise either by conscious creation by the previous owner of the property (the settlor), or because some other legally significant circumstances are present. (Ibid. 2).

between the borrower and the agent. The borrower then secures its obligations to the agent under the parallel debt. As a result of the parallel debt, the security taker can remain the same entity, i.e. the agent, also if the composition of the lenders changes. Also, it removes the concern that a security right cannot be validly created in favour of a party who is not the creditor of the secured claim, as is generally assumed under Dutch law.[36]

10.5 Further reading

The Association of Corporate Treasurers and Slaughter & May, *The ACT Borrower's Guide to LMA Loan Documentation for Investment Grade Borrowers* (ACT and Slaughter & May, London 2013), supplemented June 2014, available at www.treasurers.org/loandocumentation/investmentgrade.

Boyle, AJ, *Boyle and Birds' Company Law* (9th edn Jordan, Bristol 2014) Chapter 32 ('Debentures, Charges and Registration')

Cranston, R, *Principles of Banking Law* (2nd edn Oxford University Press, Oxford 2002)

Davies, P, and Worthington, S, *Gower and Davies: Principles of Modern Company Law* (9th edn Sweet & Maxwell, London 2012) Chapter 31 ('Debentures') and 32 ('Company Charges')

Dignam, A, and Lowry, J, *Company Law* (7th edn Oxford University Press, Oxford 2012)

Ellinger, EP, Lomnicka, E, and Hare, CVM, *Ellinger's Modern Banking Law* (5th edn Oxford University Press, Oxford 2011)

Gardner, S, *An Introduction to the Law of Trusts* (3rd edn Oxford University Press, Oxford 2011)

Haynes, A, *The Law Relating to International Banking* (2nd edn Bloomsbury Professional, 2015)

Hudson, A, *Hudson: The Law of Finance* (2nd edn Sweet & Maxwell, London 2013)

McKendrick, E, *Contract Law: Text, Cases, and Materials* (5th edn Oxford University Press, Oxford 2012)

McKendrick, E, *Contract Law* (10th edn Palgrave Macmillan Law Masters, London 2013)

MacQueen, HL, and Thomson, J, *Contract Law in Scotland* (3rd edn Bloomsbury Professional, Edinburgh 2012)

Moffat, G, *Trusts Law: Texts and Materials* (4th edn Cambridge University Press, Cambridge 2005)

Peel, E, *Treitel: The Law of Contract* (30th edn Sweet & Maxwell, London 2010)

Proctor, C, *The Law and Practice of International Banking* (Oxford University Press, Oxford 2010)

Wood, PR, *International Loans, Bonds, Guarantees, Legal Opinions (The Law and Practice of International Finance Series, Vol. 3)* (2nd edn Thomson/Sweet & Maxwell, London 2007)

Wood, PR, *Law and Practice of International Finance* (Thomson/Sweet & Maxwell, London 2008)

Wright, S, *The Handbook of International Loan Documentation* (2nd edn Palgrave Macmillan, London 2014)

36 Cf., e.g. REG Masman and PNJ van Welzen, 'Securitization', in M van den Nieuwenhuijzen (ed), *Financial Law in the Netherlands* (Kluwer Law International, Alphen aan den Rijn 2010) 381–2.

10.6 Questions

10.1 A company needs working capital. Advise the board whether to issue new shares or apply for a loan.

10.2 Lenders commonly consider it important to be able to transfer their (participation in a) loan to a third party lender. Discuss: (i) how such a transfer may be effectuated; and (ii) how this is provided for in typical loan documentation.

10.3 Discuss the merits and risks of mezzanine finance or venture capital.

10.4 Explain why lenders will typically discourage any prepayment.

10.5 Explain the differences (if any) between a representation, warranty and covenant.

10.6 'In view of the provisions that are commonly found in loan documentation that protect the lenders' interests, real or property law security rights granted to the lenders are superfluous and overly burdensome on the borrower.' Discuss.

Chapter 11

Derivatives

Chapter contents

11.1 Introduction

Derivatives are agreements whereby one party contracts with another to receive a financial benefit from the variation of a specific, underlying asset, or to seek protection against the same variation. The parties to a derivative agreement are usually a bank with another bank, but also a bank and a non-financial counterparty, and also even non-financial parties conclude derivative agreements between themselves. The asset that underlies a derivative is the yardstick for (the value of) the derivatives on which the derivative's value is calculated. Thus, the value of derivatives is not fixed in advance by the parties, rather it is derived from the underlying asset that the parties have decided to indicate in the contract.[1]

Historically, derivatives have a lineage which can be traced back to a bygone era; in ancient Greece, the price of olive oil was fixed at the time of the conclusion of the contract of sale – in seasonal terms, this could have occurred in springtime – although the product itself would not reach the customer until the following autumn, as harvest time brought it to fruition. Thus, the producer as much as the customer was protected against any fluctuation of the olive oil price that might have occurred between the sale and harvest time. Although this contract can hardly be equalled with a 'future' on olive oil in the present day financial sense of the word, some aspects of the transaction unquestionably bear the hallmarks of the contemporary 'financial future on a commodity', to be discussed more extensively below. Similar derivative transactions were prevalent in the Dutch Renaissance of the seventeenth century, when the most venerable of its local products, the tulip, succeeded the olive oil of ancient Greece as the pre-eminent underlying product to represent this specific commodity derivative.[2]

Derivatives may be concluded over the counter, i.e. may be concluded between parties outside the securities exchange.[3] Thus, the contracting parties will fix their contractual relationship by way of a one-to-one negotiation over the relevant terms and conditions, and may or may not elect to use a standardised contract (see also below). But derivatives may also be traded on an organised exchange. In that case, the agreements are necessarily standardised.

As indicated above, the reason for entering into a derivative may be, from an economic point of view: (a) a hedging one; or (b) a speculative one.[4] In the first case, a party seeks to obtain protection against a possible variation in value of a pre-existing asset or a loss. A classic risk against which parties may seek protection is the credit risk a lender runs on his borrower, i.e. the risk that the borrower/debtor defaults and thus causes the lender/creditor to incur a loss. The lender may enter into a financial derivative for the purpose of hedging, so that the lender pays a fixed amount to his counterparty (commonly a financial institution) and this counterparty undertakes to supply the lender a cash flow at short notice, should the borrower actually default.

---

1 P de Gioia-Carabellese, '"Derivatives" in the Light of the Recent Financial Crises (Lehman Brothers) and through Glimpses of Comparative Analysis' (2010) 3 *Rivista Trimestrale di Diritto dell'Economia* 234, 257. From a non-legal point of view, see among others R Masera and G Mazzoni, 'Derivatives' Pricing and Model Risk' [2013] *Law and Economics Yearly Review* 296, 311.

2 A Hudson, *The Law on Financial Derivatives* (5th edn Sweet & Maxwell, London 2012) 26.

3 A Hudson, *Hudson: The Law of Finance* (2nd edn Sweet & Maxwell, London 2013) 1172.

4 Considerations on the construction of financial contracts can also be read in C Bamford, *Principles of International Financial Law* (Oxford University Press, Oxford 2011) 308, 340.

Thus, the lender has swapped his credit default risk for a payment obligation of a fixed amount and has created the potential to counterbalance the loss originating from the loan.[5,6] Contrary to hedging, the speculative purpose occurs when the party (or both parties) to a derivative 'speculate on the performance of some identified, underlying marketplace', although in reality 'the investor does not necessarily need to invest directly in that marketplace because derivatives replicate the performance of a real market in a virtual form.'[7] More specifically and by way of example, parties may enter into the very same credit default swap ('CDS') as just discussed, while that CDS does not protect against an actual credit risk one of the parties runs under a loan to a borrower. Thus, the derivative has become a gamble between two parties on the default occurring in a contract between two other parties.

From a legal perspective, the dichotomy between hedging and speculative purposes entailed to the investment in derivatives was underlined by numerous court decisions in Britain, dating back to the early 1990s. In a controversy concerning a number of banks selling derivatives to local authorities,[8] it was held that the sole reason for such authorities acquiring derivatives was of a speculative, rather than a hedging nature, given the fact that they were exclusively seeking a profit from the fluctuation of interest rates.[9] In these circumstances, such a speculative purpose endangered the enforceability of the derivative, thereby rendering the bank ineligible to claim money arising from any transactions concluded in the interim.[10] Thus, the actual purpose entailed to the purchase of a derivative may be a concern for the bank selling the product in cases where the counterparty is prohibited, under the applicable law or by its articles of association,[11] from concluding derivatives for speculative purposes.

In the same vein, the validity of financial derivatives becomes doubtful when speculative derivatives may potentially be qualified as 'gaming or wagering' contracts. Historically, this category of contracts are regarded as 'null and void' under English legislation,[12] mainly as a matter of public policy, coupled with the moral concern that accruing (and surrendering) money in this fashion is unethical. Under English law, which is statistically speaking the jurisdiction governing the vast majority of derivative transactions in the European market, the precedent upon which financial institutions and market operators confidently (or conveniently) opt to rely is *Morgan*

5 Cf. A Hudson, *The Law on Financial Derivatives* (5th edn Sweet & Maxwell, London 2012) 74, 75.

6 Ibid.

7 A Hudson, *Hudson: The Law of Finance* (2nd edn Sweet & Maxwell, London 2013) 1176.

8 In the specific case, boroughs belonging to Greater London Council.

9 See particularly Lord Templeman's statements in *Hazell v Hammersmith and Fulham LBC* [1991] 1 All ER 545 at 549–50: 'The swap market enables a borrower to raise funds in the market to which the borrower has best access but to make interest and principal payments in its preferred form of currency . . . Swaps may involve speculation or may eliminate speculation.'

10 In some jurisdictions, such as the Italian one, the widespread sale of derivatives to public local authorities (such as *communi* or *regioni*) has also sparked off, doctrinally, serious issues as regards their consistency with the Constitution of that country (i.e. arts 81 and 97) and, particularly, the obligation to ensure balanced budgets and public debt sustainability (see M Passalacqua, 'Derivative Financial Instruments and Balanced Budgets: The Case of the Italian Public Administration' [2013] *Law and Economics Yearly Review* 447, 479).

11 Alternatively, as far as public authorities are concerned (such as municipalities/councils and, more generally, local authorities), reference shall be made to the regulations applicable to them.

12 An example, among others, is English law, where, as early as the Gaming Act 1845, particularly section 18, it is stated as follows:

> All contracts or agreements, whether by parole or in writing, by way of gaming or wagering, shall be null and void . . . no sum shall be brought or maintained in any court of law and equity for recovering any sum of money or valuable thing alleged to be won upon a wager.

Grenfell v Welwyn Garden and Hartfield DC,[13] where the possibility of assimilation (i.e. derivatives being tantamount to gaming or wagering, and thereby invalid) was unceremoniously quashed. Thus, and despite *decisa* to the contrary in the past,[14] scholars[15] have acknowledged that financial derivatives are unlikely to be regarded, nowadays, as gaming or wagering, at least under English law, as they are typically entered into at arm's length and in good faith.

11.2 Main categories of derivatives

In contemporary financial practice, derivatives can, in essence, be distinguished between the option, the forward and the swap. These main types of derivatives will be subsequently discussed below. Additionally, specific attention will be paid to credit derivatives. All these types share the characteristic that they typically have the capacity to be sold or transferred to third parties, although their value, despite these events, will continue to be dependent on the market value of the underlying asset.

11.2.1 Options

An option affords a beneficiary the right to buy or to sell an underlying asset (e.g. a commodity such as oil, wheat or gold, or a security such as shares or government bonds) specified in the contract at the time of its conclusion. More specifically, the right to sell an underlying product at some point in the future (a put option) is a contract deriving its value from that of the underlying asset at the future juncture. The party entitled to sell the share at this prospective juncture (the 'holder' or 'beneficiary' of the option) will exercise the option, probably, if the value of the underlying asset at the given time specified in the contract (the settlement date) is lower than the value at the time of the conclusion of the contract. Conversely, an option to buy an underlying asset at some point in the future (call option) will allow the beneficiary to exercise the option (and, therefore, purchase the underlying asset) if the value of the asset at the future time agreed between the parties (the settlement date) is higher than the value agreed at the conclusion of the contract.

For example, if a party wants to negotiate a call option relating to shares for an overall amount of Euro 100, it is likely that the premium paid to the other party will be a percentage of the nominal amount of the transaction, for instance 5 per cent, therefore Euro 5. It can be presumed that the holder will exercise the option, at the settlement date, if the value of the shares concerned with the negotiation has risen to more than Euro 105. In this case, the transaction will be defined, from the holder's economic point of view, as 'in-the-money'. Conversely, if the overall value of the shares has decreased to, for instance, Euro 50, it is likely that the holder will not exercise the call option; it does not make sense to him to buy shares the current value of which is Euro 50 for a price as much as twice that initially stipulated in the contract. From the holder's

13 [1995] 1 All ER 1.

14 *Universal Stock Exchange v Strachan* [1896] AC 166 (HL). The case, concerned with a pure contract for differences, where parties were speculating on an underlying price and its performance, was regarded void because it was qualified as gaming.

15 A Hudson, *The Law on Financial Derivatives* (5th edn Sweet & Maxwell, London 2012) 339.

economic point of view, the transaction will be 'out-of-the-money'. In this second case, the holder will probably not exercise the option and will lose the premium.

It is worth noting that in both cases (call option and put option), the decision to exercise the option is not an obligation, but rather a right for the holder/beneficiary. However, this right bestowed on the beneficiary to exercise the option is not gratuitous, rather it is the outcome of a price paid to the other party – a price which is commonly referred to as a premium. Thus, if the value of the underlying asset has not played out as the holder of the option hoped, he will elect not to exercise his option and his loss is confined to the premium. The counterparty or 'writer' of the option, on the other hand, is always under the obligation (both in call options and put options) to deliver or accept the asset, respectively, should the beneficiary elect to exercise the option. Thus, the financial risk is far greater for the writer of an option than for the holder/beneficiary.

As far as the settlement is concerned, the typologies of options fall into two categories: the European one, in which the right can be exercised by the holder at a specific date agreed at the outset in the contract, and the American option in which the right can be exercised by the holder within a specified window of opportunity, rather than on a fixed date.

11.2.2 Forwards

The legal feature characterising this form of financial derivatives is the promise to supply an underlying asset at a specified price and on a pre-arranged date. Differently from the option, though, the forward does not permit the holder (i.e. the party paying the price) to choose whether or not to fulfil his obligation in connection with the conditions of the market; in dealing with a forward, irrespective of the conditions of the market and, therefore, irrespective of whether the transaction is in-the-money or out-of-the-money, the two main contractual obligations (to pay money, on the one hand, and to consign the underlying asset on the other) are mandatory.

11.2.3 Swaps

The third main category of financial derivatives is swaps. We have already discussed one example above (section 11.1.1), the CDS. As another classic example, parties may wish to protect themselves against the risk associated with the payment obligation arising from a floating interest rate on a loan. In such instance, the floating interest rate may increase to the point that the debtor, i.e. the borrower to the loan, may incur a loss. In order to secure protection against that risk, the borrower may enter into a financial derivative with a counterparty for the purpose of hedging, so that the borrower pays the counterparty a fixed rate, and receives the floating rate in return which the borrower may then forward to his creditor, i.e. the lender. Thus, the borrower has swapped his payment obligation of a floating interest rate for a payment obligation of a fixed interest rate, and has created the potential to counterbalance the loss originating from the floating rate.[16]

---

16 Cf. A Hudson, *The Law on Financial Derivatives* (5th edn Sweet & Maxwell, London 2012) 74, 75. In *Hazell v Hammersmith and Fulham LBC* [1990] 2 QB 697, the swap has been defined as follows: '[A]n agreement between two parties by which each agrees to pay the other on a specified date or dates an amount calculated by reference to the interest which would have accrued over a given period on the same notional principal sum assuming different rates of interest are payable in each case.'

11.2.4 Credit derivatives

Credit derivatives may be regarded as a specific category of financial derivatives. Under these contracts, the parties do not hedge or speculate on a variation in value of an underlying asset (as typically happens with other derivatives), but rather on the credit worthiness of an entity, or a 'reference entity' as is the technical term applied in the contractual frameworks. The reference entity may be connected with the holder of the derivative, for instance if the holder of the derivative holds a bond issued by the reference entity. Pursuant to the credit derivative, the holder will receive an amount calculated on the credit performance of this reference entity. For instance, if the reference entity has issued a bond and the interest on the bond turns out to be less than agreed upon, the derivative counterparty (usually a bank or another financial institution) will pay the deficit to the holder of the credit derivative. A recent spate of transactions has shown how credit derivatives can also be entered into not to avail of a specific protection, but rather with a speculative purpose, relating to the prospective and/or expected default of a reference entity.

The terms of a credit derivative commonly refer to a 'calculation agent', i.e. a party (either an external entity or one of the two parties to the contract) charged with the task of assessing whether the 'credit event', i.e. the event giving rise to an amount to be paid under the derivative relating to the credit performance of the reference entity, has materialised. Credit events will usually transpire under actual and defined circumstances, such as the non-payment of an underlying asset. However, in more complex credit derivatives, credit events may refer to publicly available information. In such instance, the degree of discretion placed in the hands of the calculation agent in consideration of whether a credit event has actually occurred, may cause a certain level of legal contention.[17]

11.3 Contractual frameworks

11.3.1 ISDA Master Agreement

Parties entering into financial derivatives are unlikely to draft new contracts from scratch each and every time they engage in a derivative transaction. Rather, it is common practice that parties agree on over-arching or umbrella documentation to regulate the various derivative transactions which they will thereafter engage in. Such umbrella documentation is widely referred to as a master agreement for the reason that, in anticipation of the series of derivative transactions that the contracting parties will effect in the future, they contain the general terms and conditions applicable to each of them. The rationale behind the adoption of a master agreement between two parties is predominantly practical in nature; two parties committed to undertaking several financial derivatives in the future may prefer to rationalise the contracts in a unified document. Proponents of master agreements also argue that they allow for the

17 *Deutsche Bank AG v ANZ Banking Group Ltd* (High Court, 24 May 1999) as recalled by A Hudson, *Hudson: The Law of Finance* (2nd edn Sweet & Maxwell 2013) 1194.

parties concerned with the transactions to benefit from minimised risks under standardised and uniform terms and conditions.[18]

Among the various frameworks available in the market for derivatives, market participants tend to adhere mainly to the ones drafted by the International Swaps and Derivatives Association ('ISDA').[19] This chapter will therefore focus on the derivatives documentation made available by ISDA, of which the latest version dates from 2002 but is updated regularly.[20] In essence, the ISDA derivatives documentation consists of: (i) a 'Master Agreement' ('MA') encompassing the main clauses applicable to the contractual relationship between the two parties concerned; (ii) a 'Schedule', in which the intention of the parties to conclude the MA is formalised, and which Schedule contains derogations and/or amendments to the main clauses of the MA;[21] and (iii) the 'Confirmation', a document specifying the specific transaction that, from time to time and during the efficacy of the MA, the parties may elect to conclude.

Section 14 of the ISDA MA 2002 defines the various typologies of transactions to which the MA will apply. The MA defines these transactions as 'Specified Transactions' which include, for instance, swaps, options and futures. In principle, the Schedule does not derogate from this wording, meaning that the MA will apply to all transactions falling within the ambit of the standard definition of Specified Transactions. Nevertheless, contracting parties may opt to either: (i) expand the list of transactions falling within the scope of the MA; or, conversely, (ii) restrict the scope of the definition by means of an express exclusion of one or more of the transactions specified under section 14. In any case, should the parties enter into a transaction which corresponds with one of the categories specified under both the MA and the relevant Schedule, the same transaction will automatically fall within the contractual ambit of the MA and the accompanying terms and conditions (as derogated by the Schedule, as the case may be) will apply automatically. Consequently, no new separate contract needs to be signed and the existing MA and Schedule will suffice for the purposes of the relevant transaction.[22]

11.3.2 Principal terms and conditions

The ISDA Master Agreement comes replete with clauses and terms which give rise to subtle interpretations and, sometimes, contentious wrangling. In the following, we will briefly analyse those which crop up most frequently.

---

18 This is called 'legal safety'. As emphasised by scholars, the 'terms have been considered in depth and so are more likely to be legally safe and sophisticated. Hence, market confidence' (see P Wood, *Law and Practice of International Finance* (Thomson/Sweet & Maxwell, London 2008) 440).

19 Ibid.

20 The latest version of the ISDA Master Agreement (2002) is available at www.isda.org. For a brief commentary on the ISDA MA, see P Wood, *Law and Practice of International Finance* (Thomson/Sweet & Maxwell, London 2008) 440, 443; C Proctor, *The Law and Practice of International Banking* (Oxford University Press, Oxford 2010) 428, 431 and extensively P Harding, *Mastering the ISDA Master Agreements: A Practical Guide for Negotiation* (3rd edn FT Press, 2010).

21 Fundamentally, the Schedule will override the MA for provisions of the latter that the Schedule refers to as expressly deleted or redrafted therein (see A Hudson, *The Law on Financial Derivatives* (5th edn Sweet & Maxwell, London 2012) 201, 202).

22 Even if the MA is terminated, section 2(a)(i) of the ISDA MA prescribes that the payment made by each party (or the delivery under the Confirmation) is subject to the remaining provisions of the MA. The proviso suddenly becomes crucial and essential, if regarded in connection with the termination of the entire framework. In brief, such a termination will transpire, triggered by the non-defaulting party, in cases where such an obligation to pay was not fulfilled.

11.3.2.1 Conditions precedent

Section 2(a)(iii) of the MA prescribes that the obligation on each party is subject to two preceding conditions: (a) that no instance of default with respect to the other party has occurred or is having an enduring impact; and (b) that no early termination in respect to that transaction has transpired. The two preceding conditions afford a right to the party with control over the payment, i.e. the right to play that card and terminate the MA if, at a future juncture, it emerged that either of the aforementioned conditions had not been satisfied at the time the payment is due.[23]

11.3.2.2 Events of default

A default on the part of either one of the two parties to a contract is sometimes not regulated under the contract but is left to the rules of the applicable general contract and insolvency law, including those rules which determine how the contractual relationships relevant to the insolvent or defaulted party shall be treated. Given the heterogeneity of rules of contract and insolvency law prevailing across various jurisdictions, the MA ensures that the remedies are stipulated uniformly. Under section 5(a), for instance, a series of events is listed which are regarded to be 'events of default' in respect to the implicated party. Consequently, the non-defaulting party may be entitled not only to terminate the MA, but to claim termination, acceleration and set-off of all transactions based on it.

Of these events of default, specific reference can be drawn to the 'failure to pay or deliver' (section 5(a)(i)). Under normal rules of applicable contract law, a failure to fulfil an obligation arising from a contract may entitle the non-defaulting party, depending on the jurisdiction, to either claim damages, terminate the contract, or even seek both remedies. As the MA is used by parties operating in different jurisdictions, section 5(a)(i) serves to regulate uniformly the consequence of any failure to pay or deliver, i.e. the termination of all transactions in place between the parties based on the MA.

Similarly, the bankruptcy or insolvency of a party to an MA is uniformly regulated under the terms of the MA at section 5(a)(vii). As rules of insolvency law are multifarious in various jurisdictions, the MA strives to align and uniformly define insolvency events as 'events of default' so that, irrespective of the applicable insolvency law, they shall be categorised for purposes of the MA as tantamount to insolvency and allow the other party to terminate. It could be argued that it is necessary to format these events into a contract, if only to bring some uniform order to a set of events or circumstances, which otherwise would not be considered in a harmonised manner across the different jurisdictions. A pertinent example would be the appointment of an administrator, provisional liquidator or trustee. These appointments may be treated as insolvency events by a particular jurisdiction but not necessarily so by another. In light of this, the MA, under section 5(a)(vii)(6), defines them as events of default, thereby leaving little room for doubt that any such appointment entitles the other party to terminate the contract.

Moreover, the insertion within the MA of insolvency events serves to further enlarge the perimeter of termination. For example, the general assignment of goods under many jurisdictions would not qualify as insolvency. The MA, conversely,

23 A Hudson, *Hudson: The Law of Finance* (2nd edn, Sweet & Maxwell, London 2013) 1226.

adopts a practical approach on the assumption – irrefutable from a practical point of view – that a number of activities such as the general assignment of goods may be an indication of its insolvency (although technically speaking they are not). Under the MA, their occurrence would not permit the party to raise any objection and they will allow the other party to terminate.[24]

11.3.2.3 Automatic termination versus termination by notice

A dilemma which parties usually face when negotiating the Master Agreement arises over which events should lead to the automatic termination of the contract, i.e. which events take effect immediately, and of which events, conversely, notice should be given by the non-defaulting party. The ISDA Master Agreement in its 2002 version specifies that as a general rule, termination is to be initiated by way of a notice served by the non-defaulting party, informing the counterparty that a termination event has occurred. Pursuant to section 6(a) of the MA, the exception to the rule is the bankruptcy event discussed above, which leads to an automatic early termination. However, parties may also decide either to apply automatic early termination to all termination events rather than exclusively to bankruptcy,[25] or, conversely, have the bankruptcy event exempt from automatic early termination so that termination of the MA shall require the notice of the non-defaulting party also in the instance of any bankruptcy event as defined under the MA.

From a non-legal perspective, it is no mean feat to establish whether automatic early termination or termination by notice would be appropriate for which events. Automatic early termination might be advisable where parties are poorly acquainted with one another, for instance when they are geographically disconnected, and the non-defaulting party would be oblivious to whether or not a termination event has occurred.[26] Yet automatic early termination is not without complications; a situation may develop where the defaulting party continues to honour its obligations under the contract regardless of the occurrence of a termination event. Should this transpire, the non-defaulting party would prefer to benefit from the payment which occurred subsequent to the termination event, rather than be required to relinquish these monies as would be the case if the termination event had qualified as an automatic termination event.[27]

11.3.2.4 Netting

One of the most important features of the ISDA Master Agreement constitutes its netting arrangement. Netting under the umbrella of an MA allows each party to add outstanding obligations and set off the aggregate value of those obligations against the aggregate of the counterparty's obligations. Thus, netting is a concept inexorably

24 Interestingly, the 'events of default' apply not solely to each party, but also to any relevant credit support provider or specified entity. The credit support provider is an entity acting as guarantor to one of the parties. If so indicated in the Schedule, the other party shall be entitled to terminate the contract if one of the events of default occurs in connection with this third party. In a similar vein, with respect to the specified entity, other parties may also be referred to, such as a corporation belonging to its company group. If this has been drafted in the Schedule, the occurrence of one of the events of default in respect to that party will allow the other party to claim the termination of the MA.

25 A Hudson, *The Law on Financial Derivatives* (5th edn Sweet and Maxwell, London 2012) 202.

26 Ibid. 203.

27 Ibid. 205.

linked with set-off.[28] The following forms of netting will subsequently be discussed: settlement netting, close-out netting and insolvency netting.

Settlement netting allows the parties to an MA to determine a net balance, i.e. set off their reciprocal obligations which follow from the derivative transactions that are due on the same date.[29] For instance, upon completion of a specific working day, the various amounts resulting from the transactions concluded over the course of that day may be converted into a single balance, which is due to be paid by one party to the other or, indeed, due to be received by that party from the other, depending on whether the sum is negative or positive. In the underpinning philosophy of the ISDA MA, the netting applies to transactions of the same nature[30] and conducted in the same currency. In contrast to some national laws of contract, however, the ISDA MA would also allow the parties to apply netting to different (outstanding) transactions, so long as a uniform currency is adopted. Settlement netting is typically contractual in nature, given that it is created by contract.

Perhaps even more importantly, close-out netting entails, subsequently: (i) the cancellation of the outstanding contracts of two parties to an MA, for instance by virtue of the default of one of the two parties; (ii) the valuation of all outstanding obligations under the cancelled contracts, which valuation is usually done by the non-defaulting party; and (iii) the determination of a net balance. Thus, close-out netting hinges upon the cancellation of the non-performed contracts within the MA which, via valuation of obligations, result in a set-off of 'gains and losses of each contract so as to produce a single net balance owing one way or the other.'[31]

Third, insolvency netting occurs in cases where one of the parties to an MA becomes insolvent. Insolvency netting is virtually identical to close-out netting, save for the reason for termination, i.e. the event that one of the parties becomes insolvent: (i) first, the outstanding contracts between the two parties are cancelled; (ii) then all outstanding obligations under the cancelled contracts are valued; and (iii) a net balance is determined which the non-insolvent shall receive from or have to pay to the insolvent.[32] The insolvency netting clause is catered for by common law jurisdictions, whereas in some civil law jurisdictions (particularly in the French legal tradition) its legal validity could be called into question by the court upon request of the non-insolvent party.[33]

---

28 PR Wood, *Conflict of Laws and International Finance* (Thomson/Sweet & Maxwell, London 2007) 224. The set-off is usually regarded as a form of payment. 'A debtor sets off the cross-claim owed to him against the main claim which he owes his creditor. Instead of paying money, he uses the claim owed to him to pay the claim he owes' (ibid.).

29 Ibid. 225.

30 As a result, it is possible to set off different transactions of swaps between the same parties, but not a swap with an option.

31 PR Wood, *Conflict of Laws and International Finance* (Thomson/Sweet & Maxwell, London 2007) 224.

32 Ibid. 225. Without the insolvency set-off, the non-insolvent party (A) would incur a potential risk of uncertainty. To elaborate, as regards two reciprocal obligations on a future maturity, A would be under an obligation to discharge immediately to the insolvent party (B) his obligation, whereas, as far as his reciprocal credit is concerned, A should prove it to the liquidator of B and, once this condition is met, A would have to compete with the other (unsecured) creditors in B's insolvency and thus receive, seemingly, only a part of his credit.

33 An example is Italian legislation. The bankruptcy legislation of that country, hinged upon an entrenched statute still in force (Royal Decree no 267 of 17 March 1942, also referred to as the 'Italian Bankruptcy Law'), does not clearly cater for a specific termination of derivative contracts in the case of insolvency of one of the parties. This is due to the fact that art. 76 of the Italian Bankruptcy Law applies exclusively to 'forward stock exchange contracts', i.e. not over-the-counter derivatives (*contra*: Court of Appeal of Milan, 17 October 1986, where it

11.4 Statutory framework

11.4.1 General

Derivatives have, for many years, not been the subject of specific legislation and regulation. The financial crisis of 2008, which some claim has been caused to some extent by an absence of legislation in the matter of over-the-counter ('OTC') speculative transactions, has prompted a general rethink of this area and a call for stricter regulation. Warren Buffett, for instance, famously wrote in 2002: 'In my view, derivatives are financial weapons of mass destruction, carrying dangers that, while now latent, are potentially lethal.'[34] On the global level, the G20 in Pittsburgh on 26 September 2009 called for mandatory centralised clearing for derivatives.[35] On 4 July 2012, the EU legislature followed up and adopted the European Market Infrastructure Regulation ('EMIR').[36] Under EMIR, in short, mandatory centralised clearing and reporting requirements are introduced. ESMA (the European Securities and Markets Authority) is made responsible for supervising the application of the Regulation and implementing secondary legislation in this area.[37] By virtue of this innovative body of rules, it is hoped that the market of OTC derivatives, which has been described by EU Commissioner Michel Barnier as a 'Wild West territory' prior to the 2008 crisis,[38] can now be regarded as more transparent, clearly defined and less pernicious.

11.4.2 EMIR

The first salient feature of EMIR is that it imposes on two counterparties dealing with derivatives the use of an intermediary to facilitate the clearing of the transaction. The intermediary may be a central counterparty ('CCP'). Pursuant to art. 2 of the EMIR a CCP means:

---

continued

was held, controversially, that art. 76 applies also to contracts for the exchange of currency concluded outwith the stock exchange). However, after the passing of Legislative Decree no 58 of 24 February 1998 (the Italian 'Consolidated Finance Act'), particularly art. 203 therein, the mandatory rescission of derivatives in the case of insolvency of one of the parties, whether or not the contract is over-the-counter, is eventually unquestionable in that jurisdiction too. PR Wood, *Set-off and Netting, Derivatives, Clearing Systems* (Thomson/Sweet & Maxwell, London 2007) 132, 193; P de Gioia-Carabellese, '"Derivatives" in the light of the Recent Financial Crises (Lehman Brothers) and through Glimpses of Comparative Analysis' (2010) 3 *Rivista Trimestrale di Diritto dell'Economia* 234, 257.

34 Berkshire Hathaway annual report for 2002. Cf. also A Hudson, *Hudson: The Law of Finance* (2nd edn Sweet & Maxwell London 2013) 1198: '[OTC derivatives have] contributed to the spreading of the crisis beyond its point of origin . . . and to magnifying it into a full-blown global financial crisis that almost brought the financial system, and with it the global economy, to its knees.'

35 On the concept of clearing, clearing house and CCP, see above, section 9.3.

36 In full: Regulation (EU) No 648/2012 of the European Parliament and of the Council of 4 July 2012 on OTC derivatives, central counterparties and trade repositories, OJ L 201/1. See also the EU Commission, *Driving Economic Recovery*, published on 4 March 2009, preceded by the 'de Larosière Report' published in February 2009 (The High-Level Group of Financial Supervision in the EU, *Report*, Brussels, 25 February 2009, http://ec.europa.eu/internal_market/finances/docs/de_larosiere_report_en.pdf, accessed 3 August 2014).

37 Theoretically, the supervision on derivatives could have been granted to the European Central Bank. However, the de Larosière Report dismissed this option, on the assumption that this different architecture would hamper the main role of the central bank, that of guaranteeing monetary stability (A Hudson, *The Law on Financial Derivatives* (5th edn Sweet & Maxwell, London 2012) 877).

38 *Driving Economic Recovery*, published on 4 March 2009.

> an entity that legally interposes itself between the counterparties to the contracts traded within one or more financial markets, becoming the buyer to every seller and the seller to every buyer and which is responsible for the operation of a clearing system.[39]

Also, parties to a derivative may use institutions ('clearing members'), one for each party, that participate in the clearing system operated by a CCP. The purpose is to ensure that operational and systemic risks that originate from entering into derivatives are reduced given the safety net of the entity or entities that step into the shoes of the counterparty, thus also taking over any default risk of that counterparty.

More specifically, in accordance with art. 4(1) of the EMIR, any OTC derivative entered into between financial counterparties is subject to the centralised clearing requirement.[40] As far as derivatives concluded between a financial counterparty and a non-financial one are concerned or, alternatively, between two non-financial counterparties, the clearing will be mandatory if the magnitude of the derivative transaction of this non-financial counterparty exceeds a specified threshold, fixed under art. 10(1)(b) of the Regulation at stake.

The EMIR also imposes on the parties to a derivative transaction the obligation to provide a 'trade repository' with detailed reports of the derivatives which they have entered into, modified or terminated. The requirement that channels of communication are maintained, which applies to both parties equally, must be fulfilled within one working day. The trade repository to which the information must be communicated is defined in the EMIR as an entity that collects and maintains the records of OTC derivatives, holding them for a period of five years. The trade repository can also be defined as an information agency that operates under the supervision of ESMA for the sole purpose of accumulating data relating to financial derivatives to which the legislation at stake is applicable.

Finally and importantly, the EMIR requires that a CCP must be in position to transfer, or, to use the appropriate technical term, 'port' the positions in derivatives held by any clearing member to another clearing member should the former clearing member default.[41]

11.4.3 MiFIR

The regulation stage in the matter of derivatives has become populated by additional characters: a significant development has been the recent enactment of the EU Markets in Financial Instruments Regulation ('MiFIR').[42] The MiFIR, enacted on 15 May 2014, is geared towards ensuring that all trading is conducted on either exchanges, i.e. multilateral trading platforms ('MTF'), or through organised trading facilities ('OTF').[43] Coupled with this provision is the norm under art. 25 of the MiFIR granting

39 Again, on the concept of clearing, clearing house and CCP, see above, section 9.3.

40 More specifically, financial counterparties include any investment firm authorised under the MiFID (on the MiFID see Chapter 8 above), any authorised bank, any authorised insurance company, an occupational pension fund, or any hedge fund properly licensed.

41 Art. 48 of the EMIR.

42 In full: Regulation (EU) No 600/2014 of the European Parliament and of the Council of 15 May 2014 on markets in financial instruments and amending Regulation (EU) No 648/2012, OJ L 173. On the MiFIR, see also Chapter 8 above.

43 Art. 24 of the MiFIR.

the operator of a regulated market the responsibility of ensuring that every class of derivatives is subject to clearing by a CCP as prescribed by the EMIR.

11.5 Further reading

Bamford, C, *Principles of International Financial Law* (Oxford University Press, Oxford 2011)

de Gioia-Carabellese, P, '"Derivatives" in the Light of the Recent Financial Crises (Lehman Brothers) and through Glimpses of Comparative Analysis' (2010) 3 *Rivista Trimestrale di Diritto dell'Economia* 234, 257

Harding, P, *Mastering the ISDA Master Agreements: A Practical Guide for Negotiation* (3rd edn FT Press, 2010)

Hudson, A, *Swaps, Restitution and Trusts* (Sweet & Maxwell, London 1999)

Hudson, A (ed), *Credit Derivatives: Law, Regulation and Accounting Issues* (Sweet & Maxwell, London 1999)

Hudson, A (ed), *Modern Financial Techniques, Derivatives and Law* (Kluwer, London 1999)

Hudson, A, *The Law on Financial Derivatives* (5th edn Sweet & Maxwell, London 2012)

Hudson, A, *Hudson: The Law of Finance* (2nd edn Sweet & Maxwell, London 2013)

Masera, R, and Mazzoni, G, 'Derivatives' Pricing and Model Risk' (2013) *Law and Economics Yearly Review* 296, 311

Passalacqua, M, 'Derivative Financial Instruments and Balanced Budgets: The Case of the Italian Public Administration' (2013) *Law and Economics Yearly Review* 447, 479

Proctor, C, *The Law and Practice of International Banking* (Oxford University Press, Oxford 2010) 425, 434

Wood, PR, *Conflict of Laws and International Finance* (Thomson/Sweet & Maxwell, London 2007)

Wood, PR, *Set-off and Netting, Derivatives, Clearing Systems* (Thomson/Sweet & Maxwell, London 2007)

Wood, PR, *Law and Practice of International Finance* (Thomson/Sweet & Maxwell, London 2008)

11.6 Questions

11.1 What is a financial derivative contract?

11.2 What is an OTC derivative?

11.3 Are financial derivatives always legally valid?

11.4 Explain the ISDA Master Agreement, its structure and most important provisions.

11.5 Describe and analyse 'netting' with reference to the main clauses of the ISDA Master Agreement.

11.6 'Netting under the ISDA Master Agreement runs foul of general insolvency law principles; it creates unjustified preference for certain creditors and should be forbidden.' Discuss.

11.7 Describe the impact of the EMIR on OTC derivatives and refer to specific provisions of this Regulation.

Chapter 12

Collateralised finance

Chapter contents

12.1 Introduction and prime examples

This chapter deals with collateralised finance arrangements. Such arrangements are typically entered into by commercial or central banks and other big players on the financial markets, such as insurance companies, investment firms and certain government bodies. The most important and well-known examples of collateralised finance arrangements are probably the repurchase agreement and securities lending agreement. Both agreements aim to provide one party with cash or securities for a fixed period of time. In exchange, the other party receives assets as collateral for the same period (this other party is therefore also referred to as the 'collateral taker'). At maturity date, the cash or securities has to be repaid/resold to the collateral taker against retransfer of the collateral. By means of this collateral and various contractual terms and financial mechanisms to be discussed below in this chapter, parties try to limit possible risks as much as possible.

In the context of collateralised finance arrangements, collateral serves as security, but also as a means of enhancing financial market liquidity. Collateral usually consists of securities and cash, but other assets are also used. For the collateral taker, it is essential that he is allowed to dispose of the collateral during the contract and until the maturity of the transaction, so that he may use it for further trading and increase the return on those assets. Consequently, from the collateral taker's perspective, collateral both makes these finance arrangements quite safe and enables him to enter into additional trading.

Collateralised finance arrangements may thus reduce the cost of credit and enlarge the liquidity of both cash and securities markets. However, these arrangements were primarily governed by domestic laws of contract and property, which laws vary considerably across Europe. Therefore, the European Union aimed to create a clear, uniform pan-EU legal framework for the use of collateral in finance transactions by means of the Collateral Directive.[1] Its purpose is to contribute to the greater integration and cost-efficiency of European financial markets. It is based on the idea that harmonised collateral rules should lower credit losses, encourage cross-border business and competitiveness, and thereby stimulate liquidity.

As stated above, financial collateral arrangements are not entered into by commercial banks only. As a means to conduct monetary policy, they are also very important to central banks. Moreover, central banks can use them for purposes such as the management of foreign reserve assets, as clarified below, under section 12.1.3.

12.1.1 Examples

As alluded to above, the most important financial transactions that make use of financial collateral are the repurchase agreement and the securities lending agreement. However, collateral is also an important element in derivatives transactions. In the following section, these three types of collateralised finance will be discussed in more detail.

1 Directive 2002/47/EC of the European Parliament and of the Council of 6 June 2002 on financial collateral arrangements, OJ L 168.

12.1.1.1 Repurchase agreement

Repurchase agreements are also known as 'repo' transactions. A repo transaction can be simplified as follows: at a certain moment (T_0), Seller (A) sells and transfers a specified amount and type of security to Buyer (B) in exchange for an amount of cash (the purchase price; E_0). The terms are that Buyer (B) will resell and retransfer equivalent securities to Seller (A) after a specified period (T_{0+x}), at a price which reflects the original sale price plus an interest component (the repurchase price plus repo interest; E_{0+i}). Thus, a repo is effectively a combination of a 'spot' sale and a 'forward' repurchase of securities, which can be qualified as a call option for the Seller and a put option for the Buyer.

From the perspective of the Seller, the need for cash usually is the principal reason for entering into a repo. The cash flow therefore is the principal flow at the outset of the transaction. The collateral flow is the flow of securities in return for this principal flow. The Seller pays interest to the Buyer for the use of the purchase price until maturity of the transaction. The level of the repo interest to be paid is determined by market interest rates, the creditworthiness of the seller and the quality of the securities involved.

Although a repo is structured as a sale and repurchase of securities, it may economically be regarded as a financing transaction having an effect similar to that of a secured loan of cash. A repo allows a seller to convert securities held by it into cash against an interest rate. However, such interest is usually below the average interbank lending rates, reflecting the secured nature of the transaction. In addition thereto, sellers may use repos to increase the return on their security portfolio. This applies especially to institutional investors, such as insurance companies and pension funds, holding large portfolios of securities. Buyers are usually commercial banks or treasury departments of large corporates. For these parties a repo is typically a means of limiting credit risk when lending money.

There are a variety of different forms of repos, which may be distinguished by means of maturity, parties involved and object of the repo.

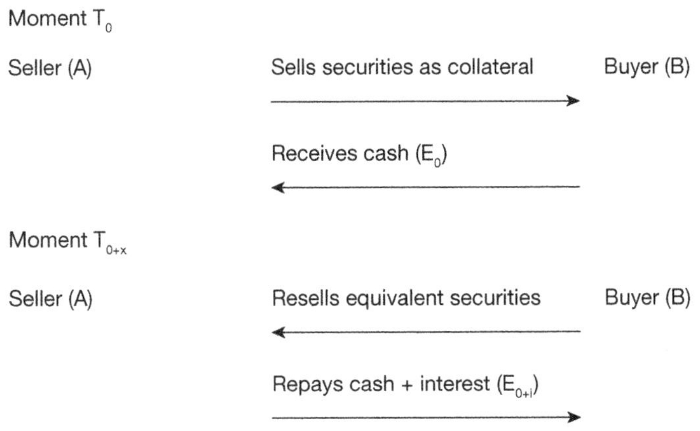

Figure 12.1 A simplified repo transaction

Maturity – Most repos are concluded for a specific time. For example, 'intra-day' repos are terminated on the same day that they are entered into, 'overnight' repos are concluded for one night only, whereas 'term' or 'open' repos are concluded with or without a fixed ending date. Sometimes the repo has a fixed maturity date, but with the possibility for one or both of the parties to extend this maturity date ('rolling repos').

Parties involved – Most commonly, only a buyer and a seller are parties to a repurchase agreement. On some occasions, however, a third party also gets involved with the transaction (tri-party repo). More specifically, the third party is usually a custodian bank or international clearing organisation. This tri-party agent acts as an intermediary between the two parties to the repo and is responsible for the administration, transfers and payments of the transaction including collateral allocation, marking to market (balancing out the value of the securities and the repurchase price) and substitution of collateral (see below, section 12.2.5).

Object – As stated above, collateral serves as security. Where the collateral consists of securities (as in the case of repos), parties will wish to minimise any exposure caused by securities volatility. Therefore, most commonly bonds are used as collateral, more specifically triple-A bonds, such as government bonds or bonds issued by an international or supranational organisation. Parties can also agree on a repo where equity is used as collateral ('equity repos'), but these kinds of repos are more complex to document, mainly because of the many different corporate events that can take place before the maturity of the repo, and the voting rights that may have to be exercised.

Sometimes a distinction is also made between 'repurchase' and 'reverse repurchase' transactions. This is not a real distinction because both terms refer to exactly the same agreement; to elaborate, the dual terminology only reflects the different perspectives of the seller and the buyer, respectively. In a 'repurchase' agreement the seller is obliged to repurchase equivalent securities at T_{0+x} from the buyer and in a 'reverse repurchase' agreement the buyer is obliged to resell equivalent securities at T_{0+x} to the seller. Hence, the seller executing the transaction would describe it as a 'repo', while the buyer in the same transaction would describe the very same transaction as a 'reverse repo'.

12.1.1.2 Securities lending

Securities lending agreements are very similar to repos. Where a repo is used to supply money to the seller, securities lending is used to supply securities to a borrower. A simplified securities lending transaction looks as follows. At a certain moment (T_0), Borrower (A) receives specific securities (S_0) from Lender (B) in exchange for an amount of cash or other securities as collateral. At the same time, lender and borrower commit themselves to retransfer equivalent securities and repayment or retransfer of the collateral at a later moment (T_{0+x}). At this later moment, the borrower usually pays an interest component on top of the retransfer of the securities borrowed (S_{0+i}).

From the perspective of the borrower, the need for specific securities is the main reason for entering into a securities lending transaction. Such need may arise because of various reasons. For instance, he might have sold securities 'short' (i.e. sold without actual possession) and must deliver these securities on the settlement date so as to be

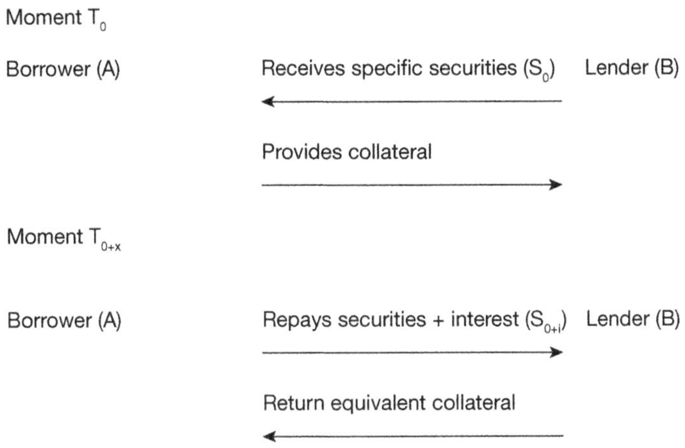

Figure 12.2 A simplified securities lending transaction

able to fulfil his contractual obligations. The flow of securities from lender to borrower is, therefore, the 'principal flow' whereas the 'collateral flow' can be defined as the flow of securities and/or cash in the opposite direction.

Lenders are usually institutional investors, such as investment institutions, pension funds and insurance companies. For these parties, securities lending transactions represent a tool to increase the return on their securities portfolios. Borrowers are usually banks or hedge funds. For them, the borrowing of securities may be a means to prevent defaulting on their own contractual obligations. The borrower may return the securities to the lender after having bought them back in the market and may make a profit if the price of the securities has fallen between T_0 and T_{0+x}.

The main difference between repos and securities lending is that in a repo, the need for cash is usually the principal reason for entering into transactions, while in the case of securities lending, it is the need for certain securities that leads to deals between parties. Other differences between repos and securities lending follow from this main difference. For example, in a repo, the seller (i.e. the party receiving cash and providing securities as collateral) is obliged to pay interest, while in the case of securities lending, the borrower (i.e. the party receiving securities and providing cash or securities as collateral) usually pays interest.

12.1.1.3 Derivatives

Derivatives transactions are discussed in Chapter 11 in greater detail. However, derivatives may be paid some attention in this chapter as well, as certain types of derivatives transactions have a structure that is comparable to that of a repurchase agreement or securities lending transaction. In certain derivatives transactions, parties also transfer cash and/or securities at moment T_0, while agreeing that they will retransfer equivalent assets at moment T_{0+x}. An example of such a derivatives transaction is a currency swap, in which party A transfers dollars to party B at moment T_0 in exchange for Euros. The amounts paid at the outset of a transaction are the 'principal amounts'. Until maturity at T_{0+x}, the parties commit themselves to a periodical exchange of interest payments received on the swapped currencies. The parties also agree that upon the

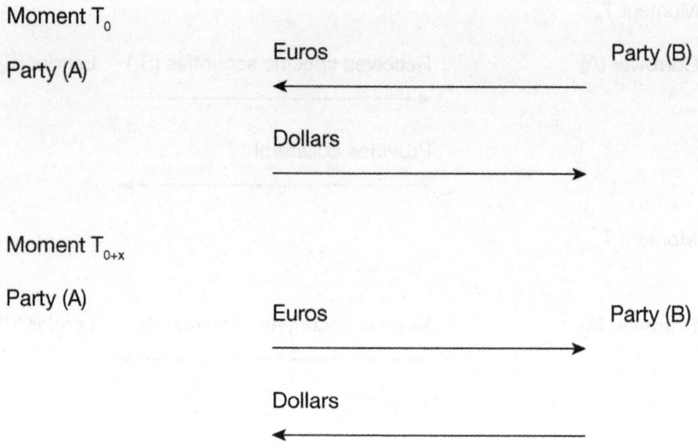

Figure 12.3 A simplified currency swap transaction

maturity date of the transaction, they will repay amounts equivalent to the principal amounts in the same currency.

Whereas 'derivatives transactions' may refer to a wide range of financial products and not all of these products have the same structure as a repurchase or securities lending transaction, the above example shows that some types of derivatives are quite similar to repurchase and securities lending arrangements. In some literature, you will therefore find that repos and securities lending arrangements are in essence types of derivatives.

12.1.2 Recovery and tradeability

From an economic point of view, the collateral provided in a repo, securities lending and derivatives transaction fulfils two functions. It serves the purpose of recourse if the collateral provider defaults on its contractual obligations (thus serving a recovery function). In addition, it can be used as a means of further trading in the market (thus serving a tradeability function). It is because of this latter function that repos and securities lending arrangements play an important role in the liquidity of international capital markets.

12.1.3 Central banks

Financial collateral arrangements are not entered into by commercial banks only. They are also important to central banks, which use financial collateral arrangements for various purposes, including for monetary policy. In the Euro area, monetary policy is carried out by the Eurosystem. The Eurosystem consists of the European Central Bank ('ECB') and the National Central Banks of the countries of the European Union that have adopted the Euro as their single currency ('NCBs'). One of the main objectives of the Eurozone's monetary policy framework is to manage the liquidity in the Euro area. The ECB may influence this liquidity by entering into collateralised finance transactions. In the case of a liquidity shortage, for example, the ECB can arrange multiple repo transactions with various European banks. Thus, the ECB prevents these banks from becoming overdrawn on their current account, as they receive cash by entering into repo transactions with the ECB in exchange for securities that the ECB receives as collateral.

12.2 Principal terms and conditions

12.2.1 Master agreement

Usually parties enter into an umbrella or framework agreement to cover all individual collateralised finance transactions between them. These so-called 'master agreements' contain general provisions; once such a master agreement has been concluded, all that is necessary for an individual transaction to be properly documented is that the transaction be agreed upon over the telephone and be confirmed by e-mail (or another messaging system), specifying the commercial terms and, if so desired, deviations or options selected from the master agreement.

Associations representing the relevant financial industry have developed special standard agreements to document repurchase, securities lending and derivatives transactions. This legal documentation aims to contribute to an orderly market in which legal risks are transparent and limited as far as possible.[2] The internationally most widely used master agreements are the Global Master Repurchase Agreement ('GMRA') for repurchase transactions, the Global Master Securities Lending Agreement ('GMSLA') for securities lending transactions and the International Swaps and Derivatives Association's Master Agreement ('ISDA Master Agreement') for the documentation of derivatives transactions. As a matter of course, parties still use ad hoc agreements because of the particularity of a transaction or because they prefer documentation that is typically domestic or the companies' own.

12.2.1.1 Repurchase agreement

The internationally most widely used master agreement to document repo transactions is the year 2000 version of the GMRA, published by The Bond Market Association ('TBMA') and the International Securities Market Association ('ISMA') currently called the International Capital Market Association ('ICMA'). The scope of the GMRA extends to virtually all repo transactions.

The structure of the GMRA is as follows. The GMRA master agreement sets out a number of general provisions that apply to all the transactions concluded under the terms of the master agreement. In order to further determine the content of the master agreement, the parties have to specify supplemental terms and conditions in Annex I to the GMRA. These supplemental terms and conditions apply to all transactions concluded between the parties. The specific content of individual transactions is determined in Annex II to the GMRA, which contains a Form of Confirmation. There are also a number of further Annexes to the GMRA which deal with special types of

2 See also Chapter 11, in which a detailed explanation of the interaction between the ISDA Master Agreement, Schedule and Confirmation is provided regarding derivatives contracts.

securities (notably bills or equities), document agency or buy/sell back transactions, and which take into account legal issues in certain countries (such as Canada, Italy, Japan and the Netherlands).

12.2.1.2 Securities lending

At present, the international market standard master agreement for securities lending transactions is the year 2010 version of the GMSLA. The GMSLA is issued by the International Securities Lenders Association ('ISLA').

The GMSLA can be used for all types of security and is intended to replace multiple older standard agreements which applied to specific types of securities lending (e.g. the OSLA for 'overseas' lenders, the MEFISLA for British lenders and the MGESLA for British government papers). The master agreement itself deals with aspects of the parties' legal relationship which are expected to be unchanging, such as definitions, representations and warranties, provisions regarding payment risk, termination, insolvency risk, governing law and forum clauses. An annex or schedule enables the parties to specify certain facts or conditions applicable to the master agreement and to deviate from provisions thereof. The commercial specifics of individual transactions are laid down in confirmations to be exchanged between the parties after such transaction has been agreed upon over the telephone first.

12.2.1.3 Derivatives

The internationally most widely used standard agreement for derivatives transactions is issued by the International Swap and Derivatives Association ('ISDA'). The ISDA is the global trade association representing the derivatives industry, and the most recent basic agreement for entering into derivatives transactions is the 2002 ISDA Master Agreement, which succeeds the 1992 standard documentation.[3]

12.2.2 Title transfer and security interest

Financial collateral can be provided in two ways: by way of (outright) title transfer, i.e. transfer of ownership, or by the creation of a security interest. In collateralised finance transactions, both possibilities are used, and the standard documentation just discussed caters for both methods.

As seen in the above section 12.1.2, collateralised finance transactions have both a recovery function and a tradeability function. In title transfer structures both functions are guaranteed. The collateral transferred serves as a security object, but at least as importantly, the transferee is allowed to dispose of the collateral received, because the transferee has a contractual obligation to provide only equivalent assets at the end of the transaction. In the case of a title transfer, it is obvious that the transferee has a 'right of use': he can dispose of the assets he has acquired as he deems fit.

A second method to provide financial collateral has been developed in the American derivatives and securities lending markets. This method combines a security interest and a general right of disposal for the collateral taker. Under traditional security interest structures, the security taker has a right to dispose of the encumbered collateral only in case of the debtor's default. But to enhance the tradability of the

3 See Chapter 11 for a more extensive discussion on the ISDA Master Agreement.

collateral provided in derivatives and securities lending transactions, under collateralised derivatives and securities lending transactions, the collateral taker is granted a general right of disposal, the so-called 'right of use'.

The (contractual) structures just discussed are subject to the applicable national (property) law. Such laws may, for instance, prohibit any title transfer for security purposes, or the combination of a security interest with a right of use. In a rare instance of European legislation concerned with property law, the Collateral Directive[4] succeeds in harmonising EU Member States' national property laws, so that both title transfer and security interest structured finance arrangements are catered for, as discussed further below, under section 12.3.

12.2.3 Flow of cash

In repurchase and securities lending transactions, different flows of cash take place, under normal circumstances as well as in the event of default. In short, the flow of cash and securities in repo and securities lending transactions under normal circumstances are as follows.

In a repo transaction, securities are transferred outright at moment T_0 from Seller (A) to Buyer (B) in exchange for a sum of money. The securities transferred at moment T_0 are usually valued at market price and a certain percentage is then discounted from this price. The percentage discounted from the market value of the securities is usually referred to as 'margin ratio' or 'haircut', while the resulting amount discounted on the basis of such percentage is called 'initial margin'. The effect of this initial margin is that the buyer (i.e. the party who provides the principal cash flow) is ensured a buffer against downward price fluctuations of the collateral provided from the outset of a transaction. This buffer is maintained during the entire course of the transaction. The initial transfer at moment T_0 is followed at moment T_{0+x} by a retransfer of equivalent securities from buyer to seller, in exchange for a sum of money equal to that transferred at the outset of the transaction plus a price differential (the 'repurchase price'). The price differential, which is a component of the repurchase price, is essentially an amount of interest. The interest percentage is called the 'pricing rate' or 'repo rate'.

In a securities lending transaction, Lender (A) typically transfers securities to Borrower (B) at the outset of the transaction, against simultaneous transfer of cash or securities as collateral from party B to party A. Just as in repo transactions, also in securities lending transactions an initial margin is envisaged to protect the lender (i.e. the party delivering the principal performance) against downward price fluctuations. This over-collateralisation is maintained during the entire course of a transaction. At the end of the transaction, Borrower (B) retransfers equivalent securities to Lender (A), and in addition pays an amount of interest, which is also called the 'lending fee'. At that moment, Lender (A) is obliged to retransfer collateral equivalent to that provided by Borrower (B) at the start of the transaction.

4 Directive 2002/47/EC of the European Parliament and of the Council of 6 June 2002 on financial collateral arrangements, OJ L 168.

12.2.4 Stabilisation instruments

Both the GMRA (for repurchase agreements) and the GMSLA (for securities lending) set out margin maintenance methods that take price fluctuations of transferred securities into account. These methods basically have the same goal: to prevent one of the parties from being exposed to a risk in relation to the other as a result of an increase or decrease in the value of the securities transferred as collateral. All margin maintenance methods have in common that the transferor of securities carries the economic risk of such price fluctuations.

Three different methods of margin maintenance can be distinguished under the GMRA for repurchase agreements: (i) margin transfers; (ii) repricing; and (iii) adjustment.

12.2.4.1 Margin transfers

The most common way of taking into account changes in the value of securities transferred as collateral is by realising margin transfers. Under a margin transfer provision, the collateral taker is obliged to deliver margin in the form of cash or securities to the collateral giver if the value of collateral securities transferred at the outset of a transaction has increased. If the value has decreased, the collateral giver is obliged to provide margin in the form of cash or securities to the collateral taker. At the end of a transaction, equivalent margin must be retransferred by the transferee of margin to the transferor.

Margin can be provided either in the form of securities or cash. Parties usually agree beforehand what they consider to be 'eligible' collateral. The determination of the market value of the loaned securities (under a securities lending agreement) and collateral securities is usually called 'marking to market'. Under the GMRA, margin transfers are usually made on the basis of a net exposure, as calculated on the basis of all transactions entered into under the same master agreement. Under the GMSLA, marking to market of collateral is possible both on an aggregated basis, as well as on a loan by loan basis (i.e. per transaction).

Consider the following example. Collateral Giver (A) receives Euro 100 from Collateral Taker (B) for 100 securities of type X with a total value of Euro 100. Because the total value of the securities X drops to Euro 90 in the course of the transaction, Collateral Giver (A) transfers 10 margin securities of type Y to Collateral Taker (B) with a total value of Euro 10. At the end of the transaction, Collateral Giver (A) is obliged to pay Euro 100 to Collateral Taker (B), whereas Collateral Taker (B) is under an obligation to transfer both 100 securities of type X with a total value of Euro 90 and 10 securities of type Y with a total value of Euro 10. The payment of equivalent margin at the end of the transaction ensures that the parties are in an economically equal position again.

12.2.4.2 Repricing and adjustment

Margin transfers are not the most appropriate stabilisation instrument in the case of extreme changes in value. This is why the master agreements provide for a possibility of repricing and adjustment.

In more detail, in the case of repricing, the original transaction is terminated, and a new transaction is entered into. The idea is that the original collateral is maintained, but its price is adjusted to the actual prices in the market. Conversely, as far as the adjustment is concerned, the parties elect to alter the securities side of the transaction, rather than the cash one, as in the case of repricing. In this instance, the original transaction is also terminated and a new transaction replaces the former one, with the parties eventually agreeing on a different kind or amount of securities as a means of credit risk mitigation. These securities will be transferred at market value at the outset of the new transaction, taking into account the margin ratio or haircut, as agreed between the parties.

12.2.5 Substitution, income payments and interest

If substitution has been agreed upon, the transferor of purchased or margin securities under a repo transaction may substitute the securities originally transferred for other acceptable securities. In a securities lending transaction, too, the transferor of collateral or margin collateral securities can call for substitution.

The rationale of substitution is different from that of adjustment. Adjustment is a margin maintenance method which takes into account changes in the market value of the securities originally transferred by replacing those securities. Substitution, in turn, reflects the desire of the transferor of securities to have the securities originally transferred returned and used for other purposes, while in exchange he transfers other securities as a substitute. Substitution must take place with the consent of the collateral taker. Such consent can be given beforehand, or in the course of a transaction.

After the transfer of securities by a transferor to a transferee in a repurchase or securities lending transaction, income payments in respect of such securities are payable to the transferee as he has become the new owner of those securities. Income payments are, for example, interest, dividends or other earnings of any kind on the securities transferred. However, it is usually (contractually) agreed that the transferee must subsequently pay through an amount equal to such income payment to the transferor.

The payment of the price differential for repos and the lending fee in securities lending may be considered as a payment of interest. In a repo transaction, this interest is paid by the seller in respect of the cash provided by the buyer at the outset of the transaction. In a securities lending transaction, the borrower pays an amount of interest for the securities provided by the lender at the outset of the transaction. The price differential in the case of a repo transaction is payable on the repurchase date. The lending fee accrues until the date when equivalent securities are redelivered.

12.2.6 Events of default, early termination and close-out netting

All master agreements contain provisions regarding events of default that lead to the termination of either a single transaction or of the entire contractual relationship existing between the parties. Various events of default are contemplated under the standard documentation, such as non-compliance with specified contractual obligations or the insolvency of one of the parties. Under the GMRA and GMSLA, an event which amounts to default results in the early termination of all outstanding transactions between the parties. However, in certain circumstances a single transaction only may be terminated. Early termination takes place automatically when certain events of insolvency occur, but in most cases, prior notice is required.

Normally a repo or securities lending agreement is terminated on a fixed date or on demand as described above, under section 12.1.1.1. In the case of a repo transaction the buyer transfers equivalent securities to the seller, in exchange for a sum of money equal to that transferred at the outset of the transaction plus the repurchase price. Likewise, the borrower under a securities lending agreement transfers equivalent securities to the lender at the outset of the transaction, and pays in addition an amount of interest (the lending fee). Vice-versa the lender is obliged to transfer collateral equivalent to that provided by party B at the start of the transaction.

However, early termination might occur in the event of a default of one of the contracting parties. Standard documentation for repo and securities lending transactions usually contains contractual close-out netting provisions in the event of default (including insolvency). The close-out netting process as set out in the GMRA and GMSLA consists of three stages. These stages are: (1) early termination and the acceleration of all rights and obligations the parties have towards each other (automatically or upon notice); (2) valuation of all rights and obligations and, if necessary, conversion into a single currency; and (3) set-off, resulting in a single monetary obligation by one party to the other.

12.3 Collateral Directive

12.3.1 Scope of the Collateral Directive

Directive 2002/47/EC of the European Parliament of the Council of 6 June 2002 on financial collateral arrangements ('Collateral Directive') has been an important step towards achieving a uniform legal regime for collateralised transactions in the European Union. The Directive aims to reduce formal requirements for the provision of collateral. Additionally, it harmonises and clarifies the legal framework existing in this area of financial law. In 2009, roughly seven years after the Directive first came into force, the Collateral Directive was amended.[5] Prior to the amendment, the Collateral Directive applied only if the collateral provided consisted of cash or securities. So as to expand the scope of the Collateral Directive and stimulate the use of collateralised finance arrangements, however, credit claims have been added as eligible financial collateral under the revised version of the Directive under discussion.[6] Yet the use of credit claims as collateral raises a number of practical questions, such as the position of the parties when the collateralised claims are paid.

Thus, the scope of the Directive is limited as it applies to certain types of collateral only. Furthermore, the Directive applies only if: (i) the transaction is concluded between certain market participants, such as public authorities, central banks and financial institutions, and not with a natural person;[7] (ii) certain formal requirements are met, including the requirement that the collateral provided should come into the possession of or fall under the control of the collateral taker (or of a

5 By Directive 2009/44/EC of the European parliament and of the Council of 6 May 2009 amending Directive 98/26/EC on settlement finality in payment and securities settlement systems and Directive 2002/47/EC on financial collateral arrangements as regards linked systems and credit claims, OJ L 146/37.

6 Art. 1(4)(a) of the Collateral Directive.

7 Art. 1(2) of the Collateral Directive.

person acting on his behalf);[8] and (iii) the transaction concerns either a title transfer financial collateral arrangement or a security financial collateral arrangement.[9]

One of the central issues of debate arising in connection with the scope of the Collateral Directive is whether the Directive should be interpreted extensively, so that a 'security financial collateral arrangement' also concerns arrangements using traditional security interests such as a pledge without a right of use. Furthermore, the Directive does not state its territorial scope, so that EU courts will have to apply their own conflict of laws rules to determine whether the Directive (as implemented into national laws) applies. On the other hand, it does provide a conflict of laws rule as regards, in short, property law aspects of securities that are to be used as collateral and credited to a securities account: these aspects shall be governed by the law of the country in which the relevant account is maintained.[10]

12.3.2 Derogations from domestic law

The Collateral Directive is intended to enhance the liquidity of the European markets for cash and securities by harmonising a number of provisions of property and insolvency law. Thus, the Directive requires Member States to protect financial collateral arrangements from a number of possibly conflicting provisions of domestic law (including insolvency law). The key protections are summarised below.

12.3.2.1 No formalities

Under the Directive, the effective creation or enforcement of a financial collateral arrangement must not depend on the performance of 'formal acts' such as registration or official notification. More specifically, Member States are not allowed to make the creation, validity, perfection, enforceability or admissibility in evidence of a financial collateral arrangement or the provision of financial collateral under a financial collateral arrangement dependent on the performance of any formal act. In other words, the only perfection requirement which national law may impose should be the possession or control requirement, and the Directive prohibits all other domestic requirements for deeds, notarisation and witnesses. On the other hand:

> acts required under the law of a Member State as conditions for transferring or creating a security interest on financial instruments, other than book-entry securities, such as endorsement in the case of instruments to order, or recording on the issuer's register in the case of registered instruments, should not be considered as formal acts.[11]

12.3.2.2 Right of use

Under the Directive, Member State national laws must cater for the effectiveness of a 'right of use', if parties to a security financial collateral arrangement wish to confer such a right to the collateral taker.[12] This right of use involves the right of the collateral

8 Art. 1(5) of the Collateral Directive.
9 Art. 2(1)(a) of the Collateral Directive.
10 Art. 9 of the Collateral Directive.
11 Arts 3 and 4(4) of the Collateral Directive.
12 Art. 5 of the Collateral Directive.

taker to use and dispose of financial collateral provided under a security financial collateral arrangement as if he were the owner of it.[13] Thus, the collateral taker may dispose of the collateral in his own name and for his own benefit the way he deems fit. This right of use derogates from many national laws of property, as under those laws a security right holder obtains no ownership of the collateral and is therefore, as a matter of principle, not entitled to full use and disposal.

As a consequence of the right of use under the Directive, the collateral provider is left with a mere contractual claim for redelivery of the collateral against the collateral taker after the collateral taker has disposed of the collateral. In this scenario, the collateral provider, on the one hand, would be able to offset this claim against his obligation towards the collateral taker to repay the collateralised debt. On the other hand, this is of no avail if the value of the collateral provided to the collateral taker goes up considerably, so that the set-off will leave the collateral provider with an unsecured residual exposure vis-à-vis the collateral taker.

12.3.2.3 Recharacterisation and fiduciary transfers

As stated above, collateralised finance transactions have both a recovery function and a tradeability function. Because of the recovery function, parties to repurchase and securities lending agreements may fear that a court would recharacterise a title transfer as a security interest. In other words, it is feared that the court treats an outright transfer of title as a security interest contrary to the intention of the parties. Such risk is particularly acute under national laws of property that prohibit fiduciary transfers of ownership, i.e. title transfers with the (sole) purpose of providing security.

The Collateral Directive intends to minimise recharacterisation risk. More specifically, the Directive seeks to protect the validity of financial collateral arrangements which are based upon the transfer of the full ownership of the financial collateral by eliminating the recharacterisation of such financial collateral arrangements as security interest. It provides that a title transfer financial collateral arrangement must take effect in accordance with its terms.[14] Consequently, Member States whose national laws of property generally prohibit fiduciary transfers of ownership must allow for a derogation for collateralised financial arrangements as defined in the Directive. It has, however, been debated whether this protection covers only outright transfers that serve both recovery and tradeability, or also fiduciary transfers of title that serve only recovery purposes.

12.3.2.4 Close-out netting and insolvency

National insolvency laws of various Member States prohibit set-off on the insolvency of one of the parties and ban the cancellation of contracts should insolvency proceedings or the like have been opened against one of them. Under the Directive, however, the effectiveness of close-out netting must be recognised, so as to reduce counterparty risks by set-off and close-out netting.[15]

Moreover, the Directive derogates from traditional rules of insolvency law such as automatic claw-back provisions, so that these rules may not be invoked to invalidate a financial collateral arrangement entered into, or collateral provided, before or around

13 Art. 2(1)(m) of the Collateral Directive.
14 Recital 13 and Art. 6 of the Collateral Directive.
15 Art. 7 of the Collateral Directive.

the commencement of insolvency proceedings.[16] Consequently, the Directive rules out any retroactive effect of a declaration of insolvency and it allows a level of protection in respect of legal acts concluded after the moment of the declaration of insolvency. More specifically, transfers of cash or securities that are made on the day of the declaration of insolvency, but before the actual moment of that declaration, are enforceable. In addition, the commencement or continuation of insolvency proceedings may not be an impediment to the immediate enforcement of financial collateral, whether provided on the basis of a security interest or by way of title transfer. Rights in respect of financial collateral can therefore be enforced without any requirement to the effect that any additional time period such as a freeze period must have elapsed.

12.4 Future developments

Since the financial crisis that started in 2008, collateralised finance arrangements have gained attention from policy-makers across the globe. Both on the regional, and on the global level, policy-makers are currently considering whether, and if so, how, these arrangements should be regulated. This new attention may be explained as follows. First, a specific type of repo was what Anton Valukas, who was appointed by the New York bankruptcy court to report on the causes of the bankruptcy of Lehman Brothers, found to be at the heart of the Lehman bankruptcy; he unearthed that Lehman Brothers was able, through the use of so-called Repo 105, to show more positive financial statements than were justified and thus to mislead investors and regulators alike.[17] Moreover, Lehman (and a similar explanation can be provided for the insolvency of Bear Stearns) failed because it was forced to increase the collateral it had posted for its repos, while other counterparties collectively terminated their repos and sold the securities Lehman had provided as collateral, thus driving down the value of these securities (which led to even more calls for collateral increase and so on).[18]

Second, many policy-makers seem to believe that collateralised finance arrangements form a category of 'shadow banking' and that regulation of such shadow banking might be instrumental in avoiding systemic financial crises in the future.[19] Following the release of its Green Paper in March 2012, the European Commission, for instance, launched a public consultation in order to gain the insights required to formulate a regulatory approach in this field. On the global level, the Financial Stability Board ('FSB') has targeted shadow banking and published a report on this subject in 2011.[20]

---

16 Art. 8 of the Collateral Directive.

17 Chapter 11 Case No 08_13555 (JMP) *in re Lehman Brothers Holdings Inc., et al.*, Report of Anton R Valukas, Examiner.

18 See, e.g. European Parliament Report on Shadow Banking (2012/2115(INI)) 20 November 2012, 12 and FT, 'Vast market has weakness for withdrawals', 5 March 2013, 7.

19 See, e.g. FSB, 'Shadow Banking: Strengthening Oversight and Regulation', 27 October 2011; European Parliament Report on Shadow Banking (2012/2115(INI)) 20 November 2012; FSB, 'Strengthening Oversight and Regulation of Shadow Banking: A Policy Framework for Addressing Shadow Banking Risks in Securities Lending and Repos', 18 November 2012; Communication from the Commission to the Council and the European Parliament, Shadow Banking – Addressing New Sources of Risk in the Financial Sector, 4 September 2013, COM(2013)614 final.

20 FSB, 'Shadow Banking: Strengthening Oversight and Regulation', 27 October 2011.

The European Parliament has required that the European Commission:

> [adopts] measures, by the beginning of 2013, to increase transparency, particularly for clients, which could include . . . allowing regulators to impose recommended minimum haircuts or margin levels for the collateralised financing markets, but without standardising them; . . . invites the Commission to engage in a comprehensive debate on margins in addition to the sectoral approaches that have already been embarked on, as well as studying and considering the imposition of limits of rehypothecation of collateral; Stresses the need to review bankruptcy law in relation to both the repo and security lending market and securitisations, with the aim of harmonisation and of addressing issues of seniority relevant to the resolution of regulated financial institutions; calls on the Commission to consider various approaches to restricting bankruptcy privileges, including proposals to limit bankruptcy privileges to centrally cleared transactions or to collateral meeting harmonised and predefined eligibility criteria.[21]

The FSB, on the other hand, is more nuanced. As regards the 'need to review bankruptcy law', for instance, it considers:

> Changes to bankruptcy law treatment and development of Repo Resolution Authorities (RRAs) may be viable theoretical options but should not be prioritised for further work at this stage due to significant difficulties in implementation.[22]

On 29 January 2014, the European Commission published a 'Proposal for a Regulation of the European Parliament and of the Council on reporting and transparency of securities financing transactions'.[23] In this proposal, the Commission follows the FSB route and it is concerned with reporting requirements only. More specifically, under the proposal, counterparties of collateralised finance arrangements (the proposal speaks of 'Securities Financing Transactions') must report the details of the transaction to trade repositories. Also, it requires fund managers of collective investment undertakings to inform investors on the use they make of collateralised finance arrangements. At the time of writing, this proposal was under consideration by the European Parliament.

12.5 Further reading

Keijser, T, *Financial Collateral Arrangements* (diss. Radboud University Nijmegen) (Kluwer, Deventer 2006)

Wood, PR, *Comparative Law of Security Interests and Title Finance* (Sweet & Maxwell, London 2007)

Wood, PR, *Law and Practice of International Finance* (Sweet & Maxwell, London 2008)

21 European Parliament Report on Shadow Banking (2012/2115(INI)).

22 FSB, 'Strengthening Oversight and Regulation of Shadow Banking: A Policy Framework for Addressing Shadow Banking Risks in Securities Lending and Repos', 29 August 2013, Recommendations 6–9 and 11.

23 COM(2014) 40 final, 2014/0017 (COD).

12.6 Questions

12.1 Describe in what ways repurchase agreements and securities lending transactions differ.

12.2 Describe four methods for collateral takers to limit their exposure to the collateral giver.

12.3 'The Collateral Directive results in unwarranted protection of collateral takers and a disruption of national private law systems.' Discuss.

12.4 'Fear for recharacterisation of an outright title transfer as a security interest in the context of a repurchase agreement is unwarranted, as repo title transfers always serve both a recovery function and a tradeability function.' Discuss.

12.5 Explain in what way the Collateral Directive introduced derogations from your national property, insolvency or private international law.

12.6 'The recent European Commission Proposal for a Regulation on reporting and transparency of securities financing transactions does not go far enough.' Discuss.

Chapter 13

Structured finance

Chapter contents

13.1 Introduction

This chapter elaborates upon two of the main forms of structured finance, i.e. securitisation and covered bonds transactions. Structured finance transactions, and, more specifically, securitisation and covered bonds transactions, are intended to pool economic assets or risks in a bankruptcy-remote entity followed by the issuance of securities (typically bonds). This transaction enables investors to invest in bonds that bear a lower risk than the underlying pool of assets does. We aim to provide insight in the law and practice of structured finance by explaining how the transactions are structured, examining the rationale of the transactions, and discussing legal issues concerning both securitisation and covered bonds transactions.

In a classic securitisation, assets are usually repackaged in bonds with different risk profiles, the so-called 'tranches' (see further below, section 13.2.2). Conventional wisdom has it that securitisation transactions and, more specifically, the repackaging of subprime mortgage receivables in bonds with different tranches, caused, at least in part, the last global financial crisis. Subprime mortgage receivables are claims arising from house loans secured with a mortgage but with a relatively high chance of default. By means of securitisation transactions, these claims were repackaged as bonds ('residential mortgage backed securities' or 'RMBS') that were rated positively. What is more, these bonds were, in their turn, repackaged as bonds so that investors ultimately relied on the ratings of these bonds rather than making their own assessment of the risks of the ultimate underlying assets, i.e. the high risk mortgage receivables. When US housing prices collapsed and the subprime loans risk of default materialised, RMBS lost most of their value, which caused, in its turn, the collapse of several financial institutions including Lehman Brothers, as these institutions had invested massively in these products.[1]

13.2 Securitisation

The most essential element of a securitisation transaction is the sale of assets, typically receivables, from the originating party ('the originator') to a special purpose vehicle ('SPV'). The SPV receives the purchase amount it has to pay for the receivables to the originator by issuing bonds, which are typically rated by a rating agency, to investors. The SPV pays principal and interest on these bonds with the proceeds on the receivables (i.e. principal and interest) that have been transferred to the SPV. In the following, we further elaborate on the structure of securitisation and the rationale behind the transaction. In the next section, some legal issues concerning the transaction are discussed. We finish with some remarks on covered bond transactions.

---

1 Cf. *The Financial Crisis Inquiry Report: Final Report of the National Commission on the Causes of the Financial and Economic Crisis in the United States*, www.gpo.gov/fdsys/pkg/GPO-FCIC/content-detail.html, accessed 15 April 2015. On Lehman Brothers and its insolvency, see above, Chapter 7 and section 12.4.

13.2.1 Transaction

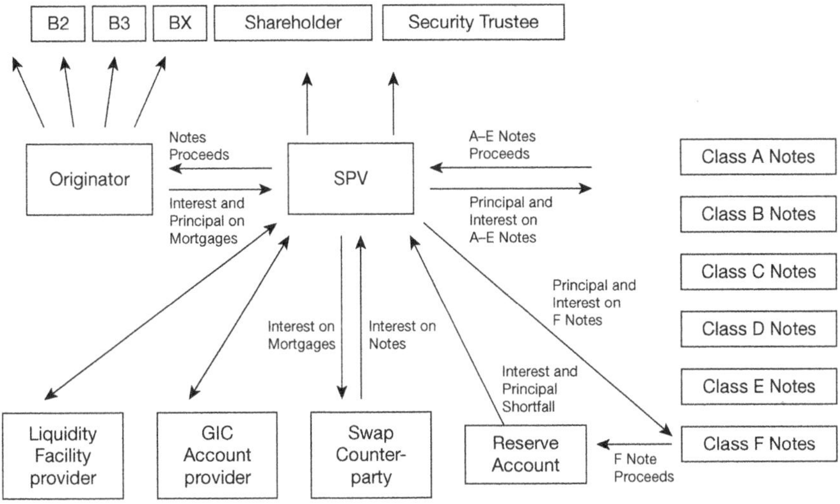

Figure 13.1 A simplified traditional securitisation

In a traditional securitisation, securitisation is achieved by the transfer of receivables (in the above illustration, claims of the originator on borrowers B2, B3 and BX) under (undisclosed) assignment from the originator to the SPV. Subsequently, the SPV issues bonds ('Class A–F Notes' in the above illustration) to investors.

13.2.2 Structure and parties

Receivables – The receivables that may be used in a securitisation transaction come in great variety and numbers. One could think of home mortgage loans, i.e. loans that have been extended to finance a house and which loans have been secured with a mortgage, and other consumer receivables such as credit card receivables, lease obligations and even monthly charges for telephones. But also loans to professional parties, such as commercial real estate mortgages, could be securitised.

One of the main objectives in a securitisation transaction is to reduce the credit risk on the receivables. Credit risk is the risk of inability to pay principal and interest. Mitigating this risk could be achieved in multiple ways. First, the credit risk on the receivables, i.e. the risk of non-payment of principal and interest on the claims, is reduced by a careful selection of which receivables are to be transferred to the SPV. In order to receive a high rating of the bonds issued by the SPV (see below), only receivables with a low default risk, i.e. claims that are highly probable to be paid, should ideally be transferred to the SPV. Second, credit risk on the receivables may be reduced by a guarantee from the originator or may be given by a third party to the SPV. Such a guarantee would secure payment on the receivables, but should not be overly extensive because of a possible recharacterisation risk (to be discussed below, section 13.2.4). A third possibility to reduce the credit risk on the receivables is by pool insurance. This means that payment of principal and interest on certain pools of claims are insured by a professional party.

Originator – An originator is the entity that initially has the receivables, i.e. that holds the claims on clients, that are to be securitised. An originating party typically is a bank, but it can also be another financial institution such as a credit card company, or any other company that has many receivables.

Debtors – Debtors of the receivables securitised can be consumers as well as companies. Consumer debts, eligible for securitisation, comprise, among others, credit card debts and mortgage loans. Company debts include long-, medium- and short-term obligations. In the vast majority of cases payment of the debt is secured, e.g. by a bank mortgage.

Servicer – The collector of the receivables is referred to as 'the servicer' and receives a fee for its work. It is very well possible that also after the transfer of the receivables to the SPV, the originator continues to collect the proceeds on the receivables and thus acts as the servicer, but this role can also be performed by a third party.

SPV – The SPV, also referred to as the issuer, is the vehicle that is essential to the securitisation transaction. It buys the receivables from the originator with capital raised by issuing different types of bonds (see further below). The SPV usually is a limited liability company and the shares of the SPV are owned by a foundation or a trust office. Thus, the SPV's shares are not held by the originator, as it is important that the SPV is not consolidated on the originator's balance sheet. Perhaps even more importantly, the SPV must be 'bankruptcy remote'. Bankruptcy remoteness is achieved by several means. First, the objects of the articles of association are limited in such a manner that the SPV is not allowed to conduct any business that does not regard the securitisation transaction. Second, all possibilities for counterparties to initiate liquidation proceedings against the SPV are excluded by incorporating a covenant in all its contracts that prohibits the contracting party to initiate liquidation proceedings against the SPV. Third, the SPV does not hire employees and retains the number of creditors to a minimum. Fourth, independent directors are appointed, e.g. by contracting a corporate service provider.

Investors – The parties buying bonds from an SPV are often other banks, institutional investors and hedge funds. With a securitisation, investors with different risk appetites may be satisfied as the bonds are commonly issued in (at least) two classes: senior and junior bonds, while the junior bonds are subordinated to the senior ones. Distinguishing senior and junior (and other classes of bonds, such as in the illustration above) is called 'tranching'.

Bonds – The risk of the SPV's inability to pay principal and interest on the bonds qualifies as a credit risk for the investors. This risk could be mitigated in several ways. First, the credit risk on the SPV is mitigated by tranching. Because junior notes are subordinated to the senior ones and thus bear the first losses, the credit risk on notes with more seniority is mitigated. Second, overcollateralisation is a way to mitigate credit risk on the SPV: the originator transfers more receivables to the SPV than are needed to pay the investors. Also, the interest the SPV receives on the receivables from the debtors is usually higher than the interest the SPV has to pay to the investors. The surplus that follows can be credited to a so-called 'Reserve Account'. Third, and importantly, the structure is set up so that investors may benefit from it, i.e. eventually exercise the security interest(s) that the debtors have granted to the originator to secure the receivables. In the most classic example of a securitisation, these security interests would be the residential mortgages the borrowers vested in the property financed by the loans from which the receivables follow. Fourth, the credit risk on the SPV is mitigated by a subordinated loan from the originator to the SPV: a loan that is only to be paid back to the originator if, should the SPV fall insolvent, all 'senior' claims, i.e. the investors' claims (including junior bonds), have first been satisfied. This loan is therefore also called the 'equity piece'. Fifth, a liquidity facility is entered into between the SPV and a 'liquidity provider' (see also below), under which facility cash must be provided to the SPV enabling it to always pay its bond holders.

Security trustee – As in the context of syndicated loans, a securitisation transaction needs a trustee to act on behalf of the entirety of bond holders (as does the trustee for the entirety of lenders in a syndicated loan) and, more specifically, execute the relevant security rights against the SPV and debtors on behalf of the bond holders.[2] The security rights securing the receivables must therefore be transferred to a security trustee, thus enabling the security trustee to execute these security rights. This transfer should enable bondholders to execute the securities in case of non-payment of the SPV, yet there are some legal issues concerning such a transfer of security rights, which will be discussed below at section 13.2.4.

Swap counterparty – As mentioned above, the SPV is able to purchase the originator's receivables by issuing bonds to investors. The SPV can pay principal and interest on these bonds from the proceeds, i.e. principal and interest, on the receivables that the originator has transferred to the SPV. The interest rate (the SPV has to pay to bond holders) on the bonds is usually floating. The interest rate (the SPV receives from the debtors) on the receivables, on the other hand, is usually fixed. To mitigate this mismatch/interest rate risk, the SPV commonly enters into a swap contract with a 'swap counterparty'. Under this financial derivative contract,[3] the counterparty accepts variable interest flows and provides fixed flows in return. The SPV thus always receives a fixed interest rate payable to the bondholders.

GIC and liquidity provider – We have just discussed the interest rate mismatch between the proceeds on the receivables and the costs of the bonds. Also, a mismatch may occur for other reasons: on the one hand, a surplus can arise, for instance when debtors prematurely repay their loans; on the other hand, a deficit may occur when debtors default. For the situation of a surplus, the SPV and an account provider may enter into a Guarantee Investment Contract ('GIC') which enables the SPV, in the case of an incidental surplus on the receivables, to invest this surplus temporarily.

2 On syndicated loans, see extensively above, Chapter 10.
3 On financial derivatives, and, more specifically, on interest rate swaps, see above, Chapter 11.

Usually the return on that temporary investment is a few basis points below LIBOR. In the case of a temporary deficit on the receivables, a liquidity facility entered into between the SPV and a 'liquidity provider' may provide cash, thus enabling the SPV to always pay its bond holders.

Rating agencies – Another party that is commonly involved in a traditional securitisation transaction is the rating agency. Its role is to rate the bonds issued by the SPV. These bonds are usually 'tranched' as rating agencies focus primarily on the credit risk of the receivables: the bonds connected with the receivables with the lowest default risk obtain the highest rating, the bonds connected with the highest default risk obtain the lowest. The rating can vary from AAA to D (also depending on the rating method used). Thus, a AAA rating ensures investors that the SPV is highly likely to pay the returns and interest on the bonds.

Profit extraction – The originator wishes to enjoy any surplus on the receivables after the investors have received their principal and interest from the SPV. A surplus could emerge in case of overcollateralisation (a method to mitigate credit risk, discussed above) and it can be agreed that the SPV must transfer the surplus to the originator.

13.2.3 Objectives

The reasons for entering into a securitisation transaction are multiple and vary for each party. From the perspective of the investors, a big advantage of buying bonds issued by an SPV in a securitisation transaction is the possibility to invest in assets with a relatively low credit risk and therefore high ratings, and high returns. Also, a securitisation enables them to invest (indirectly) in assets such as mortgage loans and credit card loans, that would otherwise not have been available for them to invest in directly.

The objectives of the originator are financial as well as regulatory. First, the originator may aim for an off-balance treatment of the receivables and a better leverage ratio. This can be achieved as the originating party no longer holds the credit risk of the receivables, but receives immediate cash (i.e. the price the SPV pays for the receivables) rather than having to wait until the receivables mature. With the cash, the originator can, for example pay its outstanding liabilities and thus obtain a better leverage ratio, i.e. a better relation between, in short, equity and debt. Note that in a synthetic securitisation (to be discussed below, section 13.2.5) off-balance treatment is unavailable since the assets are not transferred to the SPV.

Another reason for the originator to securitise its assets may be that a securitisation results in relatively cheap funding; the costs of funding, i.e. the cash the originator receives from the SPV, are relatively low since the rating of the bonds issued by the SPV is usually higher than the underlying assets would have been rated without the securitisation transaction. This can make securitisation a cheaper alternative than other funding methods, e.g. a (syndicated) bank loan or a (corporate) bonds issue.

A third reason for securitisation can be that the originator is now able to offer its assets to a broader public, because the bonds are easier to trade than the underlying assets themselves.

A fourth reason for securitisation might be the regulatory capital relief that can be achieved by the transfer of receivables from the originator to the SPV. For the credit risk the originator initially runs on the receivables, a bank must hold 'regulatory capital', so that without such credit risk on its books, the originator 'frees' this regulatory capital, i.e. needs to hold less capital, and therefore can invest it.[4]

A fifth reason for a bank to securitise receivables may lie in the acceptance of the ECB of certain SPV bonds as collateral when providing loans to banks, whereas the ECB would not accept (a security interest in) the underlying receivables.[5]

13.2.4 Legal issues

Multiple legal issues have to be taken into account when considering a securitisation transaction. These issues mainly represent regulatory and property law rules, as these rules are commonly of a mandatory nature and cannot be contracted away. In this section some of the main legal concerns will be discussed, of which the true sale requirement features most prominently.

True sale – The transfer of the receivables from the originator to the SPV must qualify as a 'true sale', because under the laws of various jurisdictions, including the US, the amount payable by the SPV to the originator may otherwise be recharacterised as a loan secured by the receivables. Also, under some jurisdictions a fiduciary transfer that is not the result of a true sale but has only security purposes, is forbidden.[6] If such 'recharacterisation' occurs, the results for the parties involved are often dramatic.[7] Off-balance treatment of the receivables will then be cancelled and the originator has thus remained liable for the credit risk on the receivables. Also, property laws are applied to the recharacterised securitisation transaction so that all regular requirements for security interests in receivables are applied – and will probably not have been complied with. This generates a host of difficulties including unsatisfied publication or registration requirements. Moreover, under most property law regimes, any surplus on the collateral needs to be returned to the creditor after realisation of the security interest, while in a securitisation transaction (at least part of) the surplus is destined for the bondholders (see also below). Finally, enforcement of a regular security interest is commonly subject to restrictive rules which are absent in the case of a full title transfer as is intended in a securitisation.

As a matter of course, the mechanics of recharacterisation depend on the applicable (property) law. Generally, however, in order to prevent recharacterisation, it is of the essence that the transaction does not contain the main characteristics of a regular security interest for a loan. First, the originator must have no remaining liability for the assets that are transferred to the SPV. This means that the originator cannot guarantee the returns and interest on the receivables and has no obligation to repurchase in case of losses on the receivables. Second, it is paramount that the SPV obtains exclusive control over the assets and is allowed to take all sorts of actions that a regular owner would be allowed to do. In other words, the SPV should obtain full power of disposal for purposes of, e.g. selling, pledging or managing the assets. Third, the assets must be isolated from the originator in case of its bankruptcy.

---

4 On regulatory capital requirements see above, Chapter 6.
5 For financial collateral transactions such as the one referred to here see Chapter 12.
6 Cf. art. 3:84(3) of the Dutch Civil Code.
7 PR Wood, *Law and Practice of International Finance* (Sweet & Maxwell, London 2008) 468–70.

Depending on the applicable law, a court might also take other circumstances into account when determining whether a securitisation transaction qualifies as a secured loan. For instance, and as already alluded to above, under common property law, a security taker is only allowed to benefit from the proceeds of the realisation of his security interest to the extent that the proceeds do not exceed the initial secured debt. Thus, he must transfer any surplus on the proceeds back to the debtor. Also in a classic securitisation, the SPV transfers back some surplus to the originator for profit extraction purposes, while other surplus is for the benefit of investors. It depends on the particular transaction whether the profit extraction is considered as material. If it is, recharacterisation might follow. Second, an originator sometimes holds a right to repurchase any surplus receivables. Whether this is considered as material also depends on the particular conditions of a transaction. In any case, the repurchase of the receivables cannot be without consideration, i.e. gratis, due to the recharacterisation risk. Third, if the originator continues to service and collect the receivables after their transfer to the SPV (see also above), this could be an indication for recharacterisation since in a true sale, the selling party is usually not committed to collect. Fourth, the originator could to some extent continue to be liable for the underlying receivables, as it usually would have made a subordinated loan to the SPV that bears losses on the receivables prior to the SPV's bondholders (the equity piece, also discussed above, under section 13.2.2). But this depends on the specific transaction and, again, it depends on the applicable (property) law whether this is a decisive factor for recharacterisation.

Security rights – As indicated above (section 13.2.2), multiple legal issues may arise regarding the transfer of the security rights that secure the receivables, to the security trustee. As a general rule of property law, security rights are accessory, i.e. they follow the claim which they secure. Thus, security rights securing the receivables would generally transfer, with the securities themselves, from the originator to the SPV. But it is quite common that the security rights securing the receivables are so-called bank mortgages. These mortgages have been vested in immovable property to secure the loan to finance that property, but under the applicable contract also secure any other claim the bank might have on the debtor, following, e.g. from overdrafts on a current account. Where a house loan is securitised and transferred to an SPV, it becomes questionable to what extent the bank mortgage securing the house loan also transfers to the SPV. Depending on the applicable law, the answer could be that the mortgage splits pro rata, which means that the percentage of the mortgage that regards the loan is transferred to the SPV while the originator retains the remainder.[8]

Where the security interests on the receivables (such as mortgages and pledges) have been transferred to the SPV, they subsequently need to be transferred to the security trustee (see above, section 13.2.2). Depending on the applicable law, this could be achieved in various ways. Under Dutch law, for instance, the mostly commonly used way is a parallel debt construction,[9] which means that the SPV obliges itself to

8 This seems the solution under Dutch law. See, e.g. MCA van den Nieuwenhuijzen (ed.), *Financial law in the Netherlands* (Wolters Kluwer, Alphen aan den Rijn 2010) 354 et seq.

9 Cf. also above, Chapter 10 on syndicated loans, where the parallel debt construct is also used.

pay the same amount to the security trustee as it has to pay to the bondholders so that the debts are parallel. The SPV subsequently vests a pledge on the receivables in favour of the security trustee to secure payment on this newly created debt. By virtue of the accessory principle discussed above, the security interests that secure the receivables (e.g. mortgages) become available, with the pledge, to the security trustee. Consequently, the security trustee has become empowered, in the case of the SPV's inability to pay principal and interest on the bonds, to enforce those security interests and recoup losses for the investors.

Assignability, notice and applicable law – Under the property laws of some jurisdictions, most notably of jurisdictions with a civil code tradition, the assignment of receivables without notice to, or consent of, the debtor cannot be asserted against third parties including the debtor itself. Since in a classic securitisation transaction several thousands of receivables on debtors are involved, noticing or asking for consent is impractical, may jeopardise the effectiveness of the transaction and is therefore expensive. This issue can be solved by the creation of an undisclosed pledge (instead of undisclosed assignment) under some property law regimes, or by a synthetic securitisation to be discussed below.

Also under property law regimes that allow for undisclosed assignments to be enforceable against third parties in securitisation transactions, debtors commonly remain empowered to discharge their obligations by paying to their original creditor (i.e. the originator) until notice of assignment (to the SPV) is given. In common law jurisdictions, such payments of debtors to the originator prior to notice of the assignment may be held in a separate trust that is unavailable for the other creditors of the originator, e.g. in its insolvency. In civil law jurisdictions that do not recognise the creation of such a trust, this may be problematic as in the originator's insolvency, payment of the debtors to the originator becomes part of the originator's insolvency estate and thus available for distribution among all ordinary creditors of the originator.

From the above, it follows that it is of paramount importance to be able to unequivocally establish which property law regime applies to the transfer of the receivables from originator to SPV. However, this is not an undisputed issue and the Rome I Regulation does not provide a definite answer, although its art. 14(2) does clarify that the law governing the assigned claim determines its assignability, the relationship between the assignee and the debtor, the conditions under which the assignment can be invoked against the debtor and whether the debtor's obligations have been discharged. Consequently, under the conflict of laws regimes of some Member States, the (proper) law of the receivables themselves (in the words of art. 14(2) of Rome I: '[T]he law governing the assigned claim') also determines the property law requirements for their transfer, while under other Member States laws,[10] the property law requirements for the transfer are determined by the law of the transfer agreement. The benefits of the last option are obvious in the context of securitisations: in such instances, the parties to the securitisation arrangement need to investigate the substantive law of the transfer agreement and comply with the property law

10 Including the Netherlands (see art. 10:135 of its Civil Code), but unlike Italy (see art. 57 of Law 31 May 1995, no. 218).

requirements of only that law, rather than having to investigate which laws apply or have been made to apply to any and all of the receivables to be transferred, and possibly comply with different property law requirements of those laws.

Set-off – Another issue regarding the assignment of the receivables is whether the debtors are allowed to set off their debts against the originator against any claim they may have against the same, also after those debts have been transferred to the SPV. Again, it depends on the particular property law applicable, but under many jurisdictions debtors are allowed to set off at least until notice has been given of the assignment.

Regulatory issues – Various regulatory concerns also have to be taken into account in a securitisation transaction. First, there is the requirement of publishing a prospectus where an issuer makes publicly available investment products, i.e. securities, to consumers. However, this requirement (which is extensively discussed above, in Chapter 2) disapplies if the bonds issued to investors are worth less than Euro 100,000 and are not listed at a regulated stock exchange.[11] Second, consumer credit regulations such as the ones discussed in sections 4.5 and 4.6 could be relevant since the SPV holds receivables that may be related to consumer debtors, e.g. mortgage and credit card loans. However, in as far as the servicing of the receivables are outsourced to a third party servicer, these regulations may disapply. As a matter of course, they apply if the SPV itself enters into a contract with consumer debtors. Third, regulations concerning data protection could apply and restrict the transfer of the receivables to the SPV (especially where the receivables concern claims on consumers), but by contracting an escrow agent that ensures compliance, the SPV may also avoid applicability of these regulations. Fourth, the SPV must comply with financial reporting requirements. This means that the SPV must make available relevant information in financial reports every year.

13.2.5 Alternative structures

In the above, we have discussed the traditional type of securitisation that is most commonly used. Alternative structures have also been developed, of which we will subsequently analyse especially one, i.e. the synthetic securitisation. But other structures are also used, such as the structure in which the SPV is a trust (as a matter of course, this is only possible in jurisdictions that recognise the trust) and the structure in which the assets securitised are securitisation bonds themselves. However, all these structures are in essence similar to the one discussed above.

In a synthetic securitisation structure, receivables are not transferred to the SPV. The reason for not wanting to transfer the receivables could be that the originator does not wish to end a confidential relation between the originator and the debtor(s) or where undisclosed assignment of claims is not possible. Therefore, in a synthetic securitisation, it is not the receivables themselves that are transferred to the SPV, but only the credit risk of those receivables that is transferred to the SPV by means of a credit

11 Art. 3(2)(c) of the Prospectus Directive.

default swap or CDS (a financial derivative discussed in Chapter 11). Thus, when credit risk on the receivables materialises as debtors default, the SPV must pay those losses to the originator under the CDS. The SPV raises the capital needed for making these payments by issuing bonds on terms that in the event of payment from the SPV to the originator, that same amount is reduced from the bonds, i.e. from the claims of the bond holders on the SPV. Of these bonds, the junior notes are first reduced and subsequently the senior notes. In as far as the SPV does not (need to) pay losses to the originator under the CDS, the capital raised by the SPV is invested in low risk assets, e.g. government bonds of financially stable countries or other relatively safe investments. The SPV can pay principal and interest to the bond holders from the fee the SPV receives from the originator for taking the risk to enter into a CDS and from the proceeds on the assets bought with the capital raised by issuing bonds.

Because under a synthetic securitisation, the credit risk on the receivables is transferred, by means of a CDS, to the SPV, synthetic securitisation provides higher capital adequacy for the originator since it does not have to retain capital against the receivables.[12] Advantages of synthetic securitisation over traditional securitisation include the avoidance of legal restrictions on the transfer of receivables (such as the recharacterisation risk of the transfer and the need for notice to, or consent of, the debtors in order to effectuate a valid transfer of a receivable under the laws of certain jurisdictions), because there is no actual transfer of receivables.

13.3 Covered bonds

13.3.1 Transaction

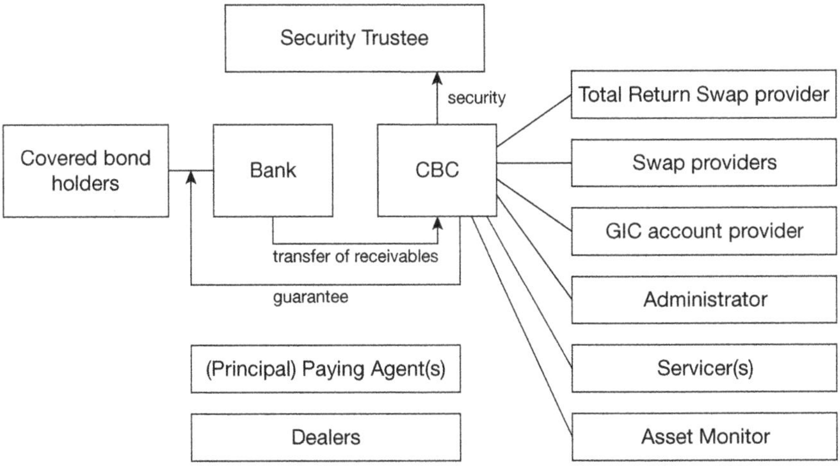

Figure 13.2 An illustration of a covered bond transaction structure

12 On capital adequacy rules, see above, Chapter 6.

In several aspects, a covered bonds transaction is very similar to a securitisation. The main difference is that in a typical covered bonds transaction it is the bank itself that issues bonds to investors, rather than the SPV as in a securitisation transaction. The bank's payment obligation of principal and interest to the investors is secured by a guarantee of a bankruptcy-remote special purpose vehicle usually denoted as a Covered Bonds Company ('CBC'). The CBC can credibly guarantee payment on the bonds issued by the bank because the bank has transferred a substantial amount of receivables to it.

Of the other differences with a securitisation transaction, we list the following. First, investors in covered bonds have a claim on the bank and (all of) its assets, rather than on an SPV that has as its only assets a specific and limited portfolio of receivables. Second, because investors in covered bonds have both a claim on the bank and (all of) its assets as well as recourse to the CBC, there is no tranching of bonds as the bonds do not relate to specific classes of receivables (as is the case in securitisations). Third, there is usually no overcollateralisation. Also, the CBC holds a dynamic pool of receivables that can be retransferred to the bank and substituted with other receivables, whereas under securitisations the SPV receives a more or less static pool. Fourth, other than in a securitisation, the transfer of receivables to the CBC does not result in cash for the bank to pay outstanding liabilities. The above characteristics also mean that the transfer does not lead to off-balance treatment of the receivables transferred.

Importantly and as already stated, as a result of the issuance of the bonds by the bank itself and the guarantee of the CBC, the investors can take recourse on both the bank and the CBC ('dual recourse'), which will commonly result in a higher rating than the underlying receivables alone would obtain. Consequently, investment in covered bonds is considered to have a low risk profile so that for risk weighing and capital adequacy purposes, covered bonds receive a favourable treatment.[13] For the same reason and as in a securitisation, the funding costs of a covered bonds transaction can be lower than ordinary loans. Also, and similar to bonds issued in a securitisation transaction, covered bonds can be eligible to serve as collateral for ECB loans, as mentioned also above, section 13.2.2.

13.3.2 Legal issues

As in a securitisation transaction, it is of critical importance that the receivables are validly transferred to the CBC. In some jurisdictions, it has been questioned whether the transfer of receivables to the CBC qualifies as a true sale as the receivables are transferred for consideration of a guarantee given to third parties rather than a price to the transferor. On the other hand, it has been argued that the same transfer of receivables must not be recharacterised as a security interest, for the purpose of the transfer is not to secure any loan or cash for the transferor (but rather a guarantee given to third parties).

13 See art. 129 of the CRR and cf. Chapter 6.

13.4 Further reading

Beale, Bridge, M, Gullitr, L, and Lomnicka, E, *The Law of Security and Title-Based Financing* (2nd edn Oxford University Press, Oxford 2012)
Benjamin, J, *Financial Law* (Oxford University Press, Oxford 2007)
Wood, PR, *Comparative Law of Security Interests and Title Finance* (Sweet & Maxwell, London 2007)
Wood, PR, *Law and Practice of International Finance* (Sweet & Maxwell, London 2008)

13.5 Questions

13.1 Why do securitisation and covered bonds transactions classify as 'structured finance'?

13.2 'Securitisation transactions have caused the Global Financial Crisis and should therefore be forbidden.' Discuss.

13.3 Discuss the advantages (if any) of a third party servicer.

13.4 Explain the security structure of a securitisation transaction to a potential investor; more specifically how he may use any security interests created to secure the receivables.

13.5 What would better secure the claims of an investor: the security structure of a securitisation transaction or a covered bonds transaction?

13.6 What laws are relevant to the transfer of receivables in both a securitisation transaction and a covered bonds transaction?

Bibliography

Adams, JN, and Macqueen, H, *Atiyah's Sale of Goods* (12th edn Pearson, Harlow 2010)

Alcock, A, 'Five Years of Market Abuse' (2007) 28(6) *Company Lawyer* 163, 171

Alexander, K, and Dhumale, *R, Research Handbook on International Financial Regulation* (Edward Elgar, Cheltenham 2012)

Alpa, G, and Capriglione, F, (eds), *Commentario al Testo Unico delle Disposizioni in Materia di Intermediazione Finanziaria* (CEDAM, Padua 1998)

The Association of Corporate Treasurers and Slaughter & May, *The ACT Borrower's Guide to LMA Loan Documentation for Investment Grade Borrowers* (ACT and Slaughter & May, London 2013), supplemented June 2014, available at www.treasurers.org/loandocumentation/investmentgrade (accessed 14 April 2015)

Bamford, C, *Principles of International Financial Law* (Oxford University Press, Oxford 2011)

Barnard, C, *The Substantive Law of the EU: The Four Freedoms* (4th edn Oxford University Press, Oxford 2013)

Beale, H, Bridge, M, Gullifer, L, and Lomnicka, E, *The Law of Security and Title-Based Financing* (2nd edn Oxford University Press, Oxford 2012)

Beale, H, Fauvarque-Cosson, B, Rutgers, J, Tallon, D, and Vogenauer, S, *Cases, Materials and Text on Contract Law* (2nd edn Hart Publishing, Oxford and Portland 2010)

Benjamin, J, *Financial Law* (Oxford University Press, Oxford 2007)

Benston, G, 'The Value of the SEC's Accounting Disclosure Requirement' (1969) 44 *Accounting Review* 515, 519

Benston, G, 'Required Disclosure and the Stock Market: An Evaluation of the Securities Exchange Act of 1934' (1973) 63 *American Economic Review* 132

Bernasconi, C, *The Law Applicable to Dispositions of Securities Held through Indirect Holding Systems* (November 2000) (Preliminary Document no 1 to the Hague Conference on Private International Law), *available at www.hcch.net*

Blair, M, and Walker, G, *Financial Services Law* (Oxford University Press, Oxford 2006)

Boyle, AJ, *Boyle and Birds' Company Law* (9th edn Jordan, Bristol 2014)

Brunnermeier, M, Crockett, A, Goodhart, C, Persaud, AD, and Song Shin, H, *The Fundamental Principles of Financial Regulation* (International Center for Monetary and Banking Studies, Geneva 2009)

Busch, D, and De Mott, DA, (eds), *Liability of Asset Managers* (Oxford University Press, Oxford 2012)

Capriglione, F, *Crisi a Confronto (1929 e 2009): Il Caso Italiano* (CEDAM, 2009)

Capriglione, F, 'Financial Crisis and Sovereign Debt: The European Union between Risks and Opportunities' (2012) 1 *Law and Economics Yearly Review* 4, 76

Chitty on Contracts, *General Principles, Volume I* (31st edn Sweet & Maxwell, London 2012)

Coffee, J, 'Market Failure and the Economic Case for a Mandatory Disclosure System' (1984) 70 *Virginia Law Review* 717

Collier, PM, *Accounting for Managers* (4th edn Wiley, 2012)

Conceicao, C, 'The FSA's Approach to Taking Action against Market Abuse' (2007) 28(2) *Company Lawyer* 43, 45

Cranston, R, *Principles of Banking Law* (2nd edn Oxford University Press, Oxford 2002)

Cranston, R (ed), *European Banking Law: The Banker-Consumer Relationship* (LLP, London and Hong Kong 1999)

Dashwood, A, Dougan, M, Rodger, B, Spaventa, E, and Wyatt, D, *Wyatt and Dashwood's European Union Law* (6th edn Hart Publishing, Oxford and Portland 2011)

Davies, PL, and Worthington, S, *Gower and Davies: Principles of Modern Company Law* (9th edn Sweet & Maxwell, London 2012)

de Gioia-Carabellese, P, '"Derivatives" in the Light of the Recent Financial Crises (Lehman Brothers) and through Glimpses of Comparative Analysis' (2010) 3 *Rivista Trimestrale di Diritto dell'Economia* 234, 257

de Gioia-Carabellese, P, 'Non-executive Directors and Auditors in the Context of the UK Corporate Governance: Two (or Too Many?) "Pirandellian" characters Still in the Search of an Author?' (2011) 22 *European Business Law Review* 759, 789

de Gioia-Carabellese, P, 'Corporate Governance of British Banks and Duties of Directors: Practical Implications of the Royal Bank of Scotland's Demise' (2014) 2 *Law and Economics Yearly Review* 134, 165

Dignam, A, and Lowry, J, *Company Law* (7th edn Oxford University Press, Oxford 2012)

Du Plessis, P, *Borkowski's Textbook on Roman Law* (4th edn Oxford University Press, Oxford 2010)

Edwards, L (ed), *The New Legal Framework for E-Commerce in Europe* (Hart Publishing, Oxford and Portland 2005)

Ellinger, EP, Lomnicka, E, and Hare, CVM, *Ellinger's Modern Banking Law* (5th edn Oxford University Press, Oxford 2011)

European Commission, 'EU Bank Recovery and Resolution Directive (BRRD): Frequently Asked Questions', MEMO/14/297, 15 April 2014, http://europa.eu/rapid/press-release_MEMO-14-297_en.htm (accessed 3 July 2014)

Final Report of the Committee of the Wise Men in the Regulation of European Securities Markets (Brussels, 15 February 2001)

Financial Stability Board, *Principles for Sound Compensation Practices – Implementation Standards* (September 2009) www.financialstabilityboard.org/publications/r_090925c.pdf (accessed 3 July 2014)

Financial Stability Forum, *Principles for Sound Compensation Practices* (April 2009) www.financialstabilityboard.org/publications/r_0904b.pdf (accessed 3 July 2014)

FSA, *The Assessment and Redress of Payment Protection Insurance Complaints* (August 2010)

French, D, Mayson, S, and Ryan, C, *Mayson, French and Ryan on Company Law* (30th edn Oxford University Press, Oxford 2013)

Furmston, M, and Chuah, J, *Commercial Law* (2nd edn Pearson, Harlow 2010)

Gardner, S, *An Introduction to the Law of Trusts* (3rd edn Oxford University Press, Oxford 2011)

Gersten, C, Klein, G, Schopmann, H, Schwander, D, and Wengler, C, *European Banking and Financial Services Law* (Kluwer Law International, Deventer 2004)

Giovannini Group, *Cross-Border Clearing and Settlement Arrangements in the European Union* (November 2001), available at http://ec.europa.eu/internal_market/financial-markets/ (accessed 14 April 2015)

Giovannini Group, *Second Report on EU Clearing and Settlement Arrangements* (April 2003), available at http://ec.europa.eu/internal_market/financial-markets/ (accessed 14 April 2015)

Gkoutzinis, A, *Internet Banking and the Law in Europe* (Cambridge University Press, Cambridge 2006)

Gleeson, S, *International Regulation of Banking. Basel II: Capital and Risk Requirements* (Oxford University Press, Oxford 2010)

Goode, R, 'The Nature and Transfer of Rights in Dematerialised and Immobilised Securities' (1996) 4 *Journal of International Banking and Financial Law* 167, 176

Grundmann, S, *European Company Law Ius Communitatis, Volume I* (2nd edn Intersentia, Cambridge – Antwerp and Portland 2012)

Gruyaert, D, and van Loock, S, 'UK Supreme Court Decision on Lehman Brothers Client Money: Equity or Lottery' (2014) 22(2) *European Review of Private Law* 217

Gullifer, L, and Payne, J, *Corporate Finance Law* (Hart Publishing, Oxford and Portland 2011)

Haentjens, M, *Harmonisation of Securities Law* (Kluwer Law International, Alphen aan den Rijn 2007)

Haentjens, M, 'Bank Recovery and Resolution: An Overview of International Initiatives' (2014) *International Insolvency Law Review* 255, 270

Haentjens, M, and Wessels, B, (eds), *Bank Recovery and Resolution: A Conference Book* (Eleven Publishers, The Hague 2014)

Haentjens, M, and Wessels, B (eds), *Crisis Management in the Banking Sector* (Edward Elgar, forthcoming 2015)

Harding, P, *Mastering the ISDA Master Agreements: A Practical Guide for Negotiation* (3rd edn FT Press, 2010)

Haynes, A, *The Law Relating to International Banking* (2nd edn Bloomsbury Professional, 2015)

Hazen, TL, *Securities Regulation in a Nutshell* (10th edn West Publishing/Thomson Reuters, St Paul (MN) 2009)

Hemetsberger, W, Schoppmann, H, Schwander, D, and Wengler, C, *European Banking and Financial Law* (2nd edn Kluwer Law International in association with European Association of Public Banks, Brussels 2006)

Hess, B, Oberhammer, P, and Pfeiffer, T, *European Insolvency Law The Heidelberg-Luxemburg-Vienna Report* (CH Beck, Hart and Nomos, Munich 2013)

Hopt, KJ, and Wymeersch, E, *European Company and Financial Law: Text and Leading Cases* (3rd edn Oxford University Press, Oxford 2006)

Hudson, A (ed), *Credit Derivatives: Law, Regulation and Accounting Issues* (Sweet & Maxwell, London 1999)

Hudson, A (ed), *Modern Financial Techniques, Derivatives and Law* (Kluwer, London 1999)

Hudson, A, *Swaps, Restitution and Trusts* (Sweet & Maxwell, London 1999)

Hudson, A, *The Law of Finance* (1st edn Sweet & Maxwell, London 2009)

Hudson, A, *The Law on Financial Derivatives* (5th edn Sweet & Maxwell, London 2012)

Hudson, A, *The Law of Finance* (2nd edn Sweet & Maxwell, London 2013)

Kaczorowska, A, *European Union Law* (2nd edn Routledge, Abingdon 2011)

Kaul, I, Conceicao, P, Le Goulven, K, and Mendoza, RU (eds), *Providing Global Public Goods* (Oxford University Press, Oxford 2003)

Keijser, T, *Financial Collateral Arrangements* (diss. Radboud University Nijmegen) (Kluwer, Deventer 2006)

Keijser, T (ed), *Transnational Securities Law* (Oxford University Press, Oxford 2014)

Kirshner, J (ed), *Business, Banking, and Economic Thought in Late Medieval and Early Modern Europe* (University of Chicago Press, Chicago 1974)

Kroes, QR (ed), *E-Business Law of the European Union* (Allen & Overy Legal Practice and Kluwer Law International, The Hague/London/New York 2003)

Kroes, QR (ed), *E-Business Law of the European Union* (2nd edn Kluwer Law International, Alphen aan den Rijn 2010)

de Larosière, J, *The High-Level Group on Financial Supervision in the EU*, Brussels, 25 February 2009, http://ec.europa.eu/internal_market/finances/docs/de_larosiere_report_en.pdf (accessed 5 August 2014)

Linklaters, 'EU "Gets Tough" on Market Abuse', 20 October 2011, www.linklaters.com/pdfs/mkt/london/Market_Abuse_briefing.pdf (accessed 15 July 2014)

McBryde, WW, Flessner, A, and Kortmann, SCJJ, *Principles of European Insolvency Law, Volume 4* (Kluwer Legal Publishers, Deventer 2003)

McKendrick, E, *Contract Law: Text, Cases, and Materials* (5th edn Oxford University Press, Oxford 2012)

McKendrick, E, *Contract Law (Palgrave Macmillan Law Masters)* (10th edn Palgrave Macmillan, London 2013)

MacNeil, IG, 'The Evolution of Regulatory Enforcement Action in the UK Capital Markets: A Case of Less is More?' (2007) 2 *Capital Markets Law Journal* 345, 369

MacNeil, IG, *An Introduction to the Law on Financial Investment* (2nd edn Hart Publishing, Oxford and Portland 2012)

MacQueen, HL, and Thomson, J, *Contract Law in Scotland* (3rd edn Bloomsbury Professional, Edinburgh 2012)

McVea, H, 'What's Wrong with Insider Trading?' (1995) 15(3) *Journal of Legal Studies* 390, 414

Masera, R, and Mazzoni, G, 'Derivatives' Pricing and Model Risk' (2013) *Law and Economics Yearly Review* 296, 311

Mezzacapo, S, 'Towards a New Regulatory Framework for Banking Recovery and Resolution in the EU' (2013) 2 *Law and Economics Yearly Review* (part 1) 213, 241

Moffat, G, *Trusts Law Texts and Materials* (4th edn Cambridge University Press, Cambridge 2005)

Mueller, RC, *The Venetian Money Market: Banks, Panics, and the Public Debt, 1200–1500* (Johns Hopkins University Press, London 1997)

Nebbia, P, *Unfair Contract Terms in European Law* (Hart, Oxford and Portland, Oregon 2007)

Ooi, M, *Shares and Other Securities in the Conflict of Laws* (Oxford University Press, Oxford 2003)

Paech, P, *Cross-Border Issues of Securities Law: European Efforts to Support Securities Markets with a Coherent Legal Framework* (European Parliament briefing note 2011)

Panasar, R, and Boeckman, P, *European Securities Law* (Oxford University Press, Oxford 2010)

Passalacqua, M, 'Derivative Financial Instruments and Balanced Budgets: The Case of the Italian Public Administration' (2013) *Law and Economics Yearly Review* 447, 479

Peel, E, *Treitel: The Law of Contract* (30th edn Sweet & Maxwell, London 2011)

Proctor, C, *The Law and Practice of International Banking* (Oxford University Press, Oxford 2010)

Proctor, C, *Mann on the Legal Aspect of Money* (Oxford University Press, Oxford 2012)

Reich, N, *General Principles of EU Civil Law* (Intersentia, Cambridge, Antwerp, Portland 2014)

Reid, A, *European Union* (4th edn W Green, London 2010)

Santen, B, and Offeren, D (eds), *Perspectives on International Insolvency Law: A Tribute to Bob Wessels* (Leiden Law School 2014)

Schammo, P, *EU Prospectus Law* (Cambridge University Press, Cambridge 2011)

Scott, HS, *International Finance* (17th edn Foundation Press, New York 2010)

Scott, HS, and Gelpern, A, *International Finance: Transactions, Policy and Regulation* (Thomson Reuters/Foundation Press, New York 2012)

Sfameni, P, and Giannelli, A, *Diritto degli Intermediari e dei Mercati Finanziari* (Egea, Milan 2013)

Siems, M, and Cabrelli, D, *Comparative Company Law: A Case-Based Approach* (Oxford University Press, Oxford 2013)

Soderquist, LD, and Gabaldon, TA, *Securities Law* (Foundation Press and Thomson West, New York 2004)

Swan, E, and Virgo, J, *Market Abuse Regulation* (2nd edn Oxford University Press, Oxford 2010)

Theissen, R, *EU Banking Supervision* (Eleven Publishers, The Hague 2013)

Thirlway, H, *The Sources of International Law* (Oxford University Press, Oxford 2014)

Todd, P, *E-Commerce* (Cavendish Publishing Limited, London 2005)

Vereecken, M, and Nijenhuis, A (eds), *Settlement Finality in the European Union: The EU Directive and its Implementation in Selected Jurisdictions* (Kluwer, 2003)

Waibel, M, and Burdeau, G (eds), *The Legal Implications of Global Financial Crises / Les implications juridiques des crises financières de caractère mondial* (Martinus Nijhoff, Leiden, forthcoming 2015)

Walker, G, and Purves, R, (eds), *Financial Services Law* (3rd edn Oxford University Press, Oxford 2014)

Weatherill, S, *Cases and Materials on EU Law* (8th edn Oxford University Press, Oxford 2007)

Weatherill, S, *Cases and Materials on EU Law* (9th edn Oxford University Press, Oxford 2010)

Wessels, B, and Moss, G, *EU Banking and Insurance Insolvency* (Oxford University Press, Oxford 2006)

Wood, PR, *Comparative Law of Security Interests and Title Finance* (Sweet & Maxwell, London 2007)

Wood, PR, *Conflict of Laws and International Finance* (Thomson/Sweet & Maxwell, London 2007)

Wood, PR, *International Loans, Bonds, Guarantees, Legal Opinions (The Law and Practice of International Finance Series, Volume 3)* (2nd edn Thomson/Sweet & Maxwell, London 2007)

Wood, PR, *Regulation of International Finance* (Thomson/Sweet & Maxwell, London 2007)

Wood, PR, *Set-off and Netting, Derivatives, Clearing Systems* (Thomson/Sweet & Maxwell, London 2007)

Wood, PR, *Law and Practice of International Finance* (Sweet & Maxwell, London 2008)

Woods, L, and Watson, P, *Steiner and Woods EU Law* (11th edn Oxford University Press, Oxford 2012)

Wright, S, *The Handbook of International Loan Documentation* (2nd edn Palgrave Macmillan, London 2014)

Wymeersch, E, *Alternative Investment Fund Regulation* (Wolters Kluwer, Alphen aan den Rijn 2012)

Wymeersch, E, Hopt, KJ, and Ferrarini, *G, Financial Regulation and Supervision: A Post-crisis Analysis* (Oxford University Press, Oxford 2012)

Zetzsche, D (ed), *The Alternative Investment Fund Managers Directive* (Wolters Kluwer, Alphen aan den Rijn 2012)

Index